COLLABORATIVE PLANNING, FORECASTING, AND REPLENISHMENT

COLLABORATIVE PLANNING, FORECASTING, AND REPLENISHMENT

How to Create a Supply Chain Advantage

Dirk Seifert

AMACOM

American Management Association

New York • Atlanta • Brussels • Buenos Aires • Chicago • London • Mexico City
San Francisco • Shanghai • Tokyo • Toronto • Washington, D.C.

Special discounts on bulk quantities of AMACOM books are available to corporations, professional associations, and other organizations. For details, contact Special Sales Department, AMACOM, a division of American Management Association, 1601 Broadway, New York, NY 10019.
Tel.: 212-903-8316. Fax: 212-903-8083.
Web site: www.amacombooks.org

This publication is designed to provide accurate and authoritative information in regard to the subject matter covered. It is sold with the understanding that the publisher is not engaged in rendering legal, accounting, or other professional service. If legal advice or other expert assistance is required, the services of a competent professional person should be sought.

CPFR® is a registered trademark of the Voluntary Interindustry Commerce Standards (VICS) Association.

Various names used by companies to distinguish their software and other products can be claimed as trademarks. AMACOM uses such names throughout this book for editorial purposes only, with no intention of trademark violation. All such software or product names are in initial capital letters or ALL CAPITAL letters. Individual companies should be contacted for complete information regarding trademarks and registration.

Library of Congress Cataloging-in-Publication Data

Seifert, Dirk.
   Collaborative planning, forecasting, and replenishment : how to create a supply chain advantage / Dirk Seifert.
      p.   cm.
   Includes bibliographical references and index.
      ISBN 0-8144-7182-X (hardcover)
   1. Business logistics.   I. Title.

HD38.5 .S45   2003
658.5—dc21   2002015915

Printing number

10   9   8   7   6   5   4   3   2   1

Table of Contents

Foreword of the VICS CPFR Committee

We want to express our sincere gratitude to Prof. Dr. Dirk Seifert and the Harvard Business School for conducting research on Collaborative Planning, Forecasting, and Replenishment (CPFR) and for writing this book. The endorsement of CPFR by a research project conducted at the Harvard Business School is a major step in the acceptance of CPFR as a creditable business process reflective of emerging global trends and the impact of technology on efficient business processes.

This book describes a practical, yet intensive, thought-provoking business process that demonstrates how to implement CPFR and gain quantifiable results, to be enjoyed by all parties to the value chain. It promotes an understanding of how to overcome the barriers to CPFR, which are primarily cultural, ignorance, and a desire to maintain the status quo. It will become clear that technology is not a barrier to implementation and that CPFR is in fact flexible and adaptable to various business conditions and circumstances.

Supply chain management has been evolving for the past twenty-five years, beginning with the traffic, order management, and warehousing departments. They were ultimately brought together under the umbrella of physical distribution. Subsequently inventory management and customer service were included, enabling integrated logistics, followed by production planning and procurement. Today we have supply chain management, which is rapidly emerging into value chain management, which recognizes the importance of demand in addition to supply.

In this continuum, sales forecasting may be the responsibility of one department or be shared by several departments, generally operating in an information stovepipe. The mission-critical information is given little, if any, import and consequently drives the supply chain with incorrect and/or untimely information. Current, fresh, visible information is a key ingredient to realizing value chain excellence coupled with defined, accepted business processes. CPFR clearly identifies the need for collaboration among trading partners throughout the value chain and identifies the financial and operational results that can be expected.

If the evolution of the supply chain has moved at the speed of sound, CPFR has evolved at the speed of light. Companies in retail, technology, textile, automotive, drug, and other industries across the globe are rapidly adopting CPFR. The case studies and other information in this book will prove to be invaluable to the practitioner and to senior leadership. We wish Prof. Dr. Seifert and the Harvard Business School the best of luck and much success as they continue their important work.

Rita Marzian,
cochair VICS CPFR, Metro AG

Jim McLaughlin,
cochair VICS CPFR, Gillette

Joseph C. Andraski,
vice chair VICS CPFR, senior vice president
OMI International

Preface

Collaborative Planning, Forecasting, and Replenishment is a determinant theme in the consumer goods economy worldwide. The prospect of enormous potential savings on the one hand, and growth through the avoidance of out-of-stocks on the other, fascinates manufacturers and retailers equally. CPFR is a further development of Efficient Consumer Response (ECR) on the supply side. It represents the second generation of ECR. Through planning and forecasting, there are clear interrelations between the supply side and departments like marketing and sales management, which until now were strongly attached to the demand side. This interdepartmental working relationship is typical of second-generation ECR. The boundaries between strategy on the supply side and the demand side are becoming more permeable.

The Globalization of CPFR

Since the emergence of CPFR in the mid-nineties, the implementation of this strategy has expanded rapidly around the world. The Voluntary Interindustry Commerce Standards (VICS) and Global Commerce Initiative (GCI) together with some of the most important companies in the North American consumer goods industry have laid the cornerstone for the success of CPFR. In Europe, ECR Europe and the national ECR organizations recognized early on the necessity of adapting CPFR to the specifics of the European market. They have done important work in recent years in developing standards for and knowledge exchange on CPFR.

CPFR has also expanded in South America, Africa, and Asia. Retailers and manufacturers in Brazil, Colombia, South Africa, and Japan are successfully using CPFR in their business processes, adapting it for their own market conditions, and creating best practices, which can be used by other countries in their respective regions.

CPFR Knowledge Transfer

The systematic transfer of CPFR knowledge will be an important task worldwide in the coming years. Creating CPFR expertise for large, medium, and small companies allows them all to enjoy the sought-after efficiencies. This is also the goal of a new CPFR educational initiative. Joe Andraski and Tom Friedman, both CPFR veterans, have created a forum with the newly grounded CPFR Institute that will enable CPFR knowledge transfer on a variety of levels. The newest CPFR findings will be adjusted to the needs of various target groups, senior management, middle management, and operations staff. The research group responsible for this volume supports the goals of the CPFR Institute.

Structure of the Book

The book is intended to give the reader insight into the current use of CPFR in the consumer goods economy through case studies and contributions by experts in the field.

The first part describes Efficient Consumer Response as the starting point for the development of the CPFR concept. Both main components of ECR, supply chain management and category management, are introduced here. The part not only covers the tasks and objectives of the individual ECR strategies, but also provides detailed explanations of things like the nine-step category management process and approaches to the reengineering of the value chain.

Part 2 begins with the value proposition of CPFR. It explains why this new management concept represents second-generation ECR. Further, the CPFR process model is introduced and its potential efficiency advantages are shown. The first chapter of this part also describes the first CPFR project by Wal-Mart and Warner-Lambert, which signaled the dawn of CPFR in the consumer goods industry. Prof. Dr. Gerhard Arminger, professor at the University of Wuppertal and chief scientist of SAF-AG, provides insights on sales and order forecasts in the CPFR process for retail. The contribution by Joseph C. Andraski, vice chairman of VICS CPFR and senior vice president of OMI International, explains CPFR as an evolutionary step in supply chain management. Julie Fraser of Industry Directions presents important results of a CPFR study done in collaboration with Syncra Systems. In it are data on actual CPFR use and the gain in utility obtained through CPFR in areas like forecast accuracy.

Chapter 3 introduces the use of CPFR in the United States. Thomas H. Friedman and Greg Belkin of MoonWatch Media discuss important trends and experiences in the use of CPFR and present two brief case studies on Wal-Mart/Sara Lee and Schering-Plough. Lawrence E. Fennell, vice president at Wal-Mart, provides the reader with background information on the current retail environment. He writes about how to get started with CPFR and suggests methods for the intelligent implementation of consumer-centered CPFR. Christopher A. Brady, who is working in supply chain management at Safeway, describes the experiences and perspectives of Safeway with CPFR. He explains where the biggest benefits are coming from and also provides insights on implementation issues. Brian Bastock (Manco), Fred Baumann (JDA Software), and Scott Smith (Ace Hardware) provide details on and list key benefits of a successful CPFR project done by Ace Hardware and Manco. Geoffrey S. Frodsham (Canadian Tire), Nick J. Miller (Global-NetXchange), and Laura Mooney (Manugistics) talk about the technology that is enabling CPFR and the use of CPFR at Canadian Tire and such GNX customers as Procter & Gamble and the successful retailer Metro. In the last chapter of this part, Michael E. Di Yeso, executive vice president and chief operating officer of the Uniform Code Council, and Joseph C. Andraski of VICS CPFR focus on the crucial importance of standards for enabling CPFR.

Part 4 switches the focus to the implementation of CPFR in Europe. The introductory article explains the differences between the North American and European consumer goods markets. Furthermore, one receives an overview of selected CPFR projects in Europe. Nils Weisphal (University of Hamburg/IDS Scheer AG), Prof. Dr. Wilhelm Pfähler (University of Hamburg), and Dr. Ferri Abolhassan (IDS Scheer AG) present major results of a European CPFR study. Saskia Treeck and Michael Seishoff of the Centrale für Coorganisation (CCG) provide backgound on current CPFR activities in Germany, Austria, and Switzerland coordinated by CCG. In particular they make reference to the CPFR management guidelines intended to ease the implementation of CPFR in the German-speaking economic regions of Europe. Gunter Baumgart (Henkel), Dr. Birgit Ester, and Christian Schick (both dm-drogerie markt, a German drug market chain) discuss the use of CPFR by dm-drogerie markt and Henkel in Germany. In comparison to the activities of Henkel and dm, the following article illustrates the activities of Procter & Gamble and dm. Peter Hambuch (Procter & Gamble) and Christian Schick (dm-drogerie markt) explain CPFR as a learning process. Donald P. Brenchley of JDA Software offers a case study from England. He talks about CPFR implementation at the British retailer Londis. The implementation of CPFR by Henkel in Spain with two trade partners is the topic of Sergio Duque, Esteban Garriga, and Hans Teuscher's contribution. Peter Hambuch further examines P&G's experience with CPFR.

Part 5 shows the possibilities for the implementation of CPFR. Robert Bruce and Ron Ireland, two former Wal-Mart executives and current senior executives at VCC Associates, identify important features of successful CPFR management and four fundamental strategies for the use of CPFR. Dawn M. Russell of Pennsylvania State University proposes a way to integrate collaborative transportation management and CPFR. Ralph W. Drayer, former chief logistics officer at Procter & Gamble and currently chairman of Supply Chain Insights, writes about the quiet revolution taking place in the industry right now. Daren K. Fairfield of Accenture points out five pitfalls of CPFR and how to avoid them. Jeffrey B. Stiely and Matthew F. Katz of Kurt Salmon Associates present a new supply chain model for the collaboration era. In the last expert contribution, Christian Koch of SAP AG and Gerhard Hausruckinger of Roland Berger Strategy Consultants conclude the part by laying out the roadmap to the network economy and offering their prognosis of the future of the consumer goods economy.

The book is to be viewed as a platform for the expression of the opinions of important players in the field: manufacturers, retailers, consulting companies, and IT-solutions providers. The opinions expressed by contributing authors do not necessarily reflect those of the editor. The articles distinguish themselves through different styles and approaches, offering the reader varying perspectives on CPFR.

Acknowledgments

The book would not have been possible without the help and the inspiration of many people and companies.

I would like to thank Accenture, JDA Software, and SAP AG, which sponsored our research on CPFR.

Special thanks in particular to the contributing authors: Dr. Ferri Abolhassan, Joseph C. Andraski, Prof. Dr. Gerhard Arminger, Brian Bastock, Fred Baumann, Gunter Baumgart, Greg Belkin, Christopher A. Brady, Donald P. Brenchley, Robert Bruce, Michael Di Yeso, Ralph W. Drayer, Sergio Duque, Georg Engler, Dr. Birgit Ester, Daren K. Fairfield, Lawrence E. Fennell, Julie Fraser, Thomas H. Friedman, Geoffrey S. Frodsham, Esteban Garriga, Peter Hambuch, Dr. Gerhard Hausruckinger, Ron Ireland, Matthew Katz, Christian Koch, Nick J. Miller, Laura A. Mooney, Prof. Dr. Wilhelm Pfähler, Prof. Dr. Dawn M. Russell, Christian Schick, Michael Seishoff, Scott Smith, Jeff Stiely, Saskia Treeck, Hans Teuscher, and Nils Weisphal for sharing the knowledge and experience of their companies.

I would like to thank the members of my research team: Alexander Adler, Mark Cicirelli, Kirstin Hornby, Julian Kurz, and Michael Lark. Heartfelt thanks also to those whose personal involvement facilitated intensive debate on many ideas contained in this volume: Fred Baumann, Claudia Beckers, Rudolf Behrens, Roland Bertsch, Steffen Bundesmann, Prof. Clayton Christensen, Hans-Gerhard Degen, Richard Downs, Eli Fel, Berthold Figgen, Dagmar Fischer-Neeb, Dr. Stephan

Friedrich, Dr. Markus Grossweischede, Prof. Janice H. Hammond, Prof. Dr. Hans Hinterhuber, Kathrin Holling, Steffen Jaeckle, Dr. Jürgen Kohr, Prof. Dr. Alexander Kracklauer, Prof. Dr. Jean-Pierre Kuliboer, Dr. Peter Linzbach, Prof. Dr. Raymond Liu, Ronald Margulis, Graham Newland, Prof. Dr. Michael Novak, Dr. Andreas Oetting, Dr. Heiner Olbrich, Dr. Olaf Passenheim, Willibald Poplutz, Achim Pütz, Prof. Dr. Philip Quaglieri, Brigitta Rodens-Friedrich, Dr. Edward J. Romar, Uwe Rosik, Wolfgang Runge, Christopher Sellers, Silke Slootz, Jim Uchneat, Jürgen Weltermann, Prof. Sean Willems, and Prof. Dr. Michael Zerres.

And, finally, my thanks to Prof. D. Quinn Mills, Prof. Michael Y. Yoshino, and the Research Division of the Harvard Business School, who all helped pave the way for the work presented here.

If you have questions, comments, and criticisms regarding this book you may contact the author via e-mail: seifert-d@gmx.de

Prof. Dr. Dirk Seifert
Harvard Business School and University of Massachusetts

1.

Efficient Consumer Response as the Origin of CPFR

Prof. Dr. Dirk Seifert,
Harvard Business School and
University of Massachusetts

In the early nineties, the American retail and consumer goods industry was confronted with massive problems. An increase in productivity was hardly to be realized; revenues stagnated at the same time that costs were rising. Competitive advantages, and thereby an increase in market share, were to be achieved only through aggressive pricing policies. The consequences of this were a negative effect on margins, contribution margins, and profits on sales. Retailing and manufacturing had to recognize that real gains through differentiation were going to be achieved only through open cooperative partnerships with one another.

The success of the retailer Wal-Mart made the consumer goods industry aware of the outstanding potential for rationalization and the possibility of improvements in productivity. Wal-Mart had concentrated on a more close-knit cooperation with its suppliers, in order to offer its customers quality products more quickly, efficiently, and at lower cost. Wal-Mart's strategy is based on a concept called Efficient Consumer Response (ECR). The results of these efforts are evidenced in the storewide records for inventory turnover, revenue per unit sales area, and operating profit.

ECR implies two essential components:

- Consumer: An orientation toward the needs of the consumer
- Efficient Response: A process-oriented optimization of the supply chain, dovetailing individual elements (orientation to value-added processes)

The deciding factor for ECR in the United States was a number of projects and studies in 1992, which were initiated by the Food Marketing Institute in Washington and affiliated work groups such as the Joint Industry Project on Efficient Consumer Response. The consultancy Kurt Salmon Associates had already done a landmark study in 1985, analyzing the supply chain in the textile and garment industry, and thereby developed the Quick Response Concept for that industry.

ECR is a comprehensive management concept for retailing and manufacturing based on a value-adding partnership between the participants. The strategy is made up of several basic strategies. Accordingly, retail and manufacturing work together to make the supply chain efficient, rational, and oriented toward the needs of the consumer. The point of departure and likewise the foundation for ECR has been partnership and cooperation-oriented thinking of retail and manufacturing. With ECR, it is about shifting from an intra- to interorganizational process organization of corporations. Exhibit 1.1 gives an overview of both main parts of the ECR concept and the associated ECR basic strategies.

On the supply side, cooperation in logistics between manufacturers and retailers should result in optimal supply chain management. On the demand side, collaboration in marketing via category management and the exchange of customer data makes it possible for all parties to achieve a more efficient marketing mix. All efforts should stand against the backdrop of improved customer satisfaction. This can result from the increase in product availability and in quality (freshness of product through more efficient logistics) or through customer-oriented assortments, which offer optimal pricing (marketing cooperation). The ob-

EXHIBIT 1.1. THE ECR CONCEPT AND ITS BASIC STRATEGIES.

Efficient Consumer Response—Concept	
Supply Chain Management (SCM)	Category Management (CM)
Efficient Replenishment (ER)	Efficient Store Assortment (ESA)
Efficient Administration (EA)	Efficient Promotion (EP)
Efficient Operating Standards (EOS)	Efficient Product Introduction (EPI)

SOURCE: CCRRGE (1994), Seifert (2001).

jective of both aspects of ECR is the reduction or elimination of all activities that do not add value, and the concentration on factors that maximize value and productivity. ECR is an interdisciplinary marketing and logistics and management task between manufacturing and retailing companies.

> **DEFINITION: EFFICIENT CONSUMER RESPONSE**
>
> ECR is a comprehensive management concept based on vertical collaboration in manufacturing and retailing with the objective of an efficient satisfaction of consumer needs. The main components of ECR are supply chain management and category management.

1.1

The Goals and Tasks of the ECR Concept

The primary goal of ECR is to transform suboptimal individual solutions of individual links in the supply chain into a comprehensive solution. The concrete goal, in the realm of cooperative logistics and thereby in supply chain management, is the elimination of inefficiency that occurs through uncoordinated sequences in the supply chain: e.g., inventory or information that lies idle for long periods or the warehousing of unnecessary safety stock.

In cooperative marketing agreements, the objective is to rectify erroneous trends in promotional activities, assortment decisions, and product introductions. The problems are rooted in nonexistent or insufficient information on customers' needs. It is category management's task to offer a platform to retailers and manufacturers that supports the exchange of consumer data and tactics for a successful entry into the marketplace of the value-adding partners.

The goal of ECR is to allow manufacturers, retailers, and consumers to participate in the creation of value and thereby a win–win–win situation. Exhibit 1.2 shows the gains for each group.

The consumer profits from ECR above all through an optimized cost–benefit ratio. Consistently low prices help maintain a constant and thereby cost-effective flow of goods, reinforcing lower prices. Basic ECR strategies like efficient replenishment ensure fresher products and higher availability. Measures like efficient store assortment bring about a customer-oriented range of products and an improved shopping experience.

Suppliers and retailers benefit through the cooperative implementation of ECR primarily through higher profits. This is made possible through the cost reductions in the supply chain and increases in revenue through an optimized marketing concept.

EXHIBIT 1.2. THE CREATION OF A WIN–WIN–WIN SITUATION AS THE GOAL OF ECR.

Consumer	Retailer	Manufacturer
Fresher products	Quicker and more efficient system	Quicker and more efficient system
Greater and more consistent value for money	Reduced inventory and capital invested Lower depreciation Less promotion handling	Reduced inventory and capital invested Optimized production planning and use of capacity
More shopping satisfaction through improved product availability	Reduced out-of-stocks Greater customer loyalty	Reduced out-of-stocks Greater brand loyalty
Easy shopping experience (optimized categories)	Customer-oriented assortment	Customer-oriented assortment
Genuine innovations	Greater customer awareness through innovative assortments	Increased market share/ competitive advantage
➡ Greater customer satisfaction	➡ Lower costs and higher revenue growth	➡ Lower costs and higher revenue growth

SOURCE: Seifert.

1.2

The Reversal of the Push Principle to the Pull Principle in the Supply Chain

ECR represents a reengineering of the supply chain in the consumer goods industry. Until now, the process flow in the supply chain was dominated by the push principle. That meant that in the traditional supply chain of manufacturing and retailing, product volume was pushed into the pipeline, regardless of retail sales. This tendency can be seen in the following facts:

- Production is not synchronized with demand and thereby overburdens the warehouses of both manufacturer and retailer. The manufacturer's own production costs are minimized; however, they cause higher costs at other stages of the supply chain.
- Buyers from the retailer's side increase the volume of their purchases to obtain discounts and are measured by the success of these efforts. These savings are often lost through higher overall costs in the supply chain.
- Within retail organizations, there is seldom coordination between the sales and purchasing departments directed toward meeting consumers' needs. This unsatisfactory relationship leads to missing information at all stages of the supply chain and large swings in the demand for product in the trade channel. The consequences of extreme surges are overly large inventories in the supply chain, suppliers with capacities that are too low or too high, as well as uncertain production planning and a low service level on fast-turning SKU (stock-keeping units).

The problem becomes more acute especially when the manufacturer is continually trying to increase deliveries of product. This leads to exorbitant deliveries of product and to cost-intensive production peaks and a taxing of capacity. The large inventories are "pressed" into retail outlets through the retailers' warehouses. Because of limited retail space, a high pressure to sell the product exists, which can be reduced only through lower prices and the resultant increase in demand. The consequences are continually sinking promotional prices and reduced margins for manufacturers as well as retailers. Consumers alter their shopping habits and no longer buy products at regular prices, but rather are always on the lookout for special offers.

Through ECR, the relationship just described is reversed. The pull principle is now the dominating idea in the supply chain. A supply chain organized according to ECR principles references itself to the consumer and does not attempt to pressure product through the channel. The consumer's needs and buying behavior stand in the middle of all considerations. Demand is determined through exact measurements obtained via market research and the analysis of scanner data. Production and distribution in the supply chain are synchronized on the basis of information from retail outlets. Distribution works as the link between the production of the manufacturer and the consumption of the customer. A seamless exchange of information operates between all participants in the supply chain. Exhibit 1.3 should serve to clarify the reversal in the prevailing attitude.

The ECR reengineering process of the supply chain described above allows the vision of a consumer-driven supply chain to become a reality. The model is based on the realization that multistage warehouse inven-

EXHIBIT 1.3. ECR—REENGINEERING THE SUPPLY CHAIN.

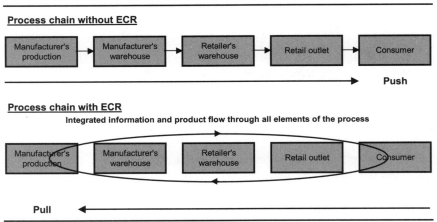

SOURCE: KSA (1993), Zentes (1996), Seifert (2001).

tory systems function decidedly better when information on orders and stock on hand in all links in the supply chain is available.

1.3

ECR—Collaboration Field Logistics: Supply Chain Management

The work between participants in the supply chain historically has led to conflicts in the trade channel. Every link in the chain was intent on minimizing its own costs. The optimization of logistics in a particular stage of production, however, often led to increased costs in preceding and following stages of the supply chain. The isolated optima of the individual stages did not lead to an overall optimum in the supply chain. Supply chain management, as the logistics foundation of the ECR concept, offers decisive differences for a comprehensive optimization of the supply chain. From supply chain management's (SCM's) perspective, the goal is a process-oriented overall treatment of the supply chain aimed at total system efficiency.

1.3.1 The Implementation of Supply Chain Planning

In the planning process of the logistics supply chain, manufacturers and retailers are supported by so-called supply chain planning (SCP) systems. Companies reach an optimal allocation of resources with these computer-based applications. Exhibit 1.4 gives an overview of the primary applications of SCP.

1.3.2 The Goals of Retailers and Manufacturers Bound to Supply Chain Management

Manufacturers and retailers have somewhat different objectives in SCM. Exhibit 1.5 lists the essential differences.

EXHIBIT 1.4. PRIMARY APPLICATIONS OF THE SUPPLY CHAIN PLANNING SYSTEM.

SCP—Application	Task
Demand Planning	Optimized quantification of demand.
Distribution Planning	Demand-oriented distribution planning, e.g., consideration of unexpected production gaps and late shipments.
Constraint-Based Master Planning	Constraint-based master planning delivers real-time planning in consideration of materials, capacities, and individual restrictions in integrated distribution, manufacturing, and suppliers' networks.
Transportation Planning	Transportation planning that gives the necessary transparency and that can accommodate all movement.
Manufacturing Planning and Scheduling	Detail planning of production. A precise time and dependencies plan is ensured.
Network Design and Optimization	Modeling of the entire supply chain and its business situation, in order to recommend the most economic strategy. Thereby, companies can quickly and easily see the course of the dovetailed process chain.
Available to Promise	Binding availability and delivery date agreements become possible through an integrated view of the supply chain. Thereby, all available inventory, orders, resource availability (transportation, production capacity, personnel, etc.) as well as alternate suppliers are considered.

SOURCE: Kansky/Weingarten (1999), Seifert (2001).

1.3.3 The Cost Savings Potential of Supply Chain Management

In order to show the possible cost savings potential available through ECR cooperation in logistics, a detailed cost structure analysis of the individual value-adding operations in the supply chain is necessary. Significant in these calculations is the share of expenditures on logistics relative to total cost. In a value chain analysis by PricewaterhouseCoopers, the essential cost components of retail and manufacturing in Europe were calculated. According to it, 21 percent of the manufacturer's total costs went toward logistics. On the retail side, the study revealed that 44 percent of total costs were attributable to logistics and thus that savings in the supply chain tended to be potentially stronger for retailers.

EXHIBIT 1.5. SCM OBJECTIVES OF RETAILERS AND SUPPLIERS.

	Market position–referenced goals	Results-referenced goals
Retailer's objectives	Expansion of logistical competence through manufacturing partner Increased consumer loyalty Better understanding of actual demand behavior Improved image through fresher products Quick logistical realization of new product introductions	Increased revenue through reduction of out-of-stocks Increased turnover of stock Inventory reduction Reduced costs of capital invested Increased earnings Reduced logistics costs Lower depreciation through expired goods (expiration of "use-by" date) Optimization of ordering and billing processes
Manufacturer's objectives	Improved image as competence partner of retailer Quick logistical realization of new product introductions Ability to influence logistics chain Creation of a competitive advantage Better understanding of actual demand behavior	Increased revenue through reduction of out-of-stocks Increased earnings Optimization of ordering and billing processes Reduction of logistics costs Optimized production Reduced inventory of raw materials and finished product

SOURCE: Seifert (2001).

A study of the Coca-Cola Retailing Research Group came to the conclusion that through SCM a cost savings potential of 1.5 to 2.5 percent of end consumer prices is achievable. Given such figures, it is astounding that many companies in the consumer goods business are not doing more in the way of ECR cooperative logistics (supply chain management). In a study by the consulting firm KPMG (in collaboration with the Kellogg School of Management) in 1998, 460 firms from twenty-four countries were asked about the degree of integration in their supply chains. The results are shown in Exhibit 1.6.

The study shows that the inclusion of suppliers (21 percent of those

EXHIBIT 1.6. DEGREE OF SUPPLY CHAIN INTEGRATION.

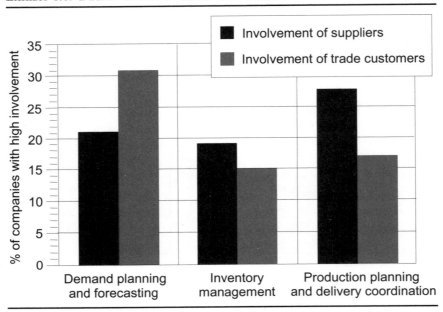

SOURCE: KPMG.

surveyed) in demand planning and demand forecasting is clearly less than that of customers (31 percent). The situation is reversed when considering production planning and scheduling. In this case consideration of the suppliers was a factor for 28 percent of those surveyed, while only 17 percent referenced customer data. KPMG perceived that insight into the advantages of increased supply chain integration is present, but that an adequate implementation has not yet occurred.

1.4

ECR—Collaboration Field Marketing: Category Management

Category management (CM) is defined as the joint process of retailers and manufacturers through which categories are managed as strategic business units in order to increase utility for the customer and thereby revenues. Whereas in supply chain management cost optimization stands in the foreground, in category management revenue optimization and the improvement of the gross margin are paramount. The full realization of cost reduction potential, however, is also the domain of CM. This comes about, for example, through more efficient structuring of promotional activities, efficient control of product assortment, or the optimized development and introduction of new products.

1.4.1 The Goals of Retailers and Manufacturers Bound to Category Management

The main idea of CM is a consistent orientation to the customer in product assortment and tender. The core of CM is, correspondingly, strategic control of product assortments. The goals of manufacturers and retailers in category management can be structured in terms of market-referenced goals (qualitative measures) and results targets (quantitative measures). Exhibit 1.7 systematizes the objectives of manufacturing and retailing.

1.4.2 The Nine-Step Category Management Planning Process

The category management planning process has the objective of assuring a structured implementation of CM. The nine-step business plan describes a series of activities, the methodology, and the responsibilities in the process. The initiation of the planning process includes the naming of clearly defined process owners with clearly laid-out responsibilities in the execution of the individual steps in the plan. In such a

EXHIBIT 1.7. CM STRATEGIES OF RETAILING AND MANUFACTURING.

	Market position–referenced goals	Results–referenced goals
Retailer's objectives	Optimized assortment regarding target group and geographic position of the retail outlet Improved image through consumer orientation, category performance, and pricing Gaining of new consumer segments Exploiting of cross-selling potentials Increased consumer loyalty Unique identity and positioning among retailers Price concept with higher value creation opportunity Early recognition of market and consumer trends Acquisition of market and marketing knowledge from manufacturers	Profit optimization of the category through increases in revenue and earnings Increased revenue through reduction of out-of-stocks Reduced costs of capital invested Increased productivity of retail space Improved reach of consumers Reduced costs through efficient promotions Increased inventory turnover Increased profit contribution of assortment Increased purchase intensity of consumers Cost optimization of new product introductions
Manufacturer's objectives	Acquisition of information about substitutions and complementary product relationships Strengthening of brand loyalty Price concept with higher value creation opportunity Better understanding of consumer behavior Access to POS data from retailers Improved placement on shelves Building of an image as a competence partner and preferred supplier Early recognition of market and consumer trends Gaining of influence at POS Test markets for innovative products Creation of a competitive advantage	Profit optimization of the category through increases in revenue and earnings Improved reach of consumers Cost optimization of new product introductions Increased purchase intensity of consumers Increased revenue through reduction of out-of-stocks Cost-effective use of advertising budget through efficient promotions

SOURCE: Behrends (1995), Feld (1996), Seifert (2001).

cooperation, it seems prudent for the manufacturer and retailer to structure the steps in common. The category management planning process creates a balance between product and process investment and takes into consideration all required activities of the whole system from manufacturer to retailer to consumer.

Only when all partners have a complete understanding of the process can the details of the individual steps be adequately addressed. In the planning process, that is, the definition, dimensioning, and structuring of the introduction of a category, one must always consider the demand structure and the buying behavior of the previously identified target group. In Exhibit 1.8, the nine steps of the CM planning process are illustrated.

Strategy Analysis

The first step of the CM planning process entails a strategy analysis of the retail organization. Essential is an understanding of the company's

EXHIBIT 1.8. THE CATEGORY MANAGEMENT PLANNING PROCESS.

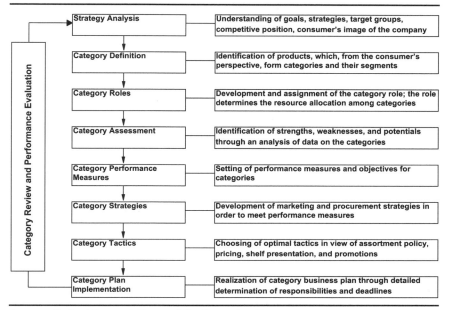

SOURCE: Roland Berger & Partner/The Partnering Group.

objectives, its niche in the marketplace, and its image in the eyes of consumers. From that, strategies can be derived for a successful penetration and loyalty. These are, for example, the assortment, marketing, and pricing strategies with quantitative measures like penetration rate and demand coverage quotas (loyalty). Particularly important for the strategy analysis is the identification of the retailer's target group.

The strategic framework consists of established corporate strategies and their connection to the category's business plan. The corporate strategy should embody the corporate vision and the resultant objectives in marketing and finance. Furthermore, a marketing strategy, a purchasing strategy, and a strategy for developing relationships to suppliers should be generated.

According to the definition of the strategic framework at the corporate level, strategies for the individual categories can be derived and thereby support a comprehensive company strategy. On the basis of this result, the business plans for the categories. Exhibit 1.9 diagrams the above-described connections.

Category Definition and Segmentation

After strategy analysis comes the definition of categories and their segmentation. Vitek describes this step as follows: "Segmentation is the

EXHIBIT 1.9. STRATEGIES OF RETAILERS AND THEIR CONNECTIONS TO CATEGORY BUSINESS PLANS.

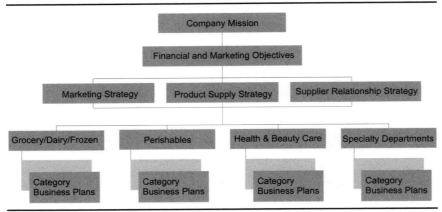

SOURCE: Roland Berger & Partner/The Partnering Group.

process where we take any category and break it down based on the consumer decision process. For example, we may see deli as a single entity but we could segment the category by flavor, pack size, or even shelf life, depending on the consumer's shopping behavior."[1] This step is critical in the joint efforts of retailer and manufacturer. This is where the basis for all following steps is established. One should pay particular attention to defining categories from the perspective of the user and not from that of the retailing or manufacturing partners.

The analysis of category structures consists of the identification of the most important categories, segments, and subsegments of the category. The deciding factor for success here is the most accurate possible reflection of how the target customer makes his purchase decisions in each of the categories. In the definition of categories, the retailers will profit from a reliable knowledge of the consumer and the market of the consumer goods manufacturer. Information on buying behavior is often presented in the form of buying decision trees.

The individual steps in the definition of categories should be correspondingly done on the basis of a thorough knowledge of the customer. In Exhibit 1.10, a model of the process of category definition according to McKinsey (Tochtermann/Lange) is shown.

The Role of the Category

After the definition of categories and their segmentation comes the fixing of the category's role. This third step is often discussed as the core of CM, as it is here that the desired high-level corporate and marketing goals, such as market image of a company, can be achieved. The determination of individual category roles offers the best approach to the differentiation from competitors. Says F. Stagliano, vice president of integrated marketing at A. C. Nielsen, "Focus on how you will distinguish yourself from competitors and put the most thought into the selection of your signature categories."

The development of category roles is also of special significance in that it determines the priority of categories in the retailer's entire organization and its resource allocation. With the assistance of adequate resource allocation, the retailer optimizes its return on investment. In Exhibit 1.11, examples of the four most important category roles and their characteristics are shown.

EXHIBIT 1.10. THE PROCESS OF CATEGORY DEFINITION.

	Understanding of the consumer´s attitudes and perceptions	Analysis of actual consumer behavior	Definition of consumer-oriented categories	Evaluation of the new category concept	Execution of market trials
Objectives	• Basic attitudes of consumer behavior • Behavior planning • Unfulfilled demand and first ideas on categories	• Connection between product/brand and buying behavior • Actual buying process	• First hypotheses on new category definition	• Agreement on category definition and opportunities for improvement	• Quantitative results of new category definition
Tasks/ Analysis	• Analysis of the planning processes of consumers (products, priorities, etc.) • Determination of influences (occasions, etc.)	• Quantitative/ qualitative analysis basket analysis • Analysis of the choice of outlet/channel • Investigation on purchase process and sequence	• Combination of attitude-based and actual consumer behavior • Determination of exceptions/ unfulfilled needs • Evaluation of new category definitions	• Creation of concept • Determination of panel size • Execution of surveys • Evaluation of data/discernment of trends • Optimization of category concept/ definition	• Evaluation of revised category definition • Generation of key learnings and impact on sales revenues, margins, etc.
Instruments	• Comprehensive interviews • Focus groups • Standard usage and attitude data	• Scanner data • Panel data • Participatory observations	• Expert workshops	• CHOICE test • Evaluation of categories based on purchase readiness, personal relevance, etc. of potential consumers	• Market tests of test market simulations

SOURCE: McKinsey.

The concrete allocation of specific roles to the individual categories is based, among other things, on the results of quantitative and qualitative analyses, as well as market forecasting. An example of quantitative allocation criteria is the profit contribution of the category to the gross profit of the company. Qualitative criteria are, for example, shopping experience and other opportunities to create consumer loyalty. Market forecasts are made drawing on projected growth in revenues and market share.

In summary, it can be seen that the determination of category roles is the most meaningful step in achieving marketing goals and consists of three interdependent steps:

1. The explicit determination within the retail organization of which category roles will be used

EXHIBIT 1.11. CATEGORY ROLES AND THEIR FUNCTIONS IN THE FRAMEWORK OF CM.

Category role	The role of the category is:	Share of categories
Destination	• To be the primary provider of these products to the target consumer • To help define the profile of the retailer in the eyes of the target consumer • To deliver consistently superior value to the target consumer • To lead all retailer's categories in the areas of turnover, market share, consumer satisfaction, service level, etc.	• 5–7% of categories
Preferred	• To be the preferred provider of these products to the target consumer • To help build the target consumer's image of the retailer • To play a primary role in delivering profit, cash flow, and ROA (return on assets)	• 55–60% of categories
Occasional/Seasonal	• To be a major provider of these products to the target consumer • To help reinforce the consumer's image of the retailer • To deliver frequent, competitive value to the target consumer • To play a secondary role in delivering profit, cash flow, and ROA (return on assets)	• 15–20% of categories
Convenience	• To help to reinforce the target consumer's image of the retailer as the place for one-stop shopping • To deliver good, everyday value to the target consumer • To play an important role in the area of generation and margin enhancement	• 15–20% of categories

SOURCE: Roland Berger & Partner/The Partnering Group.

2. The assignment of category roles to each individual category

3. The allocation of the company's resources to categories corresponding to their roles

Category Assessment

The successful management of a category requires that its status be determined. Category evaluation entails an analysis of the relevant data on the category with a view toward the market and the customer. The goal is, on the one hand, to gain a clear understanding of the current potential of the category (strengths and weaknesses) and, on the other, to identify the corresponding revenue and profit potential of the category. This potential analysis forms the basis for further advances in category management.

Category Performance Analysis

This step in the CM business-planning process establishes the essential category goals and measurement criteria for the category in question. Exhibit 1.12 shows systematically chosen indices in external (consumer-referenced) and internal (results-based) measurement criteria.

The sought-after target values must coincide with the assigned category roles from step three. Typically, the objective of a high-profile category is first and foremost increases in revenue and market share. In contrast, a supplementary category should make a contribution to profitability. As a rule, category performance criteria are developed on a yearly basis with the possibility for corrections to and modifications of

EXHIBIT 1.12. CONSUMER-REFERENCED AND RESULTS-ORIENTED MEASUREMENT CRITERIA FOR CATEGORY PERFORMANCE.

Consumer Measures	Financial Measures
• Household penetration	• Turnover category
• Purchase frequency	• Days of inventory
• Demand coverage	• Inventory turnover
• Purchase intensity	• Return on investment
• Consumer satisfaction	• Gross margin
• Image of the retailer	• Net profit

SOURCE: Seifert (2001).

the business plan occurring on a quarterly cycle. The corresponding accounting can be aided with CM scorecards.

Category Strategies

In this CM planning stage, category strategies for retailers are developed. The strategies are drawn from the previously determined category roles. For example, a high-profile category may offer the retailer the opportunity to aggressively position itself against competitors (defending turf). A seasonal or impulse category supports a strategy of building traffic. Finally, a supplementary category may support image building in that a broader assortment allows an easier and a more complete shopping experience (one-stop shopping). Accordingly, category strategies should always be in harmony with high-level corporate and marketing objectives, such as the sought-after marketing image. The strategies generated set the framework for the implementation of the instruments of retail marketing.

Category Tactics

Category tactics formulate the specific steps for the realization of the previously developed category strategies. The tactical decisions support the best possible implementation of category strategies in order to meet the objectives of the category business plan. The core areas for the development of category tactics are assortment politics, in-store presentation, pricing policies, and promotions. Exhibit 1.13 shows the relationship between category tactics and category roles.

Implementation of Category Business Plan

The implementation of the category business plan occurs in the eighth step of the CM planning process. In this next-to-last stage, the concrete activities within the category, for example, assortment optimization, promotion planning, and shelf optimization, are finalized. The implementation plan includes a clear assignment of responsibilities upon activation and a precise schedule with set deadlines (milestones). These measures go a long way toward ensuring quality during the plan's implementation. In this phase, it is the practice to bundle the different

EXHIBIT 1.13. THE RELATIONSHIP BETWEEN CATEGORY TACTICS AND CATEGORY ROLES.

Category Role	Category Tactics			
	Assortment	Shelf Presentation	Pricing	Promotion
Destination	**Complete variety** • Best variety in market • Subcategories • Premium brands	**Prime store location** • High traffic • High exposure time • High space allocation	**Leadership** • Best value (per unit of use)	**High level of activity** • High frequency • Multiple vehicles • Customized
Preferred	**Broad variety—competitive in market** • Major brands • Subcategories • Major SKUs • Private level	**Average store location** • High frequency • High space allocation	**Competitive—consistent** • Equal to competition (per unit use) • Major components of category	**Average level of activity** • Average frequency • Average duration • Multiple vehicles
Seasonal/ Occasional	**Timely variety** • Changing suppliers • Subcategories • Changing themes	**Good store location** • High traffic • Average space allocation	**Competitive—seasonally** • Close to competition • Some components of category	**Seasonal/timely** • Multiple vehicles • In-store activities (promotion teams)
Convenience	**Select variety** • Relevant brands	**Available store location** • Low space allocation	**Acceptable** • Within 15% of competition (per unit use)	**Low level of activity** • Selected vehicles

SOURCE: Roland Berger & Partner/The Partnering Group.

resources of manufacturer and retailer to secure a quick execution in the retail outlets.

Measuring Results

The last step of the category management business-planning process is the continuous control of the implementation and performance measurements. Continuous accounting of category results can be done with the help of a CM scorecard. Clearly defined polling parameters across several reporting periods enable comparative analysis.

The CM planning process offers a good basis for a structured approach to the implementation and use of category management in retail organizations. This model should not, however, be seen as a one-size-fits-all solution. The individual conditions and requirements must be adequately considered in the planning process. The efficient satisfaction of customer wishes in the framework of category management is supported by three fundamental ECR components: efficient store assortment, efficient product introduction, and efficient promotion.

1.4.3 The Management of Categories as Strategic Business Units

The task of highest priority in the competitive retail world is the development of unique characteristics and of barriers to imitation in order to be perceived as superior to one's competitors.

The key to success at the point of sale (POS) is a new definition of categories and their management as strategic business units, for which retailers and manufacturers are jointly developing new strategies. These new definitions mean a full retreat from traditional assortment structures. Until now, retailers have carried products with identical functions or homogeneous characteristics of production and materiality together as categories. The result is that most retailers' assortments are nearly identical and take the "me too" approach as opposed to one of retail competition. In strategically arranged categories, articles are bundled according to functional aspects as perceived by the customer.

Adopting the conception of categories from the customer's perspective entails the coordination of categories according to demand scenarios and cross-selling techniques that accommodate additional customer desires and that properly address the targeted market segment. This heightens the presence of an assortment among the competition and promotes a transition from POS to point of difference from the customer's perspective. Strategic categories for clearly defined market segments can be so conceived.

A concrete example of the strategically important target group of young families should make clear the revenue and profitability enhancing effects of newly defined categories. The products disposable diapers, baby carriages, toys for babies, and baby books, which were previously considered individually, can be brought together as a baby care center through their presentation as complementary articles in a common space. Unnecessary time spent searching them out on the part of the customer is eliminated and impulse buying is encouraged. In addition, this arrangement creates a small world of its own, which satisfies a clearly identified customer need. The presentation of products according to use scenarios offers the target group "young families" real additional utility and thus creates customer loyalty, which in view of future decisions on where to shop is important. The retail chain Real, a division of Metro, has introduced the concept of baby care centers with notable success in numerous outlets.

Such strategic conception of a category can be easily translated to other categories. Further themes for formation of categories might include wine (targeted at high-income households), or ready-to-eat meals (singles).

The use of CM offers the opportunity, via the introduction of strategic, customer-oriented categories, for the retailer to distinguish itself from competitors in the market. This constitutes a comparative strategic advantage. Retailers have the opportunity, via the categories they create and their added utility for the consumer, to create barriers to imitation and to be rewarded with customer loyalty as a consequence. The example of Wal-Mart and its rapid growth in the last ten years is an impressive testament to this.

Quadrant Analysis as an Instrument of Strategic Investigation of Categories

An interesting approach to an appraisal of the strategic significance of individual categories is quadrant analysis. With this method, categories are evaluated according to the determinant's revenue share and gross margin. The results testify to which objectives particular categories are well suited. This is how one differentiates between the Dogs, which produce a small share of sales and low gross receipts, and the Cash Cows, which have high values on both axes. The Traffic Builders, with their high sales volume, are good for bringing customers in the door. Because these types of items are typically sold at deep discounts, gross revenues are correspondingly low. Examples in Germany are Coca-Cola, and well-liked brands of coffee such as Jacobs Krönung or Milka-Schokolade. The last strategic group is composed of the so-called Sleepers. They are identified by their high gross revenues and low sales volume. The expansion of the sales volume of this category represents the strategic direction. Exhibit 1.14 depicts an example of quadrant analysis. The arrows indicate the direction of strategic development in each case.

EXHIBIT 1.14. STRATEGIC QUADRANT ANALYSIS FOR THE EVALUATION OF CATEGORIES.

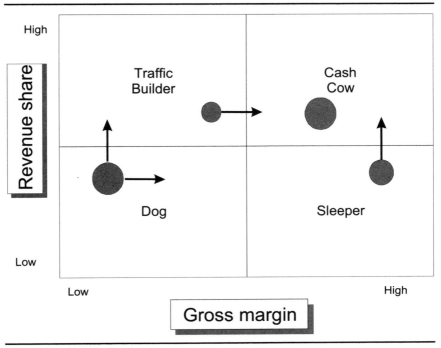

SOURCE: Beckmann (1996).

Relevant Success Factors for ECR Implementation

Since the introduction of ECR in the early nineties, the new management concept has been implemented by most large concerns in the American consumer goods economy. With a delay of one to two years, top European retailers and manufacturers successfully began to integrate ECR principles into their business processes. Several companies were able to make the necessary changes rapidly, while others needed longer or are today still in the test phase of individual ECR components.

If one analyzes the successful use of this new management concept by pioneering firms, decisive factors for the successful implementation of ECR are revealed that are also of significance for the implementation of CPFR. The ECR success factor study (Seifert, 2001) identified and prioritized the most important ones based on a poll of experts. In this study, experts from consumer goods manufacturers, retailers, and consulting firms were queried on the utility of supply chain management and CM as well as the leadership competence of the firms interviewed.

In the survey, the experts were asked about the significance of nine different factors. Based on a scale of 1 to 5 (1 = very high relevance and 5 = no relevance) the factors were rated for their relevance. Exhibit 1.15 differentiates the statements according to respondents' background, showing the difference in perspective among the different groups.

The experts rated the "involvement of top management" as the most significant factor, with an average score of 1.2. This was, however, less pronounced in the opinion of representatives from retailing, who scored this factor 1.7 compared with 1.1 given by manufacturers and consultants.

Another salient factor was "mutual trust between collaboration partners," with an average value of 1.7 for all participants. Manufacturers placed more emphasis here, with a score of 1.3, than consultants, who gave it a rating of 2.1. At the same level of significance as trust was the "implementation of modern information technology," receiving a 1.7 overall.

"Change in organizational structure" received a score of 1.9 from all participants. Manufacturing representatives gave it a 1.6, higher than the 2.0 given by consultants.

EXHIBIT 1.15. SIGNIFICANCE OF SUCCESS FACTORS BY SECTOR.

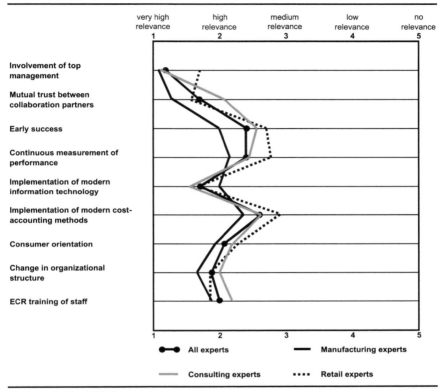

SOURCE: Seifert (2001).

"ECR training of staff," "consumer orientation." "early success," and "continuous measurement of performance" all ranked high, with values of 2.0, 2.1, and 2.4, respectively. "Early success" had more significance for manufacturers, at 2.0, than for retail, at 2.7. Similar differences of opinion were apparent with respect to "continuous measurement of performance": manufacturers rated it at 2.2 versus 2.8 for retailers.

In comparison with other factors, "implementation of modern cost-accounting methods" was considered secondary, with a value of 2.6. In the poll, participants were asked to name other success factors for ECR implementation not listed on the questionnaire. Among those cited were "consensus on joint marketing strategies," "continuity in the business relationship/business partners," "adequate incentive systems," and "continuous market monitoring." None of these was mentioned more than once.

Experience shows that the identified factors for ECR are also applicable to CPFR. Ralph Drayer, former chief logistics officer at Procter & Gamble, supports this position in his statement, "The key barrier of CPFR and its implementation is a lot like we had found with ECR. It is that you have to have trust and leadership, understand the benefits and be willing to take the pain of transition, resource it and support it. CPFR is a new business model, it's a radical change from the way things are done today." Part 2 introduces this new business model and explains key benefits and implementation requirements.

Note

1. S. Vitek, "A Work in Progress—Category Management," in *Progressive Grocer*, 5, 1998, p. 17.

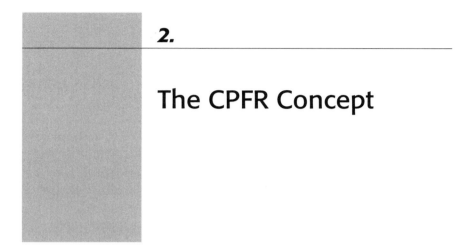

2.

The CPFR Concept

2.1

The CPFR Value Proposition

Prof. Dr. Dirk Seifert, Harvard Business School and University of Massachusetts

The ECR concept presented in the first chapter ushered in a new era in the way of cooperation between retailers and manufacturers. The cooperation in marketing (category management) and logistics (supply chain management) paves the way for new strategic approaches. Collaborative Planning, Forecasting, and Replenishment (CPFR) represents a further quantum leap in the streamlining of business processes in the value chain.

2.1.1 Integration of CPFR in the ECR Concept

For most experts in the consumer goods economy, CPFR is an evolution and refinement of the original ECR concept. Volker Schröder,

27

director of customer logistics management for Procter & Gamble, Europe, views CPFR as a "consistent and thereby more complex evolution of ECR. . . . CPFR connotes a high degree of trust and a commonly held determination to not only share data but to achieve a measurable improvement in the quality of the data." Zygmunt Mierdorf, board member of Metro AG, emphasizes, "The essence of CPFR is ECR, and the essence of ECR is the improvement of the relationship between producers and retailers. . . . In addition, CPFR was developed because of the opportunities afforded by the Internet and the B2B marketplace to better control and optimize the entire process. Common expectations and a continued sensitivity to the data direct the planning process."

In this book, and in the framework of the study of this topic at Harvard Business School, CPFR is considered a further development of Efficient Consumer Response on the supply side. The intensified efforts in cooperative supply chain management, like cross docking, vendor-managed inventories (VMI), and continuous replenishment, in evidence since the early nineties, find in CPFR a further development of collaboration. The demands on the quality of the partnerships are considerably higher than with the classic initiatives in cooperative supply chain management. The quality and the intensity of the information exchange (info partnering) demands a strong commitment to cooperation from the participating organizations. Exhibit 2.1 shows the integration of CPFR in the ECR concept.

CPFR and Collaborative Customer Relationship Management (CCRM) represent business concepts of second-generation ECR. Typical of CPFR is a strong relationship to the demand side of the equation. The planning and forecasting components demand intensive information exchange not only at the logistics level, but also in sales management, marketing, and finance planning. CPFR is thereby a tool for comprehensive value chain management of an organization. Senior management uses CPFR and its efficiency advantages in strategic supply chain management. The goal is an enduring improvement of the company's own position in the market and the optimization of its own value chain.

CCRM as a further development of the demand side enables the coordinated management of all customer touch points (point of sale

EXHIBIT 2.1. INTEGRATION OF CPFR IN THE ECR CONCEPT.

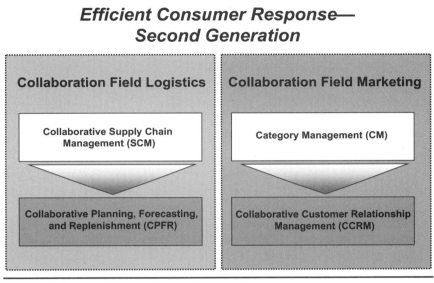

**Efficient Consumer Response—
Second Generation**

Collaboration Field Logistics

Collaborative Supply Chain
Management (SCM)

Collaborative Planning, Forecasting,
and Replenishment (CPFR)

Collaboration Field Marketing

Category Management (CM)

Collaborative Customer Relationship
Management (CCRM)

SOURCE: Seifert.

(POS), TV, radio, call center, e-mail, Internet, etc.). The intensive collaboration on the demand side beyond classic category management allows the exploitation of prominent synergy potentials in all aspects of customer management (customer identification, attraction, retention, and development). CCRM represents another focus of the research group at Harvard Business School. This topic, however, is not discussed further here relative to CPFR. A paper on this topic by Seifert, Kracklauer, and Mills appeared in June 2002 in Germany and in March 2003 in the United States.

The CPFR Opportunity

Second-generation ECR uses intensively the most modern information and communication technology. The inclusion of large B2B platforms (WWRE, GNX, CPGmarket, Transora) allows the use of state-of-the-art technology in planning and procurement. The consistent use of modern data standards and computer languages like XML supports the exchange of complex quantities of data. CPFR brings the previously distinct experiences of sales planning of both partners together and simultaneously initiates a continuously improving understanding of the system.

> **DEFINITION OF CPFR**
>
> CPFR is an initiative among all participants in the supply chain intended to improve the relationship among them through jointly managed planning processes and shared information.

2.1.2 The Birth of CPFR: Wal-Mart and Warner-Lambert's First Pilot

The first CPFR project was begun by Wal-Mart und Warner-Lambert in the United States. The IT companies SAP and Manugistics and the consulting firm Benchmarking Partners (now Surgency) supported the project with their particular know-how. The group defined Collaborative Forecasting and Replenishment (CFAR, the predecessor of CPFR), a process intended to reduce inventories across the supply chain. CFAR allowed comparisons of the sales and order forecasts of each trading partner and made visible any forecast differences early enough for the partners to resolve them. The CFAR model was first applied to Listerine mouthwash products supplied by Warner-Lambert. It included the sharing of forecasts and responding to inconsistencies between the collaboration partners' individual forecasts arising from events like Wal-Mart promotions capable of generating large swings in consumer demand. Prior to CFAR, Warner-Lambert was often caught unaware by these promotions. In order to prevent out-of-stocks it had to maintain substantial inventory as a hedge against such situations.

During the pilot, Wal-Mart and Warner-Lambert independently calculated the demand they expected six months in advance. The weekly forecast included data by week, by store, and by SKU (stock-keeping unit). Both partners shared this information with each other as it was generated, and they worked to resolve discrepancies between their forecasts on a weekly basis. Initially, the two companies exchanged forecasts on paper but the resulting manual comparison that allowed the process to be tested constrained any large-scale deployment. Eventually the Internet was used to exchange spreadsheets. As a result of the pilot, Wal-Mart began placing its order six weeks in advance to match the six-week manufacturing lead time for Listerine. Previously, Wal-Mart had placed orders nine days in advance. By receiving an order six weeks in advance, Warner-Lambert was able to construct a smoother production plan since it could manufacture according to consumer demand for Listerine rather than manufacture to maintain sufficient stock. Wal-Mart in turn saw that its in-stock position improved from 85 percent to 98 percent. The retailer also saw that sales increased by $8.5 million (U.S.) in one year with no new product introductions while inventories dropped over the course of the pilot by 25 percent. By the end of the experimental phase in fall 1996, Warner-Lambert's supply management had also improved substantially.

Over the course of the pilot, the VICS Working Group overseeing the project met every two weeks to develop a widely applicable model for sharing and responding to forecast data, which later evolved into CPFR. The pilot of Wal-Mart and Warner-Lambert represented a substantial shift in approach, since most retailers and suppliers were not used to sharing information, but Wal-Mart and Warner-Lambert had both realized benefits during the pilot. They had also developed a solid relationship in the process and continued to collaborate, paving the way for CFAR and later CPFR to be tested and improved in the future.

2.1.3 Institutions and Organizations of CPFR Development

Global CPFR implementation is greatly supported by several institutions and organizations, most of them located in the United States. The following section portrays the most relevant of these.

Voluntary Interindustry Commerce Standards (VICS)

CPFR was conceived in the United States and was first described and publicized by the Voluntary Interindustry Commerce Standards (VICS) Association. VICS was founded in 1986 and is a voluntary, nonprofit organization. The mission of the VICS Association is to take a global leadership role in the continual improvement of the flow of product and information about the product throughout the entire retail supply chain. VICS members are key retail, manufacturing, and transportation companies whose highly influential executives collaborate to develop business process standards to improve the future of the retail industry supply chain for all its participants. Since the beginning, VICS has worked to establish cross-industry standards that simplify the flow of product and information among supplier, manufacturer, and retailers.

VICS CPFR Committee

VICS maintains its original CPFR Committee, which is composed of retailers including Kmart, Sears Roebuck, Walgreens, and Wal-Mart; manufacturers like Gillette, Kellogg's, Kimberly-Clark, Mars, Nestlé, Procter & Gamble, Sara Lee, and Unilever; service providers such as Accenture, IBM, Syncra, and Retek; and e-marketplaces like Global-NetXchange, WWRE, CPGmarket, and Transora. The mission of the CPFR Committee is to create collaborative relationships between buyers and sellers through comanaged processes and shared information. The group aims to develop a set of business processes that entities in a supply chain can use for collaboration on a number of manufacturer/retailer functions toward overall efficiency in the supply chain. By integrating demand and supply-side processes, Collaborative Planning, Forecasting, and Replenishment will improve efficiencies, increase sales, reduce fixed assets and working capital, and reduce inventory for the entire supply chain while satisfying consumer needs. This is an objective that clearly agrees with the principles of Efficient Consumer Response.

In the course of its work, the CPFR Committee published the document Collaborative Planning, Forecasting, and Replenishment Voluntary Guidelines, which describes the CPFR process, its technical support, and suggestions for implementation. The guidelines created received the approval of VICS board members in June 1998. In November 1999, the CPFR committee published the follow-up document Roadmap to CPFR: The Case Studies.

Global Commerce Initiative (GCI)

The Global Commerce Initiative (GCI) is a voluntary body created in October 1999. VICS was instrumental in creating GCI for the purpose of simplifying global commerce by establishing voluntary global standards. GCI operates through an executive board composed of senior representatives from more than forty-five international companies drawn equally from the manufacturing and retailing sides of the consumer goods industry, together with eight sponsoring organizations. Four of the sponsoring bodies represent the interests of manufacturers and retailers (AIM, CIES, GAM, and FMI). Two sponsors (the ECR movements and VICS) develop working tools for the collaborative management of the supply chain. The other two bodies are the principal standards organizations, EAN International and the Uniform Code Council (UCC).

GCI has built a collaborative interbusiness process that will endorse a recommended set of standards, enabling technologies and best practices with worldwide application, in order to provide benefits to all users, large and small, wherever they operate. This global approach will be developed and documented together with international standards organizations. GCI builds from a solid foundation created by the ECR initiatives in Europe, the United States, Latin America, and Asia; the VICS Association in North America; and the work of the standards organizations EAN International and UCC. GCI is a global user group, not a standards body. Its job is to facilitate and encourage the best possible focused input on business needs on a global level, so that existing standards bodies can work with the confidence necessary to achieve true standardization.

From the initial release of the VICS CPFR Guidelines at VICS 1998, the Retail Supply Chain Business Conference, this nine-step supply chain process model has moved rapidly beyond the pilot stage to full implementation by leading retailers and suppliers in the retail supply chain. It has also been adopted by leading retail and consumer goods Internet trading exchanges such as the WWRE, GNX, Transora, and NovoPoint. In addition, UCCnet, eBXML, and the Global Commerce Initiative have incorporated this collaborative commerce process model into their open standards infrastructure development. In June 2001 GCI published its CPFR Recommendation. This recommendation for CPFR combines relevant portions of three previous VICS CPFR publications, along with new material. The process model is taken from the original VICS CPFR Guidelines document and advanced by the ECR Europe CPFR working group experiences and national ECR activities.

Some technical information derives from the Roadmap to CPFR document published in 2000. Finally, the CPFR object model and XML specification come from the VICS CPFR XML Messaging Specification.

2.1.4 The CPFR Process Model

The CPFR planning process structures the relevant steps of the implementation process of CPFR. The model is divided into three phases. Phase one consists of planning (steps 1 and 2), phase two is forecasting (steps 3–8), and phase three is replenishment (step 9). Exhibit 2.2 reflects the recommendations of VICS.

The following descriptions seek to explain the nine steps according to Voluntary Interindustry Commerce Standards.

Step 1: Develop Collaboration Arrangement

The first step of the CPFR model is to establish the rules and conventions of cooperation between retailer and manufacturer. The agreement sets the objective of both business partners. The pact also describes the actions and resources necessary for the successful application of CPFR. The jointly written paper defines the practical arrangement of the partnership, identifies the roles of the business partners involved, and establishes how the performance of the respective parties will be measured. In total, the first step consists of ten individual actions:

1. *Develop CPFR mission statement.* The development of a mission statement creates a common basis for cooperation, trust, and availability of resources. The following components of step 1 address in detail the content of the mission statement.

2. *Determine CPFR goals and objectives.* Determination of concrete goals and tasks entails agreement on the appropriate indices for measuring performance. Additionally, the business practices and criteria for exceptions purchasing and the forecasting of orders is established.

3. *Discuss competencies, resources, and systems.* The CPFR process demands a clear determination of the competencies, resources, and

Exhibit 2.2. CPFR PROCESS MODEL.

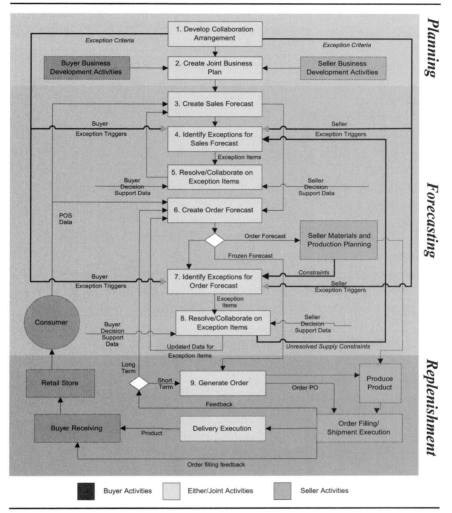

SOURCE: Voluntary Interindustry Commerce Standards (VICS) Association.

systems of all parties involved and their capability to contribute to the process. Which departmental or functional groups are ready and able to contribute to the process long term? Which additional capacities must be expanded or outsourced?

4. *Define collaboration points and responsible business functions.* Map the collaboration points to trading partner competencies and establish the responsible business functions (functional departments) that will be the key executors of the process.

5. *Determine information-sharing needs.* The CPFR process requires information from both manufacturers and retailers. Identifying the demand for information determines which information will be shared, for example, data on the identification of forecast anomalies. Furthermore, the frequency of the exchange, the medium of the exchange, the allowable response time before information requests are honored, and the forecasting method must be determined.

6. *Define service and ordering commitments.* This activity lays out the nature of order and delivery commitments in the framework of the CPFR process. This pertains especially to the phase in which collaboratively determined projections become firm orders.

7. *Determine resource involvement and commitments.* In this step, both CPFR partners establish which resources will be made available. This means, for example, how much time and how many employees will be devoted to the CPFR process. This is true of resource allocation for the work process, agreements on process management, and how initiatives like process improvement can be integrated into the system.

8. *Resolve differences between partners in the CPFR process.* This activity comprises the standardization of rules for handling disagreements and differences between partners. Should something be contested, it is important to have measures for conflict resolution in place to which all have agreed.

9. *Regularly review cycle for CPFR agreement.* This step is designed to establish a continual evaluation and to benchmark the success of the collaborative relationship. The agreement is modified whenever necessary.

10. *Publish front-end agreement.* The jointly composed agreement becomes binding for all participants in the process. The agreement

can be updated at any time to reflect new demands or developments.

Step 2: Create Joint Business Plan

In the second step of the nine-step CPFR model, both partners work out a business plan taking into account their individual corporate strategies. This is composed of defining product group roles, objectives, and articles. (The experience of category management business–planning processes can be helpful in determining product group roles, objectives, and articles.) (See also Part 1.) Contract information for the products to be optimized is continually exchanged. This is, for example, the minimum order, necessary lead time for the order, and the frequency of the order. The development of a common business plan improves the quality of projections in that available information from both partners is incorporated into the plan. Furthermore, this plan offers an appropriate platform for communication and coordination along the supply chain.

Step 3: Create Sales Forecast

The retailer's POS data and promotion planning provide the basis for the determination of sales forecasts. Sales projections become more reliable and convey the intentions of the business plan at a higher level of detail.

Step 4: Identify Exceptions for Sales Forecast

In this step, all products are identified that represent exceptions to the cooperatively determined acceptance of the sales forecast. These can be seasonal products, for example. The exception criteria for each product are determined in the front-end agreement (see step 1).

Step 5: Resolve/Collaborate on Exception Items

The fifth step concerns the joint identification and clarification of exceptions to the forecast through real-time communication between the partners. Each change flows immediately into the new forecast. The accelerated communication and decision making by producers and retailers increases the reliability of the order that is generated later.

Step 6: Create Order Forecast

In this step, data from POSs are linked to the individual inventory strategies of the partners to generate a specific order forecast. The preview represents a higher level of detail developed from the joint business plan (step 2) and the sales forecast (step 3). The order volume is based on the inventory targets per product and the destination of the goods. Consider the question: How much advance notice is necessary to transport the product to its destination? Does the order information reflect temporal differences? The short-term order forecast is used to generate actual orders. The long-term order forecast flows into the overall planning.

Step 7: Identify Exceptions for Order Forecast

In this step, all products are identified that represent exceptions to the cooperatively determined acceptance of the order forecast. The result is a list of those articles that, on the basis of the criteria in the cooperation agreement, represent exceptions.

Step 8: Resolve/Collaborate on Exception Items

The eighth step concerns the common identification and clarification of exceptions to the forecast through real-time communication between the partners. Each change flows immediately into the new forecast. The accelerated communication and decision making by producers and retailers increases the reliability of the order that is generated later.

Step 9: Generate Order

In the last step, an order forecast becomes a firm order. Order generation can be handled by either the manufacturer or retailer depending on competence in the process, access to appropriate technology, and the availability of free resources.

Inclusion of Raw Material Suppliers in the CPFR Concept

CPFR is a management concept that deals with the entire value chain as one entity. The optimization occurs not only at the intersections between manufacturer and retailer and retailer and consumer; it seeks also potential between supplier and manufacturer. Harmonized planning and production processes along the value chain offer considerable opportunities for cost reductions.

An example of a successful CPFR project comprising a supplier, a manufacturer, and a retailer is the cooperation of Henkel with the Spanish retailer Condis and the packaging company Cartisa. The cooperation between partners is described in the case study on collaboration among Henkel, Condis, and Cartisa.

CASE: CPFR COLLABORATION AMONG HENKEL, CONDIS, AND CARTISA

The consumer goods manufacturer Henkel, the Spanish retailer Condis (with 330 supermarkets in northern Spain), and the packaging company Cartisa (International Paper) have collaborated on a CPFR project since the beginning of 2001. This is one of the few operating CPFR projects where not only the business processes between manufacturer and retailer were optimized, but also those with the packaging supplier. In this way, a CPFR optimization of the whole value chain becomes possible.

According to studies done by Henkel, Spanish retailers have a 10 to 18 percent out-of-stock rate, although the service level at the distribution center is 98.5 to 99.5 percent. This fact indicates a considerable potential improvement in inventory management. According to Henkel, the problem lies in the area of promotions. The current project had already increased forecast accuracy 15 percent by May 2001 and offered the participants the chance to improve their out-of-stock situation.

Noteworthy in this example is the inclusion of the packaging supplier in the cooperation agreement. The case shows that the availability of goods, at the right time, in the right place, of the correct quantity and quality is decidedly dependent on suppliers of subcomponents. Planning, forecasting, and inventory control between supplier and manufacturer must be synchronized in the same way as between manufacturer and retailer.

2.1.5 CPFR and Value Creation

The use of CPFR makes it possible to take even greater advantage of the efficiency potential sought through ECR. The CPFR Benefits Model, developed by VICS CPFR, enables the quantification of efficiency improvements. To a limited extent, CPFR connects completely new possibilities for rationalization in the value chain.

Typical benefits of CPFR are:

- *Drastically Improved Reaction Times to Consumer Demand.* The systematic reduction of shortages and optimized turnaround times make for a more flexible and more reliable supply chain that ultimately improves product availability and customer satisfaction.

- *Higher Precision of Sales Forecasts.* Through a cooperatively developed forecast, the forecast gains in reliability. The collaborative creation of the forecast along the supply chain enables everyone in the marketplace to profit from synergies. Independent of their position in the supply chain, or their activities there, the partners can bring their differing perspectives, consumer data, previous experiences, and research into the forecasting. This combined knowledge is the basis for high reliability in sales forecasting.

- *Direct and Lasting Communication.* The establishment of direct lines of communication raises the level of exchange between phases of the value chain. Next to the continual exchange of sales data, unique developments (increased or diminished demand due to weather or stepped-up advertising, etc.) can be readily considered.

- *Improved Sales.* The cooperation of planning, forecasting, and supply dramatically reduces out-of-stock situations. Previously lost income potential is regained. All partners profit.

- *Inventory Reduction.* Imprecision in sales forecasts was the main reason for surpluses in the supply chain. Surpluses were kept on hand to even out inexact sales planning. Through CPFR, the safety stock can be reduced and availability increased.

- *Reduced Costs.* The reconciliation of production plans with raw materials suppliers and manufacturers through optimized sales projections opens up further savings potentials. Set-up time, double work, and variability are reduced. A better use of production capacity means a more efficient production process. Reduced inventories mean lower capital, handling, and administrative costs.

The CPFR concept can mean a dramatic reduction in the ramp-up time in supplying goods. Joseph C. Andraski, former vice president of customer marketing and vice chairman at Nabisco and chairman of the CPFR Committee at VICS, is designing a provocative vision with the statement: "Can you imagine the possibilities that exist when you begin production just two weeks before the product is needed?" According to Volker Schröder, director of consumer logistics management at Procter & Gamble, Europe, the current time required for replenishment is at least ten to fifteen days. The long-term goal of CPFR is to reduce this time to a mere three days, including production. Of the 130 replenishment process steps now in place, 40 should be made redundant through CPFR.

2.2

Sales and Order Forecasts in the CPFR Process for Retail

Prof. Dr. Gerhard Arminger, University of Wuppertal and SAF-AG

The general process of Collaborative Planning, Forecasting, and Replenishment (CPFR) is described in detail in other chapters in this volume. The focus in this chapter is on two of the key elements in the CPFR process, namely on problems and possible solutions for the forecast of sales and the forecast of orders. The discussion is restricted to dealing with the problems of collaborative forecasting between individual retailers and manufacturers; the extension of the CPFR process to the suppliers of raw and half-finished materials for the manufacturer is not considered here.

Section 2.2.1 gives a bird's-eye view of the supply and demand chain management process for the retailer emphasizing the role of sales forecasts and orders for different hierarchies of the supply chain from the manufacturer to the individual customer. Section 2.2.2 considers in detail the requirements for good sales forecasts on the different levels of the supply chain. Section 2.2.3 focuses on order generation based on sales forecasts and shows how order restrictions may lead to orders that may be quite different from the forecasted sales. Consequently, the forecasting of orders can be done successfully only under fairly restrictive assumptions. The final section shows how some of these principles are implemented in a CPFR pilot project between an international retailer and an international manufacturer of consumer goods.

2.2.1 Integrated Demand and Supply Chain Management

Minimizing Total Supply Chain Cost

A key objective of management in retail is the optimization of the supply chain from the manufacturer through distribution centers (DCs), which may include hubs, warehouses, and cross-docking operations, and/or direct store delivery (DSD) to the store to fulfill the individual customer's demand. The overall objective is the minimization of the total cost of the supply chain operations, which includes elements from the demand and the supply sides. The elements from the demand side are:

- *The lost profit per SKU per delivery period in any given store if an item is not available for the individual customer.* Important measures for this loss are, first, the number of items that are out of stock on any given day and, second, the number of suppressed sales on any given day multiplied by the raw profit per SKU. These measures can usually be obtained directly, or at least they can be approximated if the necessary support from the data warehouse, the transaction system, and a computer-aided ordering system with simulation facilities are available.

- *The lost profit by losing a customer completely if a customer cannot find his or her favorite item in the store and therefore changes to another store or another retailer.* This effect is significant and can usually not be measured directly and may be approximated by market research or by educated guesses.

Typical elements of the cost for stores from the supply side are:

- The ordering and capital binding cost per SKU per delivery period in the store
- The delivery rhythm or more generally the delivery plan from the manufacturer or the DC to the store generating necessary lot sizes for ordering
- The minimal number of SKUs to be ordered by the store from the DC or the manufacturer
- Logistic order restrictions on the number of SKUs to be ordered by the store from the DC or the manufacturer such as number of SKUs in a layer or on a pallet

Typical elements of the cost for a distribution center from the supply side are:

- The ordering and capital binding cost per SKU per delivery period in the DC
- The delivery rhythm or more generally the delivery plan from the manufacturer to the DC generating necessary lot sizes for ordering
- The minimal number of SKUs to be ordered by the DC or the manufacturer
- Logistic order restrictions on the number of SKUs to be ordered by the DC from the manufacturer such as number of SKUs in a layer or on a pallet or the number of pallets in a truck
- Bracketed conditions where the advantage of a lower price has to be compared to the additional capital binding, stock-keeping, and handling costs

On the DC level, the nonavailability of goods corresponds to the out-of-stock situations in the store.

The manufacturer plays an important role in decreasing the costs on the demand and on the supply side. The manufacturer can help:

- To lower the costs of suppressed sales by ensuring the availability of items in the store and in the warehouse by in-time delivery
- To lower the capital binding costs by adapting to the retailer's needs for cost-optimal minimal ordering sizes, packaging, delivery plans, and changing the bracketed conditions

These effects can be achieved only by collaboration of the retailer with the manufacturer, by sharing information about the specification of items, packaging, delivery plans, and discount systems, and, most important, by sharing information about future sales and future orders, which is typical for the CPFR process. In exchange, the manufacturer may expect to have better forecasts for the demand of a specific retailer in order to optimize its own production process, including the extension of the CPFR process to its own suppliers.

Sales forecasts and order building play a central role in this process of minimizing the total cost of the supply chain. Sales forecasts and order building constitute a process that is reverse or dual to the physical process of delivering goods from the manufacturer to the DC and/or to the store. While the process of physical delivery constitutes the process of supply chain management, the demands of the individual customer at the individual store should generate the orders by the store from the DC and by the DC from the manufacturer. The customer's demand therefore constitutes the process of demand chain management by forecasting the future sales to the customers at store level and building adequate cost-optimal orders. Since in this forecasting and order building the pull from the customer's demand and the push from the manufacturer and the retailer in the form of promotions, advertising campaigns, and special displays have to be integrated, the whole process is called integrated demand and supply chain management (IDSCM), rather than SCM alone.

Integration of Forecasts for Different Levels of the Supply Chain

If fulfilling the customer's demand in the individual store is seen as the top priority in retail, forecasting must start at the SKU level for the individual store. This priority has important consequences. The forecasting techniques that are employed on the store level must fulfill the requirements of microforecasting—that is, a specific forecast for every SKU (item level) in every store. Aggregation across items and/or across stores is not meaningful in this case; on the contrary, it may be counterproductive. The order building per store must be based on the individual sales forecast for the individual store. Since calendar events (Easter, Fourth of July, Thanksgiving, Christmas), advertising, and promotional events may have very different effects in the different stores depending on the respective locations, the forecasting techniques should not be based only on the observed time series of sales but should also be able to take this information about external influences into account. Otherwise, only trend and seasonal information can be extracted. Forecasts for sales and orders for stores are usually based on short-term forecasts, ranging from daily to between one and six weeks depending on the delivery plans of the DC or the manufacturer.

The predicted demand and the orders generated by the sales forecasts for the stores should influence the forecast for the total shipments from the DC to the stores and the orders from the DC to the manufacturer. It should be noted that the aggregated sales forecasts per item from the stores should not be used as the forecasted number of SKUs to be shipped to the stores since the sales forecasts will not be identical to the cumulated orders from the stores. A better way of minimizing the total cost of the supply chain is to use either the shipments of an item from the DC to the stores or the cumulated orders of the stores in the past to the DC as a dependent variable that is to be forecasted and then to use the aggregated sales forecasts from the stores only as an external information or input variable for the DC forecast. One should note that calendar events and promotional events are then automatically taken into account. Forecasts for shipments (or cumulative store orders) and order building for DCs are also usually based on short-term forecasts, either daily or between one and six weeks depending on the delivery plans of the manufacturer to the DC.

The sales forecast in the CPFR process is closely related to the shipment (or cumulative store orders) forecast for the DC. The order forecast is meaningful only under restrictive assumptions to be discussed later. The main difference between the sales forecasts on the store and/

or DC level and the CPFR sales forecast is the time horizon. For the CPFR process, a midrange forecast of ten to thirteen weeks is advised to enable the manufacturer to adapt the production process to the specific predicted demand of the retailer. However, like the sales forecasts on the store level and the shipment forecasts on the DC level, the CPFR sales forecast must take into account the basic demand of the customer (pull) as well as calendar events and the demand induced by promotional schemes such as different types of advertisements, displays, and price reductions (push).

The midrange time horizon may imply that other forecasting techniques should be used than for the short-time forecast in the sense that the highly adaptive forecasting mechanisms for the short-term replenishment in the store and the DC may have to be replaced by more structural models focusing on the question of how much extra demand will be induced by specific promotional schemes. However, structural forecasting models rely even more heavily on external information than do the adaptive forecasting mechanisms. Depending on how goods are distributed to the store (DC or DSD), a midrange forecast for the individual store (DSD) or for the DC should be used as an input variable for the sales and order forecast of the retailer.

Finally, a mechanism has to be found that reconciles the sales and order forecasts of the retailer and the manufacturer if they differ. This may be done by a rather time-consuming process of personal collaboration. A more effective way may be to use both forecasts as input variables for predicting the actual demand and then to weigh the retailer's and the manufacturer's forecast according to their respective ability to predict the final demand.

2.2.2 Sales Forecasts for Stores, Distribution Centers, and the CPFR Process

An accurate sales forecast is key for a successful implementation of the CPFR process. For state-of-the-art CPFR it is necessary to analyze sales forecasts on different levels of the process. The following sections present sales forecasts for stores, distribution centers, and the CPFR process.

Sales and Inventory Forecasts for the Store Level

Currently, three distinct approaches to forecasting the large number of SKUs and store combinations required for store ordering are used in semiautomatic or automatic computer-assisted ordering (CAO) systems: aggregate, profile, and microforecasting.

Aggregate forecasting manages sparse inventory and reduces processing time by grouping stores into store clusters and creating a single forecast for each item across the entire store group. This single forecast is then distributed based on each store's relationship to the store group. This method is as good, or as bad, as the quality of the group. Its specific characteristics are:

- Stores grouped into geographic or like-store clusters
- A single forecast created for the store group
- The forecast distributed by volume ratio of each store to the total
- Volume ratio based on the total store to the total or a single category to the total

The main problem of this approach is obviously that the forecast method never approaches the store SKU as unique. Therefore, the needs of the individual store may be highly over- or underestimated depending on how similar the needs of a specific store are to the aggregated demand in the store cluster. For all practical purposes, one can expect from this forecasting method for the same item many stock-outs in one store and more than necessary overstocking in another store. Also, in this approach it is practically impossible to take into account effects such as local calendar events, local advertisements, and other local promotions. In effect, CAO in the store will be only semiautomatic rather than automatic and cannot utilize the benefits of full automatization, which may be especially important if no qualified personnel is available in the store.

Profile forecasting assumes that a base forecast can be created for each store/SKU but manages sparse data by aggregating the sales influences. Therefore, it creates seasonal profiles and promotion/price lifts across store groups. Its specific characteristics are:

- Forecast individual store items without external influences.
- Aggregate external influences by item and store groups (seasons, promotions).

- Create profiles from group aggregates.
- Create static weights for the application of multiple profiles.
- Apply various profiles to base forecast to produce actual forecast.

This approach generates three major problems:

1. The results can be only as good as the quality of the cluster, and the clusters will always include outlier stores.
2. Whenever clusters are created the data must be transformed and assumptions made. These assumptions often skew the results.
3. Marrying the various profiles, such as seasonal profiles with promotional lifts, is also based on assumptions. Often the forecast is not meaningful because seasons and promotions interact. The forecast cannot be unified.

The remarks about the quality of forecasts and the inability to achieve full automatization in the store made about aggregate forecasting also hold for profile forecasting.

Microforecasting creates a single, unified forecast that takes into account trend and seasonality from historical sales as well as holidays, promotions, and price. The weight and importance of each sales influence is considered at the same time and varies by the unique store SKU. The specific characteristics are:

- Each store item is forecasted uniquely.
- Each item history and external influences are applied uniquely.
- Weight and importance of each influence varies by the store item.

The advantages of such a method are obvious:

- There are no separate profiles or promotional lifts to maintain or to merge.
- There is no clustering with its inherent problem of outliers and cluster quality.
- External information on promotions and price changes is automatically taken into account.

- The quality of the store-specific sales forecast is much improved.
- Full automatization is achieved.

The disadvantages of microforecasting are twofold:

- First, the required database implies that (daily) sales data are available for each SKU-store combination. In addition, if external information like calendar events, promotions, and price changes should be taken into account, the store-specific information for (local) holidays, promotional events, and price changes must be available for future periods. This implies that sales, calendar, promotion, and price information have to be fed into the CAO system.
- Second, the functional requirements for the effectiveness and the speed of the forecasting and optimization engine in such a CAO system are much greater than for aggregate or profile forecasting.

However, most large retailers now have data warehouses and/or transaction systems that provide the required database and automatic systems with the advanced features of forecasting and optimization. The functional requirements for a system adequate for microforecasting are given in the following subsection.

Requirements of Self-Learning Forecasting Systems

The retail user in the store should not be exposed to the complexity of the system. A self-learning or autoadaptive forecasting system automatically selects the best model from an array of statistical models by classification algorithms and continually updates the forecast interrelationships. This process is repeated for each individual store SKU with every forecast run. A complex set of models is maintained by a relatively simple set of user parameters. Additionally, the system automatically balances the sales influences based on external information such as calendar events, promotional events, and price changes in the past.

Learning from each new bit of history the system continually improves its ability to predict future sales, rapidly recognize product trends, and build dynamic seasons. The retailer not only need not marry separate profiles and promotional lifts, but the self-learning system continually and automatically analyzes the impact of each sales influence. In this way the influences of promotions, seasons, and events are considered at one time. The compound predictors can include price changes, sales promotions, calendar events, holiday information, and special circumstances, depending on the availability of data provided by the client.

Optimal Inventory Forecast

Optimal inventory sets the target shelf inventory level in the store. There is an ideal shelf set that covers both presentation stock and the possibility of preventing lost sales without exceeding the costs of carrying surplus inventory. This optimal inventory in the store sets the lower limit for the ordering process. The ordering process must order at least such a great number of SKUs of one item that the optimal inventory for the first availability day of a new delivery is equaled or exceeded. Therefore, not only a forecast of the sales per SKU in a store is needed but also a forecast of the optimal inventory.

The retail industry has depended on three primary methods: minimum stock with safety stock, minimum stock with service level, and cost-based optimal inventory.

Minimum stock with safety stock is the most traditional and most manual of the methods used by retailers to set their target shelf set (or order-up-to level). The safety stock is either a fixed numerical amount or a calculated week of supply. This is a manually set stock that the retailer decides will cover its potential need and variable need. It is not dynamic and does not create a very accurate or cost-effective result.

Minimum stock with service level is the most traditional warehouse method for calculating the ideal stock with a dynamic safety stock. The service level is based on a symmetrical (bell curve) of inventory necessary to support the risk of being out of stock. The retailer sets a desired service level that is the percentage of time that it wants to be in stock when the stock is needed, based not only on projected demand but also on risk factors such as variability in forecasted demand as well as lead-time variability.

Cost-based optimal inventory uses cost functions to redefine the traditional approach to service level and creates a shelf supply that covers volatility in forecast on a cost-optimum basis. It minimizes the total cost of lost sales and excess inventory. By recognizing the sometimes asymmetrical distribution of forecast error, especially for slow sellers, inventory more closely matches the reality of sales. This method uses the real costs associated with lost sales, which may create a significant loss of a customer's shopping basket, on the one hand, and balances it with the cost of overstocking on the shelf, on the other hand.

Regardless of the method used, a forecast of the optimal inventory is needed and made. It should be noted that the forecast of the optimal inventory is based on the sales forecast but is not identical to the sales forecast. It will usually be greater than the sales forecast. Since the ordering is based on the forecast of the optimal inventory, it is even more important than the sales forecast.

Sales and Inventory Forecasts for the DC Level

The remarks from the previous section about forecasting sales and optimal inventory for the store also hold in principle for the DC level of the supply chain. Before going into more detail, a word of caution about the variable that is to be forecasted is in order. There are two options. The first is to use as predicted (or dependent) variable the aggregated shipments of an item from the DC to the stores. The disadvantage of this approach is that an item may not be available because the manufacturer could not deliver in time. Therefore, the time series of shipments can be distorted, which makes forecasting more difficult. The second option is to use the cumulated store orders as the dependent variable. This option makes sense only if the store orders themselves are based on good SKU–store forecasts and have been optimized to fulfill logistic and other restrictions. In practice, usually only shipment data are available. However, this will quickly change, so that both options will be available in the near future.

Aggregate and profile forecasting were originally developed for application in the DC. Some of the disadvantages of these approaches for the store do not occur on the DC level. Microforecasting with self-learning systems that utilize information about external influences is also available for the DC. The disadvantage of aggregate and profile forecasting is that there is no simple way of utilizing external information as input variables for the forecasting system. The advantage of microforecasting is that external information can be utilized easily.

If the dependent variable in the DC is the shipment from the DC to the stores, then the aggregated sales forecast from the stores will be an excellent external information or input variable for the forecast of the shipments. It should be noted that the aggregated sales themselves should not be used as an input variable for the shipment forecast since the time lag between the aggregated sales from the stores and the shipments from the DC to the stores may already be considerable. In addition, the aggregate forecasts from the stores already take the effects of calendar and promotional events into account, so that there is no need to aggregate holiday events and promotional events on the DC level. The same holds true for cumulated store orders as the dependent variable.

As on the store level, the shipment forecast is short range and has to be complemented with a forecast of the optimal inventory to fix the lowest possible level of stock that has to be maintained through the ordering and replenishment process. Altogether, the microforecasting approach with self-learning and inclusion of external information is much more promising than aggregate and profile forecasting.

Sales Forecasts for the CPFR Process

The sales forecast for the CPFR process follows in many regards considerations similar to the sales forecast for the stores and the shipment forecast for the DC. The main difference lies in the following points.

First, the time horizon for the sales forecast is midrange, that is, ten to thirteen weeks ahead. This does not mean that short-term forecasts are not made. It means that every week a forecast is expected that covers each of the following thirteen weeks. From the retailer's view, these forecasts imply that a short-range forecast may be used for the first four to six weeks and that a midrange forecast will be employed for the following weeks.

Second, the forecast of the retailer (FoR) is complemented by a forecast of the manufacturer (FoM). It should be noted that the forecast of the manufacturer relies, on one hand, on the data that are shared by the retailer with the manufacturer, for instance, sales data, promotion data, or price data; on the other hand, it may also rely on information that may not be accessible to the retailer, for instance, national advertisement campaigns or information about the whole market of retailers, since the manufacturer will supply many retailers and not one retailer exclusively.

Third, the FoR and the FoM are both midrange forecasts. While the short-range forecasts typically rely on the most recent information to adapt quickly to new developments, the midrange forecasts concentrate mainly on the effects of calendar and promotional events to improve production planning for excess demand. Therefore, the highly adaptive models for forecasting on the short range should be replaced by more structural models for the midrange. Thus, information on external influences should be used for forecasting. In turn, this implies that again microforecasting should be used rather than aggregate or profile forecasting. Again, the aggregate sales from the store forecasts could be used as an input variable for the sales forecast of the retailer for the CPFR process. The manufacturer may want to use its own information about market segmentation and national advertisement campaigns as input variables for its own CPFR forecast.

Fourth, the sales forecasts of the retailer and the manufacturer have to be reconciled if large differences between these forecasts exist. This may be done in the CPFR process by setting up joint committees to deal with these differences for each item. Such a process can be handled easily if only a few items must be managed by such a process. It becomes ineffective and expensive if many hundreds or even thousands of items and many manufacturers and/or retailers are managed in this way. Therefore, such a decision-making process should be supported again by a self-learning microforecasting system where the FoR and the FoM for each item are considered as input variables for the midrange forecast of each item.

Finally, it should be noted that some retailers expect not only a joint forecast on the aggregate or on the DC level but also on the level of the individual store. In this case, the manufacturer has to undergo a forecasting process similar to a vendor-managed inventory (VMI).

2.2.3 Order Building and Forecast

While the integration of sales forecasts among the levels of store, DC, and CPFR may be complicated in detail but rather straightforward in principle, the integration of order forecasts is much more difficult and can currently be done only when fairly restrictive assumptions apply.

Order Building and Forecasting for the Store

The order building for each SKU is based on the forecasts of the sales and the optimal inventory, but it is also heavily influenced by the stock that is still on the shelf and by open deliveries, deliveries already planned for a later time point, the delivery plan of the DC or the manufacturer to the store, presentation stock, minimal order sizes, and logistic restrictions such as layers or pallets. However, all of this can be taken into account routinely by a good CAO system and can even be forecasted if only the order for the first delivery period is used as a dependent variable. The first delivery period is the time between the first day on which the goods from today's order are available and the day on which the goods from the next possible order day will be available.

It should be seen that this is a rather restrictive assumption because in practice, the determination of economic order quantities tries to optimize the logistic cost not only for the next delivery period but for a given series of successive delivery periods. Typical examples are the minimization of logistic costs for one supplier by looking at the predicted sales and optimal inventories for all items of a supplier for the next K delivery periods to fulfill restrictions such as the minimum order value (for instance $1,000) across all items of a supplier or filling a half or a full truck to lower transportation costs. In this general case, the building of the order is based on the predicted sales, but it will be almost impossible to predict how much will be actually ordered in detail with great accuracy.

Order Building and Forecast for the DC

The issues regarding the store also hold true for the DC. In the DC, the logistic restrictions will play an even greater role because the filling of pallets and trucks will be of great importance to minimize transportation and handling costs. In addition, bracketed conditions will have much greater influence than in the store. Altogether, the forecasts for the shipments to the stores and for the optimal inventory in the DC to avoid nonavailability of items will again form the basis for the actual orders, but the orders themselves may differ greatly from the shipment forecasts because of present stock, delivery plans, and logistic and financial restrictions. A meaningful order forecast will be available only if the next delivery period is considered feasible.

Order Forecast for the CPFR Process

An order forecast for the CPFR process from the retailer's view is hampered by the same difficulties as an order forecast on the store and on the DC level. Again, under the restrictive assumption that orders are made only for the first delivery period, an order forecast can be achieved by looking at that period's orders per item as the dependent variable for the forecast and by using the same forecasting methods as for the sales data. The forecasted sales and (possibly) the forecasted stock at the beginning of the delivery period may be used as input variables if a self-learning system with the possibility of including external influences is used as the forecasting engine. However, if the orders are optimized for more than the first delivery period, the order forecasts will be fairly difficult to make. To the author's knowledge it has not even been attempted yet.

2.2.4 Issues in Practical Implementation

This section discusses how some of these principles are implemented in a CPFR pilot project between an international retailer and an international manufacturer of consumer goods. The main goal of the CPFR process between these two partners is the joint sales forecast for items that will be specially advertised and promoted in the midrange future. An interesting side problem is that the sales forecasts should work not only for the aggregate but also for the store-specific level.

Both partners have powerful transaction systems for managing merchandise in place. They have also agreed on software that allows them to share information about the items that are used for the project, meaning that the sales and the forecasts can be accessed by both partners. The retailer also uses a microforecasting tool that allows the inclusion of external influences for sales forecasting and order building in the store.

The CPFR pilot process may be described briefly in the following steps:

- For each store, sales are predicted by the retailer for all weeks in the short range and midrange using historical sales as well as information on calendar and promotional events. These predicted sales are aggregated and shown to the managers in charge at the retailer and at the manufacturer.

- Retailer and manufacturer give their own forecasts on the aggregate level based on additional data or on their possibly superior judgment of external influences. These forecasts are broken down to the store level and serve as additional input variables for the forecasting tool.

- The process of forecasting on the store level is repeated with the additional input variables. The forecasts are again aggregated and sent to the managers in charge for checking and confirmation, generating a collaborative sales forecast of retailer and manufacturer.

- Since the sales forecasts are available for midrange and short range, the short-range forecasts may be used for order building at the individual stores.

This procedure combines some interesting features. First, it manages the CPFR process not only on the aggregate but also on the store level. Second, it lets empirical results decide how much weight should be given to the FoR and the FoM. Third, it still includes the element of personal communication between the responsible managers but supports it heavily with IT tools. Fourth, the problem of order forecasting is pragmatically solved by using the short-range forecast to adjust for the most recent developments.

2.3

CPFR Emerges as the Next Movement in Supply Chain Management

Joseph C. Andraski, VICS CPFR and OMI International

The advent of supply chain management (SCM) was a result of the development and implementation of a series of processes that began in the early part of the last century. It began with the development of economic order quantity (EOQ), progressing through material requirements planning (MRP), MRPII, distribution requirements planning (DRP), just in time, total quality management (TQM), theory of constraints (TOC), time-based competition (TBC), SCM, and finally what some are calling value chain management. Supporting each process was a philosophy that dealt with how to improve the effectiveness and efficiency of business.

It is fair to say that each process was flawed, and consequently there was a natural evolution from one to the next, with each step bringing improvements. Innovators dealt with organizational and cultural barriers, as senior leadership demanded operational improvements. Technology played an important role as a key enabler. On the other hand, customers were demanding reliability and flexibility, and customer service gradually became an important area of focus. It is important to note that each of the processes was essentially internally focused and the sharing of information for the most part was not considered important or relevant.

Getting to supply chain management was a journey that has taken some eighty-five years since EOQ, and some thirty-five years since the introduction of MRP. AMR Research has found that only 20 percent of all companies with sales of more than $500 million (U.S.) have invested in SCM. This is startling given the attention that SCM has received and considering the discussion of how companies will compete with their supply chains. Does this imply that senior management is not convinced that the investment in SCM will deliver on the promise? Enterprise resource planning (ERP) is a necessity for those companies that have multiple system platforms and multiple business components and operate on a global scale; however, implementation for some has been a nightmare. We believe that this is the natural evolution of the supply chain, as flaws are found and improvements are made in process, technology, and business practices.

2.3.1 Studies Reveal Supply Chain Management Benefits—Opportunities and a Path Forward

Research recently conducted by Bain & Company indicates that the returns on software investments have been elusive. Forty-four percent of three hundred executives state that they have little or only basic data, do not track forecast accuracy, do not track vendor performance, and do not communicate any of this information to senior management. They are essentially ignorant of how much supply chain inefficiencies really cost. They also reported that 80 percent of their efforts were focused within their own four walls, but that they intend to increase their external supply chain activity over the next two years.

A recent study by A. T. Kearney found five companies that used operational excellence to help deliver value 2.5 times the average of all other participants in the study. In all of the metrics used, these companies excelled: for example, 255 inventory turns of work in process, versus 65. These companies have carefully designed and effectively managed formal programs that generate continuous performance improvement.

Gartner Group reports that companies that believed that software deployment would lead to rapid ROI are in the "trough of disillusionment." Tales of failure were prevalent in 2001. The Gartner Group believes that there is a dearth of supply chain planning understanding, with only a few pockets of educated individuals and a lack of good data to drive the planning engines. It reports that the effort required for change management was greatly underestimated and that most employees felt victimized by a wave of technology. Vendors, it is postulated, were selling their vision rather than what they could actually deliver. Gartner Group also found that there was a lack of good data to drive the software engines; that is, enterprise data were often unavailable or too dirty to use.

Ernst and Young found, in a study conducted in 2000, that only 25 percent of those responding to the survey were satisfied with the results of its SCM programs. CSC found in its study that all of the subjects were internally focused and in the first or second stage of a four-stage model for supply chain best practices.

Considering these findings over the course of the history of SCM, one must acknowledge that there have been substantial gains in effectiveness, efficiency, customer service, cash flow, product quality, and availability of information. However, this is not about what was done yesterday; it is about what can be done today. Past successes are history, and expectations as to how SCM will contribute to the success of a company are what must be addressed both today and tomorrow.

Professor John Kotter of the Harvard Business School has done extensive research on companies that have succeeded through external orientation compared with those that fail to look at factors outside their own organization. He has many examples of companies that have learned from corporations outside of their industry and have reached out to their customers to create a tight bond that benefited both sides. In spite of the many examples identified by Professor Kotter, and the financial results those companies have enjoyed, we still find companies that remain internally focused relative to their customers and suppliers. The philosophy of SCM is to reach back to the supplier of raw material and carry information and product to the point of purchase. Suffice it to say, however, that most businesses and SCM professionals are thinking about what transpires within their own four walls.

2.3.2 Progressing Beyond Supply Chain Management

SCM must evolve, much as we have seen the evolution from EOQ to the present day. We have learned that the vertical silos within organizations must become horizontal and that the supply chain must evolve into a supply net, connecting all players in the game of satisfying the consumer. The critical functions within an organization must be integrated into the planning and execution process. For example, marketing has as much, if not more, influence on the success of supply chain management as production. The time frame in which products are promoted and consequently produced and distributed is a function of the plans that are developed by marketing. All customer plans are a result of the product plans created by marketing that are designed to meet company sales and financial goals. Marketing cannot be excluded from supply chain planning but must be considered an integral part to be embraced and leveraged. This takes us to value chain management, or reaching out beyond those functions that are typically considered to be SCM and/or logistical.

One should consider for a moment some of the barriers to realizing the potential of supply chain or value chain management. Apparent thus far is that senior leadership has not provided direction or support; that adequate metrics are unavailable or unused; that silos and cultural issues still exist within companies; that information is either unavailable, untimely, or inaccurate; and that individuals and corporations are slow to adapt to new ways of doing business and the new demands of the marketplace. All are relevant and exert significant influence.

While not each of these barriers are addressed here, a hypothesis is offered that suggests why companies have not realized the expected ROI from investments made in technology and business processes. Supply chain planning depends on primary information that is gleaned from a forecast, typically generated from historic sales and then run through triple exponential smoothing, various algorithms, etc. to arrive at a forecast for the out months. We have concluded that corporations are internally oriented and often operate within their organizational silos. In many cases, there are multiple forecasts within a company, each with built-in biases and safety stock calculations. The forecast used to drive DRP may not be the forecast used by the sales and marketing organization, or the forecast used by procurement, or the forecast used by the manufacturing organization. While obviously there are many opportunities for improvement, the hypothesis here is that if a forecast were developed in conjunction with a company's key trading partner, its accuracy would be substantially improved.

Collaboration Leads to New Efficiencies

That leads us to Collaborative Planning, Forecasting, and Replenishment (CPFR). While in the evolution of supply chain management, CPFR is still in its infancy, the subject of collaboration has come to the fore. Practically every trade/business magazine refers to collaboration. The scientific community has embraced collaboration and the sharing of information across the Internet. Collaborative commerce is now being practiced in the chemical, automotive, textile, and pharmaceutical industries, as well as in retail. This points to dissatisfaction with the confrontational business climate between trading partners and to the need to find another business model to help companies meet the demands of their customers and of Wall Street.

There are now recognized business gurus espousing collaboration as a business practice and a mind-set for companies to establish for internal and external relationships. Tom Peters, who wrote *In Search of Excellence*, now tells us that it is essential to collaborate with one's trading partners. Tom suggests that the new world will require companies to deal with their trading partners in a collaborative way. Well-known global consultant Michael Hammer, who wrote *Reengineering the Corporation* and several follow-up books, including *The Agenda*, says, "Knock down your outer walls, collaborate whenever you can." He goes on to say that "the walls between the supplier and the customer equal costs and the higher the wall, the higher the costs. And the walls between companies are much higher than the walls inside companies." Here is a progressive individual who believes that most companies have far to go in exploiting the potential of SCM. After strongly recommending that corporate structures and business practices be scrapped and rebuilt, he then advocates collaboration as one of the keys to success.

Reading Jack Welch's book *Straight from the Gut*, one finds that GE was collaborating both internally and externally years ago. Welch believes in boundaryless management, in which different companies collaborate on best business practices and customer satisfaction is used to measure service. His approach has a twist: He is concerned about when a part or product begins delivering a profit to the customer, not simply whether or not it is delivered on time. In a recent conference, Welch gave a presentation on the importance and value of collaboration, a significant endorsement given the success he and GE have enjoyed over the last twenty years.

2.3.3 CPFR as a Change Agent

It is obvious that there is a strong movement toward collaborative commerce independent of CPFR. This suggests an endorsement, albeit somewhat indirect. CPFR provides a framework within which trading partners can conduct collaborative business relationships with benefits to both players. There have been numerous surveys conducted by universities, trade associations, and trade journals that have addressed the subject of CPFR, its current status, plans for future implementation, etc. Generally speaking, approximately 10 to 15 percent of companies in the consumer products industry indicate that they are engaged in CPFR, another 10 to 15 percent expect to implement CPFR in 2002, and 20 percent in 2003 or 2004. Of course, there are those who believe CPFR is all hyperbole and no substance. That is to be expected, as there will always be those who will resist change and find reasons to challenge the positive experience of those who have decided to venture forward. One must keep in mind that CPFR is new, for the most part misunderstood, and a step in the natural evolution that hits at the very heart of what most companies and individuals resist: *change.*

Gary R. Forger, editorial director of *Modern Materials Handling,* has said, "the real-deal companies are the engines driving supply chain collaboration forward," and "collaboration is a much broader partnership than simply talking or sharing forecasts." He goes on to say, "If the truth be known, collaboration is still in the early evangelical stages. That's fine. There's nothing wrong with patience for (and a little faith in) an idea this new and with this much potential. Because when collaboration takes off, any company that isn't up to speed hasn't got a prayer."

There have been companies that have announced CPFR pilots and unfortunately have fallen on hard financial times. To be clear, CPFR is not a magic bullet that can remedy poor business strategy, untimely events, and unfavorable market conditions. One should consider that the retail industry has far more stores than are required to service the consumer. Retailers got caught up in the economic growth that took place over the last ten years and built stores to meet competition, on the one hand, and the expectations of Wall Street, on the other. The shakeout has begun, with the bankruptcy of Kmart, the closing of Service Merchandise, and the announcement of Toys 'R' Us closing Kids 'R' Us stores. The automobile industry can now produce approximately 18 million more vehicles per year than are needed in the marketplace. The excess capacity of the steel industry is greater than the production of the entire U.S. steel industry. This story can be told in sector after sector. CPFR could not have avoided these calamities. However, if Cisco had stayed closer to its customers and in so doing understood that demand for its products was declining in early 2001, Cisco would have slowed down production and not built inventory for anticipated sales, which ultimately resulted in an inventory write-down of $2.5 billion.

Cisco, Ford Motor Company, and Chrysler have all made great progress with SCM initiatives, reducing operating costs and inventory-carrying costs by many millions of dollars. These industry leaders have all fallen on hard times because of a number of decisions or circumstances that were not directly related to supply chain management. CPFR can have very favorable results, but it cannot abrogate poor management decisions.

Vinod Singhal, at the Georgia Institute of Technology's DuPree College of Management, and Kevin Hendricks, associate professor at the University of Western Ontario's Richard Ivey School of Business, researched SCM performance and shareholder value. They estimate that glitches (parts shortages, changes by customers, ramp-up/rollout problems, production problems, development problems, and quality problems—caused internally, by suppliers or customers) destroy about 7.5 percent of a company's shareholder value at the time of its announcement. Another 9 percent is lost in the 120 days before the announcement of the glitch, and a further 2 percent in the 120 days after the announcement. The total loss is 18.5 percent of shareholder value. Companies that have suffered such losses include Motorola, Hershey, Sony, Boeing, and Apple Computer, all of which took major hits in market value as a result of supply chain glitches.

So while it may be difficult to specifically attribute stock growth to supply chain management improvement, the negative impact on shareholder value as a result of supply chain failures is clear. The CPFR benefits model, however, does point out the financial improvement that a company can expect by implementing CPFR. This model can be found on the CPFR.org and VICS.org Web sites. It is a tool that can provide guidance based on the experience of those considered among the best in their class. Experts in activity-based costing have developed the standards. Any company considering CPFR should take the opportunity to explore this model, which is cost and obligation free.

2.3.4 Industry Standards Are Critical

Assume there is a case for a new business process that advances the progress made in SCM. That business process is CPFR, a global, open, neutral business standard for value chain partners for the coordination of plans in order to reduce the variance between supply and demand, and to share the benefits of a more effective and efficient value chain.

In every case study reported, trading partners have experienced an increase in sales, an increase in profits, and improved utilization of working capital. Interestingly enough, these are some of the very measures on which CEOs find themselves held accountable by Wall Street. Since the completion of the Voluntary Interindustry Commerce Standards (VICS) Association's Voluntary Guidelines for Collaborative Planning, Forecasting, and Replenishment (CPFR) in 1998 and its sequel, the Roadmap to CPFR, in 2000, there have been rapid advances in the application of the guidelines and the enabling technology.

Furthermore, the Global Commerce Initiative (GCI), a group of international companies that has come together to endorse global communication standards and business practices, has endorsed CPFR. The EAN-UCC Global Standards Management Process (GSMP) has recently approved the CPFR XML schema, providing a major step in the approval process that will provide the creditability the EAN-UCC seeks. Given the size and influence of these companies and those that make up the Voluntary Interindustry Commerce Standards (VICS) Association and the VICS CPFR Committee, it is fair to say that CPFR has received global endorsement. This is also supported by the fact that ECR Europe as well as ECR Brazil and IAC-EAN Colombia and Japan have joined the CPFR Committee.

There is great interest in, and adoption of, CPFR in Japan by retailers, wholesalers, suppliers, and public trading exchanges. Research on CPFR by the Distribution Economics Institute of Japan has been done for the last three years and is continuing. ECR Brazil and IAC-EAN Colombia are sponsoring educational seminars in response to the requests of their membership. Our global VICS CPFR Committee members are learning from one another, collaborating on the exchange of information, and taking into consideration the specific business requirements of the countries involved. Rarely has a new business process been so embraced by countries across the globe, with companies working together in a spirit of cooperation and with the determination to develop universal guidelines for improving the performance of companies in all industries.

Soon a new release of CPFR Guidelines will be issued that incorporates the lessons learned since the release of the Roadmap in 2000. It includes practical information for companies using CPFR. For example, the Business Planning section is greatly expanded and provides specifics on making plans between trading partners. The information in the Technology section is excellent.

"N-tier," or taking CPFR beyond the basic buyer/seller relationship to other key players in the supply chain, such as deliverers of raw material, packaging suppliers, and distribution service providers, highlights another fertile area for finding significant savings. The CPFR Committee is committed to working with the public trading exchanges, which have expressed their commitment to CPFR. We expect to provide support to, and a venue for, the exchanges to report the progress they have made with membership pilots to the VICS CPFR Committee. The importance of systems interoperability is clear, and there is support by the Committee for the recommendations recently made by the Uniform Code Council (UCC) for using a third party to evaluate and certify compatibility among software.

The Committee strongly supports UCCnet, which is a not-for-profit subsidiary of the Uniform Code Council. The business vision of UCC-net is to provide an Internet-based, easily accessible trading community, forming a cost-effective, nondiscriminatory universal platform for the synchronization of the "item information" among trading partners. The technical vision is to provide a "technology-neutral," open, scalable, distributed architecture that offers participants a secure, reliable mechanism for the synchronization of item content. Further, it hopes to encourage the voluntary participation of all solutions providers to develop service offerings and products consistent with UCCnet's open architecture and not inhibit competition in any way.

2.3.5 CPFR Addresses Several Key Pain Points

One of the problems with realizing the expected return on investment mentioned earlier was the availability and accuracy of information. Incorrect product information has cost the retail industry dearly in incorrect invoices, returned products, lost sales, customer service problems, etc. This travesty exists because of the manual and error-intensive form of information sharing that characterizes the retail industry today. Perhaps it is not as serious in department store verticals, but it is clearly a major opportunity in other retail verticals.

As CPFR is adopted and companies move to production and full-scale implementation, it will be essential to use the clean information resident in the databases of trading partners. UCCnet will enable trading partners to reap the benefits from CPFR, while significantly reducing the time consumed in category planning and essentially eliminating the unnecessary clerical effort expended on correcting invoices, prices, and promotions. Leading retailers, including Wal-Mart, Ahold, Shaw's, Wegmans, and others have clearly stated their support for UCCnet and have encouraged their suppliers to participate with them and take advantage of the benefits to be realized by using UCCnet. Technology is only effective if the information used to drive the business processes is accurate and timely.

Continuing with technology, the advancement made in SCM could not have come about without the features and functions that have been used to improve effectiveness and efficiency. For example, there is integrated supply chain management: from supply chain planning for balanced time supplies expressed in case volume, to cubic space required for distribution, dollars of inventory for cycle, and safety stock, all are based on the retail ship service level standard a company desires.

If the above are supported by CPFR, and conversely if CPFR is supported by these features and functions, the opportunities to increase sales and improve profits are compounded. Forward-moving, fledgling capabilities will mature and event management, exception processing, visibility, electronic tagging of product, and the easy exchange of operational and planning information will pave the way for the Web value chain built on the spirit of collaborative commerce and enabled by technology.

2.3.6 Implementation and Payback Can Be Quick

The time required to implement CPFR is dependent on a number of factors, which can be addressed by doing an internal assessment, outlined in the Roadmap to CPFR. The time required is also dependent on the company's decision to either start small and gain experience before moving forward, or to build the entire support infrastructure before engaging in the first CPFR relationship. Either approach is reasonable; however, those who have been the innovators believe it is prudent to start small and build on experience. Total implementation time for some companies has been as short as two to four weeks. Retail buyers typically spend minutes per week with CPFR suppliers.

Resource requirements have varied but typically involve a reallocation of resources rather than a demand for additional personnel. In many organizations, the resources are now invested in the account sales team, the continuous replenishment team, the financial team, the marketing team, and the customer service team. With CPFR, there is a significant reduction in the number of "do-overs." On the playground, disputes were settled by calling a do-over. In business, do-overs are expensive and require organizations to staff up to handle them, although the employees are never identified as "do-over experts." Most companies, although not publicly, state that some 50 percent of their resources are used to resolve problems, correct errors, and handle the requisite communications. Doing a better job of planning, through CPFR, will substantially reduce the do-overs, thus improving productivity.

The benefits of CPFR vary with the trading partnership. Case studies presented in this document highlight the opportunities identified and exploited by companies willing to share their experience. However, it should be emphasized that one of the key improvements has been in increasing sales, which points out that CPFR is truly a holistic business process that touches on practically every element of the value chain. A significant benefit is the move from a push philosophy to a pull philosophy, that is, a sales- and customer-specific plan that is driven up from the customer rather than down to the customer. It results in something unique—producing what a consumer wants to purchase rather than what a manufacturer wants to produce. There is also the joy of seeing functions within a company begin to collaborate, to share plans, to understand the challenges that their colleagues face because of top-down versus bottom-up planning.

In the past, we have dealt with partnering, strategic alliances, and other initiatives that were well intended, not well thought out, not equitable, or a combination of all three. There was never a true understanding of the benefits or of what partnership really means. While the golden rule still prevails: He or she who has the gold rules, CPFR will shift the paradigm to a more equitable sharing of opportunities because he or she will not be entirely focused on cost, but on an entire value chain, which includes sales growth and effective asset utilization.

Obstacles to Collaboration Persist

There are barriers to CPFR, which should be recognized and taken into consideration. There is, for example, the lack of internal alignment with regard to corporate goals and objectives that support a company's commitment to its shareholders and stakeholders. Other barriers include, but are not limited to, compensation that promotes a silo mentality; nonexistent change management skills; tunnel vision; the "not-invented-here mentality"; internally focused organizational silos; legacy systems; and finally, but most important, leadership that is focused on Wall Street and making the numbers regardless of the expense to the long-term prospects of the company. Just look at trade-loading practices in the grocery industry as a prime example of leadership dictated by Wall Street.

There are other barriers, like the personal comfort zones people choose not to leave, even if it means the demise of the company. Too often the argument is that "my business is different and its unique characteristics demand that the status quo must be maintained." There is nothing especially difficult about CPFR; it just takes a willingness to learn, assimilate, absorb, and implement, and to maintain the attitude that only excellence will suffice.

CPFR is a keystone of collaborative commerce, which is destined to be found in the collaborative processes identified by AMR in its January 2001 "Report on Retail E-Business":

- Collaborative demand and promotion planning
- Collaborative replenishment management—supplier to shelf
- Collaborative logistics management
- Collaborative product life-cycle management
- Collaborative trade funds management
- Collaborative product item/catalog maintenance
- Collaborative trading partner profile maintenance
- Collaborative consumer-level market intelligence management
- Collaborative category management and merchandise planning

The public and private trading exchanges, the development of technology, communications, interoperability mergers, acquisitions, etc.

will all influence the evolution of collaborative commerce. Nevertheless, the age of collaboration is here, and the funeral of the age of confrontation is taking place. Much needs to be done, but the rewards will be great and worthwhile.

CPFR Will Last the Test of Time

The future will see innovative business practices and processes that will build on what we have learned through CPFR. SCM guru Peter Drucker says it takes about ten years for a business process to become successful after going through the trials of innovation, experimentation, implementation, and failure. We strongly believe that CPFR will be the exception.

We will see change, because industry is under tremendous pressure, brought about by the options offered and the demands of the consumer for service, price, convenience, and product innovation. In response to consumer and shareholder demands, industry will begin to employ the power of the infrastructure that currently exists and become a very efficient and effective global delivery system.

Influencing factors will include the implementation of affordable technology, that is, hosting, transaction-based fees, "mini me" systems that provide basic functionality, with minimal investment in hardware that avoids the balance sheet. The economy will recover, and new ERP players will emerge. The problems related to the interfacing of best-of-breed systems will no longer cause service and operational problems.

The consolidation of retailers and wholesalers will continue, creating large companies that have a strong grip on their primary markets. Consolidation will also continue with manufacturers, third-party providers, and technology providers. This will result in a balancing of leverage and the use of collaborative efforts necessary to effectively and efficiently move products from the source of raw materials to the point of consumption. The use of statistical forecasting tools as we know them today will be replaced by interactive systems that exchange and interpret information, which will in turn drive the value chain.

Organizations and the skills that exist today will not be recognizable because of functions that will no longer be needed due to technological innovation and the use of third-party providers. Third parties, using the Internet and collaborative transportation management, will manage transportation. Finally, the dream of continuous movement and the intelligent use of motor carriers and their most important asset, the driver, will be realized.

The economy will rebound and the challenges brought on by a mobile workforce and full employment will be met with the reengineering of business practices and the implementation of integrated and compatible technologies. Productivity will improve and corporations will use some of the gains realized in profitability to help the disadvantaged around the world. After all, the age of collaboration is intended to fulfill a greater calling than what can be found in the metrics used to measure business success, and it all began with Collaborative Planning, Forecasting, and Replenishment and VICS.

2.4

CPFR—Status and Perspectives: Key Results of a CPFR Survey in the Consumer Goods Sector and Updates

Julie Fraser, Industry Directions Inc.

Syncra Systems and Industry Directions conducted a survey of manufacturers, retailers, distributors, and logistics providers, among others, primarily in the consumer goods sectors in 2000.

2.4.1 Survey Background

Our objective was to gain an understanding of whether and how companies are deploying Collaborative Planning, Forecasting, and Replenishment (CPFR) practices, the results from those that have done so, and where the industry may need further education on CPFR and its benefits.

The survey respondent base includes many types of companies. As shown in Exhibit 2.3, about a quarter of the respondents are retailers, half are manufacturers, and the remaining quarter are other types of companies, including wholesalers and distributors, logistics and transportation providers, consultants, and systems integrators.

The organizations range from under $100 million to over $5 billion, with 42 percent over $1 billion and 58 percent under $1 billion in revenues (U.S.). Note that some respondents represent divisions of larger companies.

The respondent base consists of 130 individuals from 120 companies. Many of the companies are household-name retailers and consumer goods manufacturers. They represent a range of job titles, as shown in Exhibit 2.4. Most of these respondents have multidepartmental views because of their job functions, such as MIS, management, or supply chain.

Collaborative Planning, Forecasting, and Replenishment is gaining momentum as more companies add it to their strategic initiatives and business improvement activities.

Based on the results of this and other industry data, it appeared many retail and consumer goods companies would have made significant progress in piloting or rolling out CPFR during 2000–2001. Exhibit 2.5 shows that 68 percent of the participants were actively researching, undergoing pilots, or preparing to roll out CPFR, while only 32 percent had no CPFR plans.

Exhibit 2.3. CPFR survey respondents by industry.

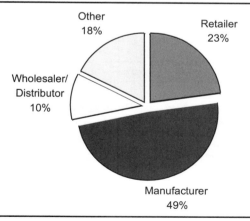

Source: Industry Directions/Syncra Systems.

Exhibit 2.4. CPFR survey respondents by job type.

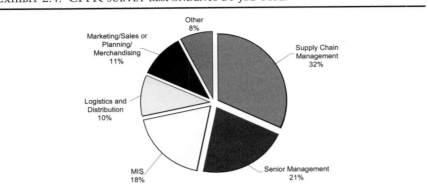

Source: Industry Directions/Syncra Systems.

Exhibit 2.5. CPFR stage.

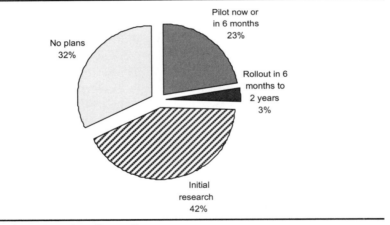

Source: Industry Directions/Syncra Systems.

As major retail and manufacturing companies now in pilot mode expand their implementations, pressure will mount on other companies to begin collaborating as well.

Companies with CPFR pilots under way, both in our study and in the VICS Roadmap to CPFR, are already gaining significant benefits. These benefits include increased service levels and sales and, at the same time, decreased inventory, as highlighted in the next section.

2.4.2 CPFR: The Next Wave

While the publicity around positive results is helping to build momentum for CPFR, industry interest is propelled even more strongly by intense pressure on companies to improve their supply chain's business performance. For example:

- Increased retail consolidation and pressure from emerging e-retailers has put greater pressure on margins and same-store revenue growth. Retailers need their suppliers to assist in lowering inventory while avoiding stock-outs.
- Consumer goods manufacturers recognize they need to better serve retailers and distributors and need parallel improvements from their material suppliers.
- Participants throughout the extended supply chain are fighting to add value and avoid the "disintermediation" that e-commerce is widely believed to allow.

In a *Consumer Goods Technology* survey on priorities for 2000, reducing supply chain costs, compressing time to market, and collaborating more effectively with trading partners were ranked as the most important business initiatives. All of these are benefits of CPFR. Companies are realizing that collaborating with their trading partners may be the only way to achieve the performance levels they and their stakeholders expect.

Further, many are recognizing that they now compete as supply chains, not just as individual enterprises. CPFR is the first recognized industry standard to provide templates for supply chain partner planning collaboration.

CPFR Processes

The term *Collaborative Planning, Forecasting, and Replenishment* makes intuitive sense. However, it's important to understand how it actually works. The starting point is an agreement between trading partners to collaborate—by developing and taking responsibility for plans, forecasts, and replenishment orders.

To collaborate, both the buyer and seller contribute to a single plan and forecast for what they will sell, and how, when, and where goods will be promoted. Each partner uses its own business systems (ERP, demand planning, forecasting, supply chain planning and execution) to develop and execute plans. The VICS CPFR communications standards and supporting software are the mechanisms that partners use to communicate plans and make subsequent changes. The result is a supply chain that is more efficient and demand driven.

Because they are sharing a common plan and forecast, it becomes possible for the buyers' order cycles to be synchronized with suppliers' production cycles. Many companies are even taking it a step further and integrating their supply-and-demand planning processes, coordinating activities between replenishment and promotional planners, and jointly identifying and creating opportunities for additional revenues.

CPFR can also reduce costs. For example, once they agree, trading partners can safely freeze a forecast and automatically convert it into a shipping plan. This eliminates the order-processing steps. Further, collaboration improves visibility of the constraints on both sides, allowing plan adjustments before, not after, plans and forecasts are finalized. Having reduced uncertainty, manufacturers and retailers alike can reduce safety stocks, stock to demand, and respond quickly to change.

2.4.3 Proven CPFR Benefits

The core objective of CPFR is to increase the accuracy of demand forecasts and replenishment plans necessary to lower inventories across the supply chain and attain high service levels of the right products in the right locations. This results in higher sales at both a category and brand level because consumers are then getting exactly what they want, when and where they want it. This is possible only when companies collaborate, sharing knowledge through a common set of processes.

Naturally, only the companies whose CPFR programs are under way can report actual benefits achieved. The results from the quarter of the participants that qualified are listed at the end of this section. However, we asked all of the respondents about what they expect could be achieved by implementing a CPFR program.

All of the companies in this study see the value of CPFR—both those that are currently involved in CPFR programs and gaining benefits, and those that have not yet begun. Eighty-nine percent of the respondents expect CPFR will provide:

- Improvements in trading partner forecast accuracy
- Decreases in inventory and safety stock
- Reduction in out-of-stock and improved service levels
- Increases in sales

Specific expectations are based on where companies are currently operating, and those with lower levels of performance will generally have the greatest potential benefit. However, in this study, those with the best performance levels are well aware of how much further CPFR might improve their capabilities.

Forecast Accuracy Levels

Half of respondents whose forecast accuracy is 90 percent or greater predict that CPFR would improve their trading partners' forecasts by at least 20 percent. Two-thirds of those with the highest level of forecast accuracy agree that their trading partners' forecast accuracy would benefit significantly from CPFR.

Inventory Levels

Forty-four percent of respondents with the lowest inventory value today believe that they would gain more than 10 percent in additional savings in inventory and safety stocks, as Exhibit 2.6 shows.

Service Levels

Half of those with over 98 percent service levels today believe that they could significantly improve by using CPFR.

Sales Increases

Of those already piloting or expecting to pilot within the next six months, 35 percent expect sales increases of over 10 percent, and over 90 percent expect some sales increase.

EXHIBIT 2.6. EXPECTED INVENTORY SAVINGS FROM CPFR.

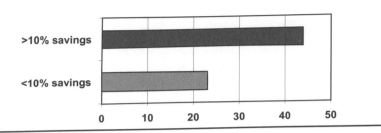

SOURCE: Industry Directions/Syncra Systems.

The one-quarter of respondents to this survey who have gained some experience operating with CPFR report the following as among the greatest benefits:

- "Weekly downloads of promotion plans means we quickly caught changes to timing, codes, and/or quantity."
- "Accurate forecasts."
- "Grew sales and reduced inventory by double digits."
- "Improved fill rates, reduced inventory, and shared the benefits."
- "Weekly downloads of actual retail sales [to a CPG company] allow us to see market reactions quickly and easily."
- "Business with the customer with whom we have CPFR in place was up 80 percent this past year."
- "Initial work improved sales $9 million."
- "Began to use data to make decisions in a way that builds business for both."
- "100 percent service level over past nine months and approaching forty annual turns."
- "We have a successful CPFR process in place with our largest customer. This past year the customer's business with us was up 80 percent."

se results match the expectations and goals of CPFR. Until recently, adopters of CPFR did not share their benefits or success factors use of the strategic advantage they were gaining.

2.4.4 Performance and Challenges

The key questions for managers are: "How can I optimize my CPFR performance?" and "What are the major challenges in future CPFR implementation?" We will try to find answers to these questions.

Forecast Accuracy

Greater accuracy in plans and forecasts is a major goal of CPFR. As such, it's important to understand where companies stand with forecast accuracy. Exhibit 2.7 displays data on forecast accuracy in the 2000 survey. It revealed that 63 percent reported less than 90 percent forecast accuracy, 18 percent reported forecast accuracy of over 90 percent, and 19 percent didn't know their organization's forecast accuracy. This latter high number suggests a lack of education about the critical nature of forecast accuracy to customer service levels and costs.

The survey data depicted in Exhibit 2.8 show the bullwhip effect. The bullwhip effect is where those partners more removed from demand have increasingly less accurate, more volatile forecasts. (The end of the whip near the "hand" of demand barely needs to move for a mighty lashing to take place at the far end of supply.)

Manufacturers—particularly   those   not   currently   involved   with

Exhibit 2.7. Forecast accuracy.

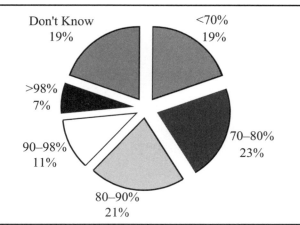

Source: Industry Directions/Syncra Systems.

EXHIBIT 2.8. FORECAST ACCURACY BY ORGANIZATION TYPE.

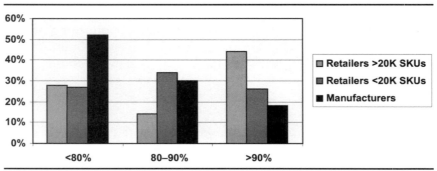

SOURCE: Industry Directions/Syncra Systems.

CPFR—have less accurate forecasts than the retailers. This common supply chain problem is particularly striking when comparing manufacturers to high mix retailers. Retailers with more SKUs tend to be more accurate than those with fewer SKUs. The retailers who handle fewer SKUs report a wide range of forecast accuracy, with no clear pattern.

In this study, smaller organizations also had more accurate forecasts than larger ones:

- Twenty percent of respondents under $1 billion and only 15 percent of those over $1 billion reported over 90 percent forecast accuracy.

- Twenty-six percent of the over $1 billion companies have less than 70 percent forecast accuracy, and only 16 percent of the smaller companies had such poor forecast accuracy.

Three-quarters of the respondents believe a more accurate sales and operations planning (S&OP) forecast would be very important to their organization. As Exhibit 2.9 depicts, 45 percent of the total rate this as extremely critical, 51 percent say it is critical or somewhat critical, and only 4 percent say it is not critical.

Impact of Inaccuracy

Companies in this survey were well aware of the problems that inaccurate forecasts cause in their businesses. They recognize that these prob-

EXHIBIT 2.9. HOW CRITICAL IS A MORE ACCURATE S&OP FORECAST?

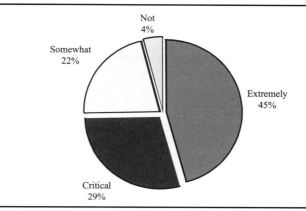

SOURCE: Industry Directions/Syncra Systems.

lems directly impact their fundamental business issues of timeliness, market share, margins, sales, and customer service levels.

Most retailers consider stock-outs a major problem, and over 40 percent have issues with materials shortages, inventory costs impacting margins, lost sales due to inability to respond to market variability, and service-level problems due to poor responsiveness to last-minute changes.

The top issue with which manufacturers struggle is the high cost of inventory and obsolescence. They also have concerns about all of the difficulties listed by retailers. Others are most concerned about inventory costs, materials shortages, and poor responsiveness to change.

Customer Service Levels

An important area that forecast accuracy affects is customer service levels. For retailers, this represents having the right product on the shelf the moment customers walk in looking for it—at a price they are willing to pay. For manufacturers, it is delivering perfect orders, or delivering the right quantity of the SKU mix requested at the specified time. This is especially critical when items are on special promotion.

Among the retailers surveyed, there is a wide range of service levels. This may be because some interpreted service as incoming perfect orders, while others viewed it as in-stock levels. As Exhibit 2.10 depicts,

EXHIBIT 2.10. CURRENT SERVICE LEVELS.

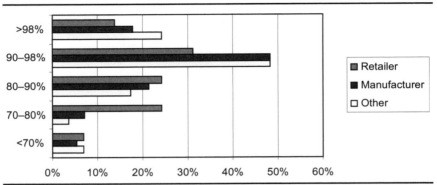

SOURCE: Industry Directions/Syncra Systems.

nearly half the retailers reported over 90 percent service levels, while a third have less than 80 percent service levels. In contrast, two-thirds of the manufacturers claimed over 90 percent perfect orders, and just 12 percent have service levels under 80 percent. This discrepancy could be the result of retailers failing to provide a buffer between demand and the manufacturers.

Of all respondents, 10 percent did not know their service levels—most of these companies have no CPFR plans. This highlights a group of companies that need internal education to understand the critical nature of service levels to supply chain success. Awareness of lost opportunity and supply chain inefficiency often provides the sense of urgency needed to spark companies to embark on CPFR.

Retail stock-outs can mean significant lost sales. Beyond the immediate loss from the out-of-stock item, customers often take their business elsewhere—for all of their shopping needs, not just for the unavailable item. Manufacturers that cannot deliver perfect orders similarly risk erosion of customer loyalty, as they may be the cause of these lost revenue opportunities, for their trading partners and themselves.

2.4.5 Leveraging Diverse Initiatives and Systems

There were multiple supply chain initiatives under way in 79 percent of the respondent companies, many of which leverage information technologies. To show them graphically, we divide them into initiatives and systems, as seen in Exhibit 2.11.

EXHIBIT 2.11. SUPPLY CHAIN INITIATIVES.

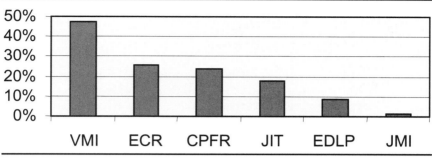

SOURCE: Industry Directions/Syncra Systems.

The breakdown shows:

- Vendor-managed inventory (VMI) is by far the most widely implemented supply chain improvement initiative, at 47 percent of those surveyed. However, of these, almost none have taken it to the next stage of shared responsibility or joint-managed inventory (JMI). This is where CPFR communication can facilitate the next step.

- ECR is the second most widely implemented initiative and is relevant to those in consumer goods retail and their suppliers.

- Almost as many are implementing CPFR, which is impressive, given how recent the guidelines are.

- Eighteen percent use just in time (JIT), which is a similar concept to ECR but used primarily by manufacturers.

- Nine percent practice every day lowest price (EDLP), a concept that some retail segments use, which would affect those retailers and their suppliers.

CPFR is the next stage in the evolution of supply chain initiatives (see Exhibit 2.12). It goes beyond current internal system implementa-

EXHIBIT 2.12. CPFR AS THE NEXT STEP IN THE SUPPLY CHAIN EVOLUTION.

SOURCE: Industry Directions/Syncra Systems.

tions and pushes the next level of information sharing out to trading partners. Using CPFR, companies are joining forces and taking responsibility for mutual plans that result in greater benefit than if they were to remain independent.

CPFR is also an enabling process for all other supply chain improvement initiatives. To quote the VICS Roadmap, "CPFR is about setting common goals for organizations and builds on and extends other Efficient Consumer Response (ECR) successes, such as category management and Continuous Replenishment Planning (CRP). It pulls them into a cohesive plan, supports better execution of the plan, and invites improved planning in the next business cycle."

CPFR leverages current investments in database and applications software, including warehouse management systems (WMS), forecasting/APS, enterprise resources planning (ERP), materials requirements planning (MRP), distribution requirements planning (DRP), and customer relationship management (CRM). All of these applications are widely used by the respondents, ranging from 46 percent using WMS and 41 percent using ERP to 9 percent using CRM. These systems store and execute plans and forecasts or track customer preferences. Very often it is advantageous to link these systems, at the partner level, to CPFR. Generally, this is not a complex process.

What can be complex is the wide variety of systems in use by each of the partners. It is not uncommon to find unique ERP, supply chain, warehouse management, or CRM system combinations in a supply chain, as we find in the respondent base (see Exhibit 2.13). There are no single leaders in these software segments.

Enterprise Resources Planning

Half the companies employing ERP use SAP, Oracle, or J D Edwards, while 42 percent are split among twenty-two other systems.

Supply Chain Planning/Forecasting

For supply chain planning or forecasting, 27 percent use Manugistics, and 9 percent have deployed i2. Of the remaining 64 percent, no more than 6 percent use any one system.

EXHIBIT 2.13. ENTERPRISE RESOURCES PLANNING IN USE.

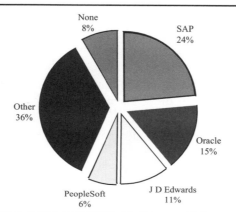

SOURCE: Industry Directions/Syncra Systems.

Warehouse Management Systems (WMS)

WMS is the application most commonly implemented among the respondents:

- Seven percent use EXE and 6 percent use OMI.
- More than 60 percent use a WMS other than the seven choices provided in the survey.
- Sixteen percent use custom-built WMS.

The enormous variety of planning and execution software in use creates an interoperability puzzle for CPFR. As a result, CPFR initiatives must use fully open, vendor-neutral CPFR communications products to support deployment in one-to-many and many-to-many trading partner environments. Since the question of software neutrality is crucial to CPFR infrastructure extensibility, it is worth noting that most of the CPFR products available are from companies that also offer supply chain planning, forecasting, or execution software. To succeed over the long haul, CPFR will need communication products that are truly open and interoperable.

2.4.6 Sharing the Knowledge

As the term *collaboration* suggests, CPFR is all about sharing knowledge with supply chain trading partners. Companies start by implementing CPFR programs with their top tier partners, based on who is ready to participate. Companies that have begun to gain the benefits are beginning to roll out CPFR to more partners.

When asked to how many partners they envision rolling CPFR out long term, most respondents indicate plans for 25 or fewer partners (see Exhibit 2.14). However, more than half the retailers expect to roll it out to more than 25 partners, and 15 percent of retailers expect to roll out CPFR to more than 100 trading partners. Manufacturers are more likely to follow the 80/20 rule, and roll out to the essential customers that make up the bulk of their business. In this set of manufacturers, less than a quarter anticipate rolling it out to over 25 partners.

The limited number of partners planned for CPFR is due in part to how few share data with their trading partners today. As Exhibit 2.15 shows, less than half of the companies in the 2000 survey share any type of data except for promotional plans, and just 56 percent of the total share promotional information.

CPFR is a program designed to enable key trading partners to improve their sales while reducing inventory and overhead. There is some early indication that such benefits might drive companies into CPFR relationships with more partners than this group of respondents anticipates today.

EXHIBIT 2.14. EXPECTED NUMBER OF TRADING PARTNERS IN CPFR LONG TERM.

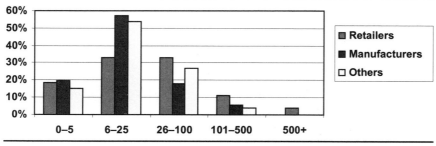

SOURCE: Industry Directions/Syncra Systems.

EXHIBIT 2.15. INFORMATION REGULARLY SHARED WITH PARTNERS.

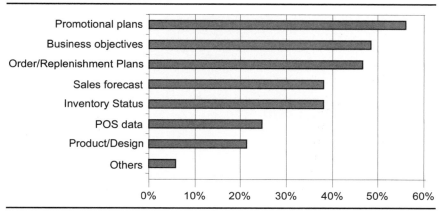

SOURCE: Industry Directions/Syncra Systems.

There are a number of respondents who see the potential to roll out CPFR quite broadly. For example, one retailer that expects to roll out to over 500 partners is a well-known nationwide chain; another expects over 200 this year. Many of the larger companies (over $250 million) expect to collaborate with over 100 partners.

Often, CPFR initiatives are pushed by one of the partners or a central "hub sponsor." Of those who know about their trading partners' CPFR initiatives, most have been asked to participate, as shown in Exhibit 2.16. However, in the total respondent base, not quite half are

EXHIBIT 2.16. PARTNER INVOLVEMENT IN CPFR.

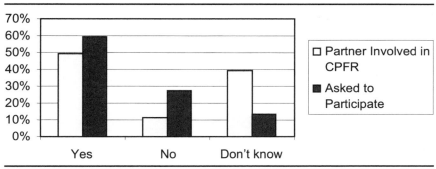

SOURCE: Industry Directions/Syncra Systems.

aware that their trading partners are involved in CPFR, and nearly 40 percent don't know whether a partner uses CPFR.

Since many of the respondents are expecting to pilot or roll out CPFR programs in the next year (and even more are conducting research to embark on a pilot), the views on participation and number of partners for CPFR are sure to change. We expect that a year from now, respondents will expand their long-term vision for CPFR to include well over twenty-five partners.

2.4.7 CPFR Implementation

While the benefits of CPFR are impressive, implementation has its challenges. Perhaps the most significant issue revolves around making what VICS calls the organizational shift to a consumer-centric, inter-enterprise orientation.

The respondents agreed, as can be seen in Exhibit 2.17. Sixty percent indicate that, indeed, internal process changes are difficult. A lack of partner trust is another major cultural issue that companies must address.

EXHIBIT 2.17. CPFR CHALLENGES.

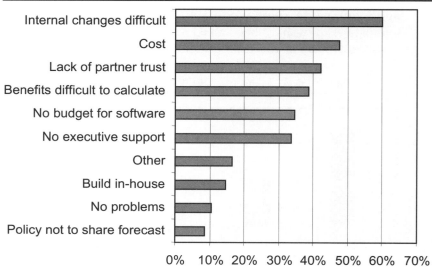

SOURCE: Industry Directions/Syncra Systems.

For those furthest along—in pilots or in planning to roll out CPFR in the near future—the top three issues are internal process change, lack of trust with partners, and cost of implementation. The other issues were not considered significant stumbling blocks by those experienced in CPFR. These companies have gained executive support and are further along in quantifying the benefits.

Many respondents are using a consultant or system integrator for their ERP and supply chain software implementation (see Exhibit 2.18). The two most widely used firms are PricewaterhouseCoopers (17 percent) and Accenture (16 percent). The other firms called upon for system implementation support include KPMG (8 percent), Kurt Salmon Associates (6 percent) and EDS/A. T. Kearney (6 percent).

Several respondents have also turned to Arthur Andersen/Senn-Delaney, Ernst & Young, and Deloitte and Touche—all grouped under "other." Since these firms have gained knowledge of the company's issues and IT infrastructure, including them in the CPFR implementation may make sense.

To reduce the cost of a CPFR implementation and accelerate its time to market, outsourcing is a viable option. Almost one in five of the respondents would consider outsourcing in their large-scale CPFR deployment plans. More (28 percent) would manage CPFR for a large number of trading partners in-house.

Interestingly, respondents in each size range had a different primary approach to how they would deploy CPFR to a large group of trading

EXHIBIT 2.18. CONSULTANT OR SYSTEMS INTEGRATOR FOR ERP OR SUPPLY CHAIN.

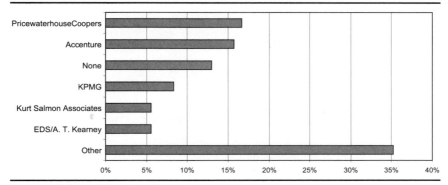

SOURCE: Industry Directions/Syncra Systems.

partners, as can be seen in Exhibit 2.19. The smallest companies would want to keep management internal. Organizations over $100 million and under $250 million are keenly interested in application service providers (ASPs), perhaps because some of these companies are highly dynamic and growing.

Half of the largest companies expect to use service bureaus to manage large CPFR implementations. Even in the remaining half, outsourcing is often a key element. They showed interest in ASPs, as well using internal management for the major trading partners and outsourcing for less strategic partners.

Key Advantages of CPFR

The companies that have already undertaken CPFR are reporting some exciting benefits. Supply chain partners are finding collaborative planning can increase sales while reducing costs. The results include:

- Increased sales of the products for which planning was collaborative

EXHIBIT 2.19. APPROACH TO LARGE-SCALE CPFR DEPLOYMENT BY COMPANY SIZE.

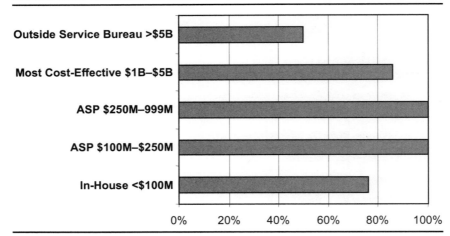

SOURCE: Industry Directions/Syncra Systems.

- Reduced forecast error
- Reduced replenishment cycle times
- Visibility to better set store-level replenishment parameters
- Improved in-stock rates for retailers
- Reduced days of supply, lower inventory levels, and higher inventory turns
- Smoother demand pattern for suppliers
- Increased service levels from suppliers to retailers
- Lower production planning and deployment costs for suppliers

Even respondents now achieving excellent performance see opportunity for further improvements using CPFR. For example, as shown in Exhibit 2.20, half the companies with over 98 percent service levels believe they could achieve significant improvement in their service levels with CPFR.

Progress Since the 2000 CPFR Research Study

One of the developments to occur since our initial CPFR research in 2000 was the emergence of widely supported public trading exchanges like Transora and World-Wide-Retail-Exchange. The attraction of a public exchange is that a single communications mechanism can enable

Exhibit 2.20. Service boost expected by CPFR.

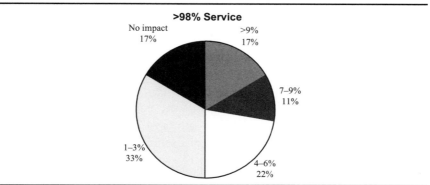

Source: Industry Directions/Syncra Systems.

collaboration with many trading partners. To date, CPFR has consisted almost exclusively of one-to-one pilots and implementations between a single retailer and a single supplier for a defined set of products. Because of the nature of CPFR, each interaction must be narrowly defined, but manufacturers would prefer a way to leverage the infrastructure and business process of CPFR across several retail trading partners and suppliers.

Quite a few manufacturers find that the trading exchanges are a logical way to do business, but some exchanges are not yet fully equipped to handle CPFR. In other cases, questions arise about how the exchanges might work together to allow members of each to collaborate across those exchange boundaries. So while some companies have based their approach to CPFR on that of one of the major exchanges, quite a few others are finding that they must move forward without full confidence in how, when, or even if public trading exchanges will fully support their efforts.

What we have seen in working with U.S. manufacturers is that CPFR is starting to gain momentum. While retail customers generally provide the first impetus, manufacturers are starting to embrace this effort as they realize the benefits as well.

Larger manufacturers in particular appear to be taking CPFR seriously, and executives are placing priority on collaboration, particularly with retail customers. As with any major initiative for process and systems change, executive support and attention are critical to success. Our observation is that the manufacturers that have made CPFR a priority and proactively pursue it, rather than simply agreeing to a customer's request to participate, are having the most success.

CPFR in Practice

One of the interesting developments of the past few years—since the publication of the VICS CPFR Roadmap—is that to get moving quickly, quite a few companies are collaborating with critical partners in a manner that is less complete than the full CPFR process. This is a traditional sequence for manufacturers taking on new businesses processes: They crawl before they walk, and walk before they run. Taking it a piece at a time can ease the challenge of transition.

Initially, quite a few manufacturers gain significant benefits just from accessing one level of the retailer's forecasts or plans and alerting the retailer to issues in an informal process when they cannot meet expectations. Ongoing identification of exceptions and collaboration to keep fulfillment in line with the latest demand movements are processes that require even further internal process and organizational change.

Companies that are further along in their CPFR implementation are finding that the role of operations increases and that of sales decreases over time. This reflects the move from only reviewing customer forecasts and providing feedback—a sales function—to collaborative planning and replenishment, where operations and supply chain functions manage the processes.

Further, most CPFR initiatives are working at the distribution center level, not necessarily the store level. This is another level of detail that may be best achieved over a period of time for some trading partners. It is also important to recognize that the internal changes required for retailers to analyze and deliver store-level demand information to trading partners may continue to be a sticking point for some time.

Many applications software vendors have also announced or improved their support for CPFR since our initial research. As a result, more U.S. manufacturers are using commercial software for CPFR than before, and some of those outsource or use an ASP rather than adding infrastructure and applications to support CPFR internally. At this point, many companies use a combination of mechanisms to support their CPFR activity, including Excel spreadsheets and internally developed software—or customer-specific software—along with these commercial products.

Today's technology would allow companies to exchange data via XML via the Internet, but our discussions suggest that many CPFR programs use EDI, flat files, and e-mail mechanisms for data sharing between partners. XML is just taking hold as manufacturers migrate from older enterprise applications to those that can transmit XML, so this transition probably will not take place any time soon for a number of the U.S. manufacturers we have encountered.

So while the VICS CPFR Guidelines outline a relatively comprehensive process for collaboration between trading partners, many companies are getting started with a more limited process. Similarly, the commercial software available that leverages XML and newer technologies is just beginning to be adopted. In practice, CPFR is being implemented and adopted incrementally.

Benefits Drive Adoption

In our initial study the respondents that had active or complete pilot projects reported stunning inventory reductions and gains in sales levels with the partner, and service level and fill rates. Our conversations more recently indicate that these benefits are still strong. Companies are also improving their forecast accuracy and, above all, their trading partner relationships. This bodes well for future expansion of CPFR activities.

Some manufacturers are finding it difficult to quantify hard benefits from CPFR because they see the largest gains in internal communications and process efficiency, as well as better trading partner relationships and becoming a preferred supplier. However, those furthest along have improved, usually simultaneously, in sales, inventory levels, and customer service. These are measurable, and as companies recognize that metrics will be key to sustaining CPFR efforts and gauging success with each partner, companies are assembling scorecards to track gains.

It's not just the largest U.S. manufacturers that are participating and gaining benefits. Quite a few $500 million to $2 billion consumer goods companies or divisions also have CPFR pilots under way or complete, and their results are at least as striking. Some of these manufacturers are also very aggressive in pursuing expansions to their pilots and adding CPFR activities with more trading partners. This is a refreshing change from all retail-driven CPFR, and we expect those aggressive manufacturers to generate even greater results from their efforts than those that wait to be invited.

The benefits to manufacturers and their suppliers are that, with a more realistic view of demand as it changes at the retail level, they can stay synchronized and work to grow sales without as much risk of inventory overages or stock-outs. The good news for retailers is that their suppliers are increasingly interested in working with them to keep the shelves stocked, and getting beyond the pain of some of the earlier VMI efforts. For U.S. consumers, all of this could add up in the long run to more pleasing retail shopping experiences, in which the brands

American shoppers prefer are easier to find and products promoted are more likely to be available in the local store.

CPFR continues to drive value for consumer goods manufacturers and their trading partners. U.S. manufacturers are incorporating it into their larger supply chain initiatives and leveraging the power of collaboration with trading partners to further the success of their value networks. CPFR has its challenges, and manufacturers are notoriously slow to change their processes, but CPFR is taking hold. In this environment, collaboration is creating win–win situations for U.S. industry and consumers.

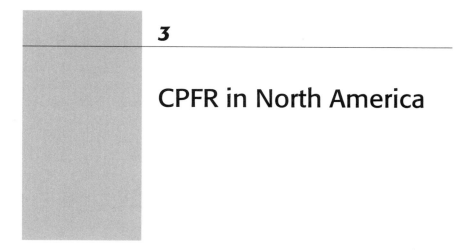

3

CPFR in North America

3.1

Major Trends in North American CPFR Adoption

Thomas H. Friedman and Greg Belkin, MoonWatch Media Inc.

The VICS Collaborative Planning, Forecasting, and Replenishment (CPFR) supply chain process initiative has become an adopted next practice globally. In its current phase of development, the objective is to extend its process model to a retailer's or supplier's full range of trading partners. Within the last three years, however, several discussions among top industry executives have occurred concerning best-practice procedures. To this end, we present analyses of five major trends involving CPFR adoption in North America, as well as some case studies.

3.1.1 Collaboration Means Restructuring Supply Chain Processes

CPFR and other collaborative processes provide true end–user benefits. Supply chain collaboration is more than visibility, information sharing, and improved technology. It also involves changing the nature of trading relationships in order to add value for end users, as well as benefiting all participants in a collaborative value chain. For example, the nine-step VICS CPFR process standard replaces traditional customer and purchase orders with collaborative demand/order forecasts and an automated replenishment order flow. These steps allow buyers and sellers to redefine how they work together and leverage each other's resources.

Actions that rely on technology to transfer functions from one side of a transaction to another, or accelerate existing work-flow processes, do not create significant added value to collaborative trading partnerships. Vendor-managed inventory (VMI), for example, moves a retailer's inventory management and replenishment role to the supplier. The supplier's greater pipeline transparency and longer span of inventory control, from the sources of supply to the retailer's selling location, simplify the coordination of product flow and work flow. However, due to a lack of shared perspective, this process creates several logistical problems. After the implementation of VMI, many retailers have discovered these hidden logistical problems and have thus been required to make additional investments.

Ace Hardware is one such retailer that at first relied on VMI but soon realized the extended benefits of CPFR. Ace's expanded single view of a supplier did not provide perfect transparency or a means of integrating retailer stock status, retailer promotions, new store openings, distribution center realignments, and total assortment management requirements into sales and order forecasts. Since each supplier used its own planning and execution processes, coordination of multiple product flows deteriorated, while competition for supply chain resources and scheduling grew exponentially as the number of VMI programs increased. As a result, inventory support for promotions was inconsistent, product shipments lacked coordination with total pipeline activity, and many independent reactive demand forecasts proliferated.

To solve this problem, Ace decided to add a single, shared demand forecast, based on the nine-step VICS CPFR model, and developed a single collaboration software suite, accessible to both supplier and retailer. The retailer and its suppliers used the CPFR process steps to jointly develop a front-end agreement and business plan to drive the supplier's planning and replenishment process execution. As an added benefit, Ace's small and medium-size suppliers were able to participate in this new collaborative model without significant systems expense or operational overhead. Supplier forecasts were seamlessly coordinated with storewide promotions, total assortment planning, and other retailer data to optimize service levels. Most important, the supplier's uncertainty over competing priorities and objectives was kept in line by jointly reconciling these data with demand and order forecasts.

Achieving effective collaboration is not a one-size-fits-all process. It is dependent on the identification of those business processes that offer the greatest opportunity for collaborative improvement. To this end, the CPFR Web site, www.cpfr.org, provides a CPFR capability assessment. It offers evaluation criteria and definitions for collaborative processes, integrated planning and forecasting, replenishment, and supply chain management and is based directly on the Global ECR Scorecard metrics developed in 1999. The assessment process allows buyers and sellers to initiate appropriate collaborative connections and set goals that can be achieved and leveraged to grow joint value chain capacity. At the same time, the Global Commerce Initiative (GCI) provides the scorecard for establishing the level of supply chain relationships. This enables companies to begin working in process areas at the correct level of engagement. It also provides a means of connecting with related key performance indicators to establish quantifiable collaborative goals and monitor performance.

Moreover, achieving the scalability of collaborative commerce relationships is directly dependent on the availability of open, neutral standards that can be used by companies of all sizes on a global basis. These standards enable trading partners to replicate new shared supply chain processes throughout the Supply Web Enterprise, spanning internal systems, processes, and intercompany transactions. The shared restructuring of supply chain processes involves the synchronization of data and a clearly defined execution of the collaborative trading partnership.

Successful supply chain management requires a focus on processes that will ultimately benefit the end user. However, this will be realized only by establishing processes that replace older technology-based supplier agreements with collaborative partnerships that benefit all participants in a collaborative value chain.

3.1.2 Scalable CPFR Requires Incremental Development

Moving beyond successful CPFR pilots to collaborative trading partner networks requires a slow, methodical approach.

The transition to a process infrastructure that will enable and support the increased transaction volume and interactive complexity of extensive CPFR trading partner relationships calls for measured steps that build on the VICS CPFR initiative. The nine-step CPFR process model of this initiative necessitates scalable technology to support exception-based decision management. It also requires feasible processes to control the complexity of relationships in a trading partner network.

The objective of CPFR pilots is to develop mutually effective processes. In the same manner, the first steps in implementing CPFR trading partner networks call for the development of process links between trading partners at an appropriate level of collaboration.

In initial collaborative process development, technology has not been the primary focus. Recent CPFR pilots, for example, demonstrated that the largest retail and wholesale companies of the global supply chain first used spreadsheets to transmit CPFR data rather than use their extensive technical resources. Scalable collaborative implementations, however, require more technological support, thereby allowing exception-based decision management to focus on process development and execution between trading partners, as opposed to the administrative issues of transaction management.

The next step in developing scalable collaborative processes involves homogeneous groups of trading partners implementing those processes. This can be aided by the VICS CPFR capability assessment worksheet, which provides a clear and objective means of segmenting trading partners within a supply chain network. By outfitting a cluster of trading partners with similar CPFR capabilities, organizations can achieve a common collaborative resolution of CPFR process improvement.

A further incremental process method would entail setting demand planning levels at the warehouse or distribution center by SKU before increasing volume and complexity at stores. In addition, firms initiating the construction of a CPFR network would simplify the complexity of process development among multiple trading partners by segmenting the product mix to focus more on stable and less on promotional or seasonal categories.

The preceding approaches provide a gradual rate of implementation, thus allowing trading partners time to mutually assess both collective progress and the capability of individual companies to manage supply chain processes and relationships. The move from a CPFR pilot of two partners to a network of fifty or more does not occur in a single step and adds significant complexity to the CPFR management process. Clusters of trading partner relationships will exist for each partner based on product mix, distribution model, promotional strategy, and systems. Limiting initial trading partner combinations will control the escalating complexity and size of the CPFR installation. This new level should be appropriate to the level of trading partner collaboration established in the initial CPFR front-end agreement process.

Future requirements for commercial implementations, however, will necessitate a scalable technology to support the gradual development of CPFR relationships. Recent announcements of the creation of an XML-based directory service standard and of application service provider (ASP) solutions by major software vendors signal opportunities for successful CPFR implementations on a large scale.

IBM, Microsoft, Novell, Oracle, Sun Microsystems, and Netscape Communications expressed support for the XML-based directory services markup language (DSML) in 1999. In addition, Logility, Oracle, Manugistics, and i2 Technologies report ASP functionality for their customers and trading partners. In particular, Logility's i-Commerce, a Web-based ASP network compliant with the VICS CPFR initiative, shows particular promise for scalable CPFR installations. These new developments will enable supply chain companies to access and manage the volume of transactions generated by multiple relationships efficiently and effectively.

In addition, the development of VICS CPFR requires that both sides learn, understand, and effectively use collaborative supply chain processes on an incremental basis. Otherwise, a rapid one-sided deployment of CPFR technology will simply become another supply chain initiative instead of a foundation for developing supply chain value.

The promise of this technology requires a disciplined gradual development of CPFR processes between trading partners. In response to this concern, the VICS CPFR committee has focused its recommendations on process first and technology second. The committee believes that the gradual maturation of each relationship is the core factor for success in building long-term commercial viability. Moreover, a premature implementation of full-scale CPFR networks can derail the initial proof-of-concept validation established by CPFR pilots.

Continued investment in incremental collaborative process development will enable high levels of cooperation, thus driving improvement in operating efficiencies for retailer and supplier.

3.1.3 The Power of One

The Voluntary Interindustry Commerce Standards Association has assumed many important initiatives of the defunct Joint Industry Project on Efficient Consumer Response in the United States. As they began focusing on the demand side of the supply chain, these two major retail business-to-business organizations found they were becoming increasingly alike. With a sharper focus on consumer satisfaction, members of these two groups are now addressing ways in which they can enable the retail industry to leverage raw point-of-sale data and to do more refined forecasting.

Both standards organizations were deeply engaged in Collaborative Planning, Forecasting, and Replenishment processes. In fact, both list the development of CPFR as having been one of their highest priorities for several years. Moreover, through its stewardship of CPFR committee meetings, VICS realized that its most active committee members were longtime participants in the ECR movement under the VICS banner.

In addition, as both supermarket and general merchandise industries grew closer over time, similarities increased. They now began to resemble each other in product lines and practices, buying from many of the same consumer product companies, such as Procter & Gamble, Johnson & Johnson, and Nabisco. Consequently, it was quite common for members of both organizations to struggle to explain the differences between them. Historically, the differences are more obvious. On the one hand, VICS was founded in the mid-1980s by a group of general merchandise retailers and suppliers, including the world's largest retailer, Wal-Mart. This group pioneered the development of interindustry communications standards, such as bar codes, shipping container marking, and electronic data interchange (EDI), that are specific to the apparel portion of the general merchandise industry. This effort was named Quick Response.

The Joint Industry Project on ECR, on the other hand, was founded in the mid-1990s by the supermarket industry. Member stores were worried that they would not be able to compete with general merchandise companies, such as Wal-Mart, Target, and Kmart, as they launched supermarkets within the superstore format. These general merchandise companies had also successfully automated their warehouses and other supply-side aspects of the business. In response, therefore, the supermarket industry created an organization with consumer product companies that focused on optimizing logistics and product flow. It also developed innovative supply chain processes, including activity-based costing (ABC) and scan-based trading.

Both industries were creating inefficiencies in standards and process development by not working together in a formal capacity. In addition, with recent consolidations in the retail industry, it was more than likely that neither organization would have enough participants or volunteers to meet its current goals domestically or globally. This same period also saw increasing numbers of similar supply chain initiatives competing for resources available to ECR and VICS members.

Moreover, with the advent of the Internet as a platform for interindustry commerce, it is possible that many current practices will quickly become outdated. New commerce opportunities such as Internet trading exchanges, built around industry hubs like UCCnet, will enable individual retailers to build either online trading communities or cooperative trading communities with like-minded retail partners. This evolution will occur during the next decade, and these communities will decide who will have the best relationships with suppliers, the most cost-efficient trading practices, and, ultimately, products for the consumer.

In response to the potential of Internet trading communities and other new technology-driven commerce practices, *Supply Chain Alert* editors successfully encouraged VICS and the ECR group to contemplate more than an informal sharing of expertise and knowledge. The general merchandise and supermarket industries have now eliminated redundancy, or better still, by evolving into a common group they have established a specific mode of communication between business-to-business retail supply chain partners.

3.1.4 CPFR Optimization Requires Order Forecasts

CPFR relationships without order forecasts do not remove uncertainty from time-phased supply chain management for suppliers. The Collaborative Planning, Forecasting, and Replenishment process model includes a single shared forecast of consumer demand at the point of sale. This forecast is the basis for the integration of trading partner supply chain processes. Such a sales forecast alone will enable improved coordination of value-chain process activities.

However, this is not enough to reduce significant constraints on supply chain effectiveness and efficiency. Shared demand forecasts alone will not optimize manufacturing flexibility or enable a make-to-order manufacturing process. Neither will they enable dynamic interenterprise scheduling to streamline asset utilization throughout the product flow from manufacturing through transportation and on to distribution centers. Therefore, order forecasts are necessary to extend the value of the CPFR process model through delivery execution. However, certain process barriers exist that make it more difficult to provide order forecasts than to provide shared demand forecasts.

One such barrier is the time horizon. Over time, the unit difference between demand forecasts of consumer demand at the point of sale and order forecasts diminishes. The long-term difference consists mainly of inventory required to fill store shelves and displays, as well as product shortage. The accuracy of demand forecasts improves when considered long term—it follows the law of big numbers. Conversely, the accuracy of order forecasts improves with its temporal proximity to actual delivery. A delivery forecast for tomorrow will be more accurate than one for next month. Manufacturing flexibility and the streamlined flow of product throughout the supply chain require closer monitoring to optimize scheduling of equipment and people.

The barrier for retailers in providing order forecasts to trading partners, after they have collaborated on shared demand, is that the temporal requirements for accuracy in demand and order forecasts are binary opposites. If the order forecast process is based on the same time frame as that used for demand forecasting, the order forecast will be unusable and inaccurate as well.

Another barrier is the process work flow in transportation management between trading partners. The industry practice of using retailer routing guides for directing suppliers to ship via collect freight creates friction in the flow of product from supplier to retailer. This is a barrier to consistent and accurate order forecasting.

In 1995, AutoZone and J. B. Hunt Logistics designed and implemented a new supply chain infrastructure that converted 77 percent of supplier inbound product from prepaid to collect freight. This change in the process work flow of inbound transportation reduced the transit time from seven days to less than two days and created a high degree of control, accuracy, and visibility in AutoZone's pipeline.

In 1997, Best Buy Company, Inc. and Sharp Electronics initiated a similar collaborative transportation management (CTM) partnership that was integrated with CPFR in 1998. That initiative enabled the trading partners to reduce the sales forecast time frame from a rolling six months to a rolling thirteen weeks. Additionally, order and shipment forecasting accuracy improved, so that orders were able to be frozen eight weeks in advance of delivery.

In order to provide usable order forecasts, retailers should use their shortest-term, netted order forecasts available as a starting point. This can begin at the time an order is transmitted from the retailer's purchase order management system to the supplier. A review of the accuracy, metrics, and synchronization of orders with the supplier will identify inconsistencies and errors that cause friction and limit the effectiveness of any order forecast. From this starting point, an extension of the order forecast time horizon will raise issues such as promotion inventory buildups, new store openings, and seasonal inventory shifts. Selecting exception criteria values; researching exceptions; and analyzing exceptions collaboratively through the use of electronic messaging, phone or videoconferencing, or face-to-face meetings will enable resolution of order forecast inaccuracy.

In some cases, logistics requirements such as trailer loads, minimum order requirements, and case packs can be solved by leveraging the systems and process knowledge of supplier trading partners. This iterative process is no different from that of developing a shared demand forecast. It simply originates from a different time frame. The lessons learned in developing short-term order forecasts will enable reasonable accuracy in the long-term order forecasts used for production and capacity planning by suppliers.

If collaborative order forecasting is not part of a CPFR trading partner relationship, the shared risk that is at the heart of an effective CPFR relationship does not exist. It also limits the ability of suppliers to engage in dynamic interenterprise scheduling, or a make-to-order manufacturing process. By removing order forecasting from the CPFR process, retailers force suppliers to minimize uncertainty in order fulfillment by maintaining excess safety stocks in trade.

3.1.5 Collaborative Efforts Drive B2B Exchanges

The future success of B2B supply Web exchanges (SWEs) requires collaborative development.

B2B exchanges enable trading partners to interact in a multiuser environment using standard transactions. The long-term viability of an exchange is dependent on developing and maintaining an attractive assortment of participating companies that will satisfy the commercial needs of buyers and sellers. Many and varied related buyers and sellers enable industry segments to find common solutions to vertical issues, as well as to integrate horizontal applications with their transactions. This, in turn, fuels an iterative work-flow process development cycle that will result in a new level of supply Web efficiency.

In the B2B community, buyers and sellers are targeting fewer and more defined segments of trading partners, with customer accounts ranging in the thousands. For example, the affiliated B2B trading exchange being created by the Big Three automotive manufacturers—General Motors, Daimler/Chrysler, and Ford—will comprise a trading community numbering over 10,000 companies, whereas traditional B2C automotive exchanges target more than several hundred million consumers. As e-commerce is extended up the supply chain, there is generally a consolidation of both the number of trading partners involved and the value of the relationships.

Purchasing decisions in B2B exchanges are generally based on strategic factors, with purchase costs being just one of several elements in the value equation. Trust, quality, reliability, product specifications, warranties, capacity, delivery, flexibility, and availability generally outweigh pure price considerations in SWE trading partner decision making. The nature of SWE relationships is essentially on a variable sum basis, as trading partners collaboratively improve the efficiency, speed, and quality of their business decisions and transactions.

Moreover, both buyer and seller make an investment in each other when they decide to conduct business. This can range from the time and expense of configuring Web catalogs to incorporating the seller's product specifications and characteristics into the buyer's internal systems and processes. In a B2B environment, changing trading partners can be costly to both sides.

In addition, collaborative B2B communities provide valuable information that was formerly unavailable in traditional supply chain relationships focusing on specific segments within the demand chain. The information exchanged is generally valuable in reengineering business processes or enhancing products and services. Collaborative transactions are integrated into transaction systems of each trading partner, enabling internal efficiencies that a one-sided relationship cannot offer. These Internet trading exchanges enable the existence of many-to-many collaborative relationships using the same standards, communication links, systems, and metrics.

For these reasons, B2B exchanges supply value for members, not only by enabling greater efficiency in processing and managing transactions, but also by providing stability and growth in the availability of relevant buyers and sellers. The presence of targeted customers, and even direct competitors, will prove to be the main initial attraction for joining a specific trading exchange.

The future development of SWE communities will be driven by the nature of the transactions supported. The initial development of trading exchanges focused on spot purchases such as maintenance, repair, and operating services, as well as shared services and commodities. Services included the provision of online vendor product catalog aggregation, procurement, bidder qualification, and financial transactions.

Internet trading exchanges are now expanding upon this initial functionality to include horizontal processes such as group buys, requests for quotation, delivery, design/build contracts, multiple vendor sourcing, and financing. Future horizontal development will focus on adding replenishment, promotion planning, new product introduction, demand forecasting, and load management to develop full trading life-cycle process support.

In addition, SWEs can add value horizontally by providing best-of-breed systems support for their members in an application service provider role. Independent B2B exchanges can use superior best-of-breed functionality to compete for members with affiliated supply Web exchanges. However, horizontal feature value will not be enough to retain members and optimize community value.

It is therefore necessary to provide nontransferable value for targeted member segments through vertical applications and functionality. Vertical features developed through community management will create benefits that are unique to the industries served by an exchange, foster member loyalty, and attract additional generated content and outreach efforts.

Vertical applications and functionality are the means by which an SWE provides nontransferable value for its targeted member segments. By adding vertical value to an SWE, the cost of moving to another trading venue is greatly increased, as the functionality is not directly transferable due to proprietary development and the smaller market for vertical applications.

Internet trading exchanges promise users significant long-term benefits. For example, they allow users to operate in a multiuser environment to exchange critical buying and selling information, and to bid for different supplier contracts. The advantages of these exchanges are dependent, however, on establishing a wide assortment of participating companies that will satisfy the needs of all users. Although the existence of targeted users, and their competitors, will provide a significant short-term attraction for joining an Internet trading exchange, future growth of specific communities will come only from the nature of transactions supported.

3.1.6 Case Study: Wal-Mart Initiates CPFR with Sara Lee

The $118 billion retailer and $20 billion manufacturer developed collaborative sales forecasting processes.

To improve the performance of product lines between their companies, Wal-Mart Stores, Inc. and Sara-Lee, Inc. recently implemented two of the nine Collaborative Planning, Forecasting, and Replenishment steps.

This collaborative effort builds on a successful long-term replenishment relationship, the improvement of which required an end-to-end process that leveraged the capabilities of all companies. In addition, the process required an industry model adaptable in a standard, yet flexible, mode by the majority of each company's trading partners without requiring complex technology.

Wal-Mart and Sara Lee therefore decided to focus initially on developing a set of standard, baseline processes and readily available technology enablers for the new collaborative sales forecasting process. Both retailer and manufacturer have taken steps to validate the CPFR industry model as the basis for further expansion of a collaborative standard within other supply chain relationships.

The retailer and manufacturer implemented the forecast collaboration process as follows:

- *Q1 1998.* As part of the CPFR pilot, Wal-Mart and Sara Lee focused on two of nine steps of the VICS CPFR business model. These involved creating a sales forecast and resolving and collaborating on exception items. At this time, the companies defined the pilot's scope, requirements, design, and metrics. Items selected for the pilot included twenty-three Hanes men's underwear styles from Sara Lee's extensive product mix. The metrics defined to measure success consisted of forecasted weeks on hand, store service level, and forecast accuracy.

- *Q2 1998.* Initial transmission of information began via a Web-based collaboration site, using secure e-mail from Wal-Mart to Sara Lee. The format used for sending forecasts and revisions incorporated the EDI 830 transaction set. On a per-item basis, the supplier validated the forecast, using a preestablished special event calendar, as well as its product knowledge, marketing programs, and promotional input from the sales and marketing department. During this period, the companies mutually calibrated the lift effects of causal factors, such as price reduction, on retail sales. In addition, exception criteria, such as store in-stock service levels and sales trends, were further refined.

- *Q3 1998.* Both companies automated the collaborative process of identifying and reconciling exceptions to the shared forecast. They also developed a weekly exception-analysis reporting format that enabled further refinement of defined item tolerances.

- *Q4 1998.* Wal-Mart and Sara Lee calculated initial pilot results through the first forty-one weeks. This included a GMROI increase, as well as a sales increase with a comp store lift. In addition, inventory turnover improved, retail inventory weeks-on-hand dropped, and product market share rose. With these initial results, the companies discerned an increase in productivity derived from increased value to the consumer as the inventory level grew. Moreover, while the established continuous replenishment partnership eliminated excess inventory from the pipeline, the CPFR partnership developed an improved ability to deliver customer value on the selling floor.

- *Q1 1999.* The companies rolled out formal collaborative processes to include other Sara Lee branded apparel products and divisions within Wal-Mart.

The new venture has clarified an understanding of consumer demand, including how to stimulate and forecast demand, as well as how to leverage individual company expertise. Sara Lee, for example, has gained a deeper understanding of forecasting dynamics for store mix within distribution center service clusters. In addition, the consistency and credibility of a single shared forecast has enabled Wal-Mart to drive the forecast deeper into its internal demand requirements planning processes.

3.1.7 Case Study: Schering-Plough Reinforces Collaborative Trading Practices

The consumer products division of $9.8 billion Schering-Plough Health Care is establishing CPFR relationships with retail trading partners.

According to the New Jersey–based health care products company, its consumer products division has established a Collaborative Planning, Forecasting, and Replenishment relationship with key retailers, including Walgreens, Kmart, and Target. In 1999 the company had enhanced retail replenishment processes with drugstore-chain The Eckerd Corporation. Since then, Schering-Plough has continued its effort to establish a consumer-based, bottom-up forecasting data program that gathers, models, and organizes data from both the company and its trading partners, to establish a single, shared source of information.

Previously, Schering-Plough's relationships with retail clients had resulted in certain logistical problems due to lack of shared product visibility. This included short and late product shipments, suboptimal product forecasting, and a lack of consumer buying-pattern research. At the same time, several unknown demand variables, such as new stores, retailer promotions, retailer stock status, and item transformation/assortment changes put additional pressure on Schering-Plough.

To further enable collaborative promotion and execution among its trading partners, the manufacturer has begun to align data from retail clients into a single data source, thus allowing collaborative promotional planning and execution from one location. In addition, it has begun to simplify supply chain management by improving in-stock positions and service levels and optimizing replenishment strategies with joint ownership.

Beginning with a decision in 1997 to establish a customer-centric forecasting program, Schering-Plough has taken the following steps to improve its data-sharing relationship with customers:

- *Q4 1998.* With the help of the E3 Corporation (now JDA Software) E3TRIM software suite, Schering-Plough executed a majority of its retail replenishment processes with Eckerd. The company reported several benefits from the project, including a 52 percent reduction in overstocks, a 33 percent drop in inventory, and a 24 percent decrease in returns.

- *Q3 1999.* Based on its success with the Eckerd project, Schering-Plough met with Illinois-based Walgreens Corporation to address the inadequate amount of sales data exchange between the two companies. The supplier and retailer agreed to work together to improve forecasting and other sales data in a single, collaborative format.

- *Q1 2000.* Schering-Plough and Walgreens employed a collaborative software suite from Syncra Systems to engage in a CPFR pilot. The two companies began with a list of selected SKUs for forecasting data exchange. Walgreen sent inventory information to Schering-Plough for review on a weekly basis and promotional and sales information was added.

- *Q2 2000.* Following the nine steps of the CPFR model, Schering-Plough and Walgreens increased the amount of SKUs involved in the project. Demand information, stock locations, and promotional and sales information were also included. At the same time, Schering-Plough approached Kmart about a similar situation regarding inaccurate and inadequate promotional information exchanged between the two companies. After several meetings, they decided to initiate a CPFR pilot with the help of the Syncra Systems solution. A pilot was initiated using a select number of SKUs.

- *Q3 2000.* After a brief realignment of staff involved in the CPFR project, Schering-Plough and Kmart increased the number of participating SKUs. Also included in this process were demand information, stock locations, and promotional and sales information.
- *Q4 2000.* Following the success of the Walgreens and Kmart CPFR efforts, Schering-Plough met with the Target Corporation and established preliminary plans to initiate a CPFR pilot involving select SKUs.

Although Schering-Plough has yet to formulate quantitative results from the CPFR relationships, it has noted several qualitative benefits. In addition to a rapid implementation time, reliable production forecasting for manufacturing operations has been identified, as well as an improved order and item fill rate. This, in turn, has helped the manufacturer identify and eradicate significant inconsistencies.

For Schering-Plough partners, high in-stock positions have resulted in increased sales, and customer demand and promotional forecasting fluctuations are now appropriately addressed by all parties involved in the transaction.

3.2

Consumer-Centric CPFR

Lawrence E. Fennell, Wal-Mart Stores

3.2.1 Current Retail Environment and Looking Forward Five Years

Before discussing the strategic necessity of moving to the platform of CPFR I believe it important to manifest the current state of retail that exists on the global stage. There are events taking place that are having and will continue to have a profound impact on retailers and suppliers. One thing will be certain over the next five years; it will be more difficult to meet the expectations of shareholders and consumers in the global retail marketplace. What are the events and issues that will be driving these challenges? Here are some of the known facts:

Fact 1: The pie is not going to get bigger. For the last several years, one company's gain has been another one's loss. This can certainly be seen in the head-to-head battles between Wal-Mart and Kmart, Kohl's and Penney's, Best Buy and Sears or Service Merchandise, Walgreens and Rite Aid. The growth retailers in the industry have made public their store opening schedules for the new year. The numbers seem to defy the current economic slowdown unless you measure them against the impact they will have on their respective competitors. Exhibit 3.1 lists the planned new stores of major American retailers.

These aggressive store-opening plans of the growth companies will be offset by the consolidation and liquidation of those retailers not prepared to compete in the competitive global retail environment.

Fact 2: Prices are going down, not up. Any holiday shopper this season could verify that there were many opportunities to buy a DVD player and movie DVD from a variety of retailers, including online, at prices far below last year's. Not only were the prices lower, but the supply was plentiful for those aggressive retailers that went after

EXHIBIT 3.1. NUMBER OF NEW STORES OF MAJOR AMERICAN RETAILERS.

Retailer	Number of new stores in 2002 (planned)
AutoZone	100
Bed Bath & Beyond	88
Best Buy	155
Costco	35
Dollar Tree	250
Home Depot	200
Kohl's	70
Lowe's	123
Staples	100
Target	100
Walgreens	475
Wal-Mart	430

SOURCE: *DSN Retailing Today,* January 7, 2002.

the business. From TVs to VCRs, from power tools to bath towels, from coffeemakers to microwave ovens, the prices have been coming down and will continue to do so. With China joining the WTO and import quotas being dismantled, the capacity for production will increase. This will be most noticeable in the textile industry; at the same time, advances in technologies will advance the deflation on pricing of hard goods.

Fact 3: Margins are going down, not up. The Kroger Company, the largest food retailer in the U.S. market, recently did an about-face from its earlier financial briefings when it stated that Wal-Mart Supercenters were not affecting its top-line growth. To quote an article by Scott Meyer in *MMR Mass Market Retailers,* dated December 17, 2001, "Kroger Co., most frustrated by its lack of topline gains, has reacted with plans to consolidate its operation and cut 1500 jobs. The cost reductions are intended to allow Kroger to cut prices as a way of driving sales. Albertson's Inc. and Safeway Inc. have also announced that boosting sales is a priority, and they are expected to make do with lower margins as a result. Analysts suggest that Kroger's move will spark further price cutting in response." As more traditional nonfood retailers move to capture the customer in the mass food industry, prices and margins will fall; you can plan on that.

Fact 4: Operations costs are going up, not down. When you have a full-time cashier at the front register who scans a TV or DVD player that sells for 10 to 15 percent less than it did three to six months ago, your productivity cost was negatively impacted for that transaction. High employee turnover and the rising cost of health care are increasing expense structures to retailers nationwide. Increases recently experienced in public utility costs, environmental impact costs for new construction, and increases in transportation and warehouse storage costs will continue to affect operating expenses and profit. Oftentimes the drive and passion to lower expense structures has been substituted for a weak effort to maintain current expense ratios.

Fact 5: Demographics and the collapsing birth rate. In most companies, it is standard practice to make exhaustive demographic studies before the approval process for retail site selection. This is an essential practice and very positive for early sales results if combined with the efforts of the marketing, merchandising, and operational functions. The problem faced by many retailers is that they fail to keep abreast of constantly changing demographics. In his book *Management Challenges for the 21st Century,* Peter Drucker states, "The most important single new certainty—if only because there is no precedent for it in all of history—is the *collapsing birthrate in the developed world.* In Western and Central Europe and in Japan, the birthrate has already dropped well below the rate needed to reproduce the population" (p. 44). He further declares, "In Japan and in Southern Europe, population is already peaking as it is in Germany. In the United States it will still grow for another twenty to twenty-five years, though the entire growth after the year 2015 will be in people fifty-five years and older" (p. 44). He concludes, "The birthrate collapse has tremendous political and social implications that we cannot even guess at today. But it surely will also have tremendous economic and business implications—and some of those can already be explored, some of them can already be tested. Above all, any strategy, that is, any commitment of present resources to future expectations—and this, to repeat, is what a strategy means—has to start out with demographics and, above all, with the collapsing birthrate in the developed world. Of all developments, it is the most spectacular, the most unexpected and one that has no precedent whatsoever" (p. 50).

Fact 6: High/low, or everyday low price? In an effort to increase sales against the likes of Wal-Mart/Sam's or Costco, many marketing/

merchandising think-tank committees are grappling with whether or not they should move into the everyday low price arena. There are examples of companies that continued to sit on the fence, or that have dived into everyday low price strategy, only to see their market share and customer loyalty plummet. Certainly Kmart is a current casualty of moving into the minefield of everyday low price with eyes blindfolded and having it blow up in its face. In the recent industry publication of *FORUM* of the GMA (Grocery Manufacturers of America) a very alarming article by Gary E. Singer, associate partner, Accenture, continues to raise serious questions regarding industrywide trade promotions. The article is titled, "The Daunting Dilemma, Redux." It begins with a look back and states, "Four years ago Accenture (then known as Andersen Consulting) released *The Daunting Dilemma of Trade Promotions,* a comprehensive consumer packaged goods (CPG) industry study on trade promotion. In the study, we concluded that CPG manufacturers are seriously undercutting shareholder value through poor trade promotions practices."

The new analysis stated, "The top line statistics were—and still are—staggering. CPG manufacturers spend $25 billion per year to generate incremental revenues of only $2 to $4 billion."

To again quote from this article, "The dilemma is that the *concept* of trade promotion can make economic sense. *Theoretically,* manufacturers can increase short-term volume, and hence profit, by offering their trading partners financial incentives to enhance product presentation to consumers. However, the failure to realize the potential benefits of trade promotions is hardly a secret. According to A C Nielsen's 2000 survey, 98 percent of manufacturers and 95 percent of retailers ranked promotion efficiency/effectiveness as a critical issue." The debate on this topic will continue to be intense.

Fact 7: It's not win-win; it's I win, you lose. In the very competitive retail arena, many retailers turn to their suppliers to give financial support to offset the losses they are trying to divert from their income statement. These offerings come under many guises, but they do not and will not promote a healthy relationship between supplier and retailer. Furthermore, the consumer loses in the long run. In a very candid and frank editorial by a long-term industry advocate, David

Pinto states in *Mass Market Retailer* (November 12, 2001), "The breakdown in retailer-supplier relations has taken the fun, creativity and excitement out of both retailing and consumer goods marketing. It has retailers increasingly turning to the supplier community, rather than the consumer, to keep them viable. It's forced suppliers to focus more on funding the retailer's efforts and less on turning out innovative new products, products which, in any event, may never gain the support at retail to see the light of a retailer's shelf." These are very strong words for someone who has been so closely connected with this business for so many years. His concerns should be taken very seriously.

Fact 8: We are still demand forecasting using the rearview mirror. Those of us in the merchandise demand forecasting business remain concerned over the lack of understanding and adoption of new technologies that can add great benefit to forecasting merchandise trends and improve the demand–planning process. There are investment market research firms employing companies like Planalytics to gauge the sales potential of key elements of the retail sector based on forecasted weather patterns for an upcoming season. These predictions are being validated with a high level of success. However, the retail community has embraced this new technology slowly. Where it is being employed, too seldom is there any thought of working it back against unit plans or allocation of product based on regional weather deviation from the previous year's record.

In the article "Your Crystal Ball" in the December 17, 2001, issue of *Computerworld*, Robert L. Mitchell observes: "Although the technology has been around for several years, many suppliers still don't use it. Market leader i2 Technologies Inc. (www.i2.com) in Dallas says that in 50 percent of new installations, no automated demand planning system is in place." The article goes on, "Microsoft [Excel] is the most widely deployed demand planning tool in the world," says Karen Peterson, an analyst at Stamford, Connecticut–based Gartner Inc. (http://www.gartner.com), "but it lacks sophisticated forecasting algorithms, can't track multiple inputs, and can't slice and dice the data for different audiences."

It certainly will be difficult for capital expenditure planning committees that have experienced slow growth these last five years to divert dwindling resources for infrastructure development given the pressure to build, buy, or expand current top-line operations. To continue non-funding of infrastructure development is just "building a house on a sandbar"; it will soon come crumbling down when the river shifts.

This concludes my review of the current and future state of the retail environment. Certainly there are other issues that are current. Those listed here appear to be grabbing the most headlines as slow-growth and nongrowth companies try to exhibit out to compete and survive in the current and future environment.

3.2.2 It's Time to Crack the Books

The history books will record that the years 1992 through mid-2000 will be noted as the greatest economic expansion in history. It certainly has been for the largest economic engine of this expansion, the United States. It is very important to understand the significance of this expansion for those companies that failed to participate. A must-read for the board members and all officers of a nongrowth retailer/supplier during this unprecedented economic expansion is *Good to Great: Why Some Companies Make the Leap . . . And Others Don't*, by Jim Collins. In the book he illustrates the Greek parable "The fox knows many things, the hedgehog knows one big thing." He writes, "The essential strategic difference between the good-to-great and comparison companies lay in the two fundamental distinctions." He develops his theory through research on eleven very successful companies, such as Walgreens. The two fundamental distinctions are:

1. Best-in-class companies found their strategies on three important dimensions:
   - What do they do better than any other company in the world (unique selling proposition)?
   - What is the key driver of their economic engine?
   - What are they really passionate about (passion for winning)?
2. Best-in-class companies translate the understanding of the above-mentioned dimensions into a clear business concept that guides their whole business.

In the early 1990s the company with which I spent nearly twenty-four years (Wal-Mart Stores, Inc.) went through a period of lackluster financial performance and execution, culminating in the first down quarter in company history. At a critical time during these very stressful days, David Glass, then CEO, asked a very insightful question at a management meeting where all division heads and corporate officers were present. His question was: "What are the ten things Wal-Mart Stores, Inc. stands for?" We were all encouraged to write our responses down along with those who reported to us out of the home office and to forward them to his office. When the several thousand replies came back, the responses showed that 80 percent of respondents had the same eight out of ten points on their list. After a review of the responses, the point was then made by Glass that, while he had confidence we understood the message and the concept of Wal-Mart, we were failing to execute them.

In what now seems like a few short months since that exercise, a top leadership change was made and two key executives, Lee Scott (now current CEO of Wal-Mart Stores. Inc) and Tom Coughlin (now current CEO of Wal-Mart Stores and Supercenters), were put in charge. *They focused on execution.* To validate what Jim Collins was saying, a "crystalline concept that guides all their efforts" was clearly demonstrated in the shareholders meeting in June 1997. One must understand that a Wal-Mart shareholder meeting is like no other in the corporate world. Fifteen thousand associates from all over the world are brought in for what some characterize as a "revival" that starts at 7:00 A.M. and goes to about 11:30 A.M. It was a very special moment, a moment like a Garth Brooks concert when the audience takes over and sings his song. Tom Coughlin started to cover the five operational execution points, which had been presented to store management teams at a year beginning meeting in January. As he started to cover the first objective, the fifteen thousand associates, without props or visuals, shouted out in unison the five points in proper order. Tom was somewhat speechless as he tried to convince investment bankers, the media, and shareholders in attendance that this was a spontaneous event. He wanted to make clear that this demonstrated the passion and commitment throughout the entire organization to execute the direction that would gain market share and customer loyalty. Certainly, the financial performance over the next five years would give testimony to that event and the clarity of that direction.

Before I move into the third phase of this article, I think it critically important to make sure that all persons involved with the enterprise of selling to the customer understand the concept of the "hedgehog or the fox." Without clarity, passion, and determination, it will be very difficult to institute the objectives and strategies of CPFR.

3.2.3 Defining CPFR

Over the last several months, the definition of CPFR has undergone several revisions. My latest, and the one I feel represents it best, is, "*A business strategy between trading partners to collaborate on a single shared vision of forecasted consumer demand at POS (point of sale) level.*" Let's take this definition apart for further analysis:

- *"Business strategy"*: Because it is a strategy, it is measurable against performance and expectation standards.
- *"Between trading partners"*: The metrics for performance are agreed upon by those involved, not made in isolation and dictated terms.
- *"To collaborate"*: The heart of CPFR is to share critical information in real time so all parties can see and have access to decision-making responses.
- *"Single shared vision"*: The measurements that will be applied to judge success must have the same basis. They cannot, for example, be independently derived forecasts from the buyer, sales/marketing, and replenishment teams. This measurement, the forecast, is a look into future events.
- *"Forecasted consumer demand"*: Based on seasonal profiles in the automated replenishment system and events that stimulate consumer demand, the effort is to collaborate on the anticipated outcome and then measure the effects on actual demand.
- *"At POS level"*: The focus is the consumer, not the distributor/warehouse or salespeople, not some static spreadsheet-predicted outcome. It's the consumer response validated by actual POS sales and then everything rolled up starting from that point of contact.

What it is not, and what it is:

- It is not about technology. It is about a business strategy to collaborate on planning, forecasting, and replenishment so as to stimulate consumer demand and meet or exceed agreed upon, mutually owned business objectives.

- It is not a paradigm shift. It is an evolving, cultural change within each organization based on trust and open dialogue developed over time.

- It is not about a new process or adding staff. It is about reanalyzing current strategies and then repositioning the structure to match the strategy.

- It is not about quarterly summit meetings, PowerPoint presentations, e-mail, or videoconferencing. It is about Internet-based, real-time communication; visibility; and feedback to all parties who can recommend changes.

- It is not about multiple forecasts (buyer, POS/warehouse replenishment, sales, marketing, and production). It is about a single shared, agreed-upon forecast that will automatically update and advance itself on a timely, forward-looking schedule.

- It is not about a strategy with a broad brush approach, or a "rising-tide-lifts-all-boats" mentality. It is about drill-downs to discover the exceptions that are not meeting expectations and then collaborating to initiate a corrective course of action.

- It is not about a targeted, specific outcome. It is about interjecting strategies into a dynamic automated replenishment program at lower levels of settings that roll up to the top-line demand forecast.

- It is not about a new "can-do-all" software package. It is about enhancing and upgrading current planning, forecasting, and replenishment systems with dedicated resources. In other words, "dance with the partner who brought you to the dance."

- It is not a retailer to primary supplier collaboration. It starts with the consumer at the POS level and then flows out to collaborative alliances made up of retailer, supplier, raw material producer, packaging, and transportation providers.

3.2.4 How Do You Get Started?

How do you get started, or maybe you have already started?

- Have you been involved in supply chain activities and strategies such as:

    Just in time

    VMI (vendor-managed inventory) at store or warehouse level

    DSD (direct store delivery)

    Comanagement at warehouse level

    Internet third-party provider

    If the answer is yes, then you have already started.

- If you have scheduled warehouse, point of sale, and seasonal forecast update meetings with your key trading partners, then you have already started.

- If the business theory (culture) of your company is to engage in a win–win environment with your trading partners, then you have already started.

- If your company looks like and resembles the "hedgehog," then you have already started. If you are more like the "fox," then you might have some work to do in defining yourself.

3.2.5 What Are the Obstacles?

Consumer-centric CPFR is moving away from the command and control atmosphere prevalent in most retailer/supplier relationships in which the retailer directs the response desired. The comanaged warehouse inventory program at Wal-Mart is a great testimony to the move away from command and control. It was designed to build relationships of high expectations and execution through Internet-based real-time information. The comanage program started in 1996 with four charter suppliers. It was built around some very basic, commonsense understandings:

- Wal-Mart, through its Information System core structure, had and still has a very highly regarded warehouse replenishment system.

- The suppliers know more about their individual items stocked in the warehouses than the Wal-Mart replenishment managers who were reordering the merchandise for the warehouse.

- If we could arrange to give access to our systems via Internet (Retail Link), wouldn't the suppliers' dedicated teams be better at ordering the merchandise, if they accommodated the guidelines and expectations they agreed upon when they entered the program?

The answer to this question has been a huge B2B success for all parties involved. It has demonstrated a move away from command and control, and toward trust building and knowledge sharing between the trading partners. It is also the platform that will move Wal-Mart and its key suppliers to the new Consumer Centric CPFR platform.

Among the obstacles are:

- The "silo mentality" between divisions of a multidivision corporation: One separate division of a supplier may enter into a CPFR look-alike endeavor with a single buying division at a multidivision retailer, only to have its efforts stifled by bureaucracies on both sides not involved in the collaborative effort. In the book *Sam Walton: Made in America,* there is a great case study on Wal-Mart and Procter & Gamble, describing how these two companies set out to break down the obstacles between them so as to give greater service and value to the customer.

- Waiting for the "one-size-fits-all" software solution, instead of improvising and enhancing what already exists: You then surround this effort with a well-trained, dedicated, and motivated team.

- The inherent resistance to abandon in an organized manner the policies and procedures, reports, and traditions that do not add value and support the strategic direction: This must be addressed and removed.

3.2.6 Where Do You Go from Here?

Try following these steps:

- Start with a pilot project. Pull a team together from both retailer and supplier. Go over the big picture, and then line up strategies, objectives, and metrics. Make sure all parties understand their responsibility to collaborate and share real-time information.

- Set up a cross-functional steering team on both sides. Encourage openness on how these changes will affect multiple layers of participants.

- Listen to the users. Upgrade, reconfigure, prioritize enhancements, but keep moving forward; do not let it stall.

- Seek out, document, and publish success stories. Make heroes out of those who show dedication and results in spite of the obstacles.

- Do not become fixated on monitoring and correcting a single issue. Remember, it is about in-stock, over-stock, out-of-stocks, planning, collaboration, flow of merchandise, replenishment, and forecast accuracy.

- When you have recorded and validated a win-win scenario, share your results in an executive review presentation. Gather support, listen for instructive feedback, and seek leadership to promote the continued implementation of CPFR.

In conclusion, please allow me to quote once more from Peter Drucker's book *Management Challenges for the 21st Century*. "Inside an organization there are only cost centers. The only profit center is a customer whose check has not bounced" (p. 122).

3.3

CPFR—Views and Experiences at Safeway

Christopher A. Brady, Safeway

Safeway operates forty-one manufacturing and processing facilities in North America. With Safeway's size and the number of suppliers from which we purchase product, the use of a process that improves order and/or sales forecasts could be effective in reducing costs. The impact could be seen not only on our "supplier to customer" supply chain costs, but on our "manufacturing plant to customer" supply chain costs as well.

3.3.1 CPFR Is About Communication

At Safeway, CPFR means communication. CPFR is a process—it is not a software application. It is not a cure-all for a company's supply chain difficulties. Basically, it is better communication between two parties (in this case a supplier and a retailer). There have been many published reports stating the "CPFR Value Proposition." Analysts have thrown out savings estimates that are in the billions of dollars annually. In the end, it may just be a better way of doing business. Any time you make the supply chain more efficient, hence lowering the cost of delivering goods to your customers, you have added value to the enterprise.

Safeway has been sharing information with its suppliers and plants for quite some time. Most of the time, however, this transfer has been unilateral. Safeway provided information about future promotions but there was no collaboration as to the forecast quantities.

3.3.2 The Application of CPFR at Safeway

First attempts at CPFR involved trading spreadsheets detailing planned promotions with selected suppliers. The scope of these pilots was not large, and the amount of data shared was limited. Recent collaborations have involved sharing additional data as well as increasing scope. The information is sent to a private exchange where the CPFR application is hosted. It is then accessed via a Web site by both Safeway and our supplier(s).

CPFR can be used to eliminate one of the biggest costs in the supply chain: the cost of last-minute changes. In a competitive environment, changes are made at the last minute that can cause increased costs to both retailer and supplier. For the supplier, these changes cause problems as it has to shift product from other customers, make last-minute changes to its production schedules (creating overtime and increased costs for procuring raw materials), or just the reverse—sit on significant amounts of inventory because of a canceled promotion. For the retailer, a last-minute change could result in a higher procurement cost or increased carrying cost for product already on hand.

Of course the retailer is where the "rubber meets the road." This is where the ultimate goal occurs: the sale. In order to manage this, the retailer does not want to be placed under constraints that will impact its ability to manage the business. If it decides to cancel a promotion because a better deal comes along, there should be no restrictions to the execution of the new plan. Some may consider this shortsighted.

Limiting last-minute changes is mostly a by-product of business process change. A comprehensive analysis detailing the actual cost to the enterprise would likely result in a process change as costs incurred by suppliers are typically passed right back to retailers in the form of higher costs or limited (or restricted) promotional dollars.

A drawback to the process is the sharing of promotional data. For years, the retail industry has been very competitive. Sharing information such as when and where a product will be promoted, the type of promotion, and the price point has been taboo. If this knowledge were shared with a competitor, it would be very easy to essentially negate a promotion. To mitigate these risks, secure transmission and hosting of data is critical. In addition, nondisclosure agreements (NDA) are necessary as well. In order for a CPFR relationship to work, there must be benefits for both the retailer and supplier that can be quantified. This allows management to make a decision to sponsor the project or not. Without executive sponsorship, the collaboration will not be successful.

In most cases, the CPFR relationship will initially be more beneficial to the supplier than the retailer. Once critical mass is reached, the suppliers will be able to realize a reduction in production costs, as they become more efficient in their production planning and raw material and packaging inventory. The retailer may see a benefit coming from increased on-shelf percentage and lower inventory carrying costs but would typically not see a lower product cost from the supplier until the supplier has realized a sustained material gain from lowered supply costs.

The biggest benefit is going to come from promotion planning. Obviously, items that are not aggressively promoted have average movement with very little variance. The benefit of better promotion planning comes from having a better in-stock percentage and not having leftover inventory after a promotion. The carrying cost of this inventory could negate some of the gains from the promotion. In addition, the decision could also be made to return the product to the supplier, which is costly as well.

3.3.3 Implementation Issues

Currently, Safeway is conducting its CPFR pilot(s) through a private exchange. It has taken on the responsibility for the technical aspects of the CPFR setup at the exchange and for providing a "roadmap" for both retailer and supplier to assist in starting and maintaining the collaboration.

Some of the issues we encountered included:

- *Number of IT Resources That Should Be Committed to the CPFR Pilot:* Since we had no verified financial benefit, we decided on an IT allocation that would be sufficient for the pilot, but that would also build a framework that could be either easily expanded or abandoned in the future. If abandoned, the resulting loss from setup costs would not be significant.

  Given these constraints, IT was able to develop a method to extract the necessary data from our proprietary systems and transmit those data to the exchange with little or no manual intervention. This was essential, as we did not want to add any labor costs to the model.

- *Timing Issues:* Initially, issues arose due to differences in timing. Safeway does its forecasts on a week-to-week (Sunday through Saturday) basis. In our first pilot, the supplier was using a monthly forecast. The supplier made a process change so that it could provide a weekly forecast as well.

- *Item Maintenance:* In the retail grocery business, items are discontinued, repackaged, or newly introduced on a weekly basis. A good CPFR tool must have the functionality to be able to easily maintain items. We ran into issues early on with discontinued items, as some of the items on the initial collaboration list were discontinued. Instead of going through the process of having the items removed from the CPFR tool, we made the decision (along with our supplier partner) to just ignore the items and remove them from any postpilot analysis.

- *Business Process:* The CPFR process needs to be minimally invasive to current processes. This is true for both the retailer and the supplier. Within that framework, the data need to be sent automatically and the supplier partner needs to review and resolve forecast exceptions prior to the retailer reviewing the remaining exceptions.

3.3.4 Suppliers Change Their Existing Processes

What Safeway found with some suppliers was that they were not generating a forecast. They would use Safeway's forecast. This limited their liability if the forecast was short. So creating a forecast was new to some suppliers. In some cases, the business unit tasked with the CPFR pilot was completely separate from the customer service personnel who had the responsibility for creating orders and, in some cases, managing inventory (vendor-managed inventory—VMI).

The supplier resolved these issues by making changes to existing processes. In order for a collaboration to be successful, the supplier needs to change the process from receiving and fulfilling orders to a process of forecasting, collaborating, and filling orders. At times, system performance has varied. The main symptom of this is slow page loading in the Internet tool. The solution for that was to make the route to the desired page as efficient as possible. This was accomplished by using hyperlinks and custom bookmarks provided in the CPFR application.

Investment buys (purchases made because of extremely favorable terms offered by suppliers) will "muddy the water" as far as measuring the benefits of CPFR. Not only is the physical inventory increased, but also the on-shelf percentage is skewed, as there is less chance of a stockout.

Safeway has seen some benefit in establishing collaborative relationships with suppliers. CPFR is one option for managing these relationships. We will continue to review supply chain costs and look for ways to reduce them or eliminate them altogether. CPFR will play a strategic role in the future but the format has yet to be determined.

3.4

CPFR Implementation at Ace Hardware and Manco

Brian Bastock, Manco
Fred Baumann, JDA Software
Scott Smith, Ace Hardware

With the ever-increasing level of competition in the hardware consumer packaged goods (CPG) sector, firms are continuing to examine new ways of optimizing existing business processes to facilitate the efficient and effective flow of product through the supply chain.

3.4.1 Primary Business Challenge

The Ace/Manco/JDA initiative focuses on the development of a strategic partnership. The primary challenge was to build a process to balance the competencies of both trading partners in a framework that allowed for agility and speed to market. The primary competencies are listed in Exhibit 3.2.

Other problems the program hoped to address:

- Replace a VMI system that was challenged to meet the new economy requirements.

- Enable real-time visibility and address the challenges of the batch processing of EDI.

- Fix inefficient labor productivity that was required in the forecasting and order-generation process.

The Business Answer

Exhibit 3.3 highlights the collaborative technology deployed and the collaborative activities encompassed in the program.

Ace utilizes a hub–and–spoke CPFR deployment model. The collab-

EXHIBIT 3.2. BALANCE OF COMPETENCIES.

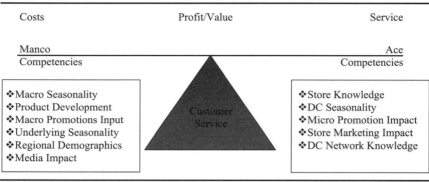

Costs	Profit/Value	Service
Manco		Ace
Competencies		Competencies

❖Macro Seasonality
❖Product Development
❖Macro Promotions Input
❖Underlying Seasonality
❖Regional Demographics
❖Media Impact

Customer Service

❖Store Knowledge
❖DC Seasonality
❖Micro Promotion Impact
❖Store Marketing Impact
❖DC Network Knowledge

SOURCE: Ace/Manco/JDA.

EXHIBIT 3.3. ACE/MANCO CPFR DEPLOYMENT.

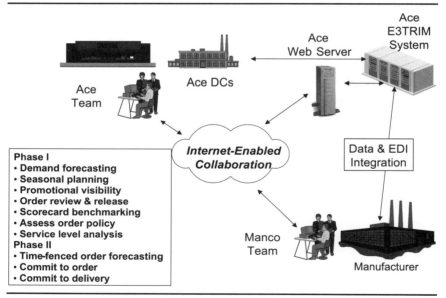

Ace Team

Ace DCs

Ace Web Server

Ace E3TRIM System

Internet-Enabled Collaboration

Data & EDI Integration

Manco Team

Manufacturer

Phase I
• **Demand forecasting**
• **Seasonal planning**
• **Promotional visibility**
• **Order review & release**
• **Scorecard benchmarking**
• **Assess order policy**
• **Service level analysis**
Phase II
• **Time-fenced order forecasting**
• **Commit to order**
• **Commit to delivery**

SOURCE: Ace/Manco/JDA.

orative technology resides at the Ace location. This is especially attractive to Ace trading partners that wish to begin a CPFR program quickly. All that the manufacturer needs technologically to begin is a PC with Internet connectivity.

During Phase I of their CPFR rollout, Manco and Ace utilized steps 1–5 and 9 of the CPFR model described in Chapter 2.1. They used the technology of JDA to create a single shared forecast of demand. Both partners had visibility *and* execution rights to update and change the forecast, the seasonal profiles that impact purchase orders, and promotional forecast quantities and timing. In addition, Manco was granted execution access to create and release purchase orders that were driven by the shared single forecast of demand. The JDA application also enables the partners to complete supply chain simulation scenarios to understand the economic trade-offs of order frequency, service level settings, and efficient ordering measures such as full-layer or pallet ordering. The EDI 830 document is delivered to Manco for information integration and contains the demand forecast numbers jointly developed through the application.

Now in the second phase of their pilot, they are utilizing additional technology to cover all nine steps of the CPFR model. How they are covering each of the nine steps is reviewed in the next section.

3.4.2 The Role of New and Standardized Techniques

The Ace/Manco/JDA project leveraged the cutting-edge processes defined by the VICS CPFR Committee. It is significant that their work did not stop with the business processes defined in the nine-step model. Their project work was segmented into two phases. Phase I addressed steps 1–5 and step 9 of the CPFR model.

Develop Front-End Agreement

In Phase I, Ace and Manco thought it important to create written documentation that would clearly define the nature of the new collaborative relationship. As part of the project kickoff, senior management from both trading partners met to articulate the expectations of their relationship. Both companies had cross-functional representation from sales, replenishment, information, logistics, and supply chain leadership. Components of their agreement included:

Metrics that would be used to evaluate the success of the relationship. Examples include forecast accuracy, sales, unit and dollar service levels, product returns, actual inventory on hand, product overstock, activity-based cost measures, freight costs, and lost sales.

Definitions and targets of each of the metrics defined for the relationship.

The frequency by which the data scorecard would be reviewed.

The execution and visibility rights that would be established through the relationship.

Roles and responsibilities for execution of the processes. Examples include data-pull owners, order creation and release responsibilities, execution rights for forecast changes, and seasonal profiles.

Create Joint Business Plan

The Ace/Manco cross-functional collaboration team works together on joint business-planning activities that are critical to the sales forecast collaboration. The group starts by defining the strategic role of the businesses involved in the collaboration; sales and service targets are established for the product line and specific merchandising tactics are laid out to meet the goals defined in the business plan. Components of the business-planning exercise include:

- Promotional event definitions and corresponding quantities to support the event
- Seasonal merchandise plans to support the flow of merchandise to their sixteen geographically dispersed distribution centers
- Assortment planning
- Space planning—planogram and shelf layout

Create Sales Forecast

The trading partners work together utilizing the technology resident at Ace to create a collaborative sales forecast. Both parties can review and adjust the sales forecast in real time. The partners can view key components in the formulation of the sales forecast:

- Historical sales
- Historical lost sales
- Previous promotional demand
- SKU variability and trending information

Exhibit 3.4 depicts collaboration on demand forecasts.

Identify Sales Forecast Exceptions/Collaborate on Exception Items

Sales forecast exception management has been critical to the success of the Ace/Manco program. The following exceptions are monitored and prioritized in the trading partnership:

- *Forecast to Actual Performance at the SKU/DC Level.* The system automatically alerts the partners when the actual performance of an SKU is other than forecasted. The exception thresholds are defined by the trading partners and the system automatically prioritizes the items that will have the highest profitability impact.
- *Overstock Exceptions.* The trading partners are alerted to items that have excessive days of supply at the locations being evaluated.
- *Lost Sales Exceptions.* The system reviews every SKU location each day and highlights the areas where the SKUs under consideration are out of stock.

Again, all exceptions are prioritized for the partners by the greatest impact to profitability.

Exhibit 3.5 highlights how the process fits within scenario C of the CPFR model.

Create Order Forecast

Based on the results that Ace and Manco realized, they wanted to move to the next level and add steps 6–8 of the CPFR model (Phase II). The

EXHIBIT 3.4. DEMAND FORECAST COLLABORATION.

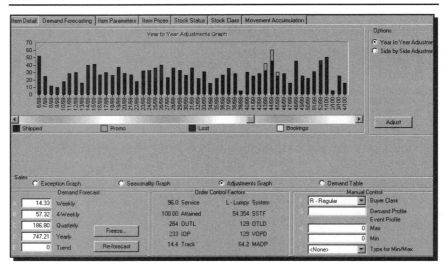

Collaborative Components:	Principles:
✓ Product seasonality	⇨Common measures
✓ Retailer promotions	⇨Demand focused
✓ Available safety stock	⇨Real-time accessibility
✓ Assortment changes	⇨Shared ownership
✓ SKU variability	
✓ Sales trends	

SOURCE: Ace/Manco/JDA.

project was kicked off in October 2000. Ace has installed the technology required to produce order forecasts and provide them via a Web interface to its manufacturers. Order forecasts can now be produced, and the project team is benchmarking the accuracy of the forecasts. The order forecasts are now dynamically translated from the collaborated sales forecast established in step 3 of the CPFR model. Critical translation variables include:

EXHIBIT 3.5. IDENTIFICATION OF SALES FORECAST EXCEPTIONS—SCENARIO C.

	I	Sales Forecast Exception Criteria are established and defined in the Front-End Agreement. Exception criteria are the factors that control the forecasting process. Retrieve the Sales Forecast Exception Criteria. (Examples include customer service measures such as retail in-stock %, or forecast measures such as forecast error.)
	II	Identify manufacturer and distributor changes or updates. (Example: a change in the number of stores.)
	III	Constrain the sales forecast based on the results of the manufacturer's comparison of the order forecast with its ability to supply. Record how the sales forecast was constrained for future demand analyses.
	IV	Compare each item's value for the selected criteria to the constraint value. (Example: Store in-stock for item X is 83%, which is less than the criteria value of 90%.)
	V	If the item's value is outside of the constraint, then identify the item as an exception item.

SOURCE: VICS.

- Minimum shipping brackets (items, total order)
- Lead-time requirements
- On-hand inventory positions
- Item service level requirements
- Product seasonalities
- Causal events
- Pack sizes/item economics
- Shipping constraints
- Receiving constraints

Identify Order Forecast Exceptions/Collaborate on Exception Items

The Ace/Manco/JDA team worked together to define the constraints that would create the most value for the next phase of their project. The following constraints are monitored to facilitate this next phase:

- *Capacity Exceptions.* Constraints that are flagged when product cannot be delivered.

- *Quantity Exceptions.* Trading partners view exceptions when either party highlights an order quantity change request to the order forecast.
- *Timing Exceptions.* Trading partners view exceptions when an order forecast cannot be delivered on a specified date.
- *Past Due Exceptions.* The system highlights exceptions on orders that have not been delivered on time.

Generate Order

Manco and Ace lead the industry with their innovation of dynamically translating their collaborative order forecast into live orders. Manco and Ace have added innovation to the CPFR model by creating multiple time fences for the order forecasts with varying levels of commitment. The most powerful concept that they are rolling out is the notion that the order forecast automatically translates to a real order when it crosses the final time fence.

Time fence parameters:

- One lead time out—Order is automatically generated
- 30 days out—Order forecast is 80 percent committed
- 60 days out—Order forecast is 50 percent committed
- 180 days out—Information only

3.4.3 Benefits Realized

Manco and Ace have experienced the following positive results:

- *Manco reduced distribution costs by 28 percent.* This came from the collaborative order flow analysis that enabled the partners to order in improved shipping economies.
- *Freight costs were reduced by 18 percent.* Order cycle simulation enabled Manco to reduce its freight costs.
- *Annual sales increased 9 percent in a flat category.* The sales improvement was delivered by several components of the program. More accurate

seasonal profiles and forecasts ensured that the product was available when the consumer was ready to buy.

- *Forecast accuracy improved by 10 percent.* This was driven by dual insight into the single shared forecast.

- *Human productivity increased.* Ace and Manco analysts have improved the productivity in the forecasting and order execution process by more than 20 percent.

- *ROI on the program was evident in less than two months.* Manco reviewed the costs of the program against the incremental margin garnered through cost savings and incremental sales.

Exhibit 3.6 shows the results, which are aggregated against all the collaborative vendors that have participated in the Ace program to date. The vendors involved in the Ace Collaborative Commerce program

EXHIBIT 3.6. RESULTS OF COLLABORATIVE EFFORTS AT ACE HARDWARE.

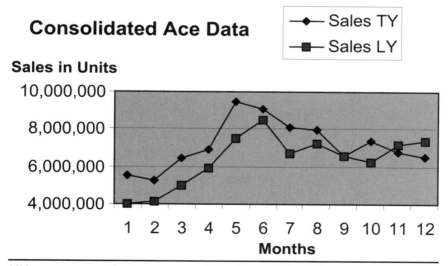

13% year-over-year sales increase versus 4% for the remainder of the company.
TY = this year; LY = last year.

SOURCE: Ace/Manco/JDA.

have improved annual sales collectively by 13 percent in 2000 versus 1999. This is compared with an Ace overall sales improvement of 4 percent. The inventory to support the improved 13 percent annual sales increase was slightly less than the year prior (approximately 1 percent less).

In 2001 the twenty-four vendors that were involved in the collaborative program increased sales 10 percent while the remaining suppliers were flat to last year. Almost $200 million of business is managed through the Ace/JDA collaborative commerce hub.

Improved service level to the stores was a key driver for the incremental sales increase delivered through the program. Across all vendors participating, the annual service level to the stores has risen by two full points on average (see Exhibit 3.7).

3.4.4 Level of Difficulty—Challenges to Be Addressed

Multiple challenges were overcome to attain the results achieved at Ace and Manco. They include:

EXHIBIT 3.7. DEVELOPMENT OF SERVICE LEVELS AT ACE HARDWARE.

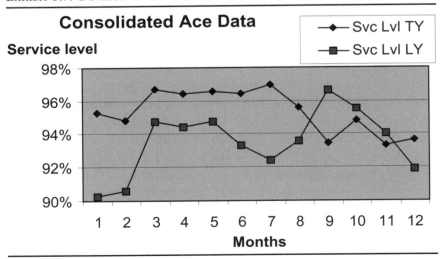

SvC Lvl TY = service level this year.
SvC Lvl LY = service level last year.

SOURCE: Ace/Manco/JDA.

Phase I Challenges

- Creation of a software solution to support collaborative forecasting and order release without compromising trading partner security requirements
- Development of an execution model that struck a balance between time-intensive relationship building and speed-to-market multiple trading partner sessions per week
- Creation of program momentum as the first CPFR initiative in the hardware industry
- Communication of the advantages of collaborative commerce over a vendor-managed inventory
- Convincing trading partners that the reward of improved performance outweighed the risks of sharing previously proprietary information and increased resource requirements
- Finding a "Just Enough Documentation" approach that worked for all parties involved
- Convincing vendor trading partners that they could execute the new collaborative forecasting and order release processes after five days of collaboration and training

Phase II Challenges

- Working with various security and firewall possibilities not encountered in a development lab
- Creation of a tool that accurately translates demand forecasts into order forecasts
- Definition of the initial time fence and order forecast commitment parameters
- Measurement of order forecast accuracy to support time fence and commitment percent parameters
- Creating an easy-to-use process and software tool supporting order forecast variance resolution

Individual Partner Contributions

The stakeholders provided the following contributions:

Ace:

- Organization of internal collaboration seminars
- Support for IT infrastructure installations

- Key contributions to Phase II design feedback
- Provision of key metrics and reports to trading partners
- Provision of cross-functional organizational resources to sponsor and support the program:

    Executive sponsorship

    Collaborative commerce project management

    On-site training

    IT project management

Manco

- Provision of cross-functional resources to support the program:

    Executive sponsorship

    Collaboration analysis

    Sales and category management expertise

- Endorsement of cross-industry adoption of CPFR practices through speaking and press engagements:

    CPFR Committee Meetings

    2000 Retail System Track

    Hardware industry meetings

    North American Collaboration Summit

- Delivery of manufacturing metrics for the evaluation of the partnership:

    Activity-based costing

    Operational metrics

Benefits from a Partnership Standpoint

The Ace/Manco/JDA initiative gives "real-time" shared open access to a common data source for the first time, thus enabling the special knowledge of both partners to be brought to bear on supply chain issues when they arise. This unique approach has led to the development of "Collaborative Communities," composed of Ace employees, Ace's trading partners, and JDA's inventory management experts (see Exhibit 3.8).

EXHIBIT 3.8. COLLABORATIVE COMMUNITIES.

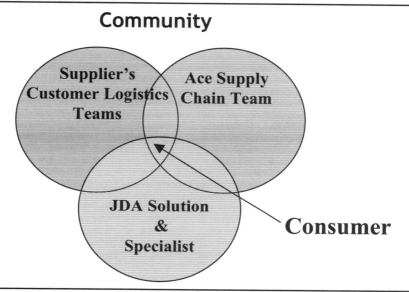

SOURCE: Ace/Manco/JDA.

The JDA methodology allows for the inclusion of trading partners and their Ace counterparts in strategic planning, forecasting, replenishment, and merchandising decisions.

In effect, supply chain collaboration provides a mechanism for the joint ownership of the three main inventory management outputs—sales forecast, order forecast, and purchase order approval. It can also be taken a step further with the integration of each partner's supply-and-demand planning processes, coordinating activities and jointly creating and identifying opportunities for additional revenues. To summarize, the program has:

1. Built greater trust between the trading partners
2. Improved supply chain visibility
3. Focused all members on the same goals
4. Created a balance of competencies
5. Facilitated easier implementation of new ideas
6. Created a stepping-stone to other opportunities

7. Increased sales
8. Improved consumer satisfaction
9. Removed inventory from the supply chain

Summary

The Ace/Manco project is an example of an innovative sustainable initiative that demonstrates clear benefits, both commercial and professional, from cooperation between trading partners. The initiative confirms the possibilities of suppliers, their customers, and third parties, working together to achieve excellence in supply chain management. Participants showed a willingness to take on an unquantifiable risk in pursuit of an uncertain reward and intuitively recognized the logistics value of better information flows. Individuals, often acting well beyond their defined responsibilities, have worked to coordinate diverse skills and knowledge in order to drive the necessary organizational and operational change.

3.5

CPFR Implementation at Canadian Tire and GlobalNetXchange (GNX)

Geoffrey S. Frodsham, Canadian Tire Corporation
Nick J. Miller, GlobalNetXchange
Laura A. Mooney, Manugistics

The rate at which organizations adopt change varies, and Collaborative Planning, Forecasting, and Replenishment (CPFR) has been no exception. From its inception in 1996 manufacturers and retailers have experimented with implementing collaborative business processes and technologies, striving to meet the nine-step process standards established by the Voluntary Interindustry Commerce Standards (VICS) Association. For some, progress has been slow, but for all that have engaged in a CPFR pilot, one thing is clear—there are considerable financial and nonfinancial benefits to be had from increasing collaboration and trust with business partners.

3.5.1 What Is Driving CPFR?

The wide range of adoption rates clearly indicates that implementing CPFR practices is not easy, so why the continued attention? Not only is CPFR still creating buzz in the retail industry, but other industries are rapidly adopting flavors of collaborative processes modeled after CPFR. In the case of retail, there are several market issues driving the need for CPFR and the benefits it brings.

Customer Centric Market Shift

Consumers have more power than ever, especially in light of the recent economic downturn. It is no longer enough simply to build brand recognition; instead, the focus is on developing strong brand loyalty among consumers. In order to build this loyalty, manufacturers must understand what consumers want—knowledge that is largely held by the retailer. Without retailer-held information on consumer buying behavior, manufacturers cannot develop the strong brands that draw consumers into retail stores. When it comes to satisfying customer needs, both the manufacturer and the retailer win; so it pays for both to share valuable information so that they can work together to better meet consumer demand. Collaboration helps distribute visibility of consumer buying habits back through the supply chain to ensure that future demand is more accurately forecast and inventory levels are appropriately maintained.

Low Margins

In an increasingly competitive environment, many manufacturers and most retailers are dealing with extremely tight margins and struggling to maintain profitability. Because CPFR facilitates the sharing of information at both regional and store levels, retailers can recognize operational efficiencies—most often through the simultaneous lowering of inventories and lowering of stock-outs—that decrease their costs. At the same time, CPFR allows both manufacturers and retailers to better manage pricing and promotions to increase profitability and win market share.

Rapid Change

The pace of change has greatly accelerated. Product life cycles are shorter, consumer behavior is less predictable, and economic events ripple through markets very quickly. In order to survive, manufacturers and retailers must be prepared to react to, and preferably predict, change. Failure to do so results in costly inventory write-offs, stockouts, and loss of market share. The more far-reaching the collaborative processes and technologies, the more synchronized the supply chain is and the better it is able to react to change. Trading partners that work together are more likely to survive today and more likely to gain competitive advantage in the future.

As can be seen in Exhibit 3.9, for retail, as well as many other indus-

EXHIBIT 3.9. BENEFITS OF CPFR.

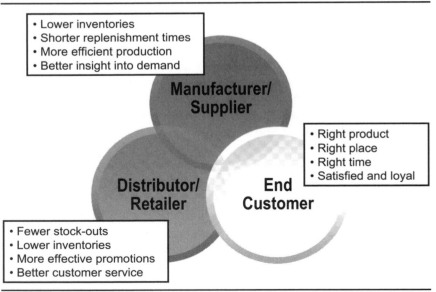

* Lower inventories
* Shorter replenishment times
* More efficient production
* Better insight into demand

Manufacturer/ Supplier

* Right product
* Right place
* Right time
* Satisfied and loyal

Distributor/ Retailer

End Customer

* Fewer stock-outs
* Lower inventories
* More effective promotions
* Better customer service

SOURCE: Manugistics.

tries, supplier-customer collaboration and the adoption of a formal CPFR program generate tremendous benefits:

Manufacturer/Supplier: Reduction in finished goods inventory, shorter replenishment times, more efficient production, increased communication with customers, and better insight into consumer demand—translating into lower costs, increased sales, higher margins, and stronger brand equity.

Distributor/Retailer: Fewer stock-outs, lower inventories, more effective promotions, and better customer service—resulting in lower costs, increased sales, higher margins, and greater customer loyalty.

End Customer: Right product, right place, right time—translating into a satisfied, repeat customer.

Phased Approach to CPFR Adoption

To realize these benefits, companies are taking steps to implement some form of collaboration with their suppliers and customers. Degrees of collaboration vary. For many companies, full-fledged CPFR on a large scale is not possible due to issues of trust, lack of head count to manage processes, or resistance to acquiring the technology necessary to support it. Rather than doing nothing in these cases, companies are leveraging the concepts on a smaller scale.

For some, a phased approach means limiting the scope of the collaborative process. For example, companies are reevaluating programs like vendor-managed inventory (VMI) and modernizing the program by adding collaborative technologies to facilitate greater communication and improve the results. Then, as trust builds and the technology infrastructure is acquired, the collaborative VMI process can be extended to take on additional aspects of the CPFR standards and produce even greater benefits. Often, coexisting VMI and CPFR programs complement each other, with more accurate forecasts from CPFR driving order-level execution for VMI.

For other companies, especially those that have grown through acquisition, extending collaboration to partners is not feasible (and will not be effective) until they get their own house in order. Recognizing that they will get the maximum value out of CPFR if they are able to combine collaborative processes with traditional supply chain management efforts, companies are consolidating software and processes to improve demand management, inventory management, and order management within the enterprise. Often, this leads to better sales and operations planning, which in turn can be expanded to include partner collaboration and offer a smooth transition to CPFR efforts.

Rather than, or in addition to, limiting the scope of the process, some companies choose to limit the scale—implementing CPFR with one partner or for one specific product line. This can also be an effective way to ease into CPFR initiatives provided that the smaller model addresses all of the components necessary to scale it to the next level, including process work flow, investments in employee training, incentive programs, and enabling technology. Often small CPFR pilots are never expanded because they are so small that manual techniques are sufficient, and a lack of focus on automating processes and implementing collaboration and event management technologies prevents companies from growing the program, thereby limiting its benefit.

Criteria for CPFR Success

The companies that have been most successful in implementing CPFR to date—reaping both financial and nonfinancial rewards on a large scale—are those that address the following critical issues (see Exhibit 3.10) during all phases of their CPFR initiatives:

Well-Defined Processes. Whether companies use the standard process prescribed by VICS or adapt the standards to customize their own CPFR process, laying out the business processes that are to be incorporated into the CPFR program is critical to establishing and managing the scope of the initiative. Once processes are established, all participants must commit to their responsibilities within the process and collaborate openly in those areas.

Focus on Building Trust. A lack of commitment to share information and honor trust between participants creates a critical barrier to success in CPFR initiatives. A focus on trust must be explicit, and incentives on both sides of the supplier-customer relationship must be established to foster a sense of teamwork and promote information sharing.

EXHIBIT 3.10. CRITICAL CPFR SUCCESS FACTORS.

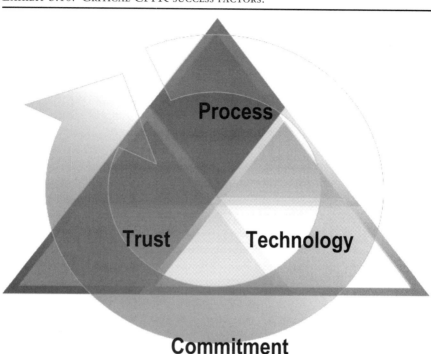

SOURCE: Manugistics.

Technology Investment. Thanks to the growth of the Internet and advances in application software, technology to support CPFR on a large scale is available and is being used successfully by many companies today. Important technology investments include Web-based collaboration software, event management and monitoring applications, and reporting and analysis tools. Often, the organization leading the CPFR effort is the most technology ready, and it must be willing to share access to collaborative technologies with partners.

Executive Commitment. Grass roots efforts within organizations can be helpful for starting up pilot initiatives or increasing the value achieved from existing programs like VMI, but for long-term success and maximum financial results, executive-level commitment to technology investment, incentive programs, and organizational change must exist.

3.5.2 Technology Enabling CPFR

To achieve maximum value from CPFR initiatives, companies must implement a core set of technology and application software. An investment in these core technologies is necessary to achieve scale and efficiency in CPFR processes, and in many cases also leads to partner confidence and trust. Critical technologies include Web-based collaboration, event management and analysis, and tracking and reporting.

Web-Based Collaboration

With its high overhead and limited data flow, electronic data interchange (EDI) is not the answer for full-scale CPFR initiatives. Instead, newer Web-based collaboration applications leverage the global infrastructure of the Internet and have been designed to allow sharing of processes and information among multiple trading partners.

Collaboration software allows processes to be tailored with each partner individually, allowing for varying degrees of information sharing across partners and providing the security rules needed to ensure privacy. This enables a manufacturer to share replenishment and manufacturing plans with one customer while sharing only replenishment plans with another.

Collaboration extends beyond simple integration. While open integration technologies are a core foundation for collaboration software, the Web-based collaboration application actually provides an interactive, easy-to-use interface for participants, ensuring that business users can do their jobs without dealing with integration complexities.

The process work flow definitions established in the collaboration software can be set up to follow VICS CPFR process standards or tailored to meet an individual company's needs. A joint business plan between trading partners can be agreed upon and published, with the collaboration software enabling information to be posted and shared by both parties to facilitate achievement of that plan. Information that can be shared in this environment includes forecasts, promotional activities, inventory plans, point-of-sale data, transportation requirements, and changes to previously agreed-to plans.

Collaboration technologies must not only give users the ability to share and review information, but also to drill down and update plans within the application, feeding changes back to supply chain management, transaction, and execution systems.

Event Management and Analysis

Given the abundance of data being shared, especially in a large-scale CPFR effort, long-term success depends on the technology's ability to monitor and alert participants to exceptions, status changes, and discrepancies. Otherwise, the number of employees and time required to manage the process becomes unwieldy and infeasible.

Working in conjunction with the collaboration software, event management and analysis technologies continually compare data being posted and evaluate the data for consistency. When unexpected variations are found between sets of data, the application issues a notification, or alert, to the appropriate participants so that they can get online, review the exception, and take action as needed.

Event management and analysis technology allows for smooth execution of a defined business process, automating work flow and allowing participants to engage in exception management. This increases efficiency and allows more information to be shared, ultimately increasing the scale and benefit of the CPFR program.

Tracking and Reporting

Enabling technology for CPFR must also be able to track changes and report on results. The system's ability to track who publishes and changes data, and when, maintains version control and establishes an audit trail. This versioning capability improves communication among trading partners, improves data accuracy, and instills a sense of accountability. In many cases, it is the tracking capability that helps to build trust between partners because it becomes difficult to hide information or engage in deceptive business practices.

Reporting technology provides the capability to analyze performance against key indicators and to generate management reports. The performance information contained in these reports can be used to refine and continually improve CPFR processes. In addition, it helps to measure return on investment generated from the program.

Where Is CPFR Going?

While companies continue to strive toward implementing the nine-step Collaborative Planning, Forecasting, and Replenishment process as currently defined, a group of leading-edge companies is working on initiatives that extend CPFR in both breadth and depth.

Collaborative Promotion Management One way to extend the value of CPFR is to expand the scope of processes and information that is shared between trading partners. For example, joint promotion management holds great potential. Value can be obtained by coordinating promotions to avoid duplicate or conflicting promotions and to ensure that increased demand from promotional activity can be met.

Canadian Tire, a large Canada-based retailer, is actively engaging in joint promotion forecasting with its CPFR partners. The program, developed by Canadian Tire and supported by Manugistics, is rapidly being scaled to include hundreds of business partners to help the retailer better forecast and manage promotions to meet customer demand. Because Canadian Tire has addressed technology as well as process implementation, collaboration among many partners is feasible. In addition, the agreed-to promotional forecasts can be seamlessly fed into supply chain management applications for planning and execution.

Other companies working with Manugistics to implement collaborative promotion management include GlobalNetXchange (GNX) and a major office supply retailer. While collaboration on promotions for forecasting and management in itself provides significant financial benefits and planning synergies, new advances in optimization technology actually allow trading partners to determine the optimal promotion to run to maximize margins and increase market share, adding even greater value.

Joint promotion planning is seen by many retailers as a way to gain competitive advantage, especially when they have already achieved low inventories and high customer service levels from ECR or VMI programs. Collaborative promotion management can help companies achieve the next level of benefit.

Similarly, collaboration for category management is also gaining interest among retailers that see the value of working with suppliers to maximize the profitability of specific categories of goods. Suppliers are motivated to strengthen their brands, and they welcome the opportunity to gain more insight into customer activity at the retail level by engaging in joint category management.

Collaborative Transportation Management Companies are also exploring the expansion of collaborative processes to transportation management. Collaborative transportation management (CTM) allows participants to collaborate with carriers and suppliers to better manage the transportation network, driving greater efficiency and lower costs.

Fundamental concepts of transportation revolve around the acquisition of capacity and physical product movement. By leveraging collaborative technologies, both shippers and carriers can experience significant incremental benefits in asset utilization, transportation costs, and improved speed to market. Additionally, emerging technologies are being introduced by Manugistics that provide a technology platform for multienterprise collaboration, which extends the value proposition outside the traditional realm of the enterprise to other supply chains.

As companies continue to deploy technologies to help optimize internal transportation management processes, forward-thinking companies are also embracing collaborative technologies to achieve competitive advantage. Carriers are implementing technologies to help balance their capacity relative to forecasted consumer demand, and shippers are establishing closer, real-time collaboration with carriers to help manage promotional demand surges and shifts in raw material supply locations. These capabilities, added to existing transportation execution infrastructure, leverage the Internet as a medium for information sharing that drives significant business value.

Increased Visibility In addition to broadening CPFR through collaborative promotion management and CTM, companies can also increase value by extending deeper into the supply chain the visibility that collaboration fosters. "N-tier" CPFR initiatives take the processes defined in a two-tier CPFR program to the next level by implementing them in a hub or private trading network, allowing multiple tiers of suppliers and customers to collaborate.

Using technology and software applications from Manugistics, GNX is the first retail exchange to offer CPFR services in a hub environment. GNX is serving large retailers and suppliers in the food, consumer packaged goods, hard goods, and apparel industries. By accessing CPFR applications in a hosted environment, participants in the exchange benefit from the ability to improve forecast accuracy, manage promotions, plan production, improve replenishment times, and procure raw materials—with a very short implementation time. As an added benefit, the neutral third party, GNX, helps accelerate trust among participants. Aggregated results to date have been in the range of a 2–12 percent increase in on-shelf availability and a 5–20 percent reduction in inventory.

The "N-tier" approach works because the deeper the visibility, the more efficiency and costs that can be squeezed out of the supply chain and ultimately the more responsive the supply chain becomes to consumer demand.

3.5.3 Merging of Optimization and Collaboration

The ultimate challenge for companies is to achieve the optimal balance of lower costs and increased margins while meeting customer service and market share objectives. Although Collaborative Forecasting, Planning, and Replenishment programs today focus on collaboration, the value of optimization cannot be overlooked. New technologies emerging in the area of pricing and revenue optimization and continued advances in supply chain planning and optimization solutions offer early adopters an opportunity for market leadership and competitive differentiation.

In the future, the most successful CPFR programs will merge optimization and collaboration, leveraging optimization technologies to determine the right way to configure trading networks, price products, plan promotions, and distribute inventory, and then collaborating with both customers and suppliers to execute seamlessly on agreed-to plans.

Collaboration rests on the premise that increased communication and trust will lead to improved visibility into information that drives the supply chain: forecasts, customer sales, product promotions, inventory levels, delivery capacity. It is a valid premise, but what happens when the shared information is wrong? The fragile trust among trading partners quickly dissolves and the benefits and ROI derived from the CPFR program erode. Incentive and motivation to continue collaborative efforts also suffer, making future gains difficult.

Consider, for example, a supplier and customer that have collaborated and agreed to a forecast. The forecast takes into account added lift for a planned promotion, and the supplier manufactures and carries product to meet the expected increase in demand. In reality, the promotion is not as effective as predicted, and someone is stuck with the excess inventory—either the supplier is forced to reallocate it and take a costly write-off, or the customer must find a way to liquidate the inventory, most likely taking a loss. They collaborated on both the forecast and the replenishment plan, so who is to blame?

Had optimization technology been used to plan the promotion, the situation would likely have turned out much differently. Promotion scenarios could have been run and optimized before being incorporated into the demand forecast, giving both parties more accurate information. By optimizing one decision—the promotion—an entire series of more intelligent decisions on production, storage, and delivery could have been made, resulting in increased sales and lower costs for both the supplier and the customer.

Similar benefits can be derived on the replenishment side of the equation. Collaborating and agreeing on what product to place where and when will help ensure that customer demand is met. But to get even greater value, add the ability of suppliers and distributors to optimize inventory placement and transportation schedules, while still meeting or exceeding the agreed-to replenishment plan. The result, as seen in Exhibit 3.11, will be lower costs and increased margins for the supplier and most likely shorter order lead times for customers.

Although optimization may seem to lie outside the scope of CPFR, the value that optimization offers within the collaborative framework is enormous. Partners can now collaborate on technology-generated scenarios that are optimized across millions of variables—cost, customer service levels, competitor actions, time, and profitability—instantly gaining visibility into the options that will best help them realize their joint business plan and financial objectives. Optimized decisions can then be planned and executed back through the supply chain, with continual event monitoring and analysis, ensuring that any change in the base assumptions triggers an alert for collaboration. Partners can then jointly reoptimize the plan and quickly execute on changes, avoiding costly mistakes.

EXHIBIT 3.11. MERGING OF OPTIMIZATION AND COLLABORATION.

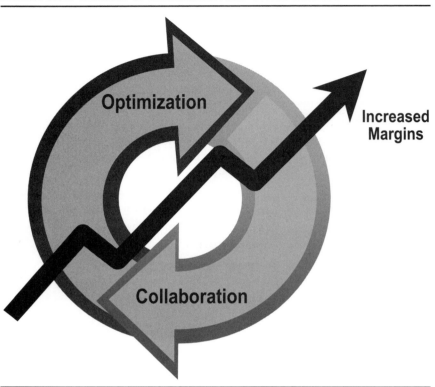

The technology for supply/demand chain optimization exists today. Companies already engaging in Collaborative Planning, Forecasting, and Replenishment initiatives have an opportunity to leverage this technology to dramatically increase the value from their current programs. Companies that see the value of merging optimization and collaboration and that have the ability to organize their trading network into a formal CPFR program will emerge as the ultimate leaders in their industries, in both market share and profitability.

3.5.4 The Use of CPFR at Canadian Tire

What is the value of finding the right approach to CPFR, including process, technology, and trust? The following case study of retailer Canadian Tire outlines one successful approach to starting a CPFR program, the benefits realized to date, and the lessons learned along the way (see Exhibit 3.12).

Canadian Tire Overview

Canadian Tire Retail (CTR) and its associate dealers are together Canada's leading hard goods retailer, offering consumers over 100,000 stock-keeping units (SKUs) of automotive parts, as well as offering over 65,000 SKUs in categories covering automotive accessories, sporting goods, lawn and garden, hardware, housewares, and home improvement. Canadian Tire is distinctive among Canadian retailers in offering such a unique range of goods and services. Canadian Tire's retail network includes more than 440 associate dealer stores, plus their online Web store.

Canadian Tire has one of the largest retail CPFR programs in place today. With fifteen suppliers live in the program, Canadian Tire originally focused its efforts on the promotional activity in its business—collaborating with suppliers on promotional forecasts and agreeing to replenishment plans to meet the consensus demand forecast. The process has evolved over time to review all components of the demand forecast.

Exhibit 3.12. Canadian Tire—Enabling collaboration in the retail supply chain.

Goal:	To collaborate with suppliers to improve forecast accuracy in order to enhance customer service, reduce inventory costs, and lower suppliers' costs.
Strategy:	Engage select suppliers into CPFR contracts in which both parties agree to share and discuss planning, forecasting, and replenishment information and collaborate on promotional and seasonal forecasts to meet jointly defined goals.
Solution:	Manugistics CPFR Solution: • Demand • Collaborate • Hosting services
Results:	• Formal CPFR program in place with 15 suppliers • Achieving near 100% consensus on demand forecasts • Significantly improved forecast accuracy • Inventory turns increased

Implementing Technology

Prior to starting its CPFR initiative in 1999, Canadian Tire invested heavily in improving forecasting and replenishment processes and implementing advanced planning applications from Manugistics for demand and fulfillment management. With these investments, Canadian Tire was able to move from a purchase order–driven replenishment environment to a proactive time-phased forecasting process in which the company was able to consider consumer demand and generate a time-phased store demand forecast. Improving the supply chain planning processes and forecast accuracy gave CTR the foundation it needed to extend the solution to suppliers for forecast collaboration. Through its own forecasting and replenishment planning improvements, which were implemented from 1996 to 1999, Canadian Tire was able to:

- Significantly increase store service levels.
- Reduce inventory by 10 percent; increase inventory turns by 2.6.
- Reduce delivery cycle times by 67 percent.

A key driver of the above achievements was the introduction of a Planned Order Forecast. By using the Manugistics Demand product, Canadian Tire was able to project a replenishment plan over a period of twenty-six to fifty-two weeks. This planned order information was then shared with suppliers using a traditional EDI document. The supplier base was expected to review this information and where necessary adjust procurement and production schedules based on the projected orders.

Suppliers were also instructed to advise Canadian Tire if they anticipated problems in meeting quantities and ship dates outlined in the Planned Order Forecast. If this were to occur, Canadian Tire would consider adjustments to its promotional planning schedule or could work with a supplier to build inventory to meet projected store demand requirements. This process was implemented prior to the VICS CPFR model being introduced.

Spurred by the success of these programs, Canadian Tire began to define its strategy for a formal CPFR program, believing that collaboration with suppliers was the next step to realizing even greater results. Through this program, the focus was placed on improving forecast quality.

To support CPFR, Canadian Tire added the Manugistics Collaborate application to the existing Demand management implementation. This provided the Web-based environment the company needed to post and share information with suppliers. In addition, Collaborate enables the event management and analysis capabilities needed to support an exception-driven review process. The CPFR applications are currently installed in a hosted environment that is managed by Manugistics and accessed by all of the suppliers in Canadian Tire's CPFR program.

By implementing the right technology to support the process, Canadian Tire will be able to scale its CPFR program in 2002 to include more suppliers and more data.

Establishing Commitment

Exhibit 3.13 shows Canadian Tire's relevant dimensions in selecting suppliers.

The retailer also takes into account:

- Supplier relationship and performance
- Value of sales
- Unit sales
- Value of items sold on promotion
- Number of SKUs promoted
- SKUs with a history of poor forecast accuracy
- Buying team preferences

Once a supplier is selected for the program, Canadian Tire undergoes an education program with the supplier, explaining what is required for participation and detailing the benefits that the supplier is likely to recognize from the program.

To officially join the program, a supplier must agree to a written "collaboration contract" that clearly outlines the responsibilities of Canadian Tire and of the supplier. In addition, the contract lays out per-

EXHIBIT 3.13. CANADIAN TIRE SUPPLIER SELECTION CRITERIA FOR CPFR.

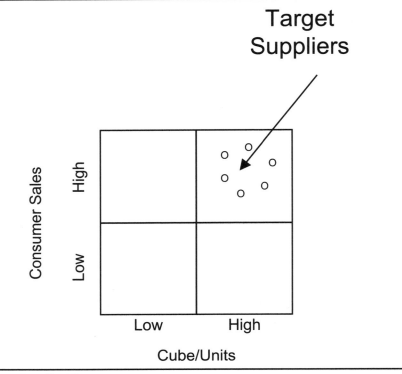

SOURCE: Canadian Tire.

formance objectives in the form of improvements across key performance indicators, including forecast accuracy, inventory reduction, and service-level objectives. These performance objectives are continually evaluated to ensure that both parties are fulfilling their commitment and meeting defined goals.

Canadian Tire CPFR Process

As part of the CPFR program, Canadian Tire shares and discusses planning, forecasting, and replenishment information with suppliers. True collaboration on demand forecasts results in a consensus forecast, which ensures that both parties understand, and are accountable for, the resulting replenishment plan.

With CPFR, Canadian Tire shares the aggregate demand forecast, representing demand for 440 stores, for a thirty-nine-week time horizon. Both base and promotional demand are identified as part of the forecast. They also share information on purchase orders outstanding, planned orders, and current and projected inventory levels at their distribution centers. Manugistics Web-based collaboration application (NetWORKS Collaborate) is used as the mechanism to publish data and collaborate with suppliers on the forecast. In Canadian Tire's case, collaboration is focused on total demand, although the promotional and seasonal demands are a major contributor for many product lines. The process and the technology allow the user to work at the total level, but also allow drill-downs to occur to understand various demand components as needed.

The supplier enters the item forecast into the application on the Web, and Canadian Tire publishes the forecast directly from the Manugistics forecasting application (NetWORKS Demand) to NetWORKS Collaborate, where it becomes visible to authorized suppliers. NetWORKS Collaborate triggers an e-mail notification to participants when items in the forecast comparison fall outside of the tolerance ranges set by Canadian Tire and that supplier. These variances are then discussed and resolved between Canadian Tire and the supplier. Replenishment plans are also published to NetWORKS Collaborate, giving suppliers visibility into planned shipments.

Canadian Tire Results

Canadian Tire is beginning to transition from a production pilot to a fully rolled out CPFR process with its top 100 merchandise suppliers. A complete evaluation of results will be executed after one year of experience is gained. Canadian Tire believes that every supplier that can gain insight into demand patterns will be better equipped to work with the retailer in fulfilling consumer demand. This understanding will enable Canadian Tire and its suppliers to drive the benefits promised in the VICS CPFR process model. The absolute size of the benefits will vary with the size of the business relationship and with the quality of each individual implementation.

Canadian Tire Lessons Learned

Having successfully established Canadian Tire's CPFR program, and as Canadian Tire continues to scale the initiative to add more suppliers, Canadian Tire and Manugistics have gained valuable insight into what it takes to be successful with CPFR. They offer the following insights:

- Having a strong forecasting solution implemented—in Canadian Tire's case, Manugistics NetWORKS Demand—provides a solid foundation for beginning collaboration.
- Exception-based event management and analysis capabilities in the Collaborate application help to keep participant workload manageable because only exceptions to predefined rules need to be reviewed each week, rather than every line item in the forecast.
- Gaining suppliers' insight through collaboration provides immense value.
- Having formal collaboration "contracts" in place with suppliers helps build commitment and keep parties engaged in the CPFR program.
- By defining the process scope for its CPFR initiative up front, Canadian Tire was able to clearly articulate the objectives of the program to suppliers and to keep the project focused as suppliers were brought into the program.
- Collaboration is needed at several levels. Total demand provides the basis for identifying exceptions and understanding product flow requirements. The ability to drill down into the demand forecast is key to ensuring that suppliers understand, or can evaluate, promotional events.
- Collaboration at the SKU level is one form of collaboration. Forecasts can be aggregated at a seasonal or category level. These aggregations are helpful to use in validating a total business against broader economic expectations, such as GDP growth.
- Collaboration can also be extended to physical operations planning.
- The CPFR process will not solve all inventory and service-level issues. Seasonal carryovers and excess inventory can still occur. However, the CPFR process definitely reduces the frequency of carryovers.

- On the technology side, make sure suppliers understand what is required to collaborate online: gain supplier CIO support for accessing Web applications and encourage broadband or high-speed connectivity.

3.5.5 The Use of CPFR at GNX

How can companies realize the benefits of Collaborative Planning, Forecasting, and Replenishment while minimizing up-front infrastructure costs and avoiding costly mistakes? The following case study of retail exchange GNX outlines how accessing CPFR services through an experienced third-party provider can get a CPFR program up and running quickly, delivering faster results and ensuring long-term scalability (see Exhibit 3.14).

GNX Overview

Because GlobalNetXchange is a trading exchange serving the entire retail industry, its success is directly tied to the quality of the services and solutions it delivers. GNX chose Manugistics to power its CPFR offering and to help it get the CPFR services up and running in a hub environment.

EXHIBIT 3.14. GLOBALNETXCHANGE—BUILDING A GLOBAL CPFR HUB.

Goal:	To establish a successful trading exchange that would make Collaborative Planning, Forecasting, and Replenishment services and technology available globally to retailers and suppliers.
Strategy:	Gain the backing of industry business leaders, sign on early adopters in the retail industry, and implement a comprehensive collaboration suite within a secure hub infrastructure that can be accessed globally.
Solution:	GNX Collaboration Suite, powered by Manugistics, consisting of four integrated modules: • Collaborate • Market Manager • Monitor • ONEview
Results:	• Live implementations in place with five retailers and six of their key suppliers • 5–20% reduction in inventory across CPFR participants • 2–12% increase in on-shelf availability across CPFR participants • Validation that exchange-based collaboration works

As part of its comprehensive CPFR offering, called GNX Collaboration Suite™, GNX provides processes and technology to support collaboration, promotion management, reporting, and event management and analysis. The services are hosted by Manugistics and are available in a secure, Web-based environment accessible from anywhere in the world.

As the first retail exchange to install and become operational with its CPFR application, GNX has had live installations since March 2001. GNX provides a single source for CPFR services, including a CPFR-hosted application environment, rapid implementation and scalability, training and consulting services, and significant licensing and hosting cost savings.

While early CPFR programs focused on food and consumer packaged goods, GNX is expanding the CPFR process and benefits to the entire retail industry, including automotive, apparel, hard goods, and general merchandise.

3.5.6 GNX Client Results: Metro AG and Procter & Gamble

Metro, Europe's third-largest trading group, operates Cash & Carry stores in twenty-four countries and is the world's leading wholesaler. Cash & Carry stores sell a comprehensive offering of fresh foods and nonfood products for commercial buyers in 350 worldwide markets.

A key component of any retailer's business, promotions are even more important at Metro's Cash & Carry chain, where the stores run frequent strategic promotions to improve sales and move inventory. Metro found that in Cash & Carry's past promotions, inefficient collaboration often resulted in a chain reaction of problems for both Metro and its suppliers. Forecasts that varied significantly from actual demand led to high or low warehouse inventory levels, which affected on-shelf availability, which in turn compromised sales. Metro's challenge: How could it improve communication with its partners to boost forecast accuracy, while executing more effective retail promotions?

To meet this challenge, Metro chose the GNX Web-based CPFR solution as the foundation for a pilot program with Procter & Gamble, one of its leading suppliers. GNX Collaborate, powered by Manugistics, leverages the information-sharing capabilities of the Internet to facilitate communication and extensive data flow between trading partners, enabling them to jointly manage the planning process, share real-time information, and gain visibility into key supply chain processes.

P&G, a global marketer of nearly 250 brands to consumers in over 130 countries, shares a history of partnership and collaboration with Metro. Using GNX Collaborate, Metro and P&G shared an unprecedented level of information, including pre-promotion store order quantities, daily inventory data, and aggregated weekly forecasts, to develop a single sales forecast from which promotions could be executed and monitored.

Beginning with 27 SKUs in June 2001 and expanding to 78 SKUs across two categories in August 2001, the first phase of the CPFR pilot program lasted twelve weeks and measured improvements across a number of key performance indicators, including forecast accuracy and distribution inventories.

Results at the completion of the first pilot phase were quite positive. Forecast accuracy has improved, warehouse inventory levels have been reduced by as much as two weeks, and on-shelf availability has been maintained at high levels. In addition, both parties have found that GNX software facilitated a less labor-intensive collaborative process that was substantially more efficient and cost-effective than traditional off-line communication.

Because both parties were so pleased with initial results, collaboration via the GNX Collaborate solution continues as an ongoing program between Metro and P&G, with the initiative expanding to include approximately 130 SKUs of P&G paper, fabric, and home-care products.

These positive results have also prompted Metro to plan CPFR roll-outs using the GNX Collaboration Suite with ten of its major suppliers in 2002.

GNX Lessons Learned

Having successfully established a CPFR hub and helping several major retailers and suppliers implement CPFR programs, GlobalNetXchange and Manugistics have gained valuable insight into what it takes to be successful with CPFR. They offer the following insights:

- CPFR implementation across the entire supply chain all at once is not necessary. There are multiple points of entry into CPFR, with efficiencies to be gained at each point, so companies can target areas of pain to realize immediate benefits.

- Select collaborative partners on the basis of room for improvement versus technological sophistication.

- CPFR is a cultural change, not just a process or system.

- An exchange as a neutral third party can be effective in facilitating trust and collaboration between trading partners.

Initial gains will be qualitative: The sharing of business processes and internal challenges will improve visibility and understanding, and collaboration on promotional processes and schedules can help in problem prevention. Long-term gains will show more quantitative results in the form of increased forecast accuracy, lower inventory levels, and fewer stock-outs.

3.6

The Power of Standards-Based Collaboration: The Uniform Code Council and CPFR

Joseph C. Andraski, VICS CPFR and OMI International
Michael Di Yeso, Uniform Code Council

Today, efficient and optimized business practices cannot be achieved in isolation. Companies seeking peak supply chain performance must reach beyond the four walls of their individual enterprises and work in close cooperation with trading partners. The key components of this business equation are standardized business processes, a commitment to collaboration, and the efficient exchange of clean business data.

Today, the business landscape is driven and defined by technology, globalization, and converging supply chains. Rapid advancements in technology and transportation have made global commerce a reality for virtually every company, breaking down barriers and opening up potential new markets. This evolution, while providing companies with new business opportunities, is simultaneously presenting more competitors than ever before. Across virtually every major industry, supply chains are converging, blurring traditional lines of business and increasing competition and bottom-line pressures. The combination of these forces is making it more challenging for companies to survive and succeed.

3.6.1 Standards: The Foundation for Collaboration

As industries moved toward a global market, the need for open, broad-based standards grew. One of the first breakthroughs in standards was the development of the Universal Product Code (U.P.C.) by the Uniform Code Council (UCC). In the 1960s, leaders of the U.S. grocery industry recognized the need for greater collaboration to solve common business problems. Working in an atmosphere of consensus and cooperation, they came together with leading technology providers to find a standardized way to mark and identify products and streamline the checkout process.

When the UCC introduced the Universal Product Code in 1974, it was originally developed for a single, domestic industry application. The U.P.C.'s success in the U.S. grocery industry clearly demonstrated its benefits and broad applicability. The U.P.C. gained interest from the international business community. It quickly crossed over national borders and was adopted by other industries.

The worldwide success of the U.P.C. became the foundation of the EAN-UCC System, a global system of standards that brings greater speed and efficiency to the flow of physical product and electronic information through the supply chain. Recognized as one of the most important innovations in the history of commerce, this powerful global system removes billions of dollars of costs from the supply chain every year, improving productivity and facilitating global trade. Today, nearly one million member companies conducting business in 141 countries worldwide use these tools to speak in a *Global Language of Business*®, enabling them to uniquely identify products, assets, locations, and logistics units, as well as related electronic communications.

In today's competitive global marketplace, speed and efficiency are critical to success and survival. Managing the physical flow of product with the electronic flow of business data is a major challenge in today's intensely competitive environment. A system, built with standardized processes and a common business language, is needed to monitor and manage the movement of product and information through every component along the supply chain.

The EAN-UCC System is based on the user-driven development of open, multi-industry standards to eliminate the supply chain roadblocks and bottlenecks that hampered timely and efficient trade and business practices. The UCC and EAN work closely with users of all industries to develop standards, solutions, and best practices that allow companies to enhance every aspect of their operations.

3.6.2 Standards: Critical for Business Innovation

While innovation is essential to improve business, new ideas must travel a long path before they become widely adopted supply chain solutions. Throughout business history, emerging technology could not deliver its full potential until standards drove wide adoption. The growth of the railroads in the 1800s did not occur until the industry agreed to standards. Surprisingly, fax machine technology has been around since the early 1900s but had limited usage due to technical incompatibility. The industry's efforts to standardize in the 1960s and 1970s provided a common technical foundation to allow fax technology to reach a critical mass of users. Thanks to the cost efficiency of standards, fax machines experienced explosive growth in the early 1980s, going from 300,000 machines in use domestically to over 1.5 million in just a few years.

Whether it's the growth of the railroads, the fax machine, the U.P.C., or the development of a next-generation computer chip, standards are at the core of every business innovation. They provide a common, consensus-based platform that reduces time, costs, and technical roadblocks. However, companies cannot reap the benefits of standards unless they're fully implemented into their supply chain. Simply stated, standards cannot be idle; they must be put to work.

The standards and tools of the EAN-UCC System enable companies to communicate and trade in a common business language. As this system gained a critical mass of users across the global supply chain, it created a more collaborative atmosphere. By implementing and adhering to these standards, trading partners began to see across-the-board benefits. As industries started to see the value and benefit of standards, they began to work more closely together in search of new ways to achieve optimum supply chain efficiency.

3.6.3 Collaboration: The New Culture of Business

There has been a fundamental culture change in the way companies interact with trading partners. Years ago, trading partners were known as "vendors" or "distributors." The relationships were often adversarial. Regardless of the industry, the common view was solely focused on wearing vendors down with fierce determination to get the best, rock-bottom terms. There were equal parts mistrust, perpetual disagreements, unreasonable demands, and a stubborn refusal to be reasonable and compromise. Today, most psychologists would call that type of relationship "dysfunctional."

And yet, the very success and future of a company was solely dependent on these dysfunctional relationships. It's no surprise that these relationships were usually not as productive or efficient as they could have been. Fortunately, more enlightened thinking has prevailed. Today, more and more trading partners are working together with a shared view that the end consumer is their *common customer*, producing more effective solutions and improved business practices.

Collaboration has changed the confrontational game and brings trading partners together as never before. The results of CPFR relationships have been amply reported, with numerous case studies presented at global forums. Without a doubt, CPFR delivers results that include increased sales, increased profits, reduced inventory, and the potential for reducing a company's infrastructure. A company that is conditioned to internal collaboration is more capable of collaborating with upstream and downstream trading partners.

In order to realize the full potential of CPFR, it is critical that companies recognize that the culture of collaboration must be both external and internal. CPFR is not just about companies reaching out to their trading partners; it must include an integrated internal organizational approach. While supply chain management focuses on the processes that enable the flow of product and information from raw materials to final consumer, CPFR's focus is on how organizations can work together to make that process better and more efficient by creating a joint go-to-market strategy. Sales and marketing do not normally consider their input as critical in successful supply chain strategies, but they are absolutely essential in CPFR planning because collaborative demand creation and accurate forecasting are the points of difference between the way business is done today and the way business should be conducted. Effective CPFR implementations cannot occur without a culture that facilitates strong internal collaboration between all departments.

3.6.4 The EAN-UCC System: Gateway to CPFR Global Adoption

In order to realize the full value and benefits of CPFR, a critical mass of users is essential. If CPFR provides a process that can lead to improved performance, then the next question is how do we get it to scale, and how soon? The answer lies in the global standards that have been built by the EAN-UCC System, which serve as the very foundation for a collaborative business platform.

The EAN-UCC System provides a proven platform for companies seeking to implement CPFR and use it on a global basis. It is a global system that is already in place, with an active user body that encompasses nearly one million member companies doing business in twenty-three major industries. EAN-UCC communication standards are not in development but available now, for all to utilize in order to efficiently exchange and communicate information with their trading partners. The proven track record of EAN-UCC Standards and its critical mass of active and engaged users make the case for the scaling CPFR.

Successful implementation of CPFR requires a standardized way to electronically share business information. The explosive growth of the Internet has led more companies to view it as a cost-efficient gateway to conduct global e-business. As the Internet matures, standardized solutions will enable more companies to affordably participate in e-business.

Previously, EDI standards did not cross national boundaries, so any multinational corporation would have to deal with multiple means of communicating throughout the globe. A standard called EDIINT (using the Internet to communicate EDI transactions) has been developed to enable EDI-based companies to exchange relevant information expeditiously and securely. The UCC and EAN have expanded the e-business user base with the development of the first global XML (Extensible Markup Language) standards. Now the call to standardization really does mean that there is one format that can be used throughout the globe to reduce costs and confusion.

3.6.5 Data Synchronization: Essential for Accurate Data Exchange

One of the greatest obstacles to achieving efficient collaborative commerce has been the lack of accurate business data. Costly supply chain bottlenecks occur when trading partners cannot exchange information quickly and accurately. Manual means of managing and updating trading information result in inaccurate data that create a financial ripple effect throughout the supply chain. Without quality data, collaboration and critical business processes will be far from efficient.

Companies have recognized the cost of inaccurate data. The lack of an open, standards-based solution has prevented companies from solving this issue on a broad basis. However, that has not stopped companies from throwing money at this problem. Recent surveys and research have revealed the dissatisfaction that companies have expressed with technology investments. Morgan Stanley estimates that U.S. companies threw away $130 billion in the past two years on unnecessary software and other technology. The Gartner Group estimates that companies waste as much as 20 percent of the $2.7 trillion spent annually on technology. Obviously there are a lot of reasons that this waste exists, but we can point to a few that have to do with the lack of standards or collaboration.

Today's estimates are that between 30 and 60 percent of information at the retail level is incorrect. Without a strong business foundation based upon common and accurate data, truly efficient supply chain management cannot be realized. Technology investments must be planned carefully to facilitate the efficient exchange of accurate and up-to-date information. It should provide a gateway to communicate with its trading community any time, any place, and in the same manner. A company should be able to access product location, specifications, price, and availability instantaneously. Without the clean quality data that are produced through data synchronization, the ability to effectively implement CPFR will be hampered.

One example that highlights the importance of data synchronization is UCCnet, a wholly owned subsidiary of the Uniform Code Council. Based on the open standards of the EAN-UCC System, UCCnet provides standards-compliant item registry and data synchronization services in an open and technology-neutral environment. UCCnet provides an open repository for item, location, and trading partner capabilities, enabling suppliers to communicate new or changed product data throughout the product life cycle over the Internet in near real time. This ensures that all trading partners are using identical, accurate, and standards-compliant item information. UCCnet subscribers are able to considerably reduce errant purchase orders, returned shipments, reductions, logistics systems errors, and associated costs throughout the supply chain.

UCCnet has a tool called the Benefits Calculator (www.uccnet.org) that is intended to help trading partners identify some of the benefits associated with UCCnet and data synchronization. The tool's calculations are based on the number of customer orders per year and the number of nonquality orders per customer per year. A nonquality order is any order that requires further processing due to errors or lack of information. The potential savings are calculated for both the manufacturer and the retailer.

The tool calculates potential savings in the following areas:

- Time spent handling nonquality orders—calculates the extra number of hours per year spent handling nonquality orders
- Administrative handling costs—calculates the administrative costs incurred in the form of deductions taken for inaccurate or missing item-related data
- Paper administrative time saved—calculates the number of hours spent handling the paper errors, i.e., contracts and keying

The total potential savings are calculated for both the manufacturer and retailer for a single manufacturer-retailer relationship. The potential savings for the retailer is then extended based on the percentage the particular manufacturer represents of the retailer's total business. While this is not an "apples-to-apples" relationship, this extended figure provides an approximate total potential benefit for the retailer, making the assumption that all manufacturers will utilize UCCnet and comply with UCCnet standards accordingly.

While UCCnet is used only for example purposes, it emphasizes the important role data synchronization plays in the collaborative process. Unless companies are communicating current, accurate, and "clean" data on a timely basis, the full benefits of CPFR and supply chain management cannot be achieved. Data synchronization solutions must be in place so that quality data travel along every point of the supply chain.

3.6.6 CPFR in Action

The first step toward building a CPFR relationship is to complete the CPFR Capability Assessment that can be found in the CPFR Roadmap at www.CPFR.org. Complete the assessment and arrive at a base case. The base case can help determine what areas are in need of improvement and consequently the opportunity horizon. The CPFR Roadmap lays out the process for creating a CPFR relationship. While all of the nine steps in the Guidelines do not need to be followed, the Roadmap does provide a view as to how others have implemented CPFR.

A simple tool that is available to all companies is the CPFR Benefits Calculator, which can help a company determine the potential benefits it can expect by employing CPFR. It is easy to use, secure, and available on www.CPFR.org, and there is no expense. The Benefits Calculator can help to answer the question of where resources are to be expended to create the most benefit.

To avoid overcounting the benefits, it is suggested that the benefits developed by the Benefits Calculator be reduced by a percentage that is considered reasonable by the management team. For example, if a company has implemented aspects of supply chain management and has already taken credit for gains made in inventory management, then it is prudent to avoid double counting and to be as conservative as possible.

Establishing expectations that cannot be realized is one of the reasons that investments in technology over the last few years did not meet ROI expectations.

A recent article highlighted the fact that a $1 billion company that reduces inventory by 2 percent will see an improvement in cash flow of $100 million. That amount of money can be reinvested into the company to fuel further growth. The bottom-line benefits of CPFR and EAN-UCC Global Standards allow companies to focus on growing their business, rather than worry about the costs of doing business.

By marrying CPFR with the efficiencies produced by UCCnet's data synchronization, the benefits of each become exponential. For example, for a company that is experiencing an increase in sales and profits, while reducing inventory, on 10 percent of its sales, CPFR relationships can scale to 50 percent of its sales by using the EAN-UCC standards and a registry and data synchronization service such as UCCnet. The impact is substantial. The profit picture is greatly enhanced because going to scale will require minor, if any, changes in staffing requirements.

While this suggestion dealt with a retailer and a supplier, another comparison can assess the benefits of a manufacturer engaging a raw material provider and bring this entity into the collaborative loop of planning, forecasting, and exchanging information. The raw materials supplier wins, the supplier wins, and the retailer wins. When a company collaborates with all of the members of its value chain, the benefits grow and it also spreads the seeds of further collaboration. This growth of "N-tier" collaboration is still a relatively untapped source of benefits. As companies see the benefits of CPFR with their customers, it is only natural that they will look to reap the same benefits with their suppliers.

It is this expansion of CPFR to the N-tier and the realization of benefits throughout the value chain that have driven the cause for interoperability and conformance among solution providers. To this end, the UCC and the Drummond Group have sponsored a series of interoperability and conformance testing to ensure that the CPFR process and techniques are truly scalable and effective, regardless of the technical environment. To truly gain the benefits of multiple collaborative relationships, the business community must trade and communicate via an open, interoperable, and global foundation of commerce. Simply stated, business cannot afford to allow the costs of multiple, unique systems to arise.

3.6.7 Standards, Collaboration, and Communication: Formula for Supply Chain Success

Business today is more global, competitive, and complex, and there is greater pressure than ever before to control and reduce costs while delivering improved bottom-line results. In order to achieve this, successful and efficient business practices must be built on a collaborative foundation that brings all trading partners together to work cooperatively. But despite the best of intentions, this effort cannot succeed without a standardized means of communicating business data throughout the supply chain.

CPFR holds enormous global potential as a process that engages trading partners in closer collaboration. As with any innovation, it must be built on a standards-based foundation so that it can scale across technology platforms and reach a critical mass of users. By using the global EAN-UCC System, the standardized exchange of business data can be successfully accomplished. The incorporation of a data synchronization solution will ensure that the communication process is current, accurate, and up-to-date for all participants in the trading community. By bringing collaboration, standards, and communication together, trading partner relationships will become truly productive and profitable partnerships.

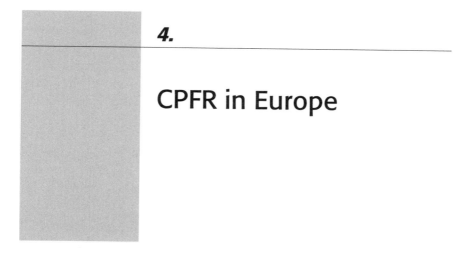

4.

CPFR in Europe

4.1

CPFR: Ready to Take Off in Europe

Prof. Dr. Dirk Seifert, Harvard Business School and University of Massachusetts

CPFR was originally developed by VICS and was thus characterized by the conditions of the American consumer goods market. The specific characteristics of European industry were not originally considered in the VICS prototype. The European market is not homogenous, but rather is comparable to a conglomerate of country-specific business structures. The independently developed structures and cultural preferences vary considerably in the planning and forecasting process. This holds true even when comparing the same economies of scale.

4.1.1 Major Differences Between the United States and Europe

One of the essential differences between the United States and Europe is a higher degree of promotional activity. In Europe, the planning of promotions stands out in the relationship between manufacturers and retailers. According to industry benchmarks, the average number of promotional activities is about 25 to 150 per year. The high frequency of promotions in Europe demands a regular, detailed coordination of business activities, which must happen in a small period of time. The CPFR prototype considers this only to a limited extent. The European organization ECR Europe has set as its goal the adaptation of CPFR to the European market. The higher promotions frequency in Europe is considered in the recommendations made by ECR Europe in its detailed description of an additional step called Planning of Promotions. In the nine-step model (shown in Exhibit 2.2 on page 35), this is inserted between steps 2 and 3. The additional step includes such necessary activities as the creation of a promotions plan, the identification of exceptions, and the cooperative handling of deviations from the plan. Depending on the original situation, coordination can occur monthly, daily, or weekly. For situations with intensive promotional activities, a rolling weekly cycle is recommended.

4.1.2 ECR Europe as a CPFR Pacemaker in Europe

One of the pacemakers in the European implementation and development of ECR and CPFR is ECR Europe. ECR Europe is a joint trade and industry body, launched in 1994 to make the grocery sector as a whole more responsive to consumer demand and promote the removal of unnecessary costs from the supply chain. With its headquarters in Brussels, the organization works in close cooperation with national ECR initiatives in most European countries (ECR Austria, ECR Belgium, ECR Czech Republic, ECR Denmark, ECR Finland, ECR France, ECR Germany/CCG, ECR Hellas, ECR Ireland, ECR Italy, ECR Nederland, ECR Spain, ECR Sweden, ECR Switzerland, and ECR UK). Participation in projects at European and national levels is open to large and small companies in the grocery and fast-moving consumer goods sectors, including retailers, wholesalers, manufacturers, suppliers, brokers, and third-party service providers such as logistics operators.

The vision of ECR Europe is "Working together to fulfill consumer wishes better, faster, and at less cost." The ECR Europe Executive

Board has equal representation from retailers and manufacturers from various European nations. The initiative is supported by four industry organizations: EAN International, Eurocommerce, CIES—The Food Business Forum, and AIM—European Brands Association. Such consulting firms as Accenture, A. T. Kearney, Roland Berger & Partner, and PricewaterhouseCoopers support the studies of ECR Europe.

ECR Europe supports the use and development of CPFR in the European consumer goods economy with numerous publications and forums. Since 1996 ECR Europe has organized an annual ECR conference at which retailers and manufacturers present current thinking on best practices on the topics of ECR and CPFR. To date, ECR conferences have taken place in Geneva (1996), Amsterdam (1997), Hamburg (1998), Paris (1999), Turin (2000), Glasgow (2001), and Barcelona (2002). A further prominent initiative is the ECR Academic Partnership, strengthened by the ECR academic network under the leadership of Daniel Corsten of the University of St. Gallen, Switzerland.

4.1.3 CPFR Gets Rolling in Europe

Since the beginning of 2001, CPFR has picked up the tempo in its implementation in the European market. A number of companies have initiated collaborations and begun CPFR projects. Other large European companies are about to begin pilot projects. Exhibit 4.1 shows selected CPFR projects currently operated or planned in Europe. Next to the respective partners, the relevant e-marketplace and the software application are noted.

Important European retailers like Carrefour in France, Metro in Germany, and Tesco in the United Kingdom understood early on the significance of CPFR and are consistently working toward the exploitation of potential improvements in efficiency. The prominent position of retailers in their respective home markets gives encouragement to the hope that the system will take root on a broader basis. The suppliers to these companies will increasingly have to ask themselves: "Will I still be in a position in three to five years to supply my primary trade partner if my business systems are not CPFR compatible?" Many consumer goods manufacturers have already answered this question for themselves and are currently developing, alone or with the help of outside consultants, their own CPFR strategies.

EXHIBIT 4.1. SELECTED CPFR PROJECTS IN EUROPE.

CPFR Collaboration Partner	Country	Involved B2B Exchanges	Involved Software
Ahold/Proctor & Gamble	Netherlands	WWRE	i2/Syncra
Boots/Johnson & Johnson	Great Britain	Unknown	Syncra
Carrefour/Henkel	France	GNX	Manugistics
Carrefour/Kimberly-Clark	France	Unknown	Syncra
Condis/Henkel/Cartisa	Spain	Unknown	Unknown
Dansk Supermarket/Proctor & Gamble	Denmark	None	Syncra
Delhaize/Masterfoods	Belgium	WWRE	i2
Delhaize/Vandermoortele	Belgium	WWRE	i2
dm-drogerie markt/Henkel	Germany	Unknown	Unknown
dm-drogerie markt/Unilever (planned)	Germany	Unknown	Unknown
dm-drogerie markt/L'Oréal	Germany	Unknown	Unknown
Eroski/Henkel	Spain	None	Manugistics
Globus/Unilever (planned)	Germany	Unknown	Unknown
KarstadtQuelle	Germany	GNX	Manugistics
Ketjuetu/Valio	Finland	None	Own software
Londis/16 supplies	Great Britain	None	JDA
Marks & Spencer	Great Britain	WWRE	i2
Marks & Spencer/Gunstones	Great Britain	Unknown	Syncra
Marks & Spencer/Teifer Foods	Great Britain	Unknown	Syncra
Metro/Henkel	Germany	GNX	Manugistics
Metro/Kimberly-Clark	Germany	GNX	Manugistics
Metro/Procter & Gamble	Germany	GNX	Manugistics
Metro/SCA	Germany	GNX	Manugistics
Sainsbury's/Johnson & Johnson	Great Britain	GNX	Manugistics
Sainsbury's/Kimberly-Clark	Great Britain	GNX	Manugistics
Sainsbury's/Kraft Foods	Great Britain	GNX	Manugistics
Sainsbury's/Nestlé	Great Britain	CPGmarket	Unknown
Sainsbury's/Unilever	Great Britain	GNX	Manugistics
Schöller/Europa Carton	Germany	None	Logility/Pipechain
Superdrug/Johnson & Johnson	Great Britain	Unknown	Syncra
Superdrug/Wella	Great Britain	Unknown	Syncra
Systeme U/Lesieur	France	None	Unknown
Tesco	Great Britain	WWRE	i2
Veropoulos/P&G/Unilever/andere	Greece	None	Microsoft

SOURCE: Accenture, Seifert (2002).

4.2

Results of a CPFR Study in Europe

Nils Weisphal, IDS Scheer AG and University of Hamburg/Germany
Prof. Dr. Wilhelm Pfähler, University of Hamburg/Germany
Dr. Ferri Abolhassan, IDS Scheer AG

In most markets around the world, industries face fierce competition. This holds true especially for the consumer goods industry and retailing. Main reasons are globalization, the intensifying market concentration on the supplier side, saturation of the markets, the introduction of SCM concepts and the fast imitation and adoption of successful strategies for securing competitive advantages. New and better concepts and strategies are needed in ever shorter cycles just to stay that bit ahead of the competition.

In the current situation, the use of CPFR could mean a competitive advantage. This can be expected if it can be shown how relevant competitive strategies are supported by the use of CPFR. At the same time one might expect that the use of CPFR will influence the competitive situation itself, by influencing not only the members of the CPFR-using supply chain, but also competitors, substitute products, and potentially new competitors, which will be directly affected by dramatic changes to the marketplace. The use of CPFR may also be expected to lead to an internal reorganization of companies and require new communication platforms.

This article shows the benefits of using CPFR as well as CPFR's influence on the external competitive situation and the internal company setup on the basis of an empirical study conducted by Hamburg University in cooperation with IDS Scheer AG from June to November 2001. This empirical study is the largest to date on the topic of CPFR in Europe.

4.2.1 Data Basis of the Study

After comprehensive research and data gathering, a total of 1,142 people at 382 European companies were contacted. Legally independent foreign subsidiaries of major international companies were treated as separate companies owing to their usually autonomous degree of freedom in their regional markets. The companies contacted were either directly affected members (possible use of CPFR) or indirectly affected members (competitors might use CPFR) of the supply chain in the consumer goods sector. The empirical study involved seventy-two participants.

The questionnaire was in three parts. The first part contained general questions on the company, the importance and potential of CPFR, and online marketplaces. This part was to be answered by all participants. The purpose of the second part was to document the current CPFR planning and was directed at those companies that had not yet implemented a CPFR project but were already at the concrete planning stage. In the third part, those companies that had already carried out at least one CPFR project were asked to report their experiences.

Participants

As contacts, the authors chose "decision takers," whose positions could be affected by CPFR:

- Senior manager/assistant to senior management
- Head of IT/vice head of IT (and similarly for the following positions)
- Head of organization
- Head of production
- Head of procurement
- Head of marketing
- Head of sales
- Head of logistics
- Head of market research
- SCM project leader

Exhibit 4.2 shows the breakdown by position of the participants.

Seventy-two people from sixty-eight different companies agreed to participate in the study. This equates to a response rate of 6.3 percent of the people contacted or 17.8 percent of the companies contacted. (This difference in the response rates reflects the good coordination within the companies. In many cases one response was given for several employees.) The fact that nearly every fifth company participated in the study shows just how topical and important the issue of CPFR is for companies.

The high importance already enjoyed by CPFR in the sector is reflected by the fact that one in six of the participants held a leading managerial position in his or her company.

EXHIBIT 4.2. POSITION OF PARTICIPANTS IN THEIR COMPANY.

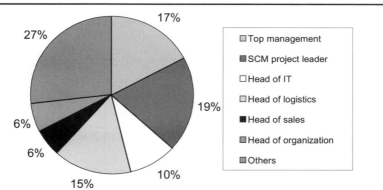

SOURCE: University of Hamburg.

The consumer goods manufacturers and retailing companies participating in the study were allocated to the following categories for comparison purposes:

- Suppliers/subcontractors
- Manufacturers
- Logistics companies
- Retailers

The largest group was formed by the manufacturers (see Exhibit 4.3).

However, on a sales basis, retailers rank equally with manufacturers (see turnover ratio in Exhibit 4.3).

The total sales of the companies that participated in the study amount to over DM 1 trillion (over EUR 500 billion). Because the sales may have been counted twice by companies doing business with each other vertically, these sales are not the same as the actual value added. The breakdown is:

- Approximately 30 percent accounted for by companies with annual sales of less than DM 1 billion
- Approximately 20 percent accounted for by companies with annual sales of DM 1 billion to 2 billion

Exhibit 4.3. Composition of participating companies and turnover ratio.

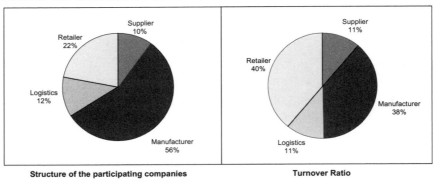

Structure of the participating companies   **Turnover Ratio**

Source: University of Hamburg.

- Approximately 30 percent accounted for by companies with annual sales of DM 2 billion to 10 billion
- Approximately 20 percent accounted for by companies with annual sales of more than DM 10 billion

An important factor is the activities of the participating companies in the various European countries. It is apparent that the majority of the participating companies are involved in cross-border activities. Exhibit 4.4 shows the countries in which the participants do business.

The national companies are regarded as being located in and responsible for their own countries only, unless they stated that they were also responsible for other countries (e.g., in many cases the Benelux market is supplied from France or vice versa). As the market structures can vary quite significantly, different strategies are often called for in individual countries.

The central European region D/A/CH has a great deal of catching up to do with regard to CPFR implementation. It and France (both 77 percent) come in last on this measure. However, this situation is obviously being corrected, because 93 percent of the companies doing business in this region are at the planning stage. The high number of CPFR rollouts in Great Britain (92 percent) might be explained by the fact that the British economy and society are geared more toward the United States than continental Europe.

Exhibit 4.4. Country activities.

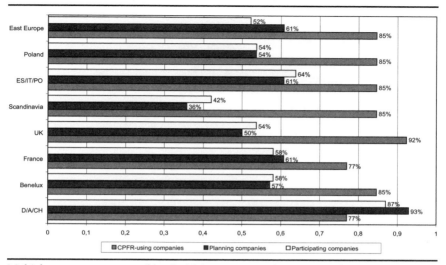

☐ CPFR-using companies	■ Planning companies	☐ Participating companies

Multiple responses were possible; the high percentage of companies in the D/A/CH (Germany/Austria/Switzerland) market can be explained by its favorable central position in Europe and also by the fact that 57 percent of the participating companies are based in this region.

Source: University of Hamburg.

Propagating the CPFR Concept

The newness of CPFR could lead one to conclude that it is not yet very widespread. In 1999 some 40 percent of the participants in the European study had already learned of the idea (see Exhibit 4.5). Two years later, the figure had already reached 92 percent. Some two-thirds of all companies are already planning CPFR projects or are using CPFR.

In reply to the question of how the participants had come across CPFR, about 30 percent responded that they had heard about it from customers, suppliers, consulting companies, or competitors, (see Exhibit 4.6). About half (48 percent) of all participants stated that they had learned about CPFR through their own efforts or groups such as VICS.

The level of CPFR knowledge in the companies, however, is not yet all that overwhelming (see Exhibit 4.7). In a self-assessment of their knowledge on a scale of 1 ("nonexistent") to 7 ("excellent") the parti-

EXHIBIT 4.5. YEAR THE COMPANY BECAME AWARE OF CPFR.

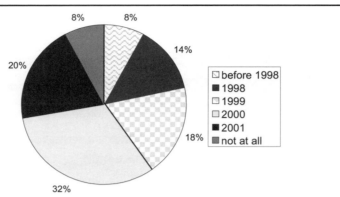

SOURCE: University of Hamburg.

EXHIBIT 4.6. SOURCE OF KNOWLEDGE ABOUT CPFR.

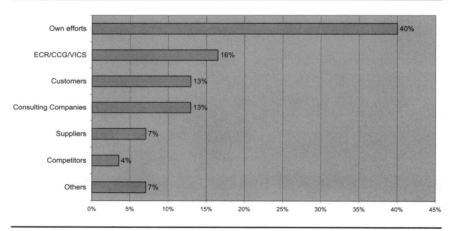

SOURCE: University of Hamburg.

cipants recorded an average of 3.51. Noteworthy here is that over half stated that their knowledge was "basic" or worse. Merely a third evaluated their knowledge as "good" or better. Most of these were companies already using CPFR.

A total of thirty of the seventy-two participating persons said that their company was planning a CPFR project, or about 42 percent.

EXHIBIT 4.7. LEVEL OF CPFR KNOWLEDGE.

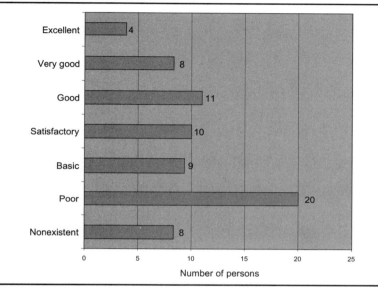

SOURCE: University of Hamburg.

Compared with the overall population of participating companies, retailers are much more strongly represented (see Exhibit 4.8).

Planned Implementation Procedure

In general, changes to business processes are subjected to a pilot project first before embarking on companywide rollout. Most companies seem to be in such a pilot phase where CPFR is concerned. This is also clearly reflected in the number of planned CPFR partners for the CPFR project (see Exhibit 4.9). More than half of all companies in the planning stage will be including only three or fewer partners in the CPFR project. Telephone conversations and e-mail exchanges with various participants underline the fact that companies are looking to gain experience with CPFR first before entering into large-scale implementation. Once the pilot projects have been completed, there will

EXHIBIT 4.8. RATIO OF COMPANIES WITH CPFR PLANNING.

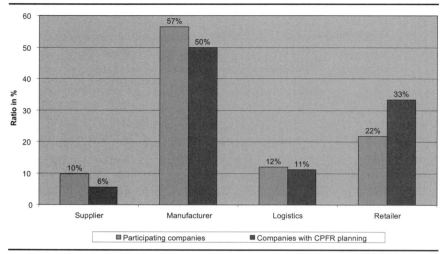

SOURCE: University of Hamburg.

EXHIBIT 4.9. NUMBER OF PARTNERS.

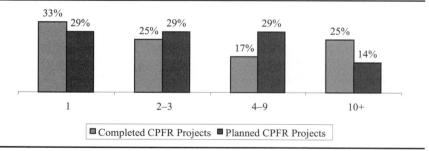

SOURCE: University of Hamburg.

presumably be CPFR projects on the same scale as already being planned by 14 percent of the participating companies. The number of partners involved in already completed CPFR projects differs only marginally from the number in those being planned.

For implementation 73 percent of all companies have set a goal of less than one year (see Exhibit 4.10). Thirty percent of all companies at the planning stage assume that project rollout will take less than six months. Companies working on the basis of two years or more are in

EXHIBIT 4.10. TIME NEEDED TO IMPLEMENT CPFR.

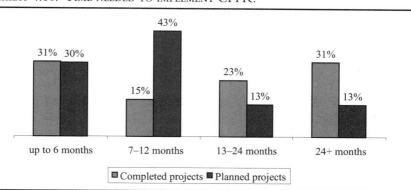

SOURCE: University of Hamburg.

the main those companies with more than ten partners, that is, those already past the pilot phase.

The actual implementation period of previous CPFR rollouts is longer than that of planned projects. This may be due to the larger size of the projects. An alternative reason may be that rollout was simply delayed because of various problems.

4.2.2 Which Strategies Are Companies Following with CPFR?

The foremost goal of a company should be long-term maximization of profit or market value. There are various strategies available for generating a competitive advantage that will lead to the achievement of this goal. One tool for reaching this foremost goal is CPFR. More than a quarter of all those surveyed stated that of all areas, CPFR had the greatest influence on corporate strategy (see Exhibit 4.11).

How can CPFR generate competitive advantages with respect to classic competitive strategies? And how will the various methods to pursue these strategies via CPFR perform compared with each other? The following discussion will try to answer these questions.

Overall Cost Leadership

Overall cost leadership helps a company generate higher margins from the same market prices or allows it to set lower selling prices with the same margin. Both lead to a competitive advantage over rival companies. Cost leadership can be achieved via the following methods:

- Reducing costs of production, for example, through cooperation
- Reducing inventory costs, for example, through early coordination of promotions
- Reducing costs of rejects, for example, through demand-synchronized production in the case of foodstuffs
- Reducing selling costs, for example, optimized personnel deployment planning in logistics through more accurate transport volume planning
- Optimizing advertising costs, for example, coordination between retailer and manufacturer for promotions or more accurate target group definition through pooled data administration

The individual effects of these approaches have already been described in detail in the first part of this book. Therefore, a detailed description of the impact of CPFR has been dispensed with here.

In the empirical study, the participants ranked the cost-saving potential from CPFR higher than that of all other SCM concepts (see Exhibit 4.12).

EXHIBIT 4.11. AREA OF GREATEST INFLUENCE OF CPFR.

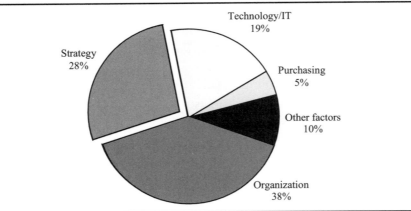

Technology/IT
19%

Strategy
28%

Purchasing
5%

Other factors
10%

Organization
38%

SOURCE: University of Hamburg.

EXHIBIT 4.12. COST-SAVING POTENTIAL OF STRATEGIC CONCEPTS.

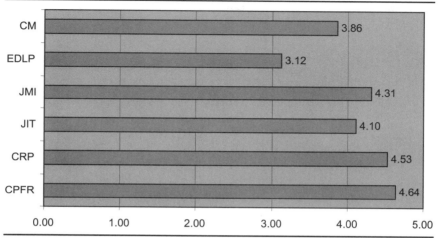

SOURCE: University of Hamburg.

Answering the questions involved a scale of 1 (inappropriate/very low) to 7 (ideal/very high). The values of the individual concepts are the averages of all participants across the concept in question.

Differentiation

To adopt a differentiation strategy a company must succeed in making its products or services so different that "they are regarded in the entire sector as being unique" (Porter, 1999). Just like the cost leadership strategy, a differentiation strategy can be applied in a number of ways:

- Increased product availability through reduced out-of-stocks thanks to joint planning
- Improved quality of service, for example, through identifying and joint placing of cross-selling pairs (ham and asparagus)
- Improved product quality, for example, through identifying weak points in the supply chain
- Increased product variety, by identifying new gaps in the market

CPFR, given a better grade here than for its cost-saving potential, is not regarded as the best method for achieving this goal (see Exhibit

4.13). Category management, which specializes in this field, comes in ahead of CPFR.

Niche Strategy/Focus

CPFR-using supply chains have much more meaningful data at their disposal than other market participants do. This paves the way to more precise forecasts for certain target groups and markets. This in turn permits competing on a broader front and penetrating new niches with an expanded product range. New submarkets can be identified in line with the philosophy of "Think Globally—Act Locally" (see Exhibit 4.14, Company B), and the development of new product variants that meet the needs of customers better than the existing ones do.

This can generate new customers who had not bought any of the existing products on the market (see Exhibit 4.14, area which without CPFR was outside all the circles and is now within one of the new circles). Alternatively, customers may be won over from a competitor because their needs are better satisfied. This results in an increase in the number of different products offered on the market. Disadvantages caused by lower output per product can be offset through lower costs thanks to CPFR.

EXHIBIT 4.13. BOOSTING CUSTOMER SATISFACTION VIA STRATEGIC CONCEPTS.

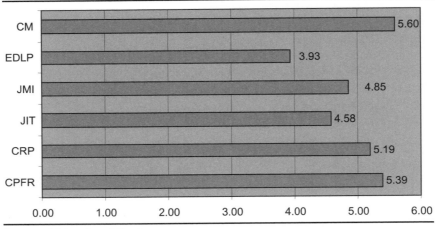

SOURCE: University of Hamburg.

EXHIBIT 4.14. PRODUCT DIFFERENTIATION IN NICHE MARKETS.

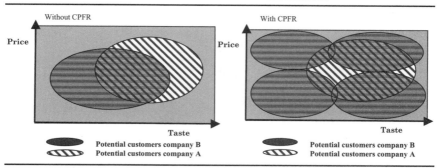

SOURCE: University of Hamburg.

Prospector/Pioneer Strategy

The prospector strategy can be applied at the corporate level and at the product level.

Prospector Strategy at the Corporate Level The trend toward concentration means that there are ever fewer manufacturers and retailers in most markets. This makes the pioneer strategy particularly important for exploiting the potential of CPFR. From an early stage, a company must try to attract the right supply chain partners before they are snapped up by rivals or risk not being able to find a powerful partner.

The pioneer strategy is very important now because CPFR groups are not realigned on a daily basis but tend to be formed for the middle and long term. Fundamental decisions will have to be made by top management especially in Europe, where CPFR will probably spread widely over the next two years.

Apart from the fear of missing the (supply chain) boat and thus the opportunity to cut costs, one notion is key, particularly for participants upstream from the end users: The initial projects have shown that a company tends to place orders with an upstream company with which it has a CPFR cooperation rather than with a nonparticipating company. Surveyed companies report more than 80 percent growth in trading volume with their cooperation partners.

There have even been cases in which order volumes have been reduced with previous suppliers and placed with the cooperation partner.

Prospector Strategy at the Product Level Better knowledge of the market and more efficient R&D allow the pioneer strategy to be applied to the product level through the goal of shorter time to market. This means that manufacturers participating in the CPFR process have better prospects for developing and launching products more quickly thanks to the greater data available.

The faster development will help the product become the quasi-standard in its segment (e.g., Coca-Cola Light). This "first mover" advantage is particularly pronounced in the consumer goods industry. Other manufacturers looking to launch me-too products would have to spend a great deal to persuade customers to give their chocolate buttons a try.

Comparison of the Measures Adopted

In order to evaluate which strategy/strategies companies are following with CPFR, the participants in the study were asked to assess a number of measures with respect to CPFR (see Exhibit 4.15).

For companies planning CPFR projects, the highest goal was increasing the quality of service for customers and cutting inventory costs. Increasing sales (both absolutely and with the CPFR partner) was followed by shortening the "time to market" (TtM) with new products.

Exhibit 4.15. Planned CPFR project goals.

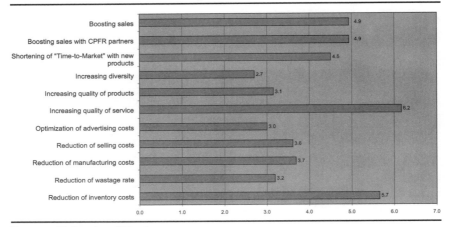

Source: University of Hamburg.

This aspect comes as a surprise. In the past it was never discussed as a goal for CPFR, and here it comes before reducing the costs of production and selling.

For companies already using CPFR, the degree of fulfillment (the quotient of the evaluation of the goal to the evaluation of the results of an action) is on the whole relatively high. Thus, CPFR seems to meet the participants' high expectations (see Exhibit 4.16). The highest degree of fulfillment was found with the two main goals, along with shorter TtM. CPFR users were disappointed about success in reducing selling costs.

Possible reasons for a low degree of fulfillment of individual goals could be overly high expectations or problems encountered during implementation. For example, the most frequently cited problem encountered by participants during implementation was incompatibility in partners' IT systems (see Exhibit 4.17).

Other problems mentioned include cost reasons, insufficient internal resources (staff), and the lack of internal technical infrastructure. The feared potential lack of cooperation between partners over the releasing of sensitive business data was not encountered as a problem.

This section shows that there is no one single strategy companies are using with CPFR but several of the classic strategies are being adopted in parallel. CPFR thus permits an increase in service quality with a

EXHIBIT 4.16. DEGREE OF CPFR OBJECTIVE FULFILLMENT.

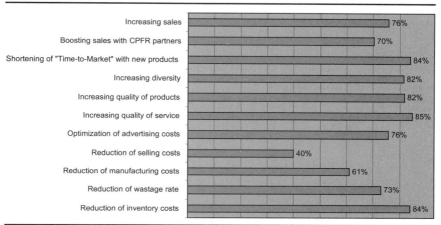

SOURCE: University of Hamburg.

EXHIBIT 4.17. PROBLEMS ENCOUNTERED IN CPFR IMPLEMENTATION.

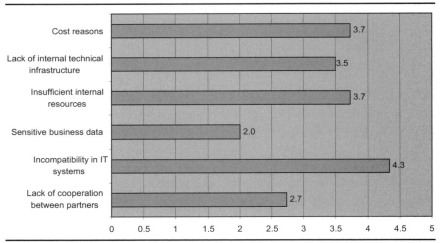

SOURCE: University of Hamburg.

simultaneous reduction in (inventory) costs and shorter development times for new products. Such a fundamental expansion of corporate strategy is possible only because of the rapid rate of development in new information technologies.

4.2.3 Influence of CPFR on the Prevailing Competitive Situation in Industry

CPFR incorporates previously independently acting upstream and downstream companies along a supply chain into a common concept. This prompts the question of what influence CPFR will or could have on the overall competitive situation in industry. To answer this question we will describe the competitive situation following Porter (1999) by examining the five well-known competitive forces.

Suppliers

In the past suppliers/manufacturers have tended to have a somewhat cool relationship to retailers. There are annual meetings to haggle over prices and conditions, often with threats of delisting being uttered, and afterwards both parties feel that they "have been taken for a ride."

The relationship between supplier and retailer has to be completely redefined if CPFR is to be used as a management tool. Since CPFR demands a very high level of cooperation and exchange of information, the win–lose attitude must be replaced by a win–win cooperative behavior. Companies that make it their policy never to release (or exchange) data, as is the case with most discounters in Germany, will never be able to embark the successful cooperation required by CPFR.

Suppliers stand to profit from CPFR in many respects. Apart from the previously scarcely accessible POS data, they gain an insight into customer requirements through the experiences contributed by retailers. The retailer data can also include information about the sales figures of competing suppliers so that sales in the individual categories can be optimized. These new data sources permit suppliers to look for new products that satisfy customer needs better than those already on the market. Other advantages can be derived from the actions previously described, such as lowering supply costs.

One disadvantage of CPFR could be that the closer ties to fewer suppliers will increase dependency on these suppliers. Therefore a company should have more than one CPFR partner per product. Apart from the risk that the loss of a supplier will lead to the product no longer being available at all, there is also a risk of worse procurement terms and perhaps a lack of information about the market. It thus remains vital that market observations are conducted. This can be done, for example, by the company running the CPFR process via an Extranet but at the same time using B2B marketplaces to keep in touch with developments in the market.

Customers

Customers here fall into two categories. If the company does not sell to consumers but supplies intermediate products to other manufacturers or finished goods to retailers, the conclusions are the same as described in the previous section (Suppliers). On the other hand, customers can refer to the final customer, or consumers, the subject here.

The customer (consumer) can enjoy many advantages from CPFR. Exhibit 4.18 shows the process for gaining customer loyalty and thus leading to a win–win situation for both sides. The cooperation of the companies involved in the CPFR process can reduce the forecast errors for promotions, sales, and orders. As a result, inventory peaks can be

EXHIBIT 4.18. INFLUENCE OF CPFR ON CUSTOMERS.

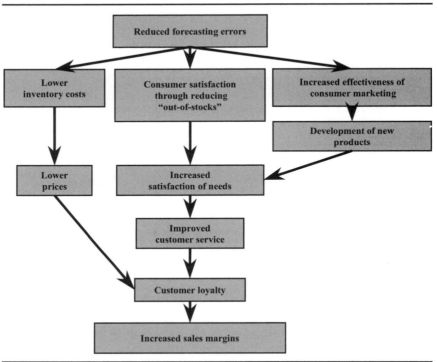

SOURCE: University of Hamburg.

reduced, leading to lower inventory costs and thus lower prices. The troughs are also lower. This means that improved sales forecasts lead to fewer forecasting errors, thus avoiding empty shelves (out-of-stocks). The continuous availability of products increases customer satisfaction. Customers will find the products they want at the right time, in the right quantity, and in the right place. The outcome is increased satisfaction of needs.

In addition, the continuous availability of each product will show producers exactly which products are really wanted (no more substitute buying). The data this generates can be used to develop existing or new products with a view toward increased satisfaction of customers' requirements.

All these actions impact the customer like an improvement in customer service (which they in effect constitute). These, together with the lower prices, lead to greater customer loyalty. The entire supply chain will benefit from the greater overall demand.

Competitors

A company in a supply chain group will enjoy many of the advantages already discussed. As a result of these advantages, a company will be able to offer its products at more favorable prices and in a more focused manner. Such a company will reap greater customer loyalty. All these advantages will be felt by competing companies as disadvantages.

The intense cooperation between the supply chain partners will lead to a growth in loyalty within the supply chain. As a result, an outside competitor may be dealt with at a lower priority. Where there are production bottlenecks, the cooperation partners will be served first. The outside competitor will sustain an irreparable competitive disadvantage. Exhibit 4.19 shows a simplified presentation of this relationship. For example, company A organizes the CPFR process via a proprietary Extranet and so can exclude company B.

Company A must strive to create an exclusive relationship (with respect to CPFR) with its SC partners.

In order to rectify this disadvantage, company B will now try as second mover to build close ties with vertical partners as well. Thus it is already possible to talk about "supply chain competition" instead of competition among companies.

However, the partners can of course be members of several CPFR supply chains at the same time. The more concentrated the market of an SC link is, the more difficult it will be for the second mover to create a close CPFR supply chain.

Potential New Competitors

Potential competitors will find it all the more difficult to enter the market. The formation of CPFR supply chains means better information and closer ties for the participants. In markets with high levels of horizontal concentration, CPFR supply chains may constitute an impenetrable barrier to entry. A new entrant must either have a high level of vertical integration or be/become a member of a supply chain if it is to survive in the market.

EXHIBIT 4.19. SUPPLY CHAIN VERSUS INDIVIDUAL COMPANIES.

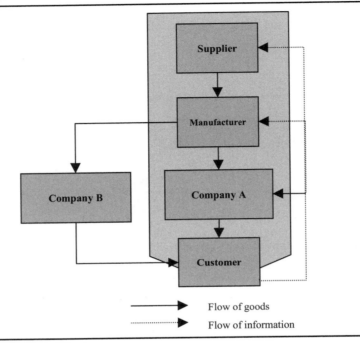

Flow of goods
Flow of information

SOURCE: University of Hamburg.

On the other hand, members of a CPFR supply chain can also become new competitors to other companies. A company that decides to
launch a new product line as part of its differentiation strategy may enter
a new market segment. The close cooperation with one (or several)
retailers leads to an immediate listing, as the retailer already has precise
information about the partner's sales, forecasts, and promotional activities, so the cooperation will also run smoothly in other market segments. This listing will increase the pressure on those companies already
doing business in that segment. On the one hand, this new competitor
will probably capture some of their market share and sales, but on the
other, shortage of shelf space may lead to their being delisted.

Substitute Products

Substitute products constitute a lower risk for a company that uses
CPFR, given the better satisfaction of customer wishes even at the mar-

gin of customer preferences. Exhibit 4.20 illustrates this context. Prod-uct A is a substitute for product B (which is sold by a CPFR-using company) in the areas X and Y, which are the margins of customer preferences. Company B can satisfy these margins better through appro-priate positioning (e.g., double positioning at the checkout). As a result, the indecisive customer will now favor one company and the overlap-ping area will fall to the CPFR-using company as an area in which the company has no competitors. The competition will now be concen-trated only on area Y.

Evaluation of the Influence of CPFR on the Competitive Situation

The study participants planning CPFR projects were asked to evaluate the impact of CPFR on the competitive forces. Potential new competi-tors and substitute products have been included under "influence on competitors" together with the current competitors. The results, seen in Exhibit 4.21, show that CPFR has had a lasting impact on the com-petitive situation and hence on the market structure. The participating companies think that CPFR will have significant influence on the com-petitive situation both vertically and horizontally. The influence on competitors is evaluated as much higher by those companies that are planning a large-scale use of CPFR (more than six planned partners)

EXHIBIT 4.20. CUSTOMER PREFERENCES.

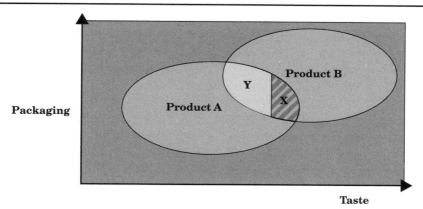

SOURCE: University of Hamburg.

EXHIBIT 4.21. INFLUENCE OF PLANNED CPFR PROJECTS ON COMPETITIVE FORCES.

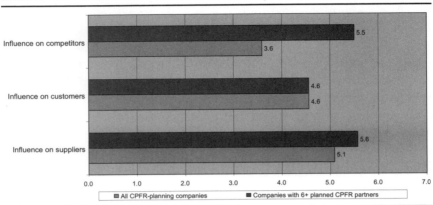

SOURCE: University of Hamburg.

than by all CPFR-planning companies. This may be because these companies are already trying to set up CPFR supply chains via vertically upstream or downstream companies and thus gain a strategic competitive advantage.

The participants were also asked about any disadvantages they had encountered with CPFR (see Exhibit 4.22). On the whole the disadvantages were not ranked all that highly. One criterion, however, does stand out: the unexpectedly high increase in dependency on customers (although not from the viewpoint of retailers).

Correspondingly, the influence of CPFR on the customers of companies already using CPFR is given a higher grade (5) than by those at the planning stage (4.6). Therefore, this disadvantage is not to be taken lightly.

4.2.4 Internal Reorganization Due to CPFR

The introduction of CPFR does not only influence the external competitive situation. It is also bound up with fundamental changes within the companies themselves. This affects restructuring within various company departments (see Exhibit 4.23) as well as the question of the optimal degree of integration (insourcing and outsourcing), and the selection of the communications media for implementing CPFR.

Together with introducing CPFR, half of all companies are already

Exhibit 4.22. Disadvantages of CPFR.

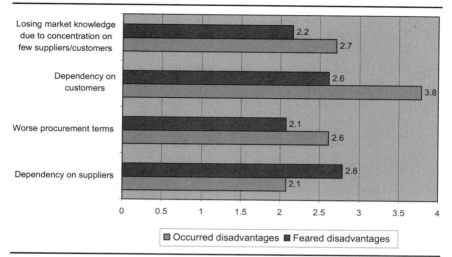

SOURCE: University of Hamburg.

Exhibit 4.23. Planned restructuring with CPFR.

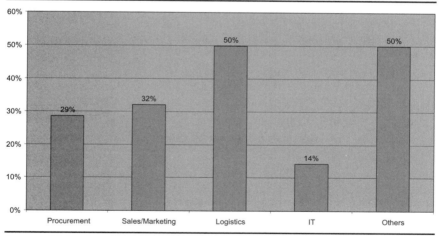

SOURCE: University of Hamburg.

planning changes to their logistics structures. Some 30 percent are planning restructuring actions for procurement and also sales/marketing.
Note that multiple responses were possible.

Although many of them are still in the pilot phase, 25 percent of all
companies are already planning on outsourcing various activities (see
Exhibit 4.24). The most frequently stated areas were logistics and transportation. This shows the necessary effort to concentrate on core competency when using CPFR.

For companies already using CPFR, the incompatibility in IT structures was one of the greatest obstacles in implementing projects. Therefore, it was interesting to learn what forms of cooperation there are and
which software is seen by the companies as having the most favorable
prospects.

Asked about the familiarity of CPFR software, SAP AG products
were named most often (see Exhibit 4.25). With respect to performance, the software from Manugistics and i2 were ranked more or less
equally with SAP AG products.

There are various possibilities for using CPFR, especially where intercompany communication is concerned. Participants were asked to
evaluate the prospects of three possibilities. All three were given above-
average grades (see Exhibit 4.26).

The prospects for intercompany Extranets, that is, operated by several companies (e.g., Covisint in the automobile industry), were ranked
lower than those for company-owned Extranets, in which the network

EXHIBIT 4.24. PLANNED INSOURCING OR OUTSOURCING WITH CPFR.

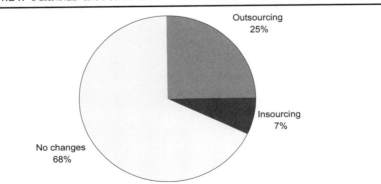

SOURCE: University of Hamburg.

EXHIBIT 4.25. ASSESSMENT OF CPFR SOFTWARE.

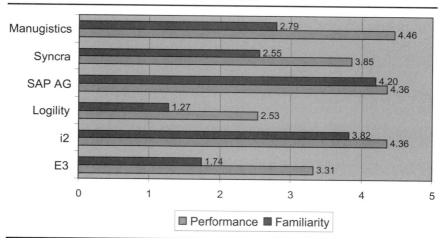

The basis for the responding participants is significantly lower given the lack of familiarity with individual products/companies with respect to the performance of the software (average of 29 evaluations/product) than for the question about familiarity (71).

SOURCE: University of Hamburg.

EXHIBIT 4.26. PROSPECTS FOR EXTRANETS AND B2B EXCHANGES.

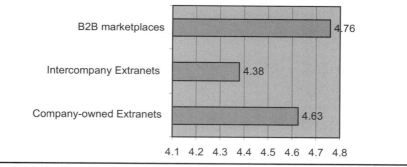

SOURCE: University of Hamburg.

belongs to one partner but is used by the other. The best marks were given to third-party-operated B2B marketplaces.

The participants were asked for their opinions in order to determine the familiarity of the outlook for these marketplaces. The most widely known (GNX and Transora) were not given the best chances (see Exhibit 4.27). This honor went to World-Wide-Retail-Exchange (WWRE).

4.2.5 Prospects

This article examines on the basis of a pan-European study the strategic possibilities of using CPFR to secure a competitive advantage, the effect of the use of CPFR on the competitive situation, and the requirement of internal reorganization for companies due to the use of CPFR. Although most companies are still in the planning phase, it is already apparent that CPFR can be used to create clear, stable ("sustainable") competitive advantages. The entire market, both horizontal and vertical, will be greatly affected by the use of CPFR. Companies refusing to

EXHIBIT 4.27. PROSPECTS OF LEADING B2B MARKETPLACES.

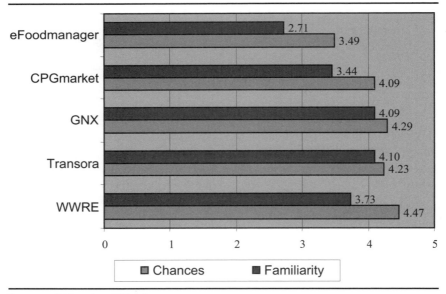

SOURCE: University of Hamburg.

embrace CPFR will sooner or later find their very existence threatened once a competitor or vertical partner moves to CPFR.

In view of the still relatively small number of companies using CPFR on a large scale, it would be interesting to see in the near future to what extent those companies currently testing or planning CPFR will change their strategic thrust. It would also be interesting to find out what impact switching to CPFR has on company earnings. Particularly in the European market, where individual companies are already using CPFR, it would be interesting to make comparisons with other companies. A study of the changes in market structure caused by CPFR and companies using CPFR and the consequences of these changes would provide an interesting field for further research. These aspects are the subject of a study that the authors at Hamburg University in cooperation with the consulting company IDS Scheer are currently working on.

4.3

CPFR in Germany, Austria, and Switzerland

Saskia Treeck, Centrale für Coorganisation (CCG)
Michael Seishoff, Centrale für Coorganisation (CCG)

Since the midnineties ECR initiatives have existed in Germany, Austria, and Switzerland. For a long time, the three countries worked independently on ECR recommendations at a national level. A close collaboration between Germany and Austria came into existence in 1997, and the logical extension of that was to expand it to include Switzerland.

4.3.1 ECR D-A-CH—The Platform for CPFR in German-Speaking Countries

ECR Germany-Austria-Switzerland was grounded in July 2000 in order to organize ECR projects more efficiently and to obtain synergy effects, particularly in view of the demands of new technologies. This platform uses the long years of experience in dealing with over 100 million consumers. Additionally, the already established ECR network was used for development and realization.

At present, many international and national initiatives on the further development of the CPFR business model are being pursued. The Global Commerce Initiative (GCI) is working closely with the Voluntary Interindustry Commerce Standards committee and ECR Europe is coordinating global CPFR activities. Beyond that, the work of realizing CPFR pilot projects at ECR Europe continues. The inclusion of the requirements of the German-speaking market in the CPFR business model are being realized through the ECR Germany-Austria-Switzerland initiative.

It is important, however, that all initiatives do not operate independently, but instead work in a continual process of coordination in order to secure reciprocal knowledge transfer (see Exhibit 4.28).

With the CPFR business model as well as the ECR concept, the objective is to fulfill the consumer's wishes efficiently and reliably. The

EXHIBIT 4.28. COLLABORATION IN THE GLOBAL NETWORK.

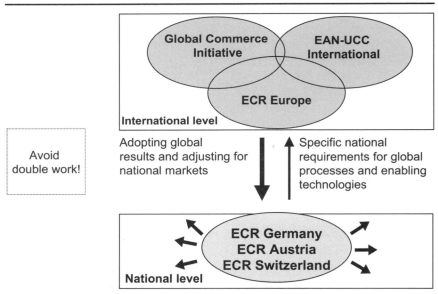

SOURCE: Central für Coorganisation (CCG).

realization of this objective can be achieved through an interorganizational collaboration on strategies and processes.

4.3.2 The Necessity of a CPFR Management Paper for the German-Speaking Market

As a consequence of the differing market conditions, a differentiated approach to the implementation of the nine-step CPFR business model is critically needed. The publications on CPFR to date reflect primarily the conditions in North America and Europe. The differences between the U.S. market and the European are considerable, but there are also essential differences within Europe with respect to sales strategy and consumer behavior.

While the sales policy in the United States is determined by the every-day-low-price (EDLP) policy, in Europe a higher percentage of sales is determined by retailers' and manufacturers' promotions. There are also differences in the execution of promotions in individual European regions. As an example, in Germany promotion activities are very important. The regional and national peculiarities lead to different approaches to corporate strategies through the CPFR business model and thereby a different approach to planning, forecasting, and replenishment processes, differentiated according to standard or promotional sales. A sufficient consideration of these connections is not a part of the VICS CPFR Guidelines.

In addition to the high significance of promotional activities, there are further important differences between the North American market, Europe, and German-speaking economic markets. The following points speak for a differentiated implementation of the CPFR business model:

- *Different Standards of Living in the Industrial Nations.* Within Europe, wages and living standards vary greatly, precipitating different degrees of purchasing power.
- *Consumer Behavior.* While in some European countries consumers have become very quality conscious, in others consumer behavior is dominated by price.
- *Business Strategies.* Recently, many retailers have promoted in-house brands, leading to independence from established brand-name manu-

facturers and a positive effect in the marketplace. Other companies have tried to obtain advantages through negotiations with their trading partners.

- *Internal Corporate Culture of Collaboration.* The willingness to collaborate with trade partners depends on the corporate culture inculcated by senior management, in particular, the preparedness to share data and risks.

- *The Extent of ECR Implementation.* The acceptance and implementation of ECR in Europe is less than in the North American market. Retailers and manufacturers in North America have understood how to overcome conflict and implement ECR by concentrating on common goals and improving business bilaterally.

- *Logistical Conditions.* Many European companies have entirely different distribution systems from those in the United States. Compared with the American market, where distribution over long distances is handled through cross-docking, in Europe companies prefer direct delivery to retail outlets, or through a central warehouse. There, cross-docking and VMI are also used. The high number of different replenishment techniques in Europe must be considered in the realization of CPFR.

Despite the individuality of the market, the CPFR concept can be adapted for Europe, and thus for German-speaking economic regions. The particulars of the market must be accommodated, however. It has been clearly recognized that the efficiency-enhancing aspects of CPFR in the supply chain will work independently of the distribution models found in North America or Europe. It is clear today that CPFR will support the integration of different ECR solutions and thereby contribute to their higher prevalence in the European market.

4.3.3 ECR Concept—CPFR Business Model

CPFR distinguishes itself through the fact that experience and information gained are systematically drawn into the control of the processes (feedback loop).

The simplified diagram depicted in Exhibit 4.29 reduces the com-

EXHIBIT 4.29. THE CPFR PROCESS MODEL ACCORDING TO THE CCG.

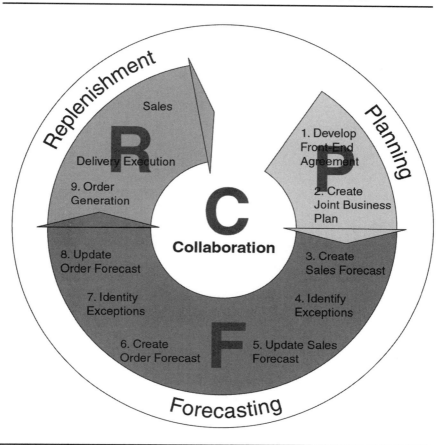

SOURCE: Centrale für Coorganisation (CCG).

plexity of the VICS nine-step work flow and shows the cyclic character of planning, forecasting, and replenishment.

While in the last few years there have been many recommendations made with respect to planning and replenishment processes, the creation of joint forecasts remains wanting. For the planning of business processes, the eight-step category management process is worth mentioning. For the realization of efficient replenishment, techniques like vendor-managed inventory and cross-docking and optimization strategies for distribution are being developed.

As an integrative step, recommendations for POS data management and sales forecasting are being developed. From the perspective of German-speaking economic regions, joint forecasting is an especially critical element in the improvement of product availability. Available publications on this topic are listed in the following section.

4.3.4 Sales Forecast

It was already apparent in early 2000 that the CPFR business model developed by VICS contained new stimuli for the optimization of business processes for German-speaking economic regions. Building on the CPFR business model, an implementation-oriented guide for the realization of joint forecasting by retailing and manufacturing was developed. It takes into account concrete recommendations from the guide published under the title *Joint Forecasting*.

The objective was the establishment of best practices for the creation of higher-quality sales forecasts, which would secure significantly better product availability and optimized levels of inventory along the supply chain. The objective documents the consistent implementation of the pull principle, including joint forecasts. The realization should be achieved through an interorganizational data exchange. Step 3 of the CPFR business model was handled in sufficient detail. These recommendations do not contradict the VICS CPFR Guidelines, rather they should be understood as supplemental to them.

The joint forecast (see Exhibit 4.30) is used as an instrument of control over product availability. To implement the forecast, reference amounts (capacities, locations, product changes, logistics concepts) from the company's strategic planning are cross-referenced with criteria from actual business (sales behavior, inventory trends).

In the context of a status quo survey, it became clear that both retailers and manufacturers currently make forecasts, but with different objectives in mind. While in retail this is often used for automated ordering, in industry the criterion of highest priority is the planning and control of production capacity. A joint estimation of the expected demand through the exchange of forecasts is not yet being done. As a consequence, out-of-stock situations occur, in particular during promotions, whether they be run by the retailer or manufacturer. As a result, all parties require security in the form of safety stock.

EXHIBIT 4.30. LEVELS OF COLLABORATION.

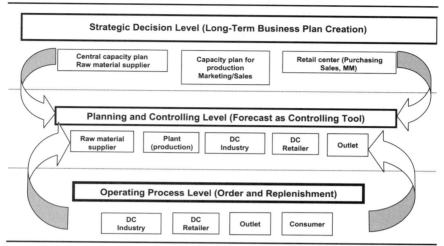

SOURCE: Centrale für Coorganisation (CCG).

The Value of Joint Forecasting

Consumers Through joint forecasting, a higher degree of planning security for product replenishment is ensured. This means that the consumer will actually find the product on the shelf when he or she goes to look for it. In particular, when a product becomes more attractive through a time-limited offer, the consumer expects it to be there through the end of the promotion. The value for the customer is also clear when new products and product variations are available in sufficient number. Furthermore, the reduction of safety stock accelerates products through the supply chain so that the customer receives fresher, more current goods.

Retailers Through the consumer's increased benefit, the retailer profits through stronger customer retention, as the consumer repeatedly visits the retail outlet. The improved image represents something of qualitative utility for the retailer.

Through joint forecasting, out-of-stocks can become the exception to the rule. Consequently, the cost of shortages through lost revenue and the undesired sales in alternative categories is avoided. Thus, the connection between distortions in the sales of a given product can be eliminated. Additionally, unused shelf space is avoided, boosting the image at the point of sale (POS).

Through the reduction of out-of-stocks, manually placed special orders are eliminated, which must always be placed when products are no longer available. Consequently, the additional costs for special orders in terms of ordering, receipt of goods, warehousing, and transportation are eliminated. Additionally, safety stocks are reduced in the central warehouse. In case an out-of-stock situation cannot be avoided by the manufacturer, it can inform the retailer in time to allow alternative measures to be taken.

Manufacturers Finally, the manufacturer also profits from the added benefit to the consumer. If the customer finds the product on the shelf, the likelihood of him choosing an alternative brand is reduced.

Rush orders by retailers lead to problems for the manufacturer, in particular when large amounts are ordered. If the amount ordered cannot be covered by inventory on hand, the planned production agenda must be quickly changed, as well as machinery taken offline, refitted, and put back into production. This can mean that shifts must be added to meet deadlines. The result is additional costs for production, warehousing, transport, and administration. Specifically, material waste through machinery breakdown and setup, the need for technicians, idle time of the production line and personnel, changes in product program, and the organization of additional workers and transportation should be noted.

Unexpected orders can lead to orders not being able to be delivered when production lines are not capable of reacting to additional demand. Thus, manufacturers, too, can suffer from lost revenues.

Through joint forecasting of anticipated demand, existing production capacity can be used more efficiently, provided critical mass among the participants is reached. The additional costs described can be drastically reduced and lead to lower per unit costs.

Additionally, safety stocks of raw materials and completed goods can be reduced along with the risk of unsalable leftovers, which is high for items produced especially for time-limited offers.

The Significance of Relevant Data Sources

Today there is a great deal of information at all levels of the supply chain that is not used for the creation of a joint forecast. It is often the case that the technical means to obtain and process these data are not in place. To the extent the data exist, appropriate tools must be delivered that are able to interpret and draw conclusions for future demand development. Next to the technical question, there must be a willingness on the part of the partners to exchange data in order to improve the process bilaterally.

To this must be added the problem of internal communication between departments that are responsible for data flowing into a forecast. The reasons can often be found in the organizational structure, insofar as different departments are directed by different areas of responsibility. In the framework of process recommendations, the various data sources of manufacturing and retailing are analyzed in order to make clear which data are necessary for the creation of a forecast.

Influences on the Creation of a Sales Forecast

The determination of demand consists of a complex relationship of logistics optimization and market-oriented measures. The many influences on the forecast throughout the supply chain characterize the long-term development of sales. A component of the process recommendation is a detailed schematic of the most important influences at each stage of the supply chain.

The consideration of all amount-relevant influences is really a theoretical illusion. A factor like the weather is nearly impossible to predict. The selection of factors that have a significant influence and the creation of systems solutions that translate these factors into the demand forecast is vital.

Detailed Creation of the Demand Forecast

Basis For all participants in the supply chain to achieve a unified definition, it is necessary to define the basis of the demand forecast. In the context of a best practices implementation, the determination should be made based on the European article number (EAN) of a trade unit. The trade unit is understood here as an amount agreed on by the trade partners that the retailer can order from the manufacturer. The following are the advantages of this approach:

- From the number of trade units, the number of consumer units can be derived.

- For planning and control of production capacity the number of trade units to be produced is necessary.

- The creation of an order forecast is made easier.

Time Line While the control of production and replenishment systems often requires considerable advance notice, order forecasts should cover a time frame of thirteen weeks.

In line with this recommendation, a realistic time line can be defined that is usable for most product mixes. This is not true for all products, obviously. Perishable goods require a considerably shorter amount of time as production and delivery systems have quicker reaction times, as determined by the nature of the product.

Amounts In the forecast, all amounts should generally be oriented to weekly net demand. In keeping with the treatment of the time frame, it can also make sense to orient to a daily basis when the planning parameters dictate.

In German-speaking economic regions, a large portion of sales runs over promotions, so the sales forecast must be accommodating. Therefore, amounts for promotions and normal sales should be represented independently.

Through this differentiation, the expecting posture of the consumer, which comes with promotions, should become more transparent not only during a promotion, but before and after the volume effect in the supply chain is apparent. The differing data sources from which amounts are determined also speak for separate representations. Exhibit 4.31 shows the most significant differences.

Rolling Actualization For high accuracy, the demand forecast cannot be static; it must reflect current market conditions. Here is where fluctuations between forecast and market should be shown. Through this approach, step 4 of the CPFR business model (recognition of exceptions) is realized. Where possible, tracking of fluctuations should be automatic so that upon recognition a manual amendment to the forecast can be made.

For the reduction of exceptions, it is necessary that the trade partners

EXHIBIT 4.31. DIFFERENCES BETWEEN NORMAL SALES AND PROMOTIONS.

Forecast for Everyday Business	Forecast for Promotional Activities
Use of historical data (time-span analysis)	Few historical data, which are seldom comparable
Future sales development can be well determined	Estimation of sales development difficult
Use of system-based forecasting possible	Unknown influences on promotion: Consumer behavior Reaction of competitors Success of advertising

define a tolerance in their joint business plan (CPFR step 2) where no manual action is necessary. Only when the threshold is crossed does a revision of the forecast become necessary.

Promotional Activities Promotions at the POS have a significant influence on the demand forecast and should be included in the forecast process. Noteworthy are:

- *Short-Term Price Reductions of More Than 5 Percent Relative to the Previous Week.* Because price is a deciding factor on anticipated demand, price information should be considered as an indicator of demand in the forecast. Especially during the promotion, high product availability at the POS is essential for the success of the promotion.
- *Product-Specific Advertising in Leaflets and Daily Newspapers.* Giving information about the advertising medium used allows one to draw conclusions about the size of the promotion.
- *Secondary Placement.* The placement of displays increases the degree of contact with the product at the POS, through which sales are increased.

These and other measures are usually done in combination with one another.

Transmission of the Forecast

Where possible, the forecast should be automatically transmitted to business partners (EDI) so that the forecast can be used without manual effort and in the in-house system. For this purpose EDIFACT Subset EANCOM® is available. For the transmission of forecasts, the EAN-COM sales forecast report is used.

The forecast can also be exchanged through Web-based procedures. At present, however, there are no general rules to ensure a standardized exchange. The necessity of Internet communication standards is, in view of e-marketplaces, a current challenge.

The management paper developed for Germany, Austria, and Switzerland as economic regions should provide a conceptual basis for creating forecasts. Access to data and the willingness of partners to change are also required.

In addition to safeguarding the results in Germany, Austria, and Switzerland, the process recommendation *Joint Forecasting* is integrated into the work of European project groups under the auspices of ECR Europe. Beyond that, the experiences of GCI are drawn upon, which has the project documentation available on its home page.

4.3.5 Conclusion

Building on the initial experiences of CPFR pilot projects in Germany/Austria/Switzerland, the CCG developed a CPFR management paper. This document gives a general overview of the structure and operation of the CPFR business model and integrates the solutions already pioneered in ECR. Additionally, there are concrete steps for the internal and external use of the CPFR philosophy. Parallel to the detailed instructions on the creation of an order forecast, the guide also contains a concrete description of an order forecast and the significance of the POS data (sales and inventory at the retail outlet level) in the CPFR business model. In describing these substantive details, the demands of the target market were considered in the guide.

To foster a better understanding, a model case for the implementation of CPFR was developed as a component of the guide. This is especially intended for companies that do not yet have any experience with CPFR. Based on a concrete project by two fictional business partners, the implementation of CPFR should be made clear.

Numerous pilots in the German-speaking market show that CPFR is not only a theory but well on the way to broad use. The road from pilot to standard practice in Germany, Austria, and Switzerland is becoming shorter. Beyond that, ECR Germany-Austria-Switzerland will continue to serve as a platform for the exchange of experience and to support CPFR through events.

4.4

CPFR Implementation at dm-drogerie markt and Henkel in Germany

Gunter Baumgart, Henkel
Dr. Birgit Ester, dm-drogerie markt
Christian Schick, dm-drogerie markt

Henkel consists of 340 companies in seventy countries, which produce more than 10,000 products. Henkel employs about 61,000 people worldwide. In Germany, Henkel is among the largest producers of consumer goods. The drugstore dm-drogerie markt (hereafter dm) has more than 1,300 outlets with 8,000 employees. The German division of dm is the second largest drugstore chain in Germany. The entire product line includes 13,000 products.

4.4.1 Development of the Collaboration Between Henkel and dm-drogerie markt

For several years, Henkel and dm have been cooperating closely at the operational level. This started in the mid-nineties with the implementation of electronic information exchange between the two companies. Initially, baseline information was exchanged through SINFOS. Thereafter, electronic ordering was done through EANCOM Format Orders, the electronic invoicing via Sedas, in Germany standard, and EANCOM Format Salesreport was used for the transmission of sales data. In 1998 continuous replenishment/vendor-managed inventory was begun based on EANCOM Format's Inventory Report.

After Henkel took over inventory control of dm's distribution center in Weilerswist, the availability of Henkel product there rose to 99.4 percent (see Exhibit 4.32). At the same time, inventory in reserve was reduced by a value of between 1.5 and 2.5 days. (see Exhibit 4.33) Deliveries by full trucks were made on an almost daily basis.

The interpretation of the individual results should be considered in light of the complexity and fragmentation of the entire replenishment process. Exhibit 4.34 shows the stages and participants in the value chain using the product Persil (laundry detergent).

In category management, there is also a high level of cooperation between Henkel and dm. Innovative placement concepts and the newest technology are being employed to work out assortment strategies. In the year 2000, dm developed, with the support of several of its suppliers, the dm Extranet. Through this system, staff at Henkel now have access to daily updated information on sales, deliveries, and inventory from dm as well as promotion planning and listing status of individual SKUs. The dm Extranet makes all relevant information immediately available for the joint business process, leading to greater transparency.

EXHIBIT 4.32. DEVELOPMENT OF SERVICE LEVELS.

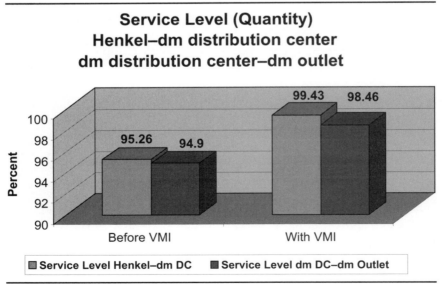

SOURCE: dm-drogerie markt.

EXHIBIT 4.33. CHANGES IN INVENTORY AFTER THE INTRODUCTION OF CRP/VMI.

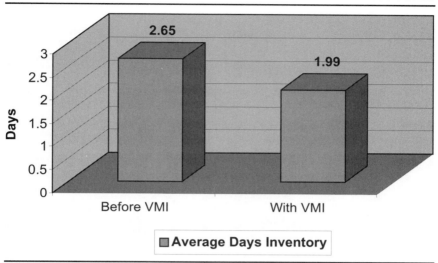

SOURCE: dm-drogerie markt.

VertiKo

The basis for the joint introduction of CPFR at Henkel and dm was, among other things, the collaboration on the research project VertiKo (vertical collaboration in the channel of distribution). At the end of 2000 both companies had begun work on this project sponsored by Germany's Federal Ministry of Education and Research. VertiKo has the objective of discerning the critical success factors for the creation of a successful cooperation between manufacturer and retailer. The results are supposed to be transferable to value-adding partnerships for their improvement. Contents of the project are all relevant complete product, data, and cash flows as well as the management relationship between the companies.

One of the first steps in the project was the completion of a jointly run SWOT (Strengths-Weaknesses-Opportunities-Threats) analysis. Everyone working at the interchange between the two companies met for a one-day workshop and paired off for SWOT analyses. At the conclusion, both viewpoints were brought together and the evaluations' similarities and differences compared.

EXHIBIT 4.34. COMPLEXITY OF THE VALUE CHAIN.

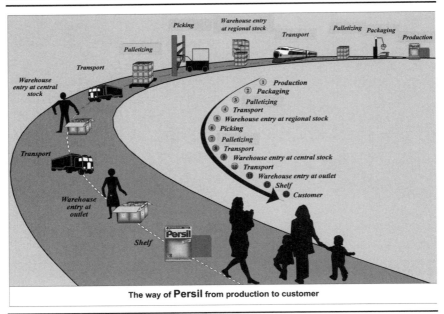

The way of **Persil** from production to customer

SOURCE: Baumgart/Bieber (2000).

One problem in the collaboration is the control of the process of product introductions and sales promotions. For parts of Henkel and dm a large information deficit and, hence, uncertainty was diagnosed. Both companies agreed with the recommendation that the entire process should be made considerably more transparent. An additional complaint on both sides was frequent delays in the process. A solution was suggested in which a common system controlled the entire process. This would include everything from order generation through promotions and the introduction of new products to performance reviews based on jointly defined indices. Such a comprehensive work flow would constantly reflect the status of the process and identify sticking points. Based on the good experience acquired with dm Extranet, the Internet was chosen for use in the pilot project.

In parallel, Henkel was jointly developing a system with other suppliers in an e-market. The system was developed using experience that Sainsbury had been accumulating at Nestlé in the United Kingdom. The central idea of this system is that events can best be controlled through a tool to which the manufacturer as well as its trading partners have access.

Henkel worked together with Nestlé and Danone on a prototype for an Internet-based work flow, which represents the information flow between the creation of a bid all the way through to the evaluation of a promotion. The system had to be tested for practicability and utility in the cooperative agreements through two pilot projects. Encouraged by the experience with dm, Henkel decided to conduct such tests. The test procedures and results are elucidated in the next chapter.

Both companies relied on the experience of their work in the CCG work groups Joint Forecasting and CPFR. Through these two forums, important foundations for a European version of CPFR were established.

The use of scanner data takes on particular significance in allowing so-called online-tracking during an actual promotion. Scanner data is compared with the forecast while a promotion or introduction is running in order to see if shortages or surpluses are to be expected. In addition to this short-term feedback loop, the information can be used strategically in the long term. This is accomplished in part through an event database where information on completed events is stored.

4.4.2 CPFR as a Further Step in the Joint Business Process

CPFR is a comprehensive model that optimizes the relationship between business partners through cooperative planning that is responsive to customers, combined with joint forecasting and improved information exchange along the supply chain. Based on a readiness to cooperate, planning, forecasting, and inventory control have been integrated into a nine-step plan.

Improvements in these areas are necessary, as they remain inefficient due to uncertainty. Up to now, companies in the supply chain have tried to optimize their processes individually. This approach leads to the following problems:

- Insufficient internal and external communication
- Different focuses in planning
- Large safety stocks resulting from missing information

CPFR is an attempt to find a complete solution. Thus, corporate boundaries are lowered to the extent that retail and manufacturing are put in the position of pursuing common objectives. Building on better relations and improvements in forecasting and planning, product availability can be increased and inventory throughout the supply chain reduced simultaneously. The benefits include increasing sales by virtue of higher customer satisfaction and cost reductions for both partners.

The C in CPFR, the collaboration, is the base for all further steps. The more pronounced the collaboration is, the higher the quality will be, and the better it will be for Planning, Forecasting, and Replenishment. Control of the collaboration is no less important for processes within a company than for those with external partners.

In the past, it was a common mistake to optimize single units and not the whole process or company. Today, many companies are restructuring their organizations to make collaboration easier in order to correct this problem. Through multifunctional process-oriented teams, collaboration in the future will become demonstrably simpler.

4.4.3 The Start of the CPFR Pilot

At the beginning of the project, it was decided who would provide which information and which common goals would be pursued. The flow of information is shown in Exhibit 4.35.

It was decided in the pilot project to send most of the data directly from Henkel to the marketplace because there was already a large, up-to-date database there, and a direct connection to the dm system or dm Extranet would have led to serious delays. Besides raising revenues through increases in product availability and the reduction of surplus at the conclusion of promotions, there were other measures to be tested:

- The synchronization of forecasting and replenishment processes
- The integration of supply and demand side
- The streamlining and standardization of communication
- The acceleration of the development of promotions
- The simplification of communication between suppliers and retailers

Exhibit 4.35. Data flow in the CPFR pilot project.

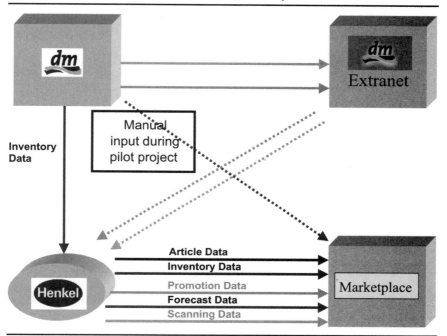

SOURCE: dm-drogerie markt.

The CPFR Work Flow in a Marketplace

The system tested in the pilot project is an Internet-supported work flow application with clearly defined phases and responsibilities, as shown in Exhibit 4.36.

Exhibit 4.37 lists who has responsibility for each step in the pilot project.

Offer Generation

The entire event process is put in motion when the key account manager enters an offer for a product introduction or promotion into the system. The manager defines the time frame for the event, chooses the appropriate products from a catalog in the system, and has the opportu-

EXHIBIT 4.36. WORK FLOW DURING THE CPFR PILOT PROJECT.

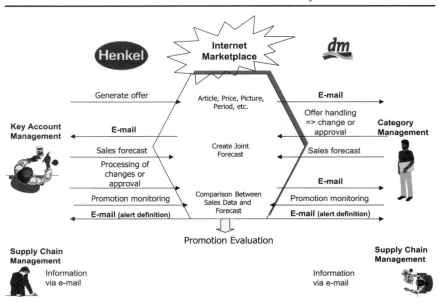

SOURCE: dm–drogerie markt.

EXHIBIT 4.37. BREAKDOWN OF RESPONSIBILITY FOR EACH PROCESS STEP.

Process Step	Responsibility
Offer generation	Key account management Henkel
Offer handling	Category management dm
Sales forecasting	Key account management Henkel/category management dm
Order forecasting	Automated
Promotion monitoring	Key account management Henkel/category management dm
Promotion evaluation	Key account management Henkel/category management dm

nity to state preferences on presentation in the outlets as well as the cost price for the retailer. It is also possible to attach supplementary information to the bid, like a picture of the product, price calculation, or a product folder. As before, initial estimates of possible sales during the event can be entered. In this step it is determined whether the further development of the bid occurs at the corporate level or through individual distribution centers. The initiator of a step can finalize it by handing it off to the next person in the work flow, canceling it, or saving it for further editing later.

Offer Handling

In the next step, the category manager at dm receives an e-mail stating that Henkel has prepared an offer on the system. Through a link in the e-mail, the manager has direct access to the bid after inputting his or her user name and password. The manager can then examine the offer, add comments, and finalize the step by accepting the offer, rejecting it, or requesting additional information.

Sales Forecasting

When both partners have agreed to run an event, the concrete planning begins. Both companies make an estimate of how much they think can be sold in which outlets. It doesn't matter which partner does this first. The step is completed when both partners agree to a forecast amount which is then translated into a percentage for each day of the week by established values already in the system.

Order Forecasting

The creation of an order forecast is a purely mathematical procedure. Based on the jointly agreed sales forecast, the size of the order is determined. The process considers existing inventories of the retailer as well as pending orders. The manufacturer then checks this value to see if it has sufficient stock or must start production to cover the demand. The earlier and more exact the forecast the manufacturer receives, the better it is able to control internal processes.

Promotion Monitoring

During a sales promotion, retail sales are compared with the forecast daily. Only in this way can product availability throughout the promotion be ensured. To utilize the recognition of an impending shortage or surplus at the end of a promotion, the supply chain must be flexible enough to accommodate fluctuations.

Promotion Evaluation

After the conclusion of a promotional event, efficiency and success are evaluated based on jointly defined indices. It is important to preserve lessons learned for application in future events. Only in this way can long-term optimization in the promotional event process be achieved.

4.4.4 Experiences from the Pilot Project and a Perspective on CPFR

The pilot project was completed at the end of October 2001. The concept and its execution have shown that the process as described is functional. It also showed that it was sensible to begin with a small scope to reduce the complexity to the lowest possible level. Likewise, it became clear that, in promotions, the discrepancies between forecasts used for production planning and actual sales could be very significant. There is still much room for improvement in their implementation.

The speed of the Internet-based system was identified as a critical factor. In comparison to intranets, the delays nullify the advantages of a work flow–based process. The participating staff agreed that the difficulties were acceptable for a test application, but that for full-scale implementation the system should be a time saver, not a time waster.

Through CPFR, and with or without the support of a work-flow tool, the network between retailing and manufacturing is growing. Beyond that, CPFR implies a closer collaboration between logistics and key account management on the manufacturing side, and assortment management on the retailing side. Through the merged planning and treatment of sales, inventory, and delivery service data, the connections of this magnitude for the overall success of an item will become apparent. Thus, a mutual understanding of the different participants in the supply chain grows, and closer coordination is the result. To that end, CPFR can be seen as a new element in the structure of ECR, which can be considered a link between the demand side and the supply side (see Exhibit 4.38).

Decisive factors in the attainment of this goal are the willingness and the determination of all participants in the supply chain, in good times and bad, to work cooperatively toward collaborative solutions.

EXHIBIT 4.38. CPFR AS A LINK BETWEEN THE DEMAND SIDE AND THE SUPPLY SIDE.

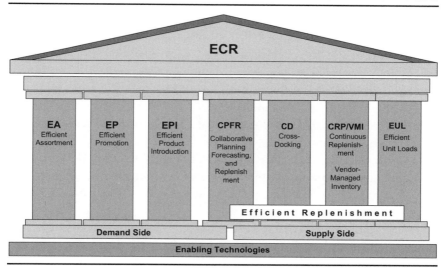

SOURCE: dm-drogerie markt/Henkel.

4.5

CPFR Implementation at dm-drogerie markt and Procter & Gamble in Germany

Christian Schick, dm-drogerie markt
Peter Hambuch, Procter & Gamble

Procter & Gamble (P&G) and dm-drogerie markt (dm) decided to carry out a CPFR pilot in Germany from May until October 2002. The pilot will follow the recommendation for the implementation of CPFR in the German-speaking economic region, which was recently published by the Centrale für Coorganisation (CCG). Both companies were actively involved in the development of the recommendation and the earlier version, *Joint Forecasting*.

In addition to following the nine steps of the CPFR model, the partners will use the preformatted templates, which are included in the CPFR recommendation, in order to document project organization, responsibilities, and work processes. The CPFR project continues the intensive and long-standing collaboration between the two partners with the mutual objective of optimizing the supply chain. For perspective, cooperation pilots were successfully managed in the past followed by broad implementation in the areas of electronic data interchange according to the EANCOM standards, vendor-managed inventory, or category management and are serving as a base for further cooperation strategies.

4.5.1 Front-End Agreement

The first step was completed with a signed front-end agreement in April 2002. The document includes:

- Committment for collaboration
- Objectives and scope of the pilot
- Corresponding effectiveness and efficiency measures

- System support and corresponding data exchange
- Necessary project support by multifunctional teams

Collaboration

Both dm and Procter & Gamble have a holistic view of the value chain (supply and demand side) and put the fulfillment of the consumers' interests at the center of their activities. By collaborating we can bundle expertise in order to further develop our business, become mutually profitable, and work jointly toward common objectives.

We are committed to making the necessary resources available to optimize business processes and support technologies, so that we improve the efficiency of the value chain and achieve profitable growth. This means we:

- Seek win–win solutions.
- Have a joint business plan in place.
- Work toward jointly defined forecast and turnover objectives.
- Treat exchanged data and information with the necessary confidentiality.
- Ensure professional project management.

Objectives and Scope

The overall objective is to ensure product availability at Procter & Gamble, from the distribution centers down to the shelf in the outlets of dm-drogerie markt for the base and promotional business via a high forecast accuracy. In particular, the objective for the promotional business was extended in a way that the remaining stocks after the promotion in the outlets should not exceed a defined maximum limit.

Both partners are also following company-specific goals:

- *dm-drogerie markt:* Via the pilot we want to find out whether it makes sense to make forecasts available for the suppliers on a broad basis so that product availability can be improved over the whole supply chain.

- *Procter & Gamble:* Many of our partners in the retail business work with merchandise-planning and control systems, which are able to generate statistical forecasts. A corresponding data exchange, based on existing EANCOM or XML standards, should bring us into position to consolidate the data in our systems and improve the forecasts for the production planning in our plants.

Measures

Key performance indicators corresponding to the objectives were chosen to measure the success of the collaboration:

- Service level from P&G to dm's distribution centers
- Service level from dm's distribution centers to the dm outlets
- Service level from the outlets to the consumers (shelf availability)
- Forecast accuracy for the promotional business
- Forecast accuracy for the base business
- Amount of remaining stock after promotions in the outlets

System Support and Data Exchange

It was agreed for the duration of the pilot that dm have online access to the Internet-based Syncra system, which is used at P&G as a collaboration tool over the whole supply chain. This includes CPFR between P&G and retailers, between P&G customer teams and the demand-planning department, which is responsible for the forecast used as a basis for production planning in the plants, and finally between plants and suppliers of raw and packaging materials. This ensures that the information on the expected demand at the POS flows through the entire chain and is available at every stage in a meaningful form.

By opening the system to a retailer for the first time, we generated for both companies an identical database enabling common considerations and evaluations. The system makes transparent the data from systems at P&G and dm, such as forecasts for the base and promotional business, P&G shipments to dm, and POS data and stock at dm. This supports an improved volume planning, tracking of plans versus actuals, and communication between the parties involved.

Common bases for data exchange are the EANCOM standards inventory report (INVRPT) and sales report (SLSRPT) as well as access to the dm Extranet.

Resources

In order to ensure a smooth project flow, both companies provide the necessary resources organized as multifunctional teams. This includes the project leaders, assortment management (buyer, account manager), enterprise resource planning (order management, customer service), and information technology.

4.5.2 Joint Business Plan

The already existing business plan was worked out in more detail for the duration of the pilot by the team members responsible for assortment management. In particular, the agreements for the promotional business accommodate the objectives of the project with regard to forecast accuracy, product availability, and the problem of remaining stock in the outlets after the promotion.

Three promotions on Pampers Jumbopacks, each with a two-week duration, will take place during the project. Jumbopacks are part of the ongoing assortment of the dm 2001 outlets, but are not carried at the dm classic outlets, although the classic outlets are allowed to participate at the promotions. In general dm differentiates among three types of outlets of which two are involved in the project.

Outlet Type: 2001 Outlets

These outlets are usually located in industrial parks or at the borders of the cities, in most cases as direct neighbors of well-known discounters. The surface area typically varies between 600 and 800 square meters. This outlet type has more selling space available than classic outlets to present the assortment to the consumer, with deeper shelves and more space to carry larger stock. The availability of free parking lots facilitates the purchasing of products with larger dimensions; thus, for example, the baby category has a significantly higher turnover compared with the classic outlet type. Some SKUs are sold only at this outlet type. The share of 2001 outlets amounts to about 20 percent at dm-drogerie markt.

Outlet Type: Classic Outlets

Classic outlets are located in near or directly in pedestrian areas. This outlet type has an average footprint of 400 to 600 square meters, smaller than the 2001 outlets, and therefore requires different operations. In particular, a more precise assortment management, a more frequent delivery cycle, and a continuous shelf replenishment are needed. The share of classic outlets amounts to about 80 percent at dm-drogerie markt. Exhibit 4.39 lists planning factors by outlet type.

It was agreed to run the volume-planning process for the first promotion according to the current procedure. Process steps will be modified toward objectives based on results and learning experiences.

4.5.3 Exchange of Forecasts and Management of Critical Exceptions

Both partners agreed to not exchange sales forecasts but to focus on order forecasts, which are loaded into the Syncra system. This doesn't mean that sales forecasts are completely out of consideration. The order forecast, particularly for the promotional business, is based on the corresponding sales forecast, which is generated by each partner according to its specific assumptions. Jointly defined were the tolerance limits for critical exceptions. A critical exception occurs if the comparison of both

EXHIBIT 4.39. PLANNING FACTORS BY OUTLET TYPE.

	dm 2001 outlet	*dm* Classic outlet
Sales history available	Yes	No
Forecast generation	Easier	More difficult
Probability of out-of-stocks during promotions	Lower	Higher
Problem of high remaining stock after promotions	Lower	Higher

SOURCE: dm-drogerie markt/Procter & Gamble.

forecasts results in a value outside of the agreed bandwidths. A joint solution will be managed according to the agreed-on work process.

Exhibit 4.40 clarifies the process for the base business.

EXHIBIT 4.40. CPFR PROCESS USED FOR ORDER FORECASTS.

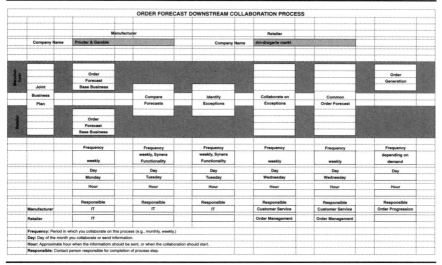

SOURCE: dm-drogerie markt/Procter & Gamble.

(Names of the responsible team members were replaced in the diagram by their functions.)

Promotional Business

Team members from assortment management (buyer, account manager) are responsible for data entry and exception management on both sides. Forecasts for promotional volumes will be exchanged about thirteen weeks in advance of the promotion and will be modified based on more recent insights, about two weeks before the promotion, when the final orders on outlet level are available. Unlike with the base business, we limit the exchange of forecasts for promotions to Pampers Jumbopacks.

Base Business

We exchange forecasts for all P&G SKUs carried in dm's outlets from the fabric and home care, health and beauty care, and paper categories.

The team members from enterprise resource management (dm order management, P&G customer service) are responsible for data flow and exception management:

- We exchange order forecasts on EAN level (shipping unit) weekly over a rolling thirteen-week horizon.
- dm generates a statistical forecast in SAP R/3 Retail using a trend model.
- P&G generates a forecast based on dm's distribution center offtake numbers adjusted by promotional volumes.

Exhibit 4.41 shows the forecasts of both partners for one variant of the Pampers Jumbopacks. Forecasts for the base business are very close together, while the values for the promotion vary but are still within the agreed bandwidth, which is effective thirteen weeks in advance of the promotion.

EXHIBIT 4.41. CPFR FORECAST ANALYSIS.

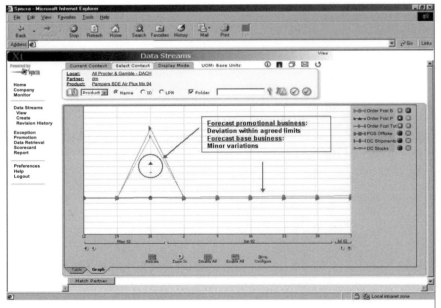

SOURCE: dm-drogerie markt/Procter & Gamble.

The forecasts of both partners are compared with Syncra's "exception reporting" functionality. In case of a critical exception both partners automatically receive an e-mail alert with an Internet link leading directly to the exception. The responsible team members take the necessary steps according to the agreed-on work process in order to start the collaboration on exceptions and come to a common forecast.

4.5.4 Order Generation

The orders for the base business are generated at P&G according to the VMI cooperation, based on the daily exchanged EANCOM inventory report (INVRPT) and the VMI system used at P&G. If necessary, orders are complemented by promotional volumes, which are ordered by dm separately.

4.5.5 CPFR—A Learning Process: Evaluation of Test Results

The results will be measured continuously during the pilot. The data needed either come from the project partners' systems or will be collected in-store from a defined panel of dm 2001 and dm classic outlets:

- Service level from P&G to dm's DC: weekly data out of P&G's order management system
- Service level from dm's DC to dm's outlets: weekly data out of dm's SAP R/3 Retail
- Service level from the outlets to the consumer (shelf availability): store checks during the promotions completed by outlet-specific offtake and stock data out of dm's data warehouse
- Forecast accuracy: weekly data via Syncra's scorecard functionality comparing forecasts with actuals
- Remaining stock after promotions at outlet level: store checks the day after the end of the promotion

We hope to learn more through field work during promotions in order to improve the volume-planning process so that from a consumer's point of view no out-of-stocks occur and from an outlet point of view a minimum of stocks remain after the promotion. This evaluation should show, on one hand, the success of the project regarding forecast accuracy and service levels and should deliver, on the other, additional insights for the further intensification of the collaboration between dm-drogerie markt and Procter & Gamble.

4.6

CPFR Implementation at Londis in Great Britain

Donald P. Brenchley, JDA Software

In this pioneering collaborative replenishment initiative led jointly by the British retailer Londis and the software company E3 (now JDA Software Group), the different partners in the supply chain were drawn together into one group. It has been the solution provider E3 that has helped to integrate Londis Holdings Ltd. (annual revenue: £500) and nineteen important suppliers in such a way that retailer as well as supplier could profit from their mutual know-how. This successful initiative shows mutual advantages, which can be achieved by a cooperation of trading partners within the supply chain.

4.6.1 The Business Problem and How It Was Solved

Like all retailers, Londis faces intense competitive pressure in the British food retail market and is looking for new possibilities to optimize the flow of goods along the whole supply chain. The company also wants to sustain good supply capabilities to ensure continued customer loyalty and to win new customers.

Method of Resolution

This initiative is based on the development of strategic partnerships with the supplier around common and open real-time access to a database of the special software E3TRIM for forecasting and inventory management of central warehouses. The initiative is managed by a steering committee and the precise goals of this project have been determined after consultations with the Londis inventory analysts:

- Increased product availability
- Customization of warehousing to the supply possibilities of retail shops
- Reduced stocks and returns
- More efficient marketing and promotional campaigns
- More revenue and profit
- Fewer lost sales

These concrete goals require a widespread strategic relationship between the trade partners. This project is based not only on the relations between two partners, but also on a large amount of interaction between the many participants, ensuring that suppliers can learn from each other.

This approach, up until now unique, has led to the development of an "e-collaboration community" that consists of Londis employees and suppliers and inventory management experts from E3. Producers have remote access to their respective segment of the Londis database and the use of the full functionality of the E3 application. Using the replenishment and inventory management software E3TRIM, suppliers have secure and open access to the information their retailers need for the order process, as well as access to all of the system functions, which makes a "perfect order" possible. We are focusing on all the factors that determine inventory and supply possibilities: promotions, product introductions, and product retirements. E3TRIM helps the supplier realize much more quickly which sales have taken place and determine the optimal amount of the expected order with the real-time data knowledge while eliminating the costs associated with poor data integrity and misunderstandings.

Result

The Londis/E3 project has shown that such a concept offers concrete advantages for all participants, as all trade partners will profit from a higher transparency of the supply chain. This will result in specific advantages for suppliers, Londis, and consumers.

4.6.2 Advantages for Suppliers

"Better communication and the possibility to exchange data now makes it possible to react faster and easier to our clients' demands. The analyzed data deliver clear demand patterns and trade will face much less problems. Our level of service is much higher than ever before."

—Ian Bullivant, Interbrew, Londis supplier

Suppliers gained the following advantages:

- Greater ability to supply: average improvement in supply abilities of 0.5 percent
- Smaller inventories: average reduction in inventories of 13.75 percent
- Shorter order times: average reduction in order times of 6.25 percent
- Better access to store inventories
- Simpler introduction of products and marketing campaigns
- Simplified control and evaluation of marketing campaigns
- The status of preferred supplier
- Higher transparency of the range of products
- Streamlining of the company through participation in an e-collaboration project

4.6.3 Advantages for Londis

"The order times have been reduced by around 40 to 60 percent. So, in some cases we are noticeably faster than other chains."

—Martyn Harvey, purchasing director, Londis, July 2000

Londis gained the following advantages:

- Improved supply: Today the ability to deliver is around 98.5 percent, an improvement of 3 percent.
- Reduced inventories: According to estimates by Londis, inventory could be reduced by 10 to 20 percent.
- Shorter order times: Correspondingly, the time for inventory management could be reduced by about 90 percent.
- Better control and evaluation of marketing campaigns.
- More coordinated approach of suppliers/manufacturers.
- Better utilization of shelf stocks.
- Expansion of commercial relationships and increased income on transportation and return cargo.
- Reduced minimum–order amounts without an increase in the costs for sold products.

4.6.4 Advantages for the Consumer

Two important advantages for the consumer were highlighted: a higher availability on all shelves and a wider choice of products.

Increasing the availability (grade of service) on the shelves is the result of an improved prognosis. The constant dialogue between the steering retailer, supplier, and JDA is the basis for responsiveness. By monitoring the promotions process, Londis and the respective supplier can ensure that the availability of promotional items in the outlet is coordinated with the campaigns.

Reducing inventory makes it possible to expand the range of products. Having monitored the conditions of purchase, the costs for the sold products could be reduced.

4.6.5 Conclusion and Perspective

In our case study, the participating project parties were willing to accept the necessary disclosure of their data. The participants realized the value of an improved flow of information and therefore could take advantage of the opportunity to add value. Members of the different teams were very dedicated in taking action, often more than they had ever intended, and in coordinating different skills and experiences, to promote organizational and operational modifications. E-collaboration as a new competitive concept will lead to a new evaluation of client and supplier processes.

So far e-collaboration has concentrated on improving business processes at the interface between the participating companies. This concept starts at the physical interface between trade and industry—the distribution center. If the cooperation in this area leads to results, there will be a new basis for cooperation, and the traditional separation of process responsibilities will become less and less important.

So, it is most likely that manufacturers will increasingly become involved in the responsibilities that traditionally were thought of as retailer areas, such as category and in-store merchandising, decision making on item presentation and weighting of categories, assortment recommendations on location, and the analysis of consumer behavior at different points of sale. At the same time, retailers will become more and more involved in areas traditionally belonging to manufacturers, and by this, influence the availability of final products, production, and the selection of presuppliers.

E-collaboration begins where already established processes exist. The second step is to reduce costs during production by using existing data. Priorities during production have to be rethought, and participants must apply standards for economical production. In the last step, we focus on the increase in sales: Weak spots in the supply chain are eliminated, and consumer data are analyzed and monitored. This approach permits all participants to respond very quickly by fitting products to more and more specific client demand. Flexibility of supply processes will lead to variable order quantities, allowing for more efficient planning and making it possible to respond to short-term demand fluctuations.

E-collaboration can lead to success: He who succeeds in reducing the width of processes in the supply chain and who at the same time succeeds in gaining more information will prevail in his sector and in the long run will extend his leading position. How successful this cooperation will be ultimately depends upon maintaining a correct balance of competence. Working as partners demands certain social capabilities of all participants and the willingness to think beyond the limits of one's own company.

In the end, the performance of a company can always be measured by the quality of its supply chain relations. In other words: Those companies that do not take advantage of the enormous potential offered by cooperation along the supply chain make a decisive mistake. Or, to say it in a positive way: The one that cares about relationships and cooperates with suppliers smooths the way to success in the trade of tomorrow.

4.7

CPFR Implementation at Henkel Spain

Sergio Duque, Henkel Spain
Esteban Garriga, Henkel Spain
Hans Teuscher, Accenture Spain

Henkel has had a very close relationship with supply chain initiatives during the last few years. Henkel has become deeply involved in different ECR work groups in order to share experiences and knowledge. CPFR has been one of these initiatives. CPFR, a cross-industry initiative designed to improve the supplier/manufacturer/retailer relationship, works through comanaged planning processes and shared information and builds on the concepts of ECR and demand planning through a structured approach to closer collaboration among value chain partners.

The implementation of CPFR processes at Henkel Spain has gone through different stages recently. It started with the implementation of a new demand-planning system, a CPFR pilot initiative (Henkel-Eroski) thereafter, and the evaluation of the results of this initiative in a business case in order to consider implementation with other partners of Henkel. The experience was then used in another pilot implementation (Henkel-Condis), which incorporates upstream processes. In the meantime, some internal procedures have already felt the impact of the collaborative approach.

The collaboration allows the companies to redefine the planning processes in order to broaden their horizons. The global process to integrate all the actors of the supply chain is structured as follows:

- Forecast generation: To generate an accurate forecast, collaboration is a key factor.
- This collaboration allows the manufacturer to integrate the knowledge of the distributor and in addition to fostering consistency in promotional communication, it allows the companies to achieve higher accuracy in their forecasts.
- A broader horizon of production planning is achieved through collaboration, which provides the manufacturer with the opportunity to collaborate with suppliers, especially with the suppliers of the critical materials.

Exhibit 4.42 highlights the different processes addressed in this last initiative that integrate all the actors in the supply chain.

So far the experience has been entirely positive, and the organization has experienced both the benefits and the initial difficulties of implementing CPFR.

EXHIBIT 4.42. GLOBAL PROCESS MAP.

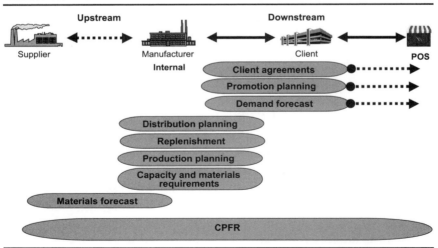

SOURCE: Henkel Spain/Accenture.

4.7.1 New Demand-Planning System

The first stage was the implementation and the integration of a new demand-planning system. Recognizing that the basis for successful CPFR is a high-quality internal forecast of the trading partners, Henkel decided to focus first internally before setting out to collaborate externally on demand planning. The demand-planning system is of particular importance, because the uncertainty in future demand is translated into inefficiencies in:

- Production (higher costs)
- High level of inventory
- Out-of-stocks, which consequently generate dissatisfaction among retailers and consumers
- Inefficiencies in logistics

The first step in implementing this new demand-planning system was to assess the initial situation, the current inefficiencies and their consequences. The main features of the initial situation were:

- Lack of a (technical) system in order to support demand forecasting
- No integration of a continuous replenishment program (CRP) in the forecast
- Increased Henkel assortment complexity
- No communication of events and knowledge of factors that influence the forecast

The consequences of that situation were:

- Costs associated with high inventories and a high number of changes in production planning
- Low service level, which generated the dissatisfaction of retailer/consumers and a high number of out-of-stocks

Project Objectives and Implementation Plan

Considering the issues mentioned above, several project objectives were established:

- Improve service level to retailer and consumer:

    Avoid internal inefficiencies: out-of-stocks, invoicing complaints, delivery mistakes, etc.

    Reduce point of sale (POS) out-of-stocks and lost sales.

    Improve Henkel's service to CRP/VMI retailers.

- Eliminate/reduce inefficiencies in the supply chain:

    Increase the demand forecasting accuracy.

    Synchronize forecasting with production.

    Integrate of the supply chain: purchasing and distribution.

- Support Henkel's management and enhance retailers' loyalty:

    Provide useful information from "demand management tool" to such areas as sales and marketing.

    Identify activities that offer advantages to retailers (CPFR).

In pursuit of the objectives defined, Henkel developed an implementation plan that was composed of these steps:

- Implement a demand-planning tool based on statistical models, which will allow Henkel to obtain more accurate demand forecasts.
- Develop adequate internal information flows in order to obtain more accurate forecasts.
- Integrate the efforts and establish information flows between sales, marketing, production, and distribution.
- Integrate the CRP management in the demand-forecasting process.

The project focused on two areas for improvement: the integration of a new demand-planning system and the reengineering of business processes.

Another important issue that the company analyzed was the complexity of the business. On the one hand, as the number of SKUs at Henkel increases, the volume per reference decreases. This leads to a significant increase in complexity in the management of the supply chain. On the other hand, the retailer structure becomes ever more complex.

As part of the implementation of the demand-planning system, the demand-planning processes were redefined as highlighted in Exhibit 4.43. At each stage of the process, the involved actors were identified and their roles and responsibilities and the key performance indicators (KPIs) defined. This involved both modules from Manugistics, the Demand-Planning Extended Edition (DPEE) and the Distribution Requirement Planning (DRP), in other words, the whole process, in which the forecast is the key input.

The main KPIs defined were related to forecast accuracy and to promotion planning. Henkel developed a fulfillment analysis tool that took into account:

- The planning and modification horizon
- The promotional volume within planning and modification
- Follow-up of Henkel's internal process of communication

Henkel defined an event plan with the objective that all of those in a position of responsibility from the different areas of the supply chain

Exhibit 4.43. Demand–planning process.

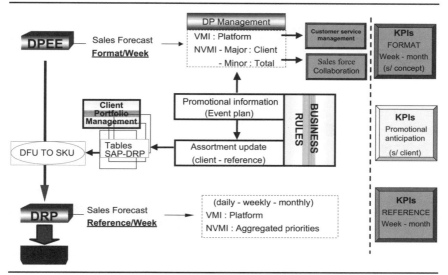

Source: Henkel Spain/Accenture.

collaborate and plan jointly the scheduling of such events as retailer and product promotions.

Due to the structure and complexity of Henkel's activities, assortment, and the market, there are many events that affect sales. However, only a few of these events are crucial for the performance of the business. Henkel also defined the DRP processes in which the forecast is the main input to the demand forecast unit (DFU) to stock-keeping unit (SKU) process. These efforts led to a considerable improvement in forecast accuracy within Henkel Spain.

The demand-planning tool implemented provides 95 percent of the total forecast at Henkel, as shown in Exhibit 4.44, with the remaining input being the latest information from marketing and sales and on assortments. Controlling, adjusting, and reviewing are the last steps in the demand-planning process.

In order to implement this new demand-planning system, Henkel analyzed information flows, procedures, organizational models, and the involved resources, tasks, and departments. The information flows among the departments were defined and established in order to avoid inefficiencies and communication problems.

The procedures and responsibilities of demand planning were defined at different levels:

EXHIBIT 4.44. THE LAST STEP IN THE DEMAND-PLANNING PROCESS.

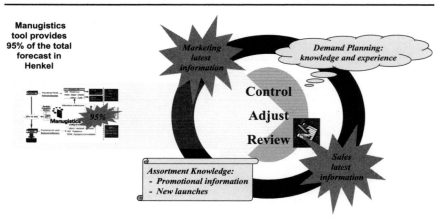

SOURCE: Henkel Spain/Accenture.

- Annual procedures:

  Forecast the demand for the following year.

  Produce forecasts for the marketing plan.

  Produce forecasts for the sales plan.

- Monthly procedures:

  Elaborate the demand forecasts for the next four months.

  Input on sales: Sales forecast for each large customer. Sales forecast for each VMI customer. Ad-hoc activities for each customer: that is, dates, products, volume, and delivery dates.

  Output: Monthly forecasts at product/format/SKU level. Detachment per week in the current month. Detachment per month in months $n + 1/n + 2$. Reporting to: top management, marketing, sales, production, trade marketing.

- Weekly procedures:

  Check the forecast of the month. See if it fits the monthly forecasts, correct if necessary.

  Analysis of deviations, specific promotions, problems (production, purchases, distribution).

  Output: Modification of the monthly forecast and detachment per week.

Demand-Forecasting Model

The company continued to generate a demand-forecasting model. The steps were:

- Design demand-forecasting model based on:

  Henkel's activities and requirements

  Specifications/functions of software available from Manugistics

- Identify, gather, and load of data into the software:

  Definition of data based on the model (sales, stocks, etc. from specific retailers, Henkel)

  Validation and cleansing of data (history)

Designing automated interfaces to introduce data from existing IT systems (CRP, SAP, etc.) into the software

- Define crucial information for the demand-planning model designed:

  Identify qualitative and quantitative inputs, retailer promotions, new product introductions, etc.

  Reengineer the business process and work-flow communications.

The differences and benefits obtained with the new demand-forecasting model were very important:

- In the past, the forecast was generated at monthly and reference levels. After the new demand-forecasting model implementation, it was generated at different levels—yearly, monthly, and weekly and always per reference. The amount of information used to generate the forecast was larger, and different inputs were provided from all departments involved.

- Henkel went from a bimonthly revision of the forecast to a weekly revision with daily adjustments.

- The method of calculation went from lineal to one that is based on the Lewandosky and Winters Series.

- The amount of data processed increased considerably, from 12,000 information units to 30,000,000 data.

- Previously staff spent 60 percent of their time processing data and 40 percent analyzing and managing. This distribution of time changed considerably, with 80 percent of their time now invested in analysis and management and 20 percent spent on data processing.

Henkel decided to implement the Manugistics demand-planning tool within the organization. This decision-support tool provided the required elements for planning supply, manufacturing, distribution, and sales and the integration of the supply chain. A demand-planning roadmap for the implementation of the tool was developed consisting of the following elements:

- Definition of the structure of the information
- Loading of the information from the last two years
- Selection and preparation of historical information
- Definition of the statistical model
- Incorporation of future events into the model
- Demand forecast

Furthermore, a continuous replenishment process implementation plan was developed covering the following:

- Training of a customer service team responsible for the forecast module (DPEE), the replenishment modules (DRP), and the interfaces and value-added tools implemented
- Communication to retailers about the objectives, potential benefits, tasks, roles and responsibilities, and critical processes
- Generation of first orders and change of IT interfaces
- Ensuring process performance
- Review and analysis of the objectives

Job Descriptions and Responsibilities

Henkel developed job descriptions for the staff involved in the processes, including their profiles, their competencies, and their requirements. The different players involved and their responsibilities were:

1. Demand manager
   - Responsibilities: This person is the owner of the process of integrated planning. He or she guarantees the process and the procedures defined for the demand planning and is responsible for the definition and collection of the information defined from the different areas involved. The demand manager elaborates the forecasts at area/format/SKU levels; follows up on the events and the impact per event; communicates the forecasts and their review to production planning; develops the definition and the control of the KPIs of the demand planning; and

checks the parameters of security stocks, service level, and costs.
- Competencies and requirements:
    Human resources management
    Analytical thinking
    Teamwork- and cooperation-oriented
    Knowledge of Manugistics tool
    Excellent knowledge of SBUs and SKUs

2. Customer services manager
   - Responsibilities: Elaborates the monthly forecast per retailer/ group level with Manugistics (VMI, Major VMI, and total Minor). Is responsible for the establishment of the CRP process and of order generation by retailer and ensures system performance and defines CRP retailer replenishment.
   - Competencies and requirements:
       Retailer orientation
       People management
       Excellent knowledge of SBUs and SKUs and retailer
       Knowledge of Manugistics tool
       Familiarity with management and control tools in processes related to the retailer

3. Production planner
   - Responsibilities: Elaborates the weekly manufacturing plan and the programs of the factories, coordinates the plan with the factory and the suppliers, and reviews the exceptions. He or she is the representative of and link with the factory and communicates the availability of products.
   - Competencies and requirements:
       Results oriented, team worker, and flexible
       Excellent knowledge of SBUs and SKUs
       Excellent knowledge of Henkel factories
       Ability to coordinate internal manufacturers

Henkel developed a matrix of responsibilities of the different processes, with different roles such as executor, consultant, and informer.

4.7.2 CPFR Pilot—Henkel and Eroski

Despite the complexity of the demand-planning system, the accuracy of the forecast was not sufficient. We realized that some final demand information had been lost. The manufacturers' drivers of the forecast are not the same as those of the retailers' (see Exhibit 4.45).

The first initiative after the implementation of this new demand-planning system was to develop a CPFR pilot with one of the most important retailers for Henkel Spain, Eroski, a Spanish retailer. This case study was one of the first European pilots to follow the CPFR process. The special aspect of the CPFR program developed by Henkel and Eroski lies in the willingness of both companies to harmonize their procedures of cooperation.

Eroski is a food-retail industry leader in Spain. The company was founded in 1969 and comprises an integrated net of 47 hypermarkets, 800 supermarkets, and 2,000 minimarkets. Its main domain is in the Basque Country, but Eroski is also present in France with 3 hypermarkets and 17 supermarkets. The group employs 23,300 people and achieves a turnover of 4,208 million euros.

Out-of-stocks in the hypermarkets revealed major shortcomings. Out-of-stocks were frequent for a number of articles (90 percent promotional). Customer service was also unsatisfactory at the central warehouse of Eroski, where products were not always delivered on time due to lack of visibility. The two companies decided to unify their attempts in order to improve their sales forecasts. The acquisition of the Demand-Planning (DP) module (Manugistics) by Henkel and the change of integrated planning processes in the supply chain were the first steps to put CPFR into place at Henkel and Eroski.

Henkel and Eroski started a CPFR pilot. All phases of the CPFR

EXHIBIT 4.45. FORECAST DRIVERS.

Manufacturer Forecast Drivers	Retailer Forecast Drivers
• Shipments • Order lead time • Capacity • Product availability • Promotions • Raw materials supply	• Consumer demand visibility • In-stock position • Shipment variance • Promotional activity • Growth plans • Distributor structure

SOURCE: Henkel Spain/Accenture.

process were put into place according to a scenario in which Henkel bore the sole responsibility for providing the forecast, calculating demand, and creating orders.

Objectives of the Pilot

The objectives of the pilot, through harmonization and improvement of the cooperation procedures, were:

- To improve customer service
- To reduce lost sales
- To increase stock turnover
- To improve punctuality of deliveries
- To reduce time required for the order cycle

Scope

All Henkel detergent products at Eroski were part of the project between the central warehouses of both Henkel and Eroski. The data exchanged were:

- Outgoing stock (once per day)
- Stock figures (once per day)
- Events calendar (once every four months)
- Sales forecasts (every fifteen days)
- Order forecasts (once per week)
- Orders (calculated once per day)

Technology Used

The data exchange is based on EANCOM standards for all messages, INVRPT, ORDERS, and INVOICES. No standard was established to transmit sales forecasts and order forecasts.

Performance Indicators

Some KPIs were defined by Henkel and Eroski, such as customer service at the central warehouse, number of out-of-stocks, number of promotions, stock rotation, full truck, full pallet, and number of urgent orders.

Resources

The multifunctional project team consisted of five employees at Henkel: one project leader, one person responsible for ECR, the key account manager of Eroski, one demand-planning expert, and one consultant from Manugistics. Four people were involved at Eroski: one project leader, one forecaster, one supplier, and one logistician.

In addition, the project relied on the external support of Accenture. As in all CPFR initiatives at Henkel Spain, Accenture helped to define the scope and the strategy for the future expansion of CPFR (rollout).

Methodology

One of the challenges of implementing CPFR was the integration of customer service representatives in the process of sales-forecasting generation due to their extensive knowledge of the retailer, especially products and promotions. After the implementation of the Demand-Planning and DRP modules from Manugistics, the project started with the central warehouse of Eroski.

The experience gained during the pilot implementation allowed Henkel to improve forecast accuracy and order generation (DRP). There were also changes to the promotion-planning process, such as new information flows, and changes in the forecasting processes, such as involving customer services in the forecasting process.

The experience with this pilot revealed the relevance of CPFR for the collaboration of commercial and operational planning. Controlled by both partners, the process helps to achieve the objective of increased sales forecast accuracy, improved customer service levels, reduced stock levels, and increased sales.

Each company tried to improve its demand reliability in order to improve internal processes and relationships with its retailers. CPFR formalizes this approach and shows how important it is to enter good quality data into systems. The internal collaboration of the sales force is also a crucial element of success.

CPFR will reach the next phase through the integration of points of sale in the future. At first, the data were gathered at the central warehouse of Eroski. Currently, the parties are working to directly include the data from the points of sale, reflecting the real demand of consumers.

4.7.3 Development of a CPFR Business Case

Once this new system was integrated and Henkel gained experience with its first pilot, the next step was to analyze the CPFR environment, its characteristics, requirements, current situation, and potential benefits that would allow Henkel to make a decision regarding the initiation of other pilots with different partners. For this reason, Henkel Spain developed a CPFR business case.

Analysis of the Background

CPFR means the cooperation of intercompany and intracompany retailers in the following processes:

- Collaboration in planning promotions and special events
- Collaboration in sales forecast values
- Collaboration in proposed orders

It must be borne in mind that the implementation of CPFR requires an important technological step forward. The major objectives of implementing CPFR were:

- Increased sales:
    Reduction of out-of-stocks
    Increased promotional activity
- Increased profitability:
    Reduction of coverage levels
- Reduction of supply chain costs:
    Optimization of promotion planning
    Integration of point-of-sale information

- Process alignment:

    Single joint forecast

    Process improvement and automation

Henkel analyzed the value and the difficulty of CPFR compared with other major initiatives (see Exhibit 4.46).

Objectives of the CPFR Business Case

The major objectives of the business case were to:

- Define alternative CPFR models in alignment with retailers' characteristics and their potential for collaboration:

    Basic CPFR: for example, just with the sales force

    Medium CPFR: for example, internally and with retailers on sales and inventory reports

    Advanced CPFR: for example, automation of forecasts and retailer orders

EXHIBIT 4.46. CPFR COMPARED WITH OTHER MAJOR INITIATIVES.

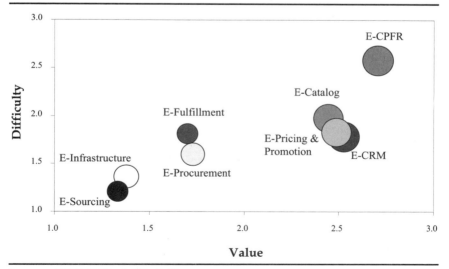

SOURCE: AECOC/Henkel Spain/Accenture.

Very Advanced CPFR: for example, promotion information and planning at point-of-sale level

- Segment retailers in alignment with their CPFR cooperation potential.
- Define the CPFR processes based on the nine-step model.
- Evaluate technological solutions in the short term and integrate them with existing HIBSA systems (e.g., SAP, Manugistics DPEE, Infoservice).
- Evaluate CPFR costs and benefits in view of their impact on the Henkel value chain with retailers, depending on the models. Seek not only quantitative benefits but also qualitative.
- Define the approach priority (retailers, CPFR models, and solutions).
- Analyze the current situation of CPFR in Spain and Europe.
- Propose an action plan taking into account short- and medium-term solutions.
- Roll out in the rest of Europe.

Definition of the CPFR Models

In order to classify the Henkel retailers in groups depending on their collaborative features, CPFR models were defined according to the type of retailer, the potential for collaboration, and the technological and information level:

- Major components in CPFR models:
  Promotion planning through EVENT PLAN
  Retailer promotions
  Chain promotions
  Product promotions
- Generation of forecasts in the Manugistics DP from:
  Henkel output
  Platform output
  Consolidated POS output

- Introduction of event effects and their description in DP
- Order generation in Manugistics DRP from:
  DPEE forecasts
  Platform stocks
  Consolidated POS stocks
- Capacity for retailers to make and send forecasts, shipments, and inventory data
- Collaboration on, and validation of, the forecasts in the collaboration tool:
  Sales, Demand Manager, CS
  Retailers

The establishment of the anticipation of collaboration is a basic point in the agreements.

The classification of the CPFR models as basic, medium, advanced, and very advanced was done according to:

- Type of retailer—classification of retailers according to their replenishment mode with Henkel: CRP Pull, CRP Push, No CRP Pull, No CRP Push
- Scope of collaboration in the processes, the interlocutor in each process
- Technological level of the retailer:
  Capacity of the retailer to send computerized shipments and inventories
  Capacity of the retailer to make and send computerized forecasts
- Information level: the level at which the retailer provides information
- Platform level
- POS level

Henkel classified the retailers into four models:

- *Basic.* The retailers included in this model are those with which no collaboration exists and which do not send any information on shipments or inventory levels. Collaboration is done internally (customer services, sales, demand planning).

- *Medium.* Retailers that provide information on shipments and inventory at platform level. Either they collaborate manually with forecast values or collaboration exists only within Henkel's internal departments.
- *Advanced.* Those retailers that collaborate and that are sufficiently developed technologically to be able to generate forecasts and send them automatically.
- *Very Advanced.* Includes those retailers that, in addition to collaborating and sending forecasts, provide information on POSs and inventories.

A preliminary assignment of retailers to the models was made. The objective was to segment retailers according to their potential for providing information on shipments, forecasts, and orders and their potential for changing their replenishment method. From this first analysis, we identified the retailers best positioned to implement CPFR: Carrefour, Eroski, and Condis.

An exhaustive definition of the processes related to the nine-step model was developed for each of the models.

Potential Benefits

The potential quantitative and qualitative benefits of applying the different CPFR models were evaluated, especially Basic CPFR and the Very Advanced CPFR, for four of our retailers, which represented approximately 30 percent of total sales. These potential qualitative benefits were:

- Increase in sales volume through:
    Reduction in out-of-stocks in stores
    Improvement in service
    Reduction of inventory on platform
- Reduction in distribution costs through:
    Improvement in production planning

Improvement in transport resource planning and utilization

- Reduction in material purchasing costs through:
  Anticipation in material purchase planning
- Reduction in marketing costs
- Better knowledge of market behavior (end consumers)
- Improvements in company image in the market

Technological Solutions

Henkel Spain analyzed the possible tools to implement CPFR, taking into account the requirements needed and the level of collaboration that we would be able to achieve. For instance, we evaluated data inputs and outputs, their collaborative components, the exception alerts, the exception resolution, the graphs, and their costs.

The conclusion was that the tools studied were oriented either toward promotion planning or collaboration in the demand forecast values. None covered both processes simultaneously. Different market-places then started offering CPFR functionality and requirements. Henkel as a direct member of one of these marketplaces made the decision to test two tools. In the meantime, it was decided to develop internal work-flow tools for the implementation of the pilots. The decision was to implement an internal tool that:

- Covers collaboration in promotion planning (Event Plan) and collaboration in demand forecast values and potentially orders and stocks
- Creates a work flow, inserting the tasks to be performed on the desktop of the persons involved in said tasks
- Uses standard protocols and development tools in the Internet environment
- Allows easy incorporation of the tool in a marketplace, whether it be the Spanish Commercial Codification Association (AECOC) or a Henkel-supported marketplace at the European level

CPFR in Europe

Furthermore, in April 2000 Henkel analyzed, with the support of Accenture, the situation of CPFR in Spain and Europe highlighted in

Exhibit 4.47 (as part of a larger study regarding the situation of B2B practices in Europe).

The most suitable levels of the potential application of CPFR varied depending on the countries studied. This was due to the differing number of retailers, the coverage level, the amount of promotional activity, and so on. The conclusion was that the best options for applying CPFR in Spain were Basic or Medium, depending on the retailers selected, in view of the market environment.

Another important conclusion of the business case was that the implementation should be in phases, starting with the collaboration with internal retailers and continuing with the adaptation of the implementation of processes to each retailer in accordance with its technology and capacity for providing information.

Three phases were defined for implementation:

- Phase 0: Collaboration with the retailer in bringing forward processes and agreements. The retailer provides all the necessary information and plans promotions sooner. Henkel makes forecasts and orders, giving the retailer access to these data.

EXHIBIT 4.47. LEVELS OF CPFR DEVELOPMENT.

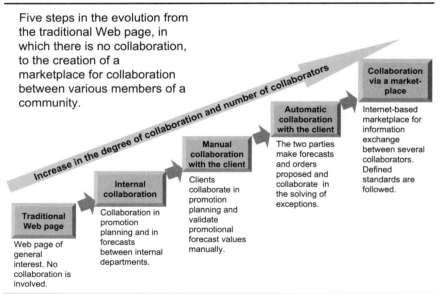

SOURCE: Henkel Spain/Accenture.

- Phase 1: Collaboration with the retailer in bringing forward processes, on agreements, and in forecast values. The retailer also makes the forecasts, thus collaborating in its values and in solving the exceptions. Henkel fills orders based on the agreed-upon forecast and gives the retailer visibility.

- Phase 2: Collaboration in all processes. Orders proposed by both parties are compared and a unique joint order is generated.

Basic Requirements

The basic requirements identified in the business case for applying CPFR were:

- Functional requirements: collaboration in the following processes with a minimum horizon of four weeks
- Promotion planning
- Forecast value
- Alignment of assortment
- Technical requirements
- Retailer's capacity to send information:

    Inventory and sales report—must be capable of automatically sending outputs and inventories and/or POSs on a daily basis

    Automatic creation and transmission of demand forecast values on a weekly basis

- Standard coding: necessary to automate processes between retailers and suppliers

Another conclusion of the business case was that the application of CPFR has great potential for improvement. The collaboration influences both internal processes and distributor processes.

CPFR is a key activity for Henkel. The development of CPFR must be aimed at including it in a marketplace, either Henkel's own at the European level or through its integration in the AECOC (Spanish commercial codification association) portal.

Therefore, the next steps after the business case was developed were to:

- Put into operation the detailed internal action plan.
- Seek out retailers prepared to collaborate in CPFR concepts.
- Put into operation the general CPFR process with the retailers chosen.

4.7.4 CPFR Pilot—Henkel and Condis

The good results obtained through the pilot with Eroski and the business case helped Henkel decide to start another initiative with Condis, a Spanish regional retailer based in Catalonia. Established in 1961, Condis is the largest supermarket chain in Catalonia, with 300 points of sale, and the second in terms of sales volume. It operates under two brand names, Condis Supermarkets and Distop. The group employs 2,900 people and achieves a turnover of 462 million euros (2000), with an increase of 17.5 percent in 1999. The group has plans to expand to other regions of Spain.

This CPFR pilot, Henkel-Condis, aims to identify the benefits of involving all the actors in the supply chain, focusing not only on the relationship between manufacturer and retailer but also on that with an upstream supplier. The objective is to integrate the entire supply chain, from one end to the other.

The pilot started in September 2000 and is planned to end in February 2002 with positive results for both partners. It will be presented during the ECR Conference in Barcelona in April 2002.

The scope of the project, from the perspective of the relationship with the retailer, is focused on the detergent category, with a particular emphasis on promotional SKUs. Within Henkel, the internal forecast, replenishment, purchasing, promotion planning, and production planning processes will be adapted to processes that are more suitable for collaboration.

Pilot Objectives

The pilot objectives defined were focused on proving the CPFR concept and validating the model. An additional objective was to generate stable delivery plans that would move the pilot toward more quantifiable objectives, such as the reduction of out-of-stocks at the point of sale, increased sales growth, improved forecast accuracy, reduction of inventories, and a broadened promotional plan horizon.

In the pilot, no specialized tool is used. The collaboration data are shared, using specially defined spreadsheets for each of the processes; collaboration will be conducted through e-mail messages and phone calls. Currently, Henkel is running several pilots in Europe, testing its own tools and retailer exchanges' tools. These will be used to develop, via the Internet, its business plans, common promotional plans, comparisons of sales forecasts of each partner, exceptions, shared sales forecasts, and order forecasts, and to obtain other information derived from different work flows.

Current Status of the Pilot

The current status of the pilot is as follows:

- Downstream collaboration with Condis completely established with collaboration on promotional planning and shared forecasts
- Replenishment of two warehouses according to the forecast
- Collaboration on solving problems directly at the POS

The key performance indicators defined by Henkel and Condis were:

- Forecast accuracy—measures of the forecast deviation
- Promotional planning—the number of days between accepted promotion plan and the day when the promotion starts
- Promotional plan changes—the number of unplanned changes in the promotional plan during the frozen period
- Service level—in terms of time, quantity, and out-of-stocks
- Inventory level—measures the number of days demand could be satisfied based on the current stockholding and previous demand
- Rush orders, full pallet, full truck

Results

The first results showed a 15 percent improvement in forecast accuracy and an improvement in the joint planning of the promotional activity.

Exhibit 4.48 highlights the improving quality of sales forecasts over a period of seven months (January–July 2001). The exhibit represents the evolution of the sales forecast generated collaboratively by Henkel and Condis:

● The "good" segment symbolizes the percentage of references with a forecast deviation of less than 20 percent, that is, references in which the difference between the sales forecast and real sales is less than 20 percent.

● The "bad" segment represents the percentage of references in which this deviation is more than 50 percent. The graph shows the positive development of the "good" segment (increasing) over the "bad" segment (decreasing) over the seven months.

In addition, initial results indicated significant improvements in a variety of areas. Sales forecast accuracy increased and this, in turn, led to a

EXHIBIT 4.48. SALES FORECAST BETWEEN CONDIS AND HENKEL (FORECAST ACCURACY).

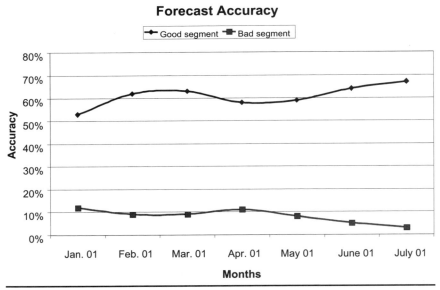

SOURCE: Henkel Spain/Condis.

customer service level of 99 percent, which was sustained without increasing inventory levels, even during promotions that traditionally experienced high out-of-stocks. Furthermore, the companies reduced supply chain costs through a 6 percent decrease in rush orders and increased the truck fill and pallet fill rates to 99 percent. Additionally, expanding the forecasting horizon to five weeks allowed Henkel and its supplier to optimize production operations.

Challenges

The results convinced the companies involved to extend the CPFR initiative in order to quickly gain critical mass and harvest additional benefits. Henkel is currently evaluating various options, including adding trading partners and applying the best practices established to other customers in order to achieve critical mass. We are increasing the level of detail of the exchanged data, expanding the geographic reach, automating data exchange through the implementation of a CPFR IT solution, and including further product categories.

These new partners will help Henkel achieve a critical mass that will allow the company to focus its efforts and processes on the critical products in promotional periods. Currently, Henkel is experiencing inefficiencies in the production of these critical products due to:

● Changes in the production planning of these formats
● Lack of packaging
● Costs of storage
● High number of obsoletes due to sales forecast deviations
● Unusual costs

Therefore, if the collaboration among the partners involved increases, and they are able to improve the collaborative processes of promotional planning and sales forecast generation of these critical products (see Exhibit 4.49), this will produce benefits for our suppliers through:

● Higher consistency with the lots ordered
● Improvement of their production cycles

EXHIBIT 4.49. STREAM MANAGEMENT OF HENKEL SPAIN AND RETAILERS.

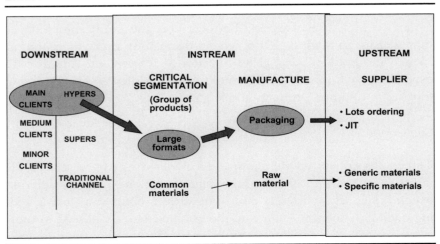

SOURCE: Henkel Spain/Accenture.

- Reduction in their delivery costs
- Improvements in transportation planning

Due to new internal processes of promotional communication in Henkel, suppliers will receive the information earlier so they will have more time for planning their production and distribution.

Another important issue, on which both companies are collaborating, is the out-of-stocks at the point of sale. Condis noted that even though service levels were improved, product availability on the shelves was significantly lower than in the stores' warehouses. Condis and Henkel have begun to analyze in-store operations with the objective of further improving product availability to the customer.

Impact on the Organization

The organization benefited by having:

- New roles and responsibilities defined
- New demand-planning process established and measured within the organization

- Availability of the promotional information with enough horizon to allow the company to plan in the middle and long term
- Willingness to collaborate with retailers in order to develop collaborative processes in forecasting and replenishment

Conclusions

Willingness to collaborate is the most critical factor for success. Companies' lack of awareness of this necessity is the most obstructive barrier to effective CPFR implementation and to achieving the potential benefits of CPFR. Another issue that requires clarification is the differences between countries, especially for multinational companies. In order to foster that awareness, the GCI (Global Commerce Initiative) is developing standards for CPFR, taking into account the knowledge and experiences of American businesses, VICS (Voluntary Interindustry Commerce Standards), and ECR (Efficient Consumer Response).

4.8

CPFR—Views and Experiences at Procter & Gamble

Peter Hambuch, Procter & Gamble

CPFR is an idea that is not simply being discussed by retailers and manufacturers worldwide, but also one that the early movers are beginning to implement. This means CPFR has become an internationally recognized and supported concept. In plain language, one can describe CPFR as follows:

- Based on commonly formulated business plans, a production level is jointly defined that:

    Is responsive to collaboratively determined demand, particularly with respect to production and warehousing

Governs the constituent flow of goods between individual participants in the supply chain

- The consumer is central to these cooperative efforts.

In addition to explaining the CPFR concept in general and presenting actual cases, an attempt is being made to locate the terms *category management*, *efficient consumer response*, *CPFR*, and *e-commerce* in their proper place with respect to one another.

4.8.1 The Objective of CPFR

CPFR is an interindustry attempt to improve the relations between business partners in the supply chain through cooperative planning and information exchange. Exhibit 4.50 shows in simplified form the interplay between participants in the process. Customer CPFR denotes the collaboration between customer teams (CBD, customer business development) and the retailing concerns. The flow of information upstream continues via the collaboration of CBD with demand planning, which we call internal CPFR, ending in production planning and manufacture. Supplier CPFR stands for the collaboration between manufacturing and its suppliers. An improved information flow (customer demand) upstream allows a synchronized flow of raw materials, packaging, and

EXHIBIT 4.50. FLOW OF INFORMATION AND FINISHED PRODUCTS IN THE SUPPLY CHAIN.

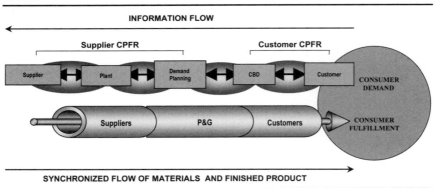

SOURCE: Proctor & Gamble.

end products downstream, resulting in the efficient fulfillment of consumer demand.

The improvement in the relationships between partners is sought, because in the contemporary supply chain, the individual participants operate in relative isolation from one another:

- Communication is insufficient and discontinuous.
- Planning is not coordinated.
- The planning process of retailing is primarily focused on revenues at the POS.
- The planning process of manufacturers is primarily focused on the size of deliveries made to the retailer's central depot.
- Planning is based on assumptions.
- Supporting systems do not exist.
- Because of uncertainty, overly large safety stock strains the supply chain, a consequence of inaccessible data on the expected demand of all other participants.

The results of a study by Benchmarking Partners in the United States makes this clear. In the year 2000, retailers achieved revenues of $3.2 trillion (U.S.). Some $1.1 trillion worth of goods and services were held in reserve in the supply chain during that time. This corresponds to a surplus equivalent to a 4.1-month supply.

Let us look more closely at the unsatisfying and costly inventory situation on both sides of the equation. The reasons why the so-called safety stock is maintained at unnecessarily high levels are uncertainty and inefficiency in the process:

- Uncertainty about consumer demand
- Uncertainty about the supply process relative to production and logistics
- Inefficiency in the process between the participants

Exhibit 4.51 illustrates the consequences of the above-mentioned problems. Although consumer demand in this example is relatively sta-

EXHIBIT 4.51. INCREASING FLUCTUATION OF ORDERS IS RESPONSIBLE FOR INCREASED STOCKS IN THE SUPPLY CHAIN.

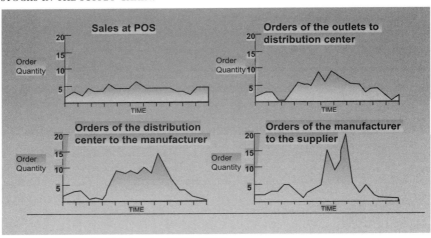

SOURCE: Lee, Stanford University/VICS (1998).

ble (graphic upper left), uncertainty and inefficiency causes observable swings in the flow of goods between:

- Warehouses and retail outlets (graphic upper right)
- The central depots of retailers and manufacturing (graphic bottom left)
- Manufacturers and suppliers of raw materials and packaging on the production side (graphic bottom right)

Manufacturers and retailers pursue the same goals:

- Both see potential for the reduction of inventories in outlets, warehouses, and at their suppliers.
- Both want to increase the availability of product throughout the supply chain.
- Both want to increase revenues and reduce costs.

Nonetheless, we find a number of inefficiencies in the supply chain:

- Overstock throughout the chain
- Unsatisfactory delivery service from manufacturer to retail, but also from the retailer's central depots to the POS

- Lost revenues through unavailability of product on the shelf, or during promotional activity
- Deficient communication between participants
- Frequent and cost-intensive "fire fighting" in the form of rush orders or short-term changes in production planning

All of the information necessary to attain these common objectives is already in existence but is scattered and not available in the required measure for all of the business partners. This information flow is hindered worldwide by the closed systems on both sides and in particular by the attitude of the business partners and their corporate culture.

This is where CPFR is instrumental in eliminating the absolute boundaries, so that a complete solution for the common good can be sought. Through CPFR and supporting technologies, it is possible that:

- Relationships between business partners improve.
- Projections for future sales and orders become more precise, thereby reducing inventories, improving delivery service, and avoiding shortages.
- Transparency is achieved through standards of measurement that allow the monitoring of progress toward the goals that have been set.

Udo Scharr of Procter & Gamble and Rita Marzian from Metro AG coined a very appropriate phrase on the occasion of the ECR Days of ECR DACH in Bonn, Germany, in September 2001. They said, "We, P&G, and Metro, want to reach the C-Level in our cooperation."

It is also important to know what CPFR is not. CPFR is not a software solution that is simply installed on the computer. Even when technology plays a significant role in the exchange of information, this is only one aspect of what makes CPFR possible. It is by no means a replacement for efficient consumer response. The concept lives through the commitment of participating retailers and manufacturers and the engagement of all employees affected. The concept is usable not only by large but also by midsize and small companies.

The Centrale für Coorganisation in Germany refers to the figure shown in Exhibit 4.52 as the ECR house. Up until now, the ECR

EXHIBIT 4.52. CPFR AND THE ECR HOUSE.

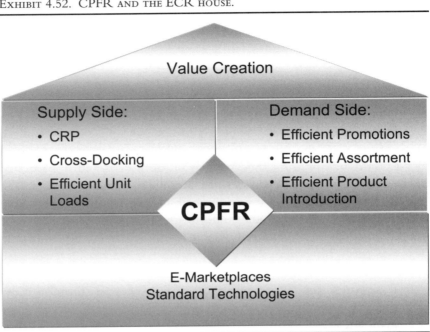

SOURCE: Centrale für Coorganisation.

house has been a duplex. In both halves, different measures were used in order to meet the objectives of ECR in order to offer the consumer more value.

One side concentrates on the supply side and increasing the efficiency in the supply chain by new logistical concepts and supporting technology like electronic data interchange. In this area supply chain managers and IT experts are working together. The other side concentrates on the demand side, ergo the consumer and thus category management. Here people from departments like purchase, operations, and marketing are working together.

The two sides work relatively separately from one another. CPFR integrates existing ECR solutions of supply and demand, previously employed in isolation, into a comprehensive approach. The core of a CPFR implementation is the willingness of the business partners to jointly control the planning, forecasting, and ordering processes. This means coordinating and linking strategic, tactical, and operative planning in pursuit of common goals.

In the lower region of the ECR house are found the so-called enabling technologies. Like those for product identification (EAN), the EANCOM standards for data exchange via EDI, or the offers becoming available in e-marketplaces. E-marketplaces have the advantage of not requiring that every participant have implemented its own complete in-house CPFR solution, but rather can obtain information through the Internet. Thus, e-marketplaces will act as pacemakers for the implementation of CPFR.

The essential elements of CPFR potential for both manufacturer and retailer are seen as:

- Increased revenues through better planning and thereby reduced inventory problems at the POS
- Improved cash flows through long-term inventory reduction
- Better coordinated organizational processes
- Reduced administrative and operational costs

In addition to the potential susceptible to measurable differences, the element of "better coordinated organizational processes" means:

- The collaboration between companies and functions is process driven.
- Responsibility is shared by business partners.
- The information exchange within and between companies is better coordinated.
- Both partners work with the same information.
- Decisions are made jointly.

CPFR—A Learning Process

CPFR is a learning process, which means that lessons learned and information gathered flow continuously into the control process. That includes gap analysis of the joint business plan, an analysis of the precision of the forecasts, or analyses of completed promotions and the flow of those insights into future forecasts.

In particular, the collaborative evaluation of the results of completed promotions versus forecasts offers important understanding and enables the comparison and use of historical data for future planning. That includes the effects on the targeted sales influenced by:

- Price
- Type and quality of promotional support
- Season and weather

CPFR as a learning process is reflected in the collaboration with our customers in North America. The following example (see Exhibit 4.53) shows in a simplified illustration the CPFR work plan that Procter & Gamble CBD (customer business development) developed together with a customer and what has happened in the course of more than a year. Included are:

- Temporal frequency of the individual steps (yearly, quarterly, weekly)
- Expected results of the individual steps (business planning, target performance comparison)
- Responsibilities (from senior management to analysts)

Taken collectively, the CPFR business model can be broken down into the three following base processes:

1. The business planning between manufacturer and retailer
2. The forecast of expected sales and delivery sizes
3. Inventory control from production and distribution through to POS

Collaboration—The Core of the Concept

CPFR is a business model, which breaks with behaviors and processes that have been superseded, offers a comprehensive solution, draws the

EXHIBIT 4.53. CPFR WORK PLAN USED BY PROCTER & GAMBLE.

Frequency	Expected Outcomes	Responsible
	Corporate Objectives/Expectations	Customer/P&G Senior Management
Annually Renew Joint Team Charter Review/Renew Joint Business Plan	A) Joint Category Goals: —Role of category —Pricing plans —Merchandising plans —New item introduction plans B) Joint Results Tracking and Review Process: —Develop scorecard to track results —Confirm gaps between goal and target —Exception resolution process —Schedule quarterly reviews C) Joint Alignment Process: —Verify goals/results will deliver corporate objectives charter	Account Manager and Buyer: Lead Process
Quarterly Joint Business Plan and Gap Analysis	—Review scorecard/gap analysis —Review merchandising results from previous quarter/gap analysis plan —Develop/revise merchandising plans, volume forecast, and calendar for next quarter —Review base volume results from previous quarter and gap analysis —Develop/revise base volume forecast for next quarter —Develop plans to resolve volume gaps —Review and revise exception criteria —Document CPFR wins	Account Manager and Buyer: Lead Process
Weekly Exception Management/ Review Actuals	—Resolve critical exceptions —Revise POS and shipment forecast	Data Analyst

SOURCE: Procter & Gamble.

customer into its considerations, and connects the demand side with the supply side. The core of the concept is the *C*. The relevant business processes involved are coordinated and synchronized across company lines. The prerequisite for this is the willingness of the business partners to guide collectively the planning, forecasting, and supply process. The *C* for collaboration is a necessary condition for integration. Business functions that were previously isolated are being bound together through CPFR. The quality of *C* becomes apparent through the fair handling of exceptional situations, when, for example, the development of business does not follow as expected and solutions must be jointly sought. The more strongly *C* is present, the higher the quality that will be achieved in the dimensions of *P*, *F*, and *R*.

The *C* fosters a cooperative culture, builds trust, aims for communication and information exchange, and creates win–win relationships between business partners. It is proactive and not reactive.

The development of joint business plans and the measurement of results throughout the supply chain are based on a cooperative process. Cooperative processes support continual improvement. Cooperation enables the necessary changes in organizational structures toward multifunctional teams, whereby the necessary training and the selection of appropriate criteria for measurement supports the formation of efficient team structures.

Technology that supports cooperation is being implemented and thereby supports the entire CPFR process. Integrated systems will close the gap between processes and technology.

CPFR leads to tangible and intangible advantages, which have been evaluated through pilot projects between manufacturers and retailers[1]:

- Improvement in forecasting accuracy 10–40 percent
- Inventory reduction in the supply chain 10–15 percent
- Improvement in service 0.5–2.0 percent
- Growth in revenues 2–25 percent (through reduced out-of-stocks on shelf and during promotions)
- Reduction in warehousing and transport costs 3–10 percent
- Improved relations between business partners
- Better internal communication/planning

Around the globe a tremendous effort is being made to prepare for the implementation of CPFR. Manufacturers and retailers are at the same time busy validating the advantages within pilot projects. These projects also seek to play a formative role in defining the CPFR service functions of the electronic marketplace (GNX, WWRE, CPG, Transora). Based on input from the real world, the tools are being improved and enhanced further in collaboration with their respective software developers. In the same way, the respective organizations (GCI, VICS, EAN-UCC) are working on the standards that will be necessary to support data exchange over the Internet.

4.8.2 Collaboration Through the Entire Supply Chain at Procter & Gamble

As we are speaking of the entire supply chain, the topic of CPFR is not complete merely with a discussion of collaboration between P&G and our trading partners. The collaboration continues internally, in order to ensure that the information flow between company divisions thrives. Essentially, this means the collaboration between the CBDs and demand planning on forecasting and product availability. The constantly updated forecast from demand planning is the basis for production planning in the factories. Logically, the CPFR concept is useful in the collaboration between the plants and the suppliers of raw materials and packaging.

Procter & Gamble has begun projects across the entire supply chain in order to bring CPFR to realization:

- Between CBDs and retail companies
- Internally, between CBDs and demand planning
- Between factories and their suppliers

4.8.3 CPFR with Retail Organizations

A whole array of projects are under way with our partners in retail, primarily in North America and in Europe. The goal is to evaluate the potential of CPFR and to jointly test and improve the necessary tools in the field and to bring us in a position to implement CPFR on a large scale. As has been presented at many conferences, in Europe we are cooperating with Metro AG in Germany, Albert Heijn in Holland, and with Dansk Supermarked in Denmark. Further agreements are in the making. We use Syncra software and the tools of the e-markets GNX and WWRE. We also have pilot projects that are developing tools for Extranets of retailers. In Europe, the focus of CPFR cooperation is on the optimization of business processes linked to promotions. This begins with the joint planning (product, week, advertising support, etc.) and continues with the forecast, sales tracking, and inventory monitoring during the promotion in the business. The success of the common business is then measured on the timeliness and sufficiency of material at various places along the supply chain (frequency of out-of-stocks and surpluses). Short-term fire fighting in the form of costly rush orders should also be avoided. Concrete results from the cooperation with Dansk include:

- Forecast accuracy for promotional revenues—improved 83–98.5 percent
- Inventory reduction in Dansk's central depot—reduced from 2.1 to 1.9 weeks reserve
- Product availability in Dansk outlets—improved from 98.36 to 99.38 percent
- Rush orders—reduced 20 percent

The pilot project with Metro AG in Germany also addressed the insufficient planning of promotions. Through collaboration, the following problems were identified:

- Inadequate communication in planning
- Insufficiently defined business processes
- Responsibilities not clearly defined
- Differing evaluation criteria (units of measure)
- Information that was insufficient, inexact, or outdated

In response to the problems identified, the following objectives were stated:

- Increase sales through a reduction in out-of-stocks.
- Reduce costs along the supply chain through, among other things, inventory optimization including promotions leftovers.

- Learn, test, and develop further.

Within the cooperative agreement the focus was placed on the following individual elements. The work process was supported through a work-flow tool.

- Planning the promotion
- Forecasting the promotion volume
- Controlling outlet orders and inventory
- Monitoring the promotion sales
- Evaluating the promotion after its conclusion

There have not yet been any results made public. The teams on both sides have expressed their views about their work:

- We do promotion management with our partner, Internet-supported with common systems, data, and processes.
- Through cooperation with our partner we are able to achieve more.
- We have an improved promotions process.
- We are convinced we can increase sales and reduce inventory.
- It is doable.
- CPFR begins with small steps. Start small and simple, be patient, and expand.

CPFR Internally

It is the assignment of our CBDs to pass on to demand planning the business plans they have developed jointly with retail concerns, where the customer-specific forecast is incorporated into a total forecast. In particular in Germany, information on planned promotions plays an essential role, as enormous spikes in the forecast, production, and delivery to the retailers and on to its outlets will result. Exhibit 4.54 clarifies this scene.

The chart shows the course of the delivery forecast, the P&G deliver-

EXHIBIT 4.54. PROCTER & GAMBLE FORECAST MANAGEMENT.

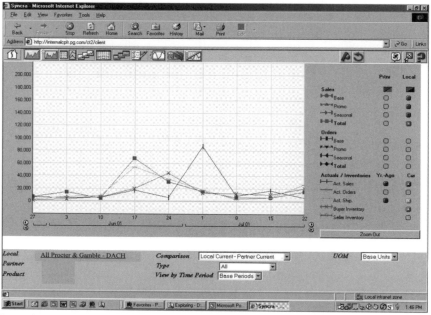

Legend:

| Line: Sales of a retail chain (sale at POS according to scanner data)
— Line: P&G deliveries to the distribution center of a retailer
■ Line: Delivery forecast for deliveries from P&G to the distribution center
X Line: Average weekly inventory in the distribution center of the retailer

SOURCE: Syncra/Procter & Gamble.

ies, and the sales in the outlets at the weekly level. The sales peak in July is readily apparent, along with the accompanying peak in deliveries, which was accurately anticipated eight weeks before shipment along with the development of inventory in the preceding two weeks. In the week of the promotion, sales with an index of 500 points over the normal volume were recorded. In order to ensure availability along the entire supply chain with such severe changes in demand, very good planning and communication are necessary on the part of all involved.

In order to support the CBDs with the planning and to improve P&G's internal communication, we began a pilot project in the first half of 2001 and tested a tool named Syncra. Syncra was developed by Syncra Systems of Cambridge, Massachusetts. The system is designed to support CPFR. It is based on e-commerce standards and supports the communication between cooperating partners. Procter & Gamble chose Syncra as its CPFR software and Transora as its e-marketplace. In principle, the customer supervisors have a large amount of data available to them, which they can use for forecasting. Depending on availability, this information is composed of items like delivery amounts from P&G to its customers, POS scanner data from its customers, details of the customer's warehouse activity and inventories, access to the customer's Extranet, or historical information on sales targets during promotions. These data come from different sources at P&G and the retail partner and are accessible through different systems.

Much effort then, on the part of the CBD is required to use all of this information and, for example, promotional volume to estimate with the expected accuracy. Generally speaking, we have defined the following requirements in order to support the process of volume planning. We want *one* tool for planning, plan supervision, and communication:

- Volume planning → Forecast
- Volume tracking → Delivery versus Forecast
- Communication → Demand planning

The tool should make transparent the data that come out of the systems at P&G and its customers. It should begin at the lowest level (week, EAN) and use a compression of customer structure and product hierarchy. It must include:

- Planned promotional business
- Planned base business
- Customer's POS data
- Customer's inventory
- P&G delivery amount

Syncra is a tool that meets these criteria, presenting the various pieces of information transparently in a tabular or graphic format. The system is readily learned and easy to work with. Access to Syncra is via a Web browser after inputting a user name and password.

With the exception of the planned promotion, we load the above-mentioned information into the system. For the calculation of forecasts for base business, we prefer to use data on our customers' drafts from inventory or our weekly deliveries to the central depot. The structuring of product hierarchies is done in consultation with the CBDs. It is the customer supervisor's job to create the forecasts in the system and to keep them current. That can take place online directly or through a tool based on Excel that automatically transfers planning data into Syncra. The planning time frame shown is three months, displayed at the weekly level.

The test with selected CBDs in Germany, Austria, and Switzerland and the chosen product categories was successful. On the technical side, the flow of information met our expectations. More important, however, was that the forecast accuracy of our CBDs markedly improved. Currently we assume that six weeks before delivery, 80 percent of the delivery amount on EAN and at the weekly level can be estimated within plus or minus 25 percent. Similarly, the tools have proven themselves with respect to communication between CBDs and demand planning. Both parties use the same system and work with the same data. In addition, there is the potential to open the system to trade partners in order to support CPFR from the retail side. The decision was made to proceed with implementation systemwide, so that by the beginning of 2002 all CBDs and all product categories in Germany, Austria, and Switzerland will be participating.

4.8.4 CPFR with Suppliers

The collaboration with factories and their suppliers is comparable to that between CBDs and their customers. Of course the information exchange doesn't relate to the finished product, but rather to raw materials and packaging. After the production planning previously described stands, the production, storage, and delivery of the suppliers is collaboratively determined with them. CPFR between all partners in the supply chain ensures that information on the expected sale at the outlet flows through the entire chain and is translated into meaningful data at every stage. On a weekly (t) time line, such a process appears as in Exhibit 4.55.

This example, which naturally does not apply to all manufacturers in all industries, nonetheless shows that forecasts, forecast accuracy, and above all communication between all parties are the keys to success. Success is product availability at the right time at the right spot in the supply chain.

Procter & Gamble has begun several projects, which, with the help of Syncra Systems, are testing CPFR between factories and suppliers. Here we use Syncra to support vendor-managed inventory (VMI) as well. This means that, based on the information in Syncra, our suppliers take over the responsibility for inventory control in our plants.

4.8.5 Experience at Procter & Gamble with Pilot Projects

The use of CPFR across the entire supply chain is realizable, even though there remain shortcomings in the system. Work is being done to rectify them. Interfaces between the systems are being developed, and we are using this unique chance to create global standards for data exchange. The desire for collaboration between business partners must be present on both sides and documented in a contract between them. CPFR must be brought to life by team leaders on both sides. The joint business plan is the basis for collaborative work in forecasting. At the outset, a collaboration must set priorities. One should not begin with all nine steps of the CPFR model at one time. Focus allows a quick start, which also allows both sides to learn quickly. One priority for

EXHIBIT 4.55. TIME LINE FOR PLANNING A PROMOTION.

Activity	Week	Information Basis
Execution of a promotion in outlets	t	EAN consumption units
Delivery to outlets	t − 1	EAN shipment units
Delivery to retail central depot	t − 2	EAN shipment units
Delivery to manufacturer's central depot	t − 3	EAN shipment units
Production	t − 4	IAN (internal article number)
Delivery of raw material to plant	t − 5	EAN, IAN
Production of raw materials	t − 6	EAN, IAN

CPFR between manufacturing and retail could be to begin with sales forecasts for promotions. Inventory buildup with new product introductions or the more complex task of product redeployment (inventory reduction with the old EAN, inventory buildup with the new EAN) are likewise appropriate for collaboration. At the beginning, partners should make analyses with the same process so that they learn from one another and jointly recognize inefficiencies in the current process. The technology is important, but at the beginning it need not be perfect. It is essential that the necessary information should flow. In the long term we need to automate forecast creation and exchange. Otherwise, the expansion of pilot projects is not scalable.

Afterword

The CPFR concept was developed in 1997–1998 by a number of manufacturers and retailers in the United States. CPFR is now being discussed around the world and becoming accepted and supported. Its potential has been validated. The coming e-markets will support CPFR with their service. The necessary standards for the required data exchange are in development. It is up to us, the participants in the supply chain, whether supplier, manufacturer, or retailer, to support the concept and to work toward the realization of its potential. No link in the chain can do it alone. It works only when we work together.

Note

1. Information provided by Transora.

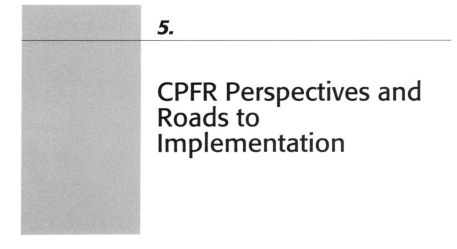

5.

CPFR Perspectives and Roads to Implementation

Migration to Value Chain Collaboration Through CPFR

Robert Bruce, VCC Associates
Ron Ireland, VCC Associates

Leading retailers are on a migration path to value chain collaboration that will allow them to surpass the competition in customer service and profitability for the shareholders. The roadmap consists of foundational, strategic, and transformational journeys that guide the organization's projects, initiatives, priorities, and goals. Collaborative Planning, Forecasting, and Replenishment (CPFR) is the initial step in a multistep process toward full value chain collaboration and competitive transformation. CPFR is the joint planning between retailers and major customers on the key elements of the demand and supply chain processes. CPFR is a core transformational strategy that takes business process, people, and technology to a higher level of performance by promoting openness, information sharing, data exchange, visibility, and joint decisions. This value chain collaboration is an important segment of a business strategy and provides a foundation for solid best practices in business processes, which include:

- Build business alliances focused on jointly managed processes.
- Develop a single, mutually owned, consumer-driven forecast.
- Achieve a higher level of accuracy than statistical measures.
- Link consumer demand with supply planning and execution.
- Improve value chain integration.

Value chain collaboration vision begins with CPFR and migrates to collaborative account/merchandise development and collaborative transportation management. Early adoption is valuable to being competitive in the marketplace.

5.1.1 Key Attributes of Successful CPFR Management

The question is not whether to embrace collaboration and more specifically CPFR, but how quickly retailers and consumer packaged goods manufacturers can implement this strategy. Being early adopters is important from a competitive point of view. Taking a significant step in enhancing the value position to improve the profitability, sales, and revenue on retailer's brands is a key to beating the competition in the marketplace. Embracing collaborative principles is more a cost of doing business and transforming the way business is done than taking a strict single project payback and return approach.

A key attribute is the joint linkage of all business units focused and aligned to the corporate vision and migration plan. Communication planning and executive ownership, sponsorship, and visible leadership are also critical components to the success of implementation. The true ownership of execution relies heavily on change management to ensure that associates embrace this new vision, own, participate in, and drive the execution. All need to be orchestrated to ensure that the organization is breaking down old barriers and paradigms while laying the foundation for a cross-functional collaborative environment.

The organization needs to be assured that all members of management support the change and are able to "walk the talk" to actually become customer centric. Being customer centric means being focused on the customer, adding customer value, and driving all decisions based upon customer demand. Making sure that everyone is working on satisfying the consumer can reinforce this customer-centric direction. If they are not contributing value to the stores servicing the customer, then they are working on the wrong things. Leadership, competency, and enabling technology are essential attributes in successful management teams that help promote and foster a collaborative atmosphere.

Leadership

To be successful, a company's leadership must preach the necessity for all employees to think in collaborative terms and act in real time. The competitive landscape is forcing the traditional retail senior management to evaluate how collaboration will affect the future of the industry. More important, senior management must determine what course if any the company will take. Will retailers take this journey? That question depends totally on the state of the retailer's leadership. Although some retailers are beginning to develop and incorporate a collaborative strategy into their overall vision and business strategies, some traditional retailers have not created or communicated a collaborative culture or mind-set throughout their organizations.

Organizations that have strong leadership have already developed and integrated their Internet initiatives within their overall business strategies. They have promoted risk taking to stimulate a collaborative culture throughout the organization. For traditional retailers to develop the new culture in their companies, they must become more adept at breaking down the impediments that have prevented them from moving forward with collaborative initiatives. Senior management leadership must champion a collaborative culture by demonstrating commitment to Internet initiatives; encouraging internal and external collaboration, openness in trading partner relationships, and risk taking with Internet-related projects; and fostering the development of stronger bonds between the IS. Some industry leaders in consumer products manufacturing and retailing have taken giant steps toward CPFR. They have management organizations committed to developing collaborative cultures and have promoted their Internet focus internally and with the investment community, customers, and suppliers.

Competency

The retail industry has traditionally used its organizational competency strengths in providing higher levels of customer service and in developing stronger relationships with supplier partners to effectively manage product delivery in the supply chain. Most retailers, however, have not discovered the ability to use the Internet to leverage their traditional strengths in customer care and supply chain management. Most traditional retailers have not utilized the Internet's potential to provide solutions for their business or operational issues.

Organizations with strong collaborative competencies have the ongoing ability to be very responsive to customer needs, the capability to execute ruthlessly and move with incredible speed. Retailers need to develop relationships with complementary collaborative players to leverage their brand or core competencies on the Internet. They must learn and understand how these initiatives could improve their own enterprise as well as the total value chain.

Technology

A key driver supporting this path to transformation resides in the arena of technology. For most traditional retailers, the industry's bottom-line focus has positioned the retailer with an IT infrastructure that is unable to meet the needs of today's New World environment in the Internet. The traditional retailer has had limited exposure and experience in implementing collaborative solutions. Success requires an IT infrastructure to implement collaborative initiatives rapidly without taking time to justify the ROI for incremental improvements in the infrastructure. Technology is the vehicle for process scalability. To ensure success, retailers and manufacturers must build and drive standards across the enterprise, having the competencies in place to develop, scale, and support collaborative Internet initiatives rapidly with trading partners.

5.1.2 Trading Partner Relationship Management

This internal focus extends outward to the trading partner community, beginning with a select group of core alliance vendors that are critical to success. A top-to-top meeting of key executives with the executive team at the retailer must occur to convince those involved that this is not the same old organization. Management needs to understand that it works for a company truly committed to addressing and resolving the ills of the past through specific action plans. This is no longer a "We win—You figure out how to win" relationship. It is now an opportunity to make a retail organization the "preferred retailer" for vendor collaborative relationships.

Formulating strong and scalable trading partner relationships takes a set of guiding principles that are continually reinforced. Within these principles a trading partner strategy can be defined, piloted, and implemented. The new evolution of these relationships focuses on a common set of goals and objectives, a high level of mutual trust, a willingness to openly share data, and a desire to link all business elements concerning win-win results for manufacturer, retailer, and customer.

Key steps in formulating strong alliance relationships are:

- Implementing executive education and training
- Defining a strategic direction and migration path
- Aligning executive sponsorship, ownership, and communication planning
- Defining the joint team mission, core objectives, metrics, rewards, and account-level profit and loss statement
- Clarifying supporting cross-functional initiatives and targeted objectives
- Formulating quarterly and monthly communication plans, performance tracking, and accomplishment reporting
- Planning executive visioning retreats semiannually or annually
- Promoting an internal and external collaborative environment

Setting a structure of strong relationships with trading partner vendors, carriers, and solution providers is paramount to support the migration to best practices. The migration may start with solidifying business operating fundamentals, but moves toward defining a dynamic and collaborative set of interrelationships internally and externally all focused and driven by the customer. This is where the real competitive strength and geometric results originate.

Leveraging the skills of others both internally and externally is a basis for collaboration cross-functionally and with trading partners. Trading partners are often experts in their categories on consumer and market analysis. As part of building a collaborative relationship with trading partners, opening retailer data to key suppliers to jointly analyze customer sales and market basket data is very important. This analysis can be focused on category/market analysis and assortment planning, as well as market and demographic analysis defining market potential, and share and gap analysis. These are important steps that will lay the foundational business processes and migration path for successful implementation of CPFR. Moving in a planned and incremental way toward Collaborative Planning, Forecasting, and Replenishment will ensure real business benefits. This process is dependent on communicating, educating, and training associates and management on a set of building blocks and sequence of actions promoting internal and external collaboration across business units.

5.1.3 Four Foundational Strategies

The four pillars for success are foundational and organizational core competencies that enable best practice migration and implementation of key transformation strategies (see Exhibit 5.1):

- Building of trading partner alliances vertically and horizontally
    - Shared consumer data for merchandising and demand planning
    - Joint collaborative decision making
    - Vertical account profitability analysis
- Consumer-driven integrated value chains
    - Vertically integrated and optimized value chains
    - Demand and supply chain linkage (from shelf to production)
- Internet-enabled collaboration
    - Planning, forecasting, and replenishment
    - Account planning and management

EXHIBIT 5.1. COLLABORATIVE VALUE CHAINS.

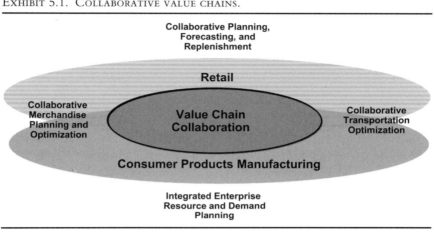

SOURCE: Bruce/Ireland, VCC Associates.

  Merchandise assortment optimization

  Transportation management

- Full value chain visibility and information/decision management

  Information visibility and real–near-real-time accessibility

  Joint decision making

  Exception management

A migration path laying key foundations and competencies must be in place to maximize execution and determine the degree of success, return on investment, and competitive positioning. These four pillars are the foundation to scalable implementation of CPFR over multiple trading partners as well as other collaborative and integrated value chain initiatives. The thread tying these strategies together blends several attributes and characteristics of a company's culture, focus, capabilities, and strategic vision.

Foundational

To lay out the roadmap to transformation, key steps must be followed to ensure sustainable success. A basic foundation must be put in place to build upon. The focus is on the basic business processes, organization, and behaviors that support all other initiatives. This is also the phase where quick hits are possible that fund further strategic initiatives giving momentum to the drive toward a transformational vision.

Strategic

Laying the cultural, basic operational, and tactical initiatives developed in the foundational stage, key strategies pull together a multifaceted approach to transformation. These strategies guide the migration path of the organization across key business units keeping the company focused and on path. This stage is where CPFR and furthering trading partner relationships reside.

Transformational

This is where the picture is painted for the organization, a picture that reflects the corporate vision that is a catapult into the marketplace, industry positioning, and a new source of competitive advantage. A transformational vision aspires toward a fully integrated value chain linking demand and supply from shelf to supply in an optimized and visible collaborative environment (see Exhibit 5.2).

5.1.4 Starting the Journey with CPFR—Nine Critical Steps

Some of the same criteria suggested in the VICS CPFR Guidelines and Roadmap documents should be used during the CPFR pilot-planning and partner selection process. Some key objectives that drive CPFR implementation help determine the selection, rate, and speed of implementation to achieve short-range, intermediate, and long-range results. Success breeds success, as the saying goes, and is valid for helping to define which trading partners are selected for your graduated rollout program. The first trading partners selected must be those that are considered industry leaders, highly competent, not resource constrained, embracing best practices, and having CPFR as a supporting corporate strategy.

Key rules for CPFR implementation are:

- *Do your homework.* Hit the calculator and determine the category and trading partners that will deliver the most impact.

EXHIBIT 5.2. MOVEMENT TO COLLABORATION.

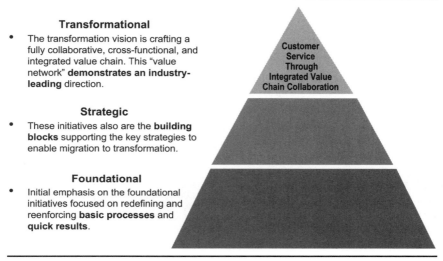

Transformational
- The transformation vision is crafting a fully collaborative, cross-functional, and integrated value chain. This "value network" **demonstrates an industry-leading** direction.

Strategic
- These initiatives also are the **building blocks** supporting the key strategies to enable migration to transformation.

Foundational
- Initial emphasis on the foundational initiatives focused on redefining and reenforcing **basic processes** and **quick results**.

(pyramid) Customer Service Through Integrated Value Chain Collaboration

SOURCE: Bruce/Ireland, VCC Associates.

- *Remember the 80/20 rule.* Define the top 10–20 percent trading partners that will give you critical mass, but don't forget about the other 80 percent.

- *Fund your program with results.* Compound the growth of results over time and communicate at every milestone.

- *Walk, don't run.* Start slow and remember it's 80 percent planning and 20 percent doing—well-thought-out and orchestrated programs—that win.

- *Success breeds success.* Competency check your trading partners—the good ones will set the pace for others, better guaranteeing results.

- *Bring in the big guys.* Discuss and implement organizational, risk, and change management issues with your executive champions.

- *Go for the gold.* Select items and categories that will deliver early business process wins and visible financial paybacks.

- *Follow the book of law.* Multitier project planning is critical in aligning business process, organizational change, and technology time lines.

- *Inspect what you expect.* Measure everything and translate it back to the key financial measurements your company uses.

- *Pick your wins.* Then communicate and celebrate with a passion.

CPFR is not rocket science and is not dependent on sophisticated technology to be accomplished. Like anything in business you must focus on business process before technology. Furthermore, being a large corporation is not a prerequisite; often CPFR can help level the playing field between the large industry leaders and more intermediate-size companies. Success with CPFR is dependent upon a company's understanding, ownership, process, and openness—internally and externally. The biggest issues I have seen with failed programs or marginal results came from a lack of understanding of what CPFR is really all about, shortchanging implementation or sitting on the sidelines and doing things the same way as always, but expecting different results.

Taking CPFR to Scale

With a solid foundation in leadership, governance, competencies, and technological architecture, the question must be asked, Is the organization in place to support the migration of collaborative processes? Piloting CPFR gives organizations the opportunity to learn, test, and otherwise lay the foundation for the business process and technology changes that must be planned for scalable rollout as well as migrating to other collaborative applications. More specifically, there are key issues that must be addressed, planned, and staged to successfully implement a scalable rollout of CPFR:

Scalability Issues
- Visioning and strategic alignment
- Business justification and case for action
- Executive ownership and sponsorship
- Migration planning to critical mass
- Multitier project planning and management
- Current process and gap analysis
- Roles and responsibility definition
- Organizational, risk, and change management
- Communication planning and project management

- Technology review and architectural assessment
- Software partner selection and implementation
- Trading partner implementation and execution

Before undertaking this journey, champions need to build internal corporate energy around a collaborative strategy, translate its support, and align it with the existing corporate strategies. Corporate impact must be defined financially and communicated over a clear time horizon while clarifying its organizational implications and requirements. Most important, in some organizations executives need to be guided and coached through the process. Executive understanding, ownership, support, and participation are critical in driving the speed and ultimately the success of implementation. Executive leadership can align the vision, issues, organization, resources, and focus to radically move the organization. In other situations executive leadership can perpetuate skepticism and near-term tactical thinking, sustain existing paradigms, and otherwise limit the potential of the organization.

The CPFR evangelists of the organization must align themselves internally with multitier champions to help drive the understanding and ownership at all levels. Additionally, selection of an executive champion is critical whether it is the president/chairman, executive, or senior vice president. Otherwise, the project will not be grounded within the company, organizational focus will be distracted, and resource assignment questionable on a consistent basis. Through proper communication planning, the organization will be in tune with the importance and role of CPFR and value chain collaboration as a key corporate transformational strategy. All too often I see companies whose executive management team does not understand what CPFR is, what it will do, and how it lays the foundation supporting the team's corporate strategic vision to competitive advantage. Even more dangerous, the team thinks it understands what CPFR is but approaches new thinking in an "old world" context.

Business Process and Change Management Issues

Companies have mentioned that technology is the easy part of piloting and implementing CPFR, but the process is difficult. Laying down the core competencies and foundations are the first two steps on the road-map to successful implementation. Technology is the enabler to scalability. It is the business process supported by the internal culture that makes CPFR successful. Defining and implementing the basic collaborative processes provide the structure needed to support the transition from piloting to scalable implementation. Many miss the importance of change management in support of the piloting and rollout process. Not addressing the organizational aspects of collaboration will limit or minimize the overall success and bottom-line financial results from CPFR.

The basic processes were redefined in the pilot stages of implementing CPFR. Existing processes need to be reinforced along with putting measures in place to make them permanent. Additional processes need to be changed to support linking the demand plan and forecasts to internal production systems for both trading partners. For the retailer forecast, quantities need to be tied through forecasting, replenishment, and order management systems. For manufacturers, forecast quantities need to be part of their internal demand planning and the advanced planning and scheduling process as well.

A blueprint must be laid out representing the current (as is) business processes compared to the new (to be) business processes required to support full implementation. The rollout plan for CPFR must be focused on business process change, associate development, and organizational alignment. The internal CPFR champions and human relations associates must drive this change management plan. Staffing capabilities and capacity issues associated with the changes in business processes along with new roles and responsibilities will need to be managed. Process roles and responsibilities need to be defined at two to three levels of detail for each related position. Communication flows should be developed reflecting inputs, decisions, and outputs prior to conducting one-on-one discussions and group training sessions with associates.

To offer permanent solutions that produce the desired results, performance metrics, measurements, incentives, and rewards need to be in place to reenforce execution. Organizational alignment and staffing issues will arise and also must be addressed as part of the change management process. Along with the multifunctional process ownership that has previously been put in place, communication planning must be a part of the change management process defining the key messages conveyed by executives to further build understanding and involvement at all levels of the organization.

It is advisable that a risk assessment be part of a change management plan. The risk assessment, milestone, and alert processes can help a company keep on track, avoid pitfalls, and otherwise make ongoing adjustments in process, change management, or technology project plans. The important issue is that the organization, governance teams, and CPFR project manager need to have three project time lines sequencing activities and running in parallel.

Technology vs. Process

Most technology is robust enough to support scalable rollout of CPFR. Three issues exist, however, one being the readiness of each company's systems architecture to support existing and future requirements of Internet-enabled collaboration, initially focused on CPFR. Second is the state of industry standards defining XML. Third are the business processes that need further definition and tailoring within each organization. Technology is the facilitator and enabler of rapid, scalable implementation and rollout. More than technology, basic process-related issues need to be addressed—do not make IT a scapegoat.

Demand Aggregation

For manufacturers, sales force demand aggregation is a paramount issue in scaling CPFR. Building critical mass is the process supporting collecting, processing, aggregating, and then separating sales/demand forecasts by retail account or, conversely, supplier. Clearly defining the organizational alignment and sales team processes for collaboration on sales forecasts, translating causal factors to a demand forecast, and processing customer-specific forecasts and feeding APS systems must be done. Within the sales forecast, collaboration process tools must be provided to standardize and translate the promotional, event, and pricing causal factors affecting the demand forecast.

Conversely, this is also a challenge for retailers. A jointly agreed upon demand plan for a retailer must be fed back into internal systems, merchandising systems, replenishment, order management, inventory deployment, distribution, transportation, and logistics forecasts. Middleware offers focused solutions to many connection issues but does not address these process-related demands. When addressed it is important that the systems are part of the natural work-flow processes to ensure timely integration.

Replenishment Fundamentals

Bottom-up consumer demand planning has the fundamental focus on consumers' buying needs at the store shelf. Consumer demand drives "pull-based" replenishment fundamentals that support the right products in the right place, at the right time, at the right price, and at the right profit margin for the business. The visibility of the consumer-forecasted demand and actual demand boosts the supply-driven optimization process.

5.1.5 Moving Toward Strategic Transformation

CPFR is not just a replacement for VMI but is a first step in a migration path to transformation and industry leadership. If you are not stepping forward then you are falling behind. You cannot be successful in your business tactics if your tactics do not complement a long-term set of strategies and support a transformational vision for your organization. It is not an issue of whether you should implement CPFR, but rather how quickly you can assess your readiness and how fast you can begin your program.

Moving from foundational to strategic initiatives requires an assessment of the organization that supports a customer-driven store process and alignment of activities and decisions. Starting from the point of customer purchase, store-level focus is on linking product on shelf with modular/planogram optimization and replenishment. Buyer and merchandising guidelines and disciplines are then redefined and reinforced to ensure accountability to supporting store performance. Further product channel development and channel strategies need to be defined and implemented to better optimize and support the stores with product flow to ensure execution. These processes are oriented to linking the following:

- Store-level ordering processes
- Planogram integration with demand planning and replenishment
- Inventory management and flow focus
- Replenishment effectiveness
- Assortment optimization and order-planning ROI maximization
- Process integration and internal collaboration
- CPFR as a gateway to other applications for collaboration
- Channel strategy definition and optimized selection

This further lays the next steps supporting demand and supply visibility, process integration, and optimal joint decision making. If you do not properly implement these strategic initiatives, you minimize the return and speed in implementing collaborative networks.

Collaborative Planning, Forecasting, and Replenishment is the initial step in a multistep process toward full value chain collaboration and competitive transformation.

5.2

Integrating Collaborative Transportation Management and CPFR—A Proposed Process and Tactics for Managing the Broader Supply Chain Collaboration

Prof. Dr. Dawn M. Russell, The Smeal College of Business Administration, The Pennsylvania State University

To successfully implement collaborative supply chain processes, whether planning, forecasting, transportation, or others, we must focus on moving beyond *coordination* to *collaboration*. In many aspects of the supply chain today we see competency in coordination, the skillful and effective interaction of movements. However, true collaboration, working together in a joint intellectual effort such as joint business planning, is less prevalent, and, consequently, full-scale CPFR implementations are not common.

To achieve the maximum potential of Collaborative Planning, Forecasting, and Replenishment (CPFR) it is necessary to focus more broadly on collaboration across the supply chain. CPFR pilots today are primarily focused on planning and forecasting, and not as directly focused on replenishment, the *R* in CPFR. Inherent in this *R* in CPFR is the fact that replenishment involves physically moving the goods via some transportation mode, for example, truck, air, rail, or ocean vessel, from origin to destination. It is this requisite physical movement of the goods that binds collaborative transportation management (CTM) via the *R* to CPFR and creates additional complexity and consequently additional barriers to implementation.

Despite the challenges, however, companies continue to pursue collaboration in a supply chain context looking for improved business-to-business relationships, revenue enhancements, and cost reductions. As a result of the work conducted through the Voluntary Interindustry Commerce Standards (VICS) organization, generally accepted guidelines for implementing CPFR exist, and successful CTM and CPFR pilots are documented.

Going forward we need to focus on developing pilots into fully scalable CTM and CPFR. In doing so we need to consider how to overcome the barriers to full-scale implementation, many of which are associated with social and organizational complexity. Accordingly, the purpose of this discussion is twofold:

1. To introduce CTM as an expansion of CPFR
2. To discuss managerial tactics for pilot teams facing the social and organizational challenges of implementing collaborative supply chain processes, including CTM and CPFR

5.2.1 Integrating CTM and CPFR

The mission of CTM is to extend the CPFR initiative to include the partnership between retailers, suppliers, and carriers through collaborative measures and shared information, in order to improve service efficiency and reduce costs of the transportation process.[1]

CTM focuses on developing appropriate information exchange links among retailers, suppliers, and carriers and enhancing the business relationship among trading partners through joint process development. CTM first focuses on the information exchange process and the business partnerships and then considers appropriate technology support tools.

Retailers should consider CTM as one approach to achieving more consistent lead times. Suppliers can leverage the opportunities offered by CTM to avoid premium unpredicted transportation expense. Finally, carriers will want to consider CTM as a means of improving asset utilization.

5.2.2 CTM Benefits Realized

Three industry leaders, Wal-Mart, Procter & Gamble, and J. B. Hunt, conducted the initial CTM pilot. In reviewing the pilot process, the interenterprise team was able to identify several important benefits, including:

- Additional and improved information availability
- Development of a standard approach for exchanging information among shipper, receiver, and carrier, which resulted in a reduction in unnecessary process steps, that is, less "scrambling" to complete the promotional events
- Improved customer service through improved shipment status visibility for the retailer
- Improved understanding of the customer's business
- Creative expediting of shipments
- Less time spent at the receiver in the form of a 16 percent decrease in unload time
- Fewer empty miles in the form of a 3 percent decrease in empty mile percentage

- Handling additional volume without introducing additional cost into the system so that other customers are not neglected while promotional events are supported[2]

5.2.3 Proposed Process Integration of CTM and CPFR

Many companies today use the CPFR guidelines developed by the CPFR Committee of the VICS organization to drive their activities in organizing and running a CPFR pilot. Recognizing the synergies between CPFR and CTM, VICS, at its February 2002 meeting, made a decision to position the committee focusing on CTM as a subcommittee of CPFR. Through this committee, there are activities in progress to leverage what has been learned from several CPFR pilots and the initial CTM pilot to develop a process standard for CTM and to integrate that standard with the existing CPFR Guidelines. Exhibit 5.3 depicts the existing CPFR guideline, a proposed CTM guideline, and the linkages between these two processes.

There are four primary linkages depicted in Exhibit 5.3: (1) involving the carrier in the front-end agreement; (2) broadening joint business planning to include the carrier; (3) translating the order forecast into a ship forecast to be used by the carrier; and (4) feeding information from the manufacturer and distributor exception triggers into the ship forecast so that exceptions can be resolved among the carrier, manufacturer, and distributor. Each of these linkages plays a key role in bringing the transportation provider into the replenishment process to execute the physical movement of goods as accurately and cost effectively as possible. Involving the carrier in the front-end agreement expands the guidelines for operating collaboratively, which facilitates the cooperative arrangement going forward with carrier involvement. Broadening the joint business planning to include the carrier facilitates more comprehensive information exchange regarding replenishment. Translating the order forecast into a ship forecast provides extended visibility for the carrier to better plan asset utilization. Feeding exception information into the ship forecast ensures that the carrier is kept in the information exchange cycle and has the opportunity to make adjustments to shipment planning as readily as possible.

Exhibit 5.3. Integration of CTM into CPFR.

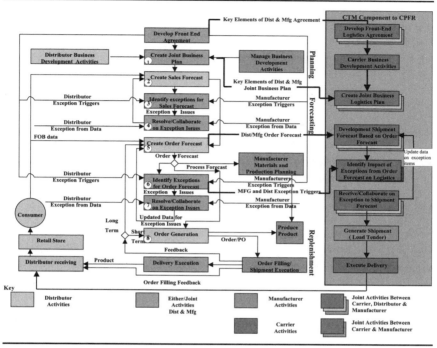

Source: VICS/Dawn M. Russell.

5.2.4 Managerial Tactics for Successful Implementation of Collaborative Processes

Whether it is collaboration in the form of CTM or CPFR, or other collaborative supply chain processes, the implementation of these processes carries with it significant social and organizational complexity, which creates barriers to implementation. To achieve full-scale CPFR and realize the maximum benefit of our efforts, we need to continue to define the elements of this social and organizational complexity and develop tactics and strategies for overcoming the barriers. This section discusses some of the tactics found to facilitate successful implementation of collaborative processes.

People Management Tactics

People are the most important aspect of a collaborative arrangement because collaboration is based heavily upon relationships and trust among trading partners. Specific tactics for managing the people aspects of a collaborative process include:

- *Focus beyond technology standards and functionality.* Although technology standards and appropriate functionality are important to successful CPFR implementation, to get the most out of the technology, companies must also focus on integration of people into the process supported by appropriate technology, technology strategy, and stakeholder management. Understanding who directly and indirectly affects, and is affected by, the CPFR initiative and obtaining their buy-in and support for the project can be leveraged to fully integrate CPFR into the business operations.

- *Leverage existing long-term relationships.* Collaboration is not something that should be initiated with all suppliers and customers. Collaboration is a strategic, joint business–planning initiative. Leveraging existing relationships with long-term business partners is an appropriate starting point. This thinking is aligned with one of the primary tenets of CPFR, which is that its success is significantly influenced by the current and historical relationships of the individuals and organizations involved.

- *Ensure leadership at all levels of the organization, not just the executive level.* We talk a good deal about the need for top-level support in CPFR, and this is true. However, we do not talk as much about the need for managerial-level and operating-level support. It is the managerial and operating levels that allow companies to execute a strategy such as CPFR. If people at these levels are not changing their behaviors, how do we expect the CPFR initiative to become part of the daily operating activities?

- *Facilitate a collaboration mind-set.* The mind-set of the individuals participating on the collaborative process team has to be one of collaboration. One team member from the CTM pilot commented: "It is almost a given that you come to the table with CPFR knowledge." While CPFR specifically may not be the requisite mind-set, a willingness to share information and jointly manage the process is critical to success.[3] *[Source: (2000) VICS/CTM/Northwestern University Research]*

- *Assess CTM readiness.* In the initial CTM pilot, it was recognized that there needs to be already in existence good processes, strong relationships, and trust among the partners. Once there is commitment to the concept and the process is well defined within each partner's business, then the CTM and CPFR processes can be used by each trading partner as a tool to build relationships with other business partners, where the existing relationships may not be as strong.[4] *[Source: (2000) VICS/CTM/Northwestern University Research]*

- *Prioritize face-to-face meetings to facilitate building relationships.* The value of face-to-face meetings is significant for maintaining momentum of the project and for ensuring the quality of the process that is developed. Team members in the initial CTM pilot commented that the only way to develop the relationship to the point where it is strong enough to enable CTM, is to conduct face-to-face meetings over time.[5] *[Source: (2000) VICS/CTM/Northwestern University Research]*

- *Look for the unanticipated opportunities resulting from the interaction.* As a result of the ongoing face-to-face, telephone, and e-mail communications, the three companies in the initial CTM pilot encountered several unanticipated opportunities along the way. There was general consensus that collaboration, especially CTM, is a great opportunity to get three companies talking, even if there is not 100 percent follow-through on initiatives.[6] *[Source: (2000) VICS/CTM/Northwestern University Research]*

Process Management Tactics

Process management in a collaborative situation takes on added complexity as two organizations are brought together. Specific tactics for managing the added complexity include:

- *Develop the facilitative processes.* To achieve scalable, sustainable collaboration, companies need to develop the facilitative processes. We spend a significant amount of time identifying the tasks that need to be completed and organizing them in a process map. However, we do not spend a lot of time considering what is required to facilitate completion of those tasks. In the case of CPFR, specific subprocesses that need to be developed to facilitate successful implementation include: the forecast model development (as opposed to model use) process, collaborative problem-solving process, stakeholder management process, communication process, joint business-planning process, performance measurement process, and the information technology strategy development process.

- *Consider customization as a viable (and potentially necessary) alternative for successful implementation.* There is no "cookie cutter" approach to CPFR. The most successful implementations are those that are developed uniquely to suit the everyday operating activities of the trading partners involved.

- *Maintain realistic expectations of elapsed and applied time.* In considering collaboration, the team needs to maintain realistic expectations regarding the time involved in developing sound relationships upon which an effective collaborative process implementation can be built. In many cases a pilot can take six to twelve months to conduct. This time estimate includes the pilot planning, implementation, and post-pilot implementation assessment.

- *Measure the process in addition to measuring the outcomes.* CPFR is for many organizations a significant shift in thinking. We have long measured *outcomes* such as inventory levels, customer service, and delivery performance, and should continue to do so. However, with the dramatic process shift associated with CTM and CPFR, measuring changes in the *process* is key to achieving the desired improvements in outcome. People act as they are motivated to act and if we want people to dramatically change how they act in a short period of time, they typically need to have an incentive to do so. Developing measures of the process provides new goals for employees to achieve in addition to their outcome-oriented goals.

- *Enforce revised performance metrics during the pilot period.* In addition to developing the right process and outcome metrics for the pilot period, these performance metrics should be incorporated into the existing performance metrics of the team members. Keeping in mind that people act as they are motivated to act, they must be motivated to act differently during the development and implementation of the collaborative processes. Considering that the pilot process can be as long as a year, people who are not bound by new performance incentives may revert back to old habits, such as end-of-quarter pushes, which can quickly derail the collaborative pilot.

- *Consider a third party to facilitate the pilot.* In order to keep the process focused, and to facilitate the interaction among companies in the process development stages, third-party unbiased guidance is recommended. For example, in the case of the initial CTM pilot, a third-party facilitator working through the VICS organization was involved during the pilot-planning stages.[7] *[Source: (2000) VICS/ CTM/Northwestern University Research]*

- *Strive to meet the scheduling challenges.* To facilitate participation in face-to-face meetings, schedule the sessions a month in advance and compel people to make the meeting a priority. Because face-to-face meetings are critical to success, the scheduling challenge must be met.[8] *[Source: (2000) VICS/CTM/Northwestern University Research]*

- *Commit to improving the broader supply chain.* While CTM and CPFR are focused on specific supply chain processes, the impacts of these initiatives reach throughout the supply chain. Therefore, to reap the full benefits, the trading partners need to be committed to improving the broader supply chain, in addition to their specific processes of interest.[9] *[Source: (2000) VICS/CTM/Northwestern University Research]*

Information Technology Management Tactics

Technology to support collaborative supply chain processes ranges from very simple spreadsheets or databases to the more sophisticated offerings serving the collaborative space from software vendors such as Syncra Systems, i2, and Manugistics. Specific tactics for managing the information technology to support a collaborative effort include:

- *Employ a suite of technology tools to support the collaborative processes.* Collaboration is a multifaceted process and by its very nature requires a wide range of information technology support tools. Collaboration requires a suite of technology to facilitate jointly:

- Developing and testing analytical models
- Sharing standard transactional data, for example, inventory availability, shipment notices, customer orders
- Exchanging nontransactional information to support decision making, for example, discussing issues between two or more individuals or groups, raising new ideas, providing feedback regarding satisfaction with the arrangement
- Developing documents, for example, the front-end agreement, joint business plans
- Obtaining and incorporating nontechnical market information, for example, changes in market conditions

A Team Support System (TSS) concept can be used to guide the development of an integrated information technology architecture. A TSS is defined as a system that provides full information systems support to the members of a team who participate in one or more specific processes or tasks. A TSS supports the individual work of each team member, as well as the members' collaborative work in various modes of interaction, and supports their collaboration whether they are working at the same location or at different locations, and whether they are working at the same time (synchronously) or at different times (asynchronously).[10]

- *Address technology issues in the design phase focusing on how to best support the unique manner in which collaborative teams think and act.* One of the characteristics of collaboration is that it is very much an intellectual effort. As a group, collaborative teams think differently than each member of the group thinks individually. Consequently, to support the workings of the group, the technology must be implemented to support the *collaborative intellectual* effort.

Although we operate in an environment of more questions than answers regarding "how" to collaborate, we continue to make strides as a community of practice toward developing useful tactics and strategies for overcoming the barriers to implementation. Social and organizational complexity is virtually uncharted territory in the field of supply chain management, but it is an area that is increasingly crucial to achieving the next significant gain in supply chain efficiency.

Notes

1. www.vics.org (2000).
2. VICS/CTM/Northwestern University Research (2000).
3. Ibid.
4. Ibid.
5. Ibid.
6. Ibid.
7. Ibid.
8. Ibid.
9. Ibid.
10. Manheim, Vlahos, and Xie (1994).

5.3

The Foundation Is in Place—It Is Time to Transform

Ralph W. Drayer, Supply Chain Insights, formerly of Procter & Gamble

Savvy executives are seeing the opportunity to drive the use of the Internet and supply chain partnerships to transform their supply chains, delivering differentiated capability, value, and competitive advantage in the process.

5.3.1 The Quiet Revolution

Much has been written about the subjects of logistics, supply chain management, value nets, and e-business, but most companies have been slow to take advantage of what has become one of the most dramatic and dynamic changes to business in the last hundred years. Leveraging the Internet with the best supply chain management techniques creates not only greater efficiencies but, more important, differentiated value and customer loyalty through the creation of entirely new business models. Witness the success of the early transformers, companies like Dell and Cisco.

When viewed in the context of today's consumer-driven market-place—extremely rapid changes in consumer preferences, behaviors, and shopping options—the need for, and opportunity of, advantages through supply chain transformation should be compelling.

5.3.2 The Foundation

Despite the slower than expected uptake in supply chain transformation, all the required foundation elements are now in place.

Tremendous strides have been made in the art and science of supply chain management as it has evolved from physical distribution and logistics to a more holistic focus on the management of upstream and downstream relationships with suppliers, distributors, and customers to achieve greater consumer value added at less cost. A fundamental principle of supply chain management is that significant leverage can be obtained by working with suppliers and customers as if they were part of an integrated, seamless pipeline. In this way, considerable improvements in total delivered cost as well as customer satisfaction can be achieved.

Supply chain management tools such as continuous replenishment and high-velocity cross-docking delivered impressive results for customers and suppliers alike and led an entire industry to come together to develop more efficient supply chain practices. Launched in 1993, Efficient Consumer Response (ECR) has changed the whole trading partner focus from adversarial "win-lose" negotiation to collaborative trading relationships focused on removing inefficiencies from the total supply chain and delivering higher consumer satisfaction and value. Perhaps most important, ECR built trust and demonstrated the value of deeper collaboration across the supply chain, preparing these companies to fully leverage the powerful capabilities of the Internet.

The dream of supply chain transparency and real-time interaction with all trading partners became a reality with the arrival of the Internet. The Internet allows unprecedented, seamless, and continuous exchanges across the supply chain. Significant efficiencies can be gained through linking the supply chain and removing unnecessary inventory, variation, and cost and reducing cycle times to create an "extended enterprise." In an extended enterprise environment, the sharing of information leads to common goals, increased velocity of trade, and a meshing of business processes.

Because the Internet is a robust commerce platform, it shifts the emphasis from simply *connecting* partners, which is mostly transaction oriented, to *coordinating* interbusiness processes. This is important because coordination is knowledge and process oriented and synchronization at this level creates more value across the chain.

5.3.3 The Opportunity

The real payoff from these three critical foundation elements: supply chain management, Efficient Consumer Response, and the Internet is enabling *business collaboration*. Collaboration occurs when companies work together for mutual benefit. It means that companies leverage each other on an operational basis so that together they perform better than they could separately. Collaboration can occur all along the value chain from design collaboration, through procurement and final distribution. This allows companies sharing information to dramatically shorten processing time, eliminate value-depleting activities, and improve quality, accuracy, and asset productivity. The overriding goal is to optimize the end-to-end supply chain for the benefit of the end consumer.

Collaborative Planning, Forecasting, and Replenishment (CPFR) is a great example of a new, collaborative business process reflecting the evolution of an ECR supply chain practice (continuous replenishment) and a demand chain practice (category management). CPFR creates a "win–win" scenario, bringing demand and supply planning together in one process and tying the buyer and seller together so that their goals are compatible. By competing as one, buyer and seller form a value chain that will easily come out ahead of other buyers and sellers still focused on win–lose price negotiation.

The ultimate business collaboration models emerging are called "value nets" and "virtual enterprises." If you have ordered a computer over the Internet, you've come in contact with this model. It transforms the traditional linear supply chain to create differentiated capability and competitive advantage. Changing the way you do business is what it is all about!

The value net business model uses advanced supply chain and ECR concepts to achieve both superior customer satisfaction and company profitability. It links increasingly specific customer requirements to flexible, cost-effective manufacturing and uses digital information to move products rapidly, bypassing costly distribution layers. It connects supply chain providers that work in concert to deliver tailored solutions. It elevates operational design to the strategic level and adapts to constant change.

As the name implies, it is no longer just about supply, it is about creating *value* for customers, the company, and its suppliers. It is also no longer a sequential, rigid, linear supply chain. Instead, it is a fast, flexible, high-performance network of customer/supplier partnerships and information flows. The value net begins with the customer, allows him or her to design products from a menu, and builds to satisfy actual demand, leveraging operations and customer choice to drive strategic advantage. Since the value net's product and service advantage is based on a collaborative set of relationships, it is also harder for competitors to replicate it.

Another powerful transformational model is the "virtual" or "extended enterprise," which changes the entire concept of what it means to be a company. In this model, each company performs just those processes at which it excels, leaving others to do the rest. A manufacturer, for instance, may concentrate on marketing and sales; its suppliers may collaborate to design the manufacturer's product, and a distributor may perform the actual assembly. Every participant in the virtual enterprise has a common focus: delivering the greatest possible value to the final customer at the lowest possible cost to the enterprise. To achieve this objective, information must be shared, redundancy eliminated, and opportunities for collaboration exploited. This in turn requires unprecedented cooperation, enterprisewide planning, alignment around common goals, and an inclusive culture.

5.3.4 The Challenge

The value net and virtual enterprise models offer a dramatic improvement in performance but also demand radical changes in thinking and behavior. There is no silver bullet. The key is good business process integration and customer focus. This requires clear consumer value identification of the business problem or opportunity, thinking externally and viewing your extended supply chain as a strategic differentiator, and changing organizational structures—multifunctional and horizontal process teams, high-commitment work systems, and flexible structures that can be easily modified. Traditional patterns of suspicion and mistrust must also give way to openness and sharing; collaboration is to be expected and rewarded. Finally, senior management's understanding and leadership are obviously critical to create the capacity for change and an environment for success.

In preparing for the transformation, companies must progress through various stages of supply chain competence:

- *Internal Supply Chain Optimization:* typically a new organizational structure for product supply, metrics, and an internal communication system
- *Network Formation:* really beginning to work with supply chain partners and customers, removing barriers and sharing information
- *Value Network Formation:* extensive use of Extranets, collaborative planning, and design systems and some process integration
- *Virtual Enterprise:* full network connectivity is achieved and the company becomes the nucleus of the extended enterprise

Ultimately, the successful companies of tomorrow will be those that push the use of the Internet and supply chain partnerships more strategically than in the past, creating new revenue opportunities and achieving new levels of efficiency, customer loyalty, and customer satisfaction. The message, then, is for companies to start building on and leveraging the transformational foundation now in place—it is time!

5.4

Avoiding CPFR Pitfalls in the Consumer Goods Industry

Daren K. Fairfield, Accenture

Collaborative Planning, Forecasting, and Replenishment and the broader notion of interenterprise collaboration across multiple business practices can, and will, be the next breakaway business advantage for early adopters that get it right. However, this requires a supporting business strategy that can be transformational in nature, with respect to an organization's culture, operating philosophy, reward system, and business processes. It is this mind shift that is not always recognized or embraced by organizations as they embark on their collaborative journeys. The result is that these organizations get constrained by their own inconsistent business models, which leads to dissatisfaction with the collaborative process. Thus, the momentum to scale collaboration remains unsupported and unachieved. This is a shame because the value of collaboration is quite compelling, necessary even, for future business survival.

An example of what CPFR is directly targeted at exposing and resolving can be found in the following statistic, which is as true today as it was in 1996, when the Coca-Cola out-of-stock study, in concert with Accenture, was published. In spite of the consumer goods pipeline in the United States containing over $1 trillion (U.S.) (see Exhibit 5.4), lost sales due to out-of-stock situations was estimated to be as high as $12 billion (U.S.). This problem is most realized on promoted items, which are out of stock 15 percent of the time, which is even more damaging as you invite the consumer in for a specific offer and are unable to fulfill that offer.

The out-of-stock situation for nonpromoted items on a typical day is characterized by the following (see Exhibit 5.5):

- A shopper in the average supermarket will find 8.2 percent of items out of stock on a typical afternoon.

EXHIBIT 5.4. INVENTORY POSITIONS.

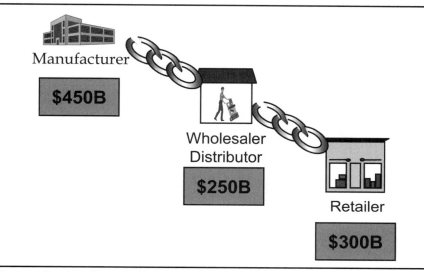

SOURCE: Benchmarking Partners, U.S. Commerce Department monthly sales and inventory reports.

- These out-of-stock occurrences represent 6.5 percent of sales.
- The consumers refuse to buy an alternative 3.4 percent of the time, which results in lost sales of 3.1 percent of the 6.5 percent of sales.
- The net result: $7 billion to $12 billion of lost sales.

CPFR can also address the issue of high promotions spend. For U.S.-based consumer goods manufacturing companies, trade promotion spend is the second largest profit and loss statement item after cost of goods, at $25 billion, which is roughly 13 percent of sales. These are the visible costs. It is also estimated that hidden costs exist of up to $5.8 billion, with fully 70 to 80 percent of this attributable to supply chain volatility and uncertainty.[1]

Our research has shown that promotions spend is not effective:

- Manufacturers estimate that only 35 percent of their promotions turn a profit.
- Sixty percent of consumers said that promotions have no influence on store selection.

EXHIBIT 5.5. STOCK POSITIONS.

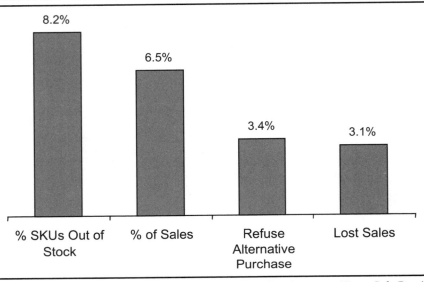

SOURCE: Retailer operation data, Prism Partner store audits, Accenture/Coca-Cola Retail Council Study.

- Only 50 percent of manufacturers surveyed are looking at incremental profitability.

Additionally, promotions often create volatility in demand resulting in significant supply chain implications, even for a single item (see Exhibit 5.6):

- High or excess inventory
- Lost sales and dissatisfaction
- Waste and write-offs
- Manufacturing disruption
- High administration costs
- Invoice queries and poor cash flow

CPFR addresses these industry ills directly and enables new avenues for performance improvement in these critical areas and many others.

EXHIBIT 5.6. IMPACT OF PROMOTIONS ON VARIATIONS IN VOLUME FOR ONE SKU.

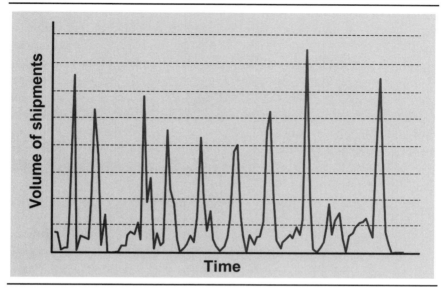

SOURCE: Accenture, Trade Promotion Study (2001).

The consumer goods industry is faced with thin margins, consolidation, and the balance of power shifting from manufacturers to retailers, which makes it critical for consumer goods manufacturers to embrace collaborative practices that allow them to establish a leadership—think preferred—relationship with retail trade partners.

The balance of this chapter conveys some of the common pitfalls of CPFR implementation and dispels some of the myths and misguided thinking of early collaborative efforts. The concepts are globally applicable. Think about your own company's situation and apply these insights to your business model for collaboration. Your trading partners, and consumers, will thank you for it.

5.4.1 Pitfall #1: CPFR Is Far Too Cumbersome to Execute Effectively

Companies have consistently mismanaged expectations with respect to what they believe they will achieve and the approach they take to executing the work. This unaligned positioning for success generally stifles momentum for CPFR efforts and causes initial pilot results to not reflect the true benefit potential of collaboration. The reported results of early collaborative efforts can be masked by the hardships faced in execution by personnel who were not positioned for success to begin with. When presented to senior management, the benefits do not seem commensurate with the effort required, and if the people executing the work were not positioned to succeed, they sour on the process and ultimately decide not to support it, for the wrong reasons (i.e., "This is too burdensome for me"). Exhibit 5.7 shows some common symptoms that can skew the results of initial CPFR pilot efforts and the true root cause.

Much of the perception of "cumbersome" activity is rooted in the fact that many companies do not have a consistent business model internally for planning, forecasting, and exception management. CPFR—note that this means collaborative planning, collaborative forecasting, and collaborative replenishment—requires a discipline in planning and forecasting that is lacking in most companies. Replenishment, by necessity, is generally the most mature in terms of consistent processes and defined execution but remains compromised as a victim of the Bullwhip Effect triggered by upstream inaccuracy. The rigor and discipline expected as part of CPFR is essential to maximizing the benefits and is why CPFR is such a powerful catalyst for "uptalenting" your organization and exposing gaps in current operating procedures and business functions.

Summary

Do not be deceived into the "CPFR is too cumbersome" assessment without looking beyond the surface symptoms and into the reality of what the drivers are specific to your organization. More often than not, the reality is that CPFR is being executed with part-time resources, without the benefit of a consistent business model for planning and forecasting, and without the alignment of key stakeholders and practitioners equally engaged and motivated to inculcate the collaborative model into their everyday activities. By addressing these symptoms, your business performance should dramatically improve and your col-

EXHIBIT 5.7. PROBLEMS WITH INITIAL CPFR PILOTS AND THEIR SOLUTIONS.

Symptom	Cause	Recommendation	Rationale	Long-Term Outlook
This takes too much time and additional steps.	Resources are executing parallel activities—current way of managing the business and new collaborative business model.	For the category or SKU set chosen, only execute according to the new business model . . . and allow focus to occur.	This alleviates the symptom of "extra" work or overtime and allows a focus that provides a pure assessment of activity. It is not the collaboration that takes too much time, but the fact that it is incremental work.	Though an additional learning curve is required initially, CPFR will alleviate much of the non–value-added "back end" time resources currently spent fixing problems—taking current reactive work away and replacing it with proactive, less expensive exception management, before business disruption occurs.
There are far too many exceptions to sort through and find anything meaningful.	Trying to catch everything rather than what are the truly major exceptions, i.e., law of Diminishing Returns.	Exception thresholds must include a real value or percent and a time component. These "values" are iterated until a reasonable level is established that meets both your and your trading partner's needs.	Exception management must be focused on the exceptions that fall within a "window of action" so as to spend valuable time on only those exceptions that require attention in a certain time frame.	This attention to only the meaningful exceptions can be narrowed to a small amount that needs to be addressed, usually requiring only minutes each week. If not, then there are deeper-rooted problems stemming from suboptimal business processes that need to be addressed.
We have been putting in all this work, but we are not seeing material benefits.	This is often because the core team is trying to shepherd the key role players into performing their duties (which they verbally committed to but are not following through on), rather than focusing on the actual work of collaboration; hence, they end up doing work that others should be responsible for and nagging others.	You must make the owners of the activities accountable for the outcomes. They vote with their time and without incentive will not actively participate.	Without this empowerment and accountability, the result is uncommitted resources, most likely because people are "too busy" with day-to-day tasks as an excuse, meaning that they again have not been positioned for success or motivated to succeed and thus are part-time based on their behavior . . . and never embrace collaboration.	True believers and sustainability in the process will come only from those that actively see the results of their personal efforts. Part-time resources rarely achieve this level of commitment.

laborative efforts will be rewarding. Remember, CPFR is meant to largely replace current reactive activities that cause business disruption with proactive activities that are intended, when properly applied, to eliminate exceptions or enable resolution of exceptions before business disruption occurs.

5.4.2 Pitfall #2: CPFR Requires All Nine Steps of the VICS Model

The Voluntary Interindustry Commerce Standards (VICS) model for CPFR is not a recipe, but a guideline for CPFR execution. For reference, the nine steps of the VICS model are:

Step 1: Develop collaboration arrangement.

Step 2: Create joint business plan.

Step 3: Create sales forecast.

Step 4: Identify exceptions for sales forecast.

Step 5: Resolve/collaborate on exception items.

Step 6: Create order forecast.

Step 7: Identify exceptions for order forecast.

Step 8: Resolve/collaborate on exception items.

Step 9: Generate order.

Rare is the case when a company can successfully implement all nine steps, since it generally does not emphasize both sales and order forecasts internally. Its trading partners also do not typically forecast both sales and orders. So, steps 1 and 2 should be followed, but steps 3, 4, 5 and 6, 7, and 8 are rarely executed together. Step 9 is always executed, or commerce is not being conducted. If you are fortunate enough to be able to execute all nine steps with your trading partner, you will be differentiated from many of your competitors and this will be to your advantage, as you get more opportunity to catch exceptions early.

Generally, consumer goods manufacturers will be receiving some type of sales forecast from the retailer that is a combination of volume and time horizon. Given this, the collaboration generally is happening on a sales forecast. However, what a manufacturer is generally more interested in is an order forecast. Retailers rarely forecast orders, since they prefer the flexibility to create an order when they wish, or let the replenishment system run its course for generating orders, which does not require orders to be forecasted, but generates orders at the point of need based on parameters of inventory on hand, lead time, safety stock, and actual and projected sales.

What manufacturers often do is use the sales forecast to create a basic order forecast that is not collaborated on with their trading partner, but is used for production scheduling and demand planning. So the insights of "predictive demand" can be achieved, even without the execution of all nine steps of the VICS model. The trap here is that trading partners can become enamored with trying to force each other into an order forecast so that they are complying with the VICS model, but then focus is lost on the outcomes and the spirit of what is trying to be achieved, and the process becomes a barrier, rather than an enabler.

Another reason all nine steps may not be executed is if a manufacturer or retailer knows that its forecasting is inferior to its trade partners', and it chooses to accept its partner's forecast as is, without the need for exception generation. This does not alleviate the need for actual collaboration, however, to ensure that deviations from base replenishment are identified through up-front planning or late-breaking events are captured that are not reflected in the forecast.

Another pitfall companies may incur when implementing the nine-step model is bypassing step 2. This was recognized early on by VICS as the practice evolved from what VICS had coined CFAR, Collaborative Forecasting and Replenishment, to include the planning component so vital to a collaborative *strategy with your trading partner*. The joint business-planning process is critical to establish common business goals, aligned operating procedures, and consumer-focused activities. Without step 2, you will have a set of business rules for exchanging data and conducting collaborative activities that are established in step 1, but you will not have the common business objectives for sales growth and category performance that are crucial to business outcome success. What happens is that you often experience counterproductive activities because the collaborative team is identifying exceptions and suggesting resolutions while another group in the organization is focusing on end results and trying to make deals that revoke the progress made collaboratively. Why? Because there are no joint plans in place that guide behaviors and business expectations. The results are suboptimized inventory in the supply chain, increased customer dissatisfaction, diluted performance measures, and greater administrative overhead to get the players on the same page with the collaborative model.

Summary

All nine steps of the VICS CPFR model do not need to be implemented to achieve significant benefits. The notion of getting to all nine steps can be an aspiration but should not be the ultimate goal. The ultimate goal is collaborating on *what is important between you and your trading partner* and *sharing the relevant information* that makes this collaboration productive and sustainable. The VICS model can serve as an excellent guideline, but remember it is just that—a guideline to be used smartly and not an end in itself.

5.4.3 Pitfall #3: CPFR Is Sharing Data with My Trading Partner, So I Am Collaborating

For clarity, perhaps the acronym CPFR should be expanded to CPCFCR, for collaboration is the special ingredient that brings the practice of CPFR to life. CPFR expects collaboration with your trading partner in *all* the areas of Planning, Forecasting, and Replenishment. Simply sharing data, which admittedly is a step in the right direction, does not account for the aligned processes and common objectives necessary for providing the context of the collaboration. Without this interaction, what you have is a more complex version of EDI-like transactions that require interpretation and cause frustration due to unknown intent when data values change or are adjusted. This results in a risk of making bad business decisions based on assumptions that may or may not be valid, and does little to promote trust with your trading partner.

By collaborating up front and throughout the process, what you establish is a trust and understanding with your trading partner that reaches unprecedented levels. By sharing each other's business processes and constraints, eye-opening insights generate new ideas. These ideas empower the removal of age-old barriers, barriers often rooted in dated practices no longer valid or contrived perception that is absent of facts. Non-value-added activities can be attacked directly throughout the demand and supply chains, together with your trade partner or independently as appropriate for maximum effect.

This insight can manifest itself in many ways and has often gone unshared simply because there was never a forum to ask for or provide this kind of information. One example related to the power of this insight includes using collaborative planning as a way to engage in a time-mapping exercise with your trading partner. The insights provided during this effort often highlight bottlenecks or ineffective processes that drive forecasting inaccuracy or inflate time and costs associated with replenishment activity. This collaborative activity alone has resulted in several days' worth of reduced lead times and mutual adjustments to ordering and replenishment systems that now have aligned parameters for maximum throughput in the correct order quantities. Another case for emphasizing collaborative planning is to have foresight into key business events such as promotions and seasonal shifts in merchandise planning so that forecasts become less volatile, more accurate, and more predictable for trade partners. This demand foresight allows for benefits that ripple back through a manufacturer's supply chain, including more effective production scheduling, less overtime for unanticipated events, better asset utilization, less obsolescence, reduced inventory carrying costs, and improved procurement activities for packaging and raw materials.

Summary

Though data sharing is a step in the right direction, it alone cannot unleash the insightful power and benefit achievement that collaboration can. Collaboration removes much of the uncertainty that remains with simple data sharing. By collaborating, the risk aversion that drives up safety stocks and inflated contingency built into service-level agreements can be reduced. Why? Because you have a knowledge context that complements the data and a forum for proactive issue/exception resolution, which reduces the profile of trade risk with your collaboration partner. Of course, the given assumption, and this is just good business in any context, is that relentless execution accompanies this insight and that words and actions are aligned and followed through on. Without this commitment and spirit of collaboration, you are back to simple data sharing or worse, sharing data that are misleading and are not a true indicator of intent.

5.4.4 Pitfall #4: CPFR Is Only Valid if Done at Scale, with All My Trading Partners and Items

CPFR delivers material benefits to both parties even with only one trading partner. Early pilots have proven this time and again. Broader application of CPFR across multiple trading partners and multiple items can and does deliver even greater benefits, and companies should look to pragmatically scale their collaborative efforts. Notice that the two prior sentences did not say *all* trading partners or *all* items. Each trading partner relationship should be deployed in a consistent way, but not all trading partners and not all items are created equal and cannot be expected to perform equally. Resources should be allocated according to the prioritized benefit objectives set for each collaboration. So *scale* is not equivalent to *all*, which is the pitfall risk that can stifle a broader change program before it gets momentum. Scale is good, but each company's definition of scale will differ, and benefits are achievable whether your end-state vision of scale is accomplished or not.

Scale is best executed and achieved when a common, pragmatic approach to scaling is used that can be applied to the two key scaling considerations: (1) scaling collaboration within a specific trading partner relationship and (2) scaling collaboration across your enterprise and multiple trading partner relationships. Companies have suffered when they do not think this through adequately to be able to accommodate both types of scale effectively. Exhibit 5.8 depicts a pragmatic approach for scaling CPFR initiatives that accommodates the two key scaling considerations.

Scale must consider several dimensions, including your organization and your trading partner's readiness in terms of culture, work flow, data management, and forecast detail information available. Even when properly applied, scale will test your internal processes and rapidly expose inconsistencies that require internal collaboration or standardization, prior to being positioned for broader collaboration across your enterprise and your trading partner community. When determining the approach to scale, the goal should not be to get all the items or all the

EXHIBIT 5.8. THE PRAGMATIC APPROACH TO SCALE.

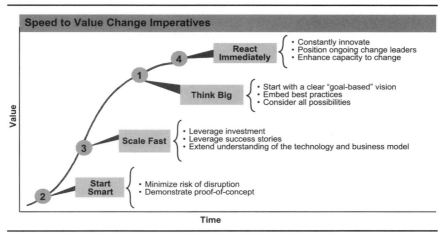

SOURCE: Accenture.

trading partners on the program as fast as possible. The goal should be to move at a fast, but manageable pace that is based on a priority of business benefit and controlled change within the business, while pushing the comfort zone for change so that momentum is not lost and actual change occurs.

Let us first consider some of the pitfalls of the items selected. For building momentum in a proof-of-concept and then looking at priority for scaling, items that have the characteristics of volume, velocity, and variability should be selected for collaboration. The pitfall is using items in early collaboration efforts that are slow movers, rarely promoted, and low in volume. Why? Because the impact to the business on these items is low, and they are not the ones causing most of the business disruption or lost sales in the supply chain. Exhibit 5.9 illustrates some of the characteristics of items for prioritization in more detail.

Now let us consider the pitfalls of trading partner selection and prioritization. Trading partner selection is often a balance of trade-offs, since most trading partners will not fit all the "best" characteristics for collaboration as you define them. The assessment process starts with the strategic intent you have for each of your trading partners and the mutual benefit that can be achieved collaboratively. If trading partners have a lower level of strategic importance, they are probably of less interest

EXHIBIT 5.9. COLLABORATION ITEM CHARACTERISTICS.

Item Characteristic	Collaboration Priority	Rationale
High Volume	Yes	High-volume items have more of an impact on the business, generally incur more carrying costs, and drive consumers' perception of overall in-stock performance and satisfaction of service.
High Velocity	Yes	High-turn items can be more difficult to replenish as mistakes are highly visible, and these items are generally more competitive so risk of lost sales is high when not available.
High Variability	Yes	These items are heavily promoted items and have sensitive price elasticity and seasonal or other stimulus buying patterns that make it hard to forecast and manage the unexpected.
Low Volume	No	Low volume means that they have less impact on the business and do not affect as broad a customer base if out of stock for a brief period.
Low Velocity	No	Low turns means that the items most likely have little impact on the bottom line and replenishment is more easily managed.
Low Variability	No	These items can be more easily forecasted on a base level of replenishment, often with little human intervention if automated replenishment systems are in place. Also, lower risk of lost sales and less price elasticity generally prevails.

or value to engage collaboratively. Strategic intent alone does not answer the prioritization question but should start the process that then allows for categorizing trading partner candidates according to tactical criteria. Exhibit 5.10 illustrates a sampling of tactical trading partner criteria and their rationale.

Though the list is not exhaustive, and the pitfall indicators are not absolute, picking your trading partners is important to the success of a broader-scaled program. Trading partners can be your biggest advocate or your biggest critic, and their influence can be significant, so it pays to manage your relationships accordingly.

Summary

The most important ways to avoid scale pitfalls are making sure you can handle scale internally (consistent business model and resources), do not

EXHIBIT 5.10. TRADING PARTNER SELECTION CRITERIA AND RATIONALE.

Trading Partner Selection Criteria	Rationale	Pitfall Indicators
Willingness to collaborate	You need to have a willing partner since it will then put in the time and resources to be successful and behave collaboratively. If a customer is requiring this commitment, then it had better be willing.	Verbal willingness, but: • Behaviors not consistent • Lack of responsiveness • Unwilling or unable to share relevant information • Shifting/turnover of resources
Customer or external requirement	A customer (think retailer or third party) may be deploying a collaborative model that either requires your commitment or can benefit you directly. If no benefit, and not a strategic or necessary customer, you may want to reconsider future business plans.	• Be sure the customer is truly willing and that you understand its expectations. • Failure to identify where the customer has prioritized your organization in its rollout plan, or its inability to tell you this, can lead to rough implementation.
Partner readiness	A trading partner needs to have a certain amount of business and technical capability to effectively collaborate. For example, this entails the ability to generate forecasts and send electronic information.	• Even though a trading partner may be willing, it may not be capable. • A readiness assessment or survey should help give you information and guide the partner's priority to you, often requiring more lead time to gain base-level capability.
Existing trading partner relationship	Do we have a good working relationship currently, and are we willing to try new things? Are we looking to build a stronger relationship, achieve preferred supplier status, or differentiate ourselves from our competitors? If our relationship is not positive, efforts are unlikely to be productive.	• Collaboration requires a relationship of trust and is a critical component of success. • This trust must be earned and backed up by behavior, so history of interaction may provide an indicator of future activity. • Also consider relationships within specific areas of your trading partner organization, since positive relationships in some areas may be hindered or affected by negative relationships in others.
Executive sponsorship commitment	The priorities are set by executives and conducted by practitioners. Without executive commitment, your trading partner may not be engaged for success, but driven only by necessity.	• Unwillingness to put in writing mutual commitments • Failure to attend important exploratory or planning meetings

equate scale with all items or every trading partner (strategic intent), and do not believe that benefits are achievable only at scale (the right level of collaboration is better than no collaboration or excessive collaboration). Scale is important to collaboration and bringing a collaborative culture to life for your organization. Unmitigated scale or scaling for the wrong reasons has the opposite effect and kills collaborative initiatives unjustly, putting your organization at a serious competitive disadvantage for the future.

5.4.5 Pitfall #5: CPFR Has No ROI, Since I Cannot Directly Quantify the Benefits

The business case for CPFR can be complex due to its pervasiveness across the enterprise, the fact that the performance metrics it affects are subject to many other influences, and that the qualitative benefits can be just as significant as the quantitative ones. This is true as you look at external performance indicators and internal performance indicators, providing further duplicity with respect to a "typical" business case. Some may look at this as a hardship, while others view this as an opportunity. Successful companies think of the latter.

A common pitfall associated with CPFR business case development is the fact that company practitioners are reluctant to claim benefits due to their fear of other influences that may call into question the validity of their benefit claims. The practitioners then dilute the true incremental benefit associated with a CPFR program for fear of reprisal or skepticism. What practitioners tend to forget is that this is true in most, if not all, business case situations. Assumptions must be made, and execution is part of the equation; other activities, known or unknown, contribute to metrics-based performance measurement. However, the key is to set a baseline of performance metrics that are understood and should show improvement based on the collaborative practice efforts. The up-front business case is based on assumptions of real or percent-based improvements across a certain size or category of business, typically targeted at sales growth (through improved in-stocks and forecast accuracy, for example) and cost reduction (through better supply chain and inventory management, for example). Then these metrics are tracked against the baseline for the specific items and locations that are part of the collaborative program, and as these indicators change, the link is made and conclusions can be drawn. Because you are tracking specific items and locations, you can also separate other influences from the effects of collaboration to provide more meaningful results and calm the skeptics. It becomes extremely difficult to argue against collaboration if these metrics are better after the program has been initiated than before. Where do the benefits come from? Exhibit 5.11 offers a typical sample of key performance measures that are used to track CPFR benefits.

Another pitfall of business case development is that qualitative or "soft" benefits are often overlooked and not balanced with quantitative or "hard" benefits. Many valuable performance improvements come from the qualitative effects of collaboration. The process of goal setting, joint business planning, and tracking performance measures as part of CPFR provides the capability to align disparate functional groups and focuses teams and individuals on outcomes rather than individual measures, which can transform an organization like never before. The "way of thinking" brought about by collaboration, and fueled by executive support, can drive new levels of innovation and cooperation internally. These changes can be noticed by customers, as organizations become easier to do business with and more responsive to their customers' needs and requests. These concepts are not lost on most executives and should not be left out of any business case discussion. Exhibit 5.12 shows how

EXHIBIT 5.11. A SAMPLING OF KEY PERFORMANCE INDICATORS.

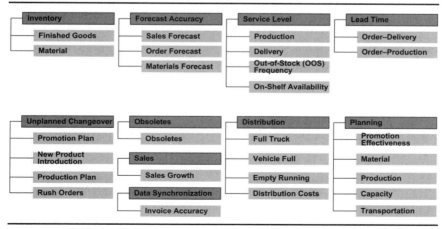

SOURCE: ECR Europe/Accenture.

Exhibit 5.12. CPFR benefits extended to new business models.

New Product Introductions	• Incorporate joint product design—speed to market • More effective private label planning and development • Able to gain product authorization/acceptance from retailer more rapidly
Trade Promotions	• Coordinated spend that is traceable for ROI analysis • Unprecedented micromarketing opportunities • Currently manufacturers' second largest P&L item, after COGS
Scan-Based Trading	• Improved level of trust with trading partners • Able to focus on the most beneficial products for SBT • Improved cash flow for SBT items • Availability of a balance of business models—SBT and/or VMI
Virtual or Extended Enterprise	• Access to trading partner expertise/experience as if they were part of your own enterprise • Retailers amplify the intelligence capture of your field sales and customer service group • Third parties act as if they are part of your organization, stronger accountabilities, aligned or even integrated business processes

Source: Accenture.

CPFR benefits can be extended into new business models for a company and bring even greater business value.

Finally, a common pitfall that constrains business momentum and benefit realization is the failure to think broadly enough about the benefit effects and the enablement capabilities of CPFR. CPFR does influence and have direct impact in a number of cross-functional areas. The underlying root of value associated with CPFR is that for the first time a business practice ties together, in a very conscious way, the demand and supply planning upon which product forecasting and replenishment is based. CPFR can link, and even better integrate, this tie of supply and demand across a wider range of influence than ever before possible, as it can extend from a raw materials supplier through to the consumer at the point of sale, and can include third-party providers along the way. This "closed" loop of information flow, work flow, and coordinated behavior eliminates or dramatically reduces the gaps that exist in today's supply chain due to insufficient information and unharmonized activity. Exhibit 5.13 represents the interactive benefit opportunities that become more achievable through CPFR.

Exhibit 5.14 illustrates the specific benefit opportunities across the broad base of core business activities.

Summary

Though business case development for CPFR can be unique and complex given its multidimensional views and breadth of influence, the pit-

Exhibit 5.13. CPFR enables interactive benefits.

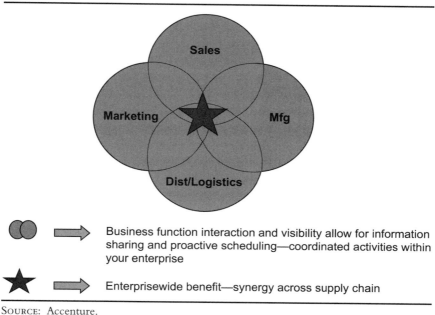

Business function interaction and visibility allow for information sharing and proactive scheduling—coordinated activities within your enterprise

Enterprisewide benefit—synergy across supply chain

Source: Accenture.

fall to avoid is trying to make the business case too fine and losing sight of the business outcomes, both quantitative and qualitative. Business case development should follow the same approach as CPFR: Think big, start small, scale fast, and react immediately. The business case that is developed can then be brought to life and evolved with the program, while showing demonstrable progress to baseline measures that can win increasing support for scale.

Conclusion

CPFR for the first time consciously brings together demand and supply planning in a collaborative context. It raises the bar for interoperability and competitive differentiation that positions early adopters for preferred relationships with their key customers and for business improvements that yield top-line results. In the current environment of thin margins, consolidation, and increasing consumer influence, those manufacturers that embrace collaboration will have a far greater chance of surviving as they tighten their bond with key accounts, gain greater

EXHIBIT 5.14. BENEFIT OPPORTUNITIES ACROSS BUSINESS FUNCTIONS.

Business Function	Benefit Opportunity
Sales	• Increase in sales through better in-stock positions • Joint planning with trade partners enabling more predictable sales results • Reduced write-offs and returns • Preferred status with retail partners • Visibility to constraints and issues prior to business impact • Proactive exception management allowing improved customer service
Marketing	• Joint promotion planning more effective, avoids promotion overlap • Direct insight into trade promotion spending and effectiveness • Enhanced coordination of activities so product, media, and point-of-sale information all converges on plan • Greater insight for micromarketing advantages
Manufacturing	• Fewer unplanned changeovers • Visibility to new product introduction, timing, volume • Enhanced capacity planning and more effective asset utilization • Reduced overtime for unplanned production cycles • Order forecast visibility for production planning • More effective procurement for raw materials and packaging
Distribution and Logistics	• Reduced inventory storage requirements • More effective inventory movement and management • Smoother labor scheduling • Improved asset utilization and third-party coordination • Less expediting • Improved transportation effectiveness and delivery

consumer insight for sales improvement, and extend their enterprise for growth and cost effectiveness like never before thought possible. When properly applied, the influence of CPFR can also bring discipline and rigor to other processes that strengthen the overall execution capabilities of the organization and uncover hidden constraints that allow for continuous improvement.

Though the pitfalls identified in this chapter are not exhaustive, they are some of the preeminent ones that often stifle early collaborative efforts or become barriers to scale. Please be on the lookout for these as you formulate your strategy for CPFR, for early consideration can alleviate or minimize these pitfalls and smooth the road to success for collaboration. There is no single, exact way to implement CPFR, but with a consistent internal business model and consistent interoperability with your trading partners, your benefit doors can be positioned to swing open through collaboration. The value potential is great, has been confirmed publicly by companies that have shared their early experiences, and carries with it the possibility of being rewarded by your customers and consumers for your efforts.

Note

1. "The Daunting Dilemma of Trade Promotion," Accenture Research (2001).

5.5

Virtually Vertical[SM]: A Supply Chain Model for the Collaboration Era

Jeffrey B. Stiely, Kurt Salmon Associates
Matthew F. Katz, Kurt Salmon Associates

Publicity surrounding the Voluntary Interindustry Commerce Standards Association's Collaborative Planning, Forecasting, and Replenishment concept abounds. Executives, however, while certainly intrigued, remain reluctant to invest heavily in full-scale implementation for a number of reasons, including doubts about pilot scalability and technology.

CPFR challenges deeply rooted and traditional business practices. And, as is often the case with major change, many companies are simply conducting the same old processes using new collaborative technologies. While this does enable faster and more efficient functionality, it is not the full-scale collaborative change effort necessary to successfully scale CPFR. Until there is a fundamental shift in the way business partners interact, CPFR, like collaborative industry movements before it, will meet expectations but will undoubtedly fall short of its full potential.

To realize maximum return and provide the greatest value to the consumer, industry leaders must step back from these functionally narrow initiatives and embrace a holistic approach to collaboration. The Virtually Vertical model encourages leaders to expand the supply chain beyond their own organizational boundaries to optimize processes that provide increased value to the consumer and eliminate those that do not.

Though this major movement began in the early 1980s with collaborative initiatives such as quick response (QR), it is now finally coming into its own. Shifting to this model is becoming a requirement for effective competition in today's marketplace.

5.5.1 From Pilot to Practice

Before describing the Virtually Vertical model in greater detail, let's look at CPFR in its current maturity to gain a better understanding of how this concept fits into the big picture. The CPFR process allows manufacturers and retailers to collaborate on common forecasts to drive replenishment. Its overall objective is to ensure that the right product is at the right place at the right time, thereby meeting consumer demand. Facilitated by technology, CPFR helps trading partners work as a team to solve business problems. Partners maintain ownership of their plans and processes but share them with others using established rules.

The philosophy behind CPFR is simple: Get supply chain partners "on the same page" earlier in the process and good things will happen. And they have. CPFR has repeatedly bolstered sales, even in traditionally "flat" categories, while reducing inventory and operating costs. Companies have also used CPFR to support new product introduction efforts. Regardless of targeted use, if applied with vigor, pilots prove successful.

Exhibit 5.15 conservatively highlights the areas in which CPFR pilots have consistently returned results. In fact, many pilots show even greater returns. While some results can be attributed to the "Hawthorne Effect"—the stimulation to output or accomplishment that results from the mere fact of being under observation—this table illustrates the long-term, scalable benefits that CPFR programs achieve. *These benefits translate to an impressive 8 percent to 12 percent increase to the bottom line.*

In addition to these remarkable benefits, retailers have seen improve-

EXHIBIT 5.15. RESULTS OF CPFR PILOTS.

Metric	Lever	Impact
Sales	• Optimized inventory levels resulting in increased in-stock	up 15% to 20%
Margin	• Reduced markdowns • Better operating efficiency from longer planning horizon and improved forecast	up 3% to 5%
Inventory	• Improved forecasting accuracy • Increased planning horizon	down 12% to 15%
SG&A	• Reduced transportation expediting costs • Reduced inventory carrying costs • Reduced overhead	down 3% to 5%

SOURCE: KSA analysis.

ments in private-label merchandise in the categories in which CPFR is piloted, and have realized a host of intangible benefits, including improved vendor relationships, enhanced visibility and understanding of the supply chain, and greater internal synchronization. It is no longer contested; CPFR packs real punch. But while the impact is profound, the real challenge lies in a company's willingness to focus on full-scale collaborative change efforts.

5.5.2 The Truth About Technology

Though it may seem like a probable culprit, and an easy scapegoat, technology is not stalling the full-scale deployment of CPFR. There are two prevalent concerns with regard to technology: first, whether it is yet possible to crunch the sheer volume of transactions inherent in CPFR, and second, whether collaborative practices are feasible given companies' diverse range of selected solutions.

With regard to the first point, carefully selected, the right technology supports high-volume transactions. Leading solutions have proven to scale, and their continued functional enhancements give users a multitude of choices. Point solutions provide strong exception management and fast engines to crunch data, while broader supply chain management solutions have developed modules to provide integrated offerings. Users have a broad spectrum of functional solutions from which to choose.

In one of the more widely circulated CPFR pilot case studies, Kmart installed scalable CPFR technology in 1999. In fact, in collaborating with forty-seven vendors on fifty-two weekly forecasts involving more than 2,000 stores, the technology supported more than five million data points. When SKUs are taken into account, the data points are exponentially higher. The selected software supported Excel file feeds, flat file transfers, and "hard links" to supply chain management software. While Kmart hit other stumbling blocks to its overall business performance that have slowed the rollout of CPFR, it certainly has demonstrated that the concept can scale from a technology standpoint.

By enabling increased collaboration, information sharing, and exception management, Internet-based CPFR technology solutions allow companies to share information regardless of the enterprise or supply chain management systems employed. This is demonstrated in pilots employing "peer-to-peer" CPFR technology, which, through industry standards, enables competing solutions to share and synchronize data and allows various parties to view the data in the same way. While some go to great lengths to promote this capability, it is a requirement and, incidentally, the foundation of electronic data interchange (EDI).

Companies should simply select solutions that are scalable and can be integrated with existing technology. The important thing to keep in mind is that a successful CPFR implementation relies on technology as the enabler, but well-defined business processes and organizational structures are the real keys to success.

Global Acceptance

A lack of awareness or interest is not impeding full-scale adoption either. The world is quite readily installing CPFR. In the United States alone, more than $15 billion in the supply chain is managed by CPFR processes. There are more than thirty significant CPFR programs currently under way in Europe, and significant pilots are active in Asia, Canada, and South America. Globally, companies such as A&P, Canadian Tire, Gillette, Hewlett-Packard, Kimberly-Clark, Marks & Spencer, Microsoft, Procter & Gamble, Staples, and Tesco and leading B2B exchanges like Transora and the World-Wide-Retail-Exchange (WWRE) have also become actively involved. Furthermore, Kurt

Salmon Associates (KSA) is leading a consortium of premier department store retailers and branded manufacturers, including Federated Department Stores, Inc.; May Department Stores Company; Saks Inc.; Jones Apparel Group, Inc.; Liz Claiborne; Estée Lauder; and Jockey International, that has built upon the CPFR process and is currently proving the concept in its industries. Various industry groups are working together to develop globally accepted standards, and trade laws are continuing to change and encourage cross-border trade and partner development.

Tripped Up by Transition

So with significant proven results, capable technology, and global acceptance, what *is* stalling the broad-scale implementation of CPFR, and why aren't companies realizing the full potential of collaboration? One executive of a successful pilot described the thrill and sorrow of his experience. On one hand, he was pleased with the financial results; on the other, he was embarrassed by some of his organization's current procedures and bureaucratic rules hindering "true" progress.

Many CPFR leaders talk of promotion sales expectations that would not have been met without this practice. Others can recite the adjusted SKU number in the forecasted order that resulted in an incremental $12,000 revenue gain in a single day. One retail executive claims he would have run out of candy corn on Halloween if not for the last-minute discovery of misaligned delivery windows and order quantities.

Across industries, many examples of CPFR pilot successes have reached the level of boardroom folklore. Sure these results easily justify the relatively small capital and related technological investments needed to pilot CPFR, but are they enough to convince executives to commit to the wholesale process and cultural change necessary for full-scale implementation? As executives ponder this question, pilots enter a critical transition phase.

Most pilots last about 100 days, and many lose momentum during the transition phase. During the pilot, organizations assign their best people and select partners who will match their level of attention and enthusiasm. They choose the SKUs that are most apt to deliver results. They realize great value and achieve success versus their original metrics.

It is here, at their pinnacle, that the programs begin to stumble. Some move forward with additional pilots—adding another vendor or product category. Others push existing pilots further in an effort to confirm ROI projections. But few see their organizations fully transform to the collaborative business model. This is because each collaborative initiative, whether CPFR or QR, is confined to the functional boundaries of that initiative. But collaborative practices require changes beyond any single function. In fact, they affect almost all functional areas.

In most organizations, the conduit between trading partners is the sales/buyer relationship. While this relationship may be ideal for selecting and moving product, this is only a subset of the issues that must be addressed to optimize service to the consumer. To reach potential, collaborative relationships require fundamental shifts in varied business practices. New business practices in logistics, product development, forecasting, and many others do not fall into the natural realm of the sales/buyer skill set or authority. These practices, therefore, are not addressed and redesigned for maximum potential.

The initial movement eventually loses wind before the full potential is reached, and the best resources are reassigned to the next "big idea." To realize its full benefit and drive true organizational change, collaboration must be approached holistically, rather than within functional silos.

5.5.3 Thinking Beyond the Organization

The collaborative business model requires that entire supply chains, with the primary goal of exceeding consumers' expectations, act as entities beyond their own organizational boundaries.

To illustrate the concept, let's look at a recent example from the rental car industry. Aware that a speedy return process was critical to customer satisfaction, rental car agencies devoted great effort and resources to minimize the time customers spend from lot entry to checkout. They issued handheld terminals, added attendants, and increased the frequency of their shuttles. Cars that were returned without a full tank of gasoline, however, slowed the car turnaround time. To address this hitch, agencies implemented stiff penalties, "punishing" consumers in hopes of reducing the exceptions. The result was a speedy, cost-effective checkout process. But that wasn't all. It also resulted in lost future business opportunity from frustrated consumers who were forced to buy gas at an inconvenient location or face punitive prices for fuel.

In January 2001, National, a division of the ANC Rental Corporation, announced its new "Save Time" fuel service exclusively for members of the Emerald Club, National's loyalty program. This timesaving refueling option allows Emerald Club members to have their returned rental cars refueled by National service agents at competitive local self-serve gas prices, plus any applicable taxes and fees.

According to National's research among its frequent renters, not having to stop for gas before returning the rental car is perceived as a desirable convenience and a big time-saver (ten to twenty minutes) for busy travelers. The refueling option was considered a very positive, meaningful, and motivating idea that members felt would save them both time and money.

By looking at the broader picture, National realized that the fast checkout process consumers desire begins *before* they reach the lot. It includes not having to take an additional exit, pull into a gas station, possibly wait in another line, and execute another credit card transaction. By discouraging the consumer from refueling on the agency property, agencies have actually *increased* the total return time, disappointed customers, and, in the meantime, lost the opportunity for additional revenue from the sale of fuel.

Many of these agencies are still guilty of looking at the problem too narrowly. Admittedly they have minimized *on-site* checkout time *given their current resources.* But by offering gas on-site, they could minimize checkout time *as the consumer defines it.* In so doing they would increase their market share (by offering better consumer value), while increasing their share of wallet (fuel sales). Rather than discourage consumers from buying gas on-site, rental agencies should encourage them. And who knows, it might not be a bad idea to partner with a fast-food chain to offer them a drive-thru window to boot!

Another example of this broader thinking is Barnes & Noble's collaborative relationship with Starbucks to provide consumers with a more enjoyable shopping experience by offering coffee in its bookstores. After learning that consumers' spending increases with the duration of their stay, Barnes & Noble formed this relationship to encourage shoppers to spend more time in the store. Recognizing that selling coffee is not its core competency, the bookseller opted for this arrangement in which both parties benefit and consumer value is enhanced.

Starbucks, in turn, recognizing a particular consumer segment's desire for doughnuts with its coffee, partnered with Krispy Kreme in select geographic locations to provide additional value to this consumer. Furthermore, Starbucks formed alliances with Compaq and Microsoft to deliver new wireless products and services to consumers as part of its unique coffeehouse experience. These activities required partners to look at their core competencies, develop new business models, and install supporting infrastructure. And while Starbucks does not benefit directly from book purchases, and Internet providers do not benefit from coffee or doughnut sales, all are adding value to the consumer experience and building loyalty, which drives profitability for everyone.

5.5.4 Building a Truly Collaborative Supply Chain

These examples highlight the two key concepts of the Virtually Vertical paradigm, which are:

1. Begin all process, organization, and system strategies with consumer value *as defined by the consumer.*
2. Fanatically meet and exceed that value equation by extending *beyond the reach of your own organizational resources.*

While both the Starbucks and National examples illustrate how this principle enabled the supply chain to broaden its service offering, it is just as capable of providing better value within an existing service offering.

It is exactly this philosophy that has driven retail's collaborative era. In fact, we are already in the midst of this major shift in the retail business model. Beginning as far back as the early 1980s, initiatives such as Efficient Consumer Response (ECR), floor-ready merchandise (FRM), and QR have all pursued this principle. CPFR is the most recent piece of the collaboration puzzle.

Take for example the concept of FRM, introduced in the early 1990s. Here we saw the industry think beyond its own organizational boundaries in an effort to lower overall cost to the consumer. It was a simple equation: Affix hangers and apply price tickets at the supplier for 15 cents per unit, or continue to do it in the retailer's DC for 35 cents per unit.

For years, retailers continued to perform the more costly operation because it was beyond their organizations' reach to have suppliers do it. But when the supply chain acted as one holistic organization, it became self-evident that the process should be changed. Of course it required great negotiation and effort to determine who would receive what percentage of the spoils, but nevertheless, it had tremendous positive consumer impact in the end and drove profit increases for many.

FRM is a simple example of what is possible with the concept of holistic collaborative thinking. The supply chain, rather than individual companies, began with the consumer's perception of value and thought beyond its own organizational boundaries to bring the solution to bear.

But while these initiatives have generally met expectations, they have fallen considerably short of their potential. These changes have only reengineered individual pieces of the total supply chain. Still missing is the holistic view of the supply chain that brings all of these pieces together. To be truly successful, supply chains, not organizations, must apply this thinking from process A to Z.

The perspective clearly shifts the focus from winning companies to winning supply chains, and in this new paradigm, improving margin or market share at the expense of the consumer, regardless of the short-term benefit for any individual organization, will no longer be a sustainable business strategy.

This new model is not unlike a vertical company in that it has the advantage of vertical efficiency (e.g., no overhead associated with intercompany operations). Exhibit 5.16 highlights how vertical companies outperform traditional supply chain partnerships.

It is interesting to note that while the disparity exists for all product categories within retail and consumer products, it is more pronounced in soft goods. Apparel and fashion retailing is an SKU-intensive, quick-cycle business that is highly complex and wrought with many processes and relationships. Emotional aspects that drive creativity and newness also drive complexity. These unique characteristics create a great need for effective communication and collaboration. Therefore, the greater

EXHIBIT 5.16. VERTICAL SUPPLY CHAIN VERSUS TRADITIONAL SUPPLY CHAIN.

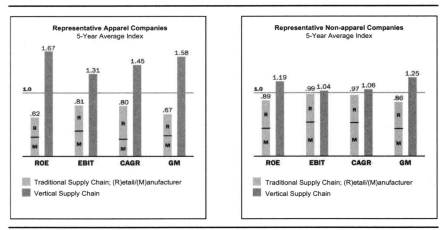

SOURCE: Annual reports and SEC filings/KSA research.

the complexity of the business, the more important the need for collaborative practices.

But the Virtually Vertical model surpasses even the vertical company's efficiency. The centralized leadership and "ownership" of the entire vertical chain limits its flexibility to meet ever-changing consumer demand. This new model, on the other hand, powerfully combines the strengths of the vertical and traditional systems, while minimizing the disadvantages of each.

Reaching Critical Mass

CPFR will achieve its original vision when it breaks from the old supply chain model, placing consumer need above organizational interests. The new hierarchy is consumer, supply chain, and *then* individual company. While this may sound utopian, or even naive, it is fundamental to the collaborative shift. Individual companies will benefit as a natural side effect of this approach. Exhibit 5.17 illustrates the progression toward meeting consumer needs.

To illustrate, let's return to the FRM example. The consumer need is lower prices. The supply chain solution is to move value-added processes, such as affixing hangers, as far back in the supply chain as possible. This reduces the number of "product touches" at a labor rate lower

EXHIBIT 5.17. CONSUMER FOCUS: THE KEY TO COLLABORATION.

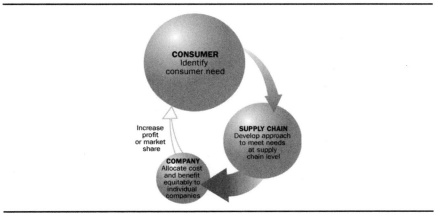

SOURCE: KSA.

than can be achieved in retail DCs. While such a solution appears to go against manufacturers' best interests, as it adds cost and time to their processes, it is not a stumbling block to designing a supply chain that meets the consumer's need for lower prices and on-time in-store delivery.

Only after the ideal solution has been designed should discussions begin regarding how to allocate new costs and benefits among individual companies. In our example, manufacturers assumed an additional 15 cents, while retailers saved 35 cents. By agreeing upon adjusted wholesale prices, the 20-cent savings was divided equitably between the partners.

Indeed, FRM was not an effortless initiative. It took years of negotiating and dealing to finally change this practice. Needless to say, a vertical company, in control of all parties concerned, would have made the shift much more quickly. In the traditional supply chain model, each new process change that requires action beyond the four walls of a company entails this long and painful transformation period.

As a result, it is easy to see why these collaborative initiatives, taken on their own, do not realize their greatest potential. On their own, CPFR and the other movements cannot justify the risk and cost of such a quantum business model transformation. And lacking the payback required to change the paradigm, we have seen these collaborative concepts implemented in diluted form. Their benefits have been limited to what can be gained without significantly changing the way the supply chain functions as a whole.

KSA believes that these individual movements are nearing critical mass. Taken with other collaborative concepts of the past and near future, CPFR is beginning to justify the risk associated with shifting to an entirely new mode of doing business. In the next few years, this model will emerge with force. Supply chains must look beyond their components to define a new model that serves the consumer first and drives individual profitability second.

5.5.5 Opportunity Unveiled

Beginning with consumer need and working back through the supply chain without the constraint of organizational boundaries would create a sudden rush of "quick hit" opportunities. CIOs would exult in the system integration opportunities, supply chain managers would recognize broad gaps in communication, and merchants would identify redundancy in head count. Entire processes not performed by vertical companies would be deemed unnecessary and costly. In short, the Business Process Reengineering (BPR) wrecking ball, so popular in the mid-1990s, would again swing. Only this time, it would swing free of the artificial boundaries of company walls, enabling it to now realize its intended potential.

Elevating perspective from the company level to the supply chain level is the key challenge that must be overcome to realize the full potential of collaborative initiatives. The Virtually Vertical model requires that companies make overarching organizational, process, and systems changes that will allow them the flexibility necessary for efficient collaboration with partners to deliver maximum value to the consumer. Success will require that new meaning be given to words like *trust, redundancy, core competency,* and *value-added.* While technology enables these process changes, it is not the driver. Rather, the impetus must be creating consumer value with the vision that the sum of the parts is greater than the whole.

While CPFR pilots have been largely successful as companies add resources to design and support new processes, this is an obstacle to full-scale rollout. Instead, focus must be placed on designing *new* processes that eliminate non-value-added functions. Resources must be able to work smarter, not harder.

In this new model, individual firms may entirely relinquish old responsibilities and acquire new ones. There may be functions, currently performed redundantly by teams in multiple organizations, that should be performed by one team consisting of members from multiple companies. It is even feasible that a given individual may have bosses from two different companies.

Without question, supplier and vendor roles will change. In a commodity category, the planner or category manager may take a broader functional responsibility while narrowing category breadth. For example, planning, replenishment, order management, logistics, and transportation may all fall under the category manager's territory. Each relationship is different, however, and each party will bring its own unique strengths to bear.

The organization in a Virtually Vertical company may, therefore, look very different from the structures to which we are accustomed today.

5.5.6 Redefining Supply Chain Processes

There are three critical steps to redefining supply chain processes such that the full potential of collaboration can be realized:

1. *Eliminate functions not valued by the consumer.* The company-centric mind-set has given birth to many unnecessary functions. The best metric for ferreting out these processes is to determine whether the consumer cares if they are performed. Examples of functions in which consumer value is not enhanced include chargebacks, formal orders between the supplier and retailer, and invoicing. In the ideal supply chain, these tasks would be eliminated.

   Would it instead be possible for a supplier to simply deliver from a frozen forecast? Is an order any more than a forecast inside a delivery window? Invoices could be eliminated in favor of auto-payment by receipt, to be reconciled at the end of a quarter, month, or year. Clear rules regarding when a forecast is truly frozen, when changes can be made, and when a change triggers an exception that warrants a discussion or meeting would, of course, be required. On the other hand, the new processes would eliminate all of the time, cost, and errors associated with the laborious order management and payment functions.

2. *Centralize functions that can be performed at a single point in the supply chain.* There are many functions performed redundantly by each member of the supply chain. While the functions are important to the consumer, doing them once is sufficient; any more is wasteful.

   In the forecasting stage, for instance, one of the parties may prove more accurate. This could be the party with the sophistication to generate better forecasts or, if the product is more fashion-oriented, the party closer to the end consumer may own the forecast. Quality assurance, while valued by the consumer, may be just as effective if performed by only one party. Efficiency is gained when tasks that were formally owned by both the supplier and retailer are shifted to the most appropriate party. Double checks and "sign-offs" often consume time and resources without providing any additional value.

3. *Define new processes to support collaborative functions where appropriate.* This third category creates the need for collaborative tools. These are the functions that are best performed by cross-organizational teams. CPFR was designed to facilitate planning, a truly collaborative function. Retailers bring insight to planned promotions, new store openings and closings, and other factors that will create an otherwise unpredictable impact on demand. Branded suppliers know their production capability and manufacturer promotions and may have better insight into consumer demand for their own products across the various distribution channels.

   In some cases, such as planning and forecasting, these functions are performed separately by both retailers and suppliers. In other cases, they are performed by only one party, and suffer from the lack of input from other relevant members of the supply chain. Product development, in some supply chains, is an example. In either case, the goal is to identify new ways of working together such that there is both efficiency *and* quality of result.

While implementation of this idea will vary from one supply chain to another, Exhibit 5.18 provides one potential approach.

EXHIBIT 5.18. REDEFINING BUSINESS RELATIONSHIPS.

	Eliminate	Assign/ Redefine	Collaborate
Consumer Research & Trend		▲	
Financial Planning			★
Merchandise & Assortment Planning			★
Buying and Selling	■		
Design		▲	
Development			★
Source & Production Planning			★
Materials Management			★
Shared Risk			★
Productions		▲	
Order Management	■		
Logistics Planning			★
Distribution			★
Quality Management & Returns		▲	
Replenishment		▲	
In-season Planning			★
Invoicing/Payment/Chargebacks	■		

SOURCE: KSA analysis.

KSA has developed a model that projects the performance of the Virtually Vertical supply chain. Exhibits 5.19 and 5.20 highlight both the areas of impact (some of which have been mentioned), and their corresponding effect on the business as a whole.

While the EBIT increase for the Virtually Vertical company is significant, the magnitude of the benefit is actually understated. This graph focuses simply on the cost savings, but Virtually Vertical companies will

EXHIBIT 5.19. REWARDS OF COLLABORATION.

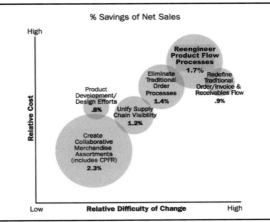

SOURCE: KSA Virtually Vertical Toolkit.

EXHIBIT 5.20. OPTIMIZING VALUE CHAINS.

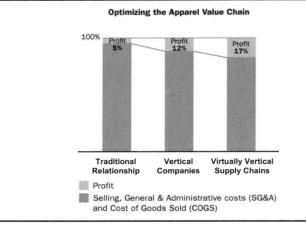

SOURCE: KSA Virtually Vertical Toolkit: annual reports and SEC filings.

also experience increased sales. As a case in point, a supply chain that implements collaborative planning will see increased in-stocks and fewer markdowns, resulting in better top-line performance. Therefore, the 17 percent profit number (shown in Exhibit 5.20) is actually taken from a greater sales volume.

Trust and Commitment to Change

This level of process redefinition requires that the trust an organization would place in itself now be placed in its collaborative partner(s). Unless this trust exists, none of these process changes are feasible and redundancy will remain. "Trust," however, does not mean blind faith. As within one's own organization, when expectations are not met, the source of the problem is rooted out, evaluated, and addressed as appropriate. This may mean tweaking the process; adding resources; or, if it is a skill set misalignment, relocating or even dismissing the employee responsible. This protocol is no different in a collaborative organization.

In addition to placing unprecedented trust in partners, organizations must be committed to change. And change of this magnitude cannot occur without the clout of industry movers. Small companies can initiate change by engaging their larger customers or suppliers but will not succeed without support. Larger, more influential companies must therefore become the drivers of change. While the presented concepts are targeted to private consortiums, exchanges, or hand-selected companies that have the sponsorship and backing of at least one "driving organization," small- to medium-size companies can and should heed this advice and begin to position themselves in the new model of collaborative commerce. In fact, their smaller size and nimble character can be an advantage in helping to orchestrate and drive change.

Summary

The retail industry is experiencing a shift in paradigm approaching the magnitude of the Industrial Revolution. The movement to the Virtually Vertical model literally requires the complete redefinition of business as we know it. Technology, among other factors, has finally provided supply chains a tool that can enable this entirely new business model. The Virtually Vertical model offers the flexibility of individual companies, while eliminating the overhead of company-to-company redundancy.

The movement to this model has been under way since the earliest days of QR and has changed business culture such that hammering suppliers or hiding information from retail partners is no longer the standard way to conduct business. The key now is to step back, align previous initiatives such as ECR, QR, and vendor-managed inventory, and use these tools to drive inefficiency out of a sequential supply chain. Doing so will require the vision and commitment to rebuild from the ground up.

This is not to say, however, that the change must occur all at once. That is something we learned from BPR. Instead, companies must find a way to implement these collaborative practices in the context of an end vision. CPFR, therefore, must be viewed as a step in the pursuit of that vision. Such a perspective will justify the significant investment and inherent risk associated with developing new relationships with trading partners.

The potential impact of this movement is tremendous, and the benefits are attainable. Supply chains can cut 10 percent of their costs while improving the quality of the end product. First movers can pass that value on to the consumer, or split it among the members of the supply chain. But, like most major movements, it isn't the reward that will drive the industry shift, but the fact that survival will depend upon it.

5.6

On the Road to the Network Economy—Developing an E-Transformation Roadmap for Profitable Growth in the Consumer Goods Industry

Christian Koch, SAP AG
Dr. Gerhard Hausruckinger, Roland Berger Strategy Consultants

What keeps CEOs of consumer goods manufacturers and retailers awake at night worrying about the future of their companies? It is the search for sustainable and profitable growth, which is not that easy given the current state of the economy. Buzzwords such as *globalization, innovation, brand* (portfolio) *management, supply chain excellence*, and *e-business* are the main planks of strategy design today. In a recent study[1], manufacturers and retailers put the potential savings from a consistent e-transformation program alone at around 1–3 percent, and the growth potential at around 5 percent of their sales. The savings are seen mainly in the supply chain, in sales organization, and in improvements to marketing and promotional processes. The study found that this generates growth, mainly through better planning processes and through more effective promotions based on collaborative processes.

The entire economy is involved in a trend toward intercompany process optimization, shifting the focus away from purely internal process improvements. Innovation is firmly focused on manufacturers' interfaces on the sales side. For ECR Europe, as a joint initiative of manufacturers and retailers, this is nothing new. For a long time now, ECR Europe has been analyzing this potential and engaging in many projects and initiatives to create strategies for implementing it in practice. What we have found is that while the concepts are undoubtedly mature enough to be used in business, the technology available is unable to support them properly. Contrary to ECR's intentions, "enabling technologies" have thus become "disabling technologies," preventing the broad-based use of the proposed models. New technology can be a major driver of collaborative processes and help achieve quantum leaps in performance only if it dovetails with corporate strategies, core business processes, and the organizational framework.

5.6.1 The Innovative Context

In the consumer goods industry, projects are focused mainly on collaborative technology that is relevant to the sales side. Trade promotion management, advanced planning and scheduling, and Collaborative Planning, Forecasting, and Replenishment (CPFR) are some of the hottest applications at present. In many ways, the Internet provides the basis for implementing processes in day-to-day business. Extranets, Web EDI, and eBXML now offer communications opportunities that enable broad-based collaborative applications. Additionally, the emergence of marketplace technologies—driven initially by public exchanges, but seen increasingly as communications platforms for individual companies—has given the outsourcing efforts of the new economy a basis in reality, even in the post–new economy age. Innovative companies are turning to these technologies and trying to establish a sustainable competitive edge as "early adopters" or "smart followers."

An extensive portfolio of technologies is now available, with portal technologies and self-service applications in purchasing and internal administration. But even conventional approaches such as data warehousing and the associated reporting and analysis features have made considerable progress. The volumes of data that can be managed today are much larger than ever before, and at the same time, far more users are in a position to analyze them.

These technologies promise companies potential benefits across the board, but the question of what action to take, when, and how to do it remains. To use a metaphor, it's all about using the right score to combine a large number of individual musicians and instruments into one orchestra playing melodious symphonies.

What makes matters worse is that, as the economy stands, short, transparent projects have a clear edge over long-term reorganization projects. Not knowing what resources will be available next year or what the economic climate will be like, people tend to focus on short-term improvements where the costs are foreseeable and the returns more or less immediate.

However, ensuring that this action maintains its innovative momentum in the long term means embedding it in a long-term technology strategy. Otherwise it could meet the same fate as many e-commerce projects in the hype phase of their life cycle. The cost of integrating stand-alone solutions into developing and thus, changing, IT structures in the long term can easily exceed the cost of introducing the solution in the first place, and so call its commercial viability into question. Or it may turn out that integration is not even feasible from a technological standpoint.

Managing Transition as a Planned and Actively Managed Total Process

To summarize, managing innovation successfully, both in technological and business terms, requires combining both levels into a single, total process. In real terms, this means:

- Taking a cold, hard business look at the status quo
- Identifying the main weaknesses and potential for improvement (looking for short-term, limited scope, and clear or measurable benefits)
- (Roughly) quantifying the benefits
- Examining existing solutions and technology options
- Putting options and potential into context
- Producing a project sequence (roadmap) for transforming the company within the network economy

Systematically linking strategy, organization, business processes, and information technology also means bringing the right know-how into the complex process of roadmap development. That is why SAP and Roland Berger Strategy Consultants have joined forces to produce a master plan for the consumer goods industry, which can be used in designing company-specific e-transformation roadmaps to suit individual needs and aims. We will look at this more closely in the next section.

5.6.2 Developing a Master Roadmap for the Consumer Goods Industry

Of course you can design a roadmap to help an individual company find its way to the network economy without using a ready-made template. The difference between the two is much the same as the difference between customized and standard software. Ultimately, customized software is rarely suited to wider applications, as the extra time and cost involved are disproportionate to the desired results.

However, as with standard software, adapting it to a specific segment or company is worthwhile and also significantly increases the value added. Here, the focus is on the FMCG (fast-moving consumer goods) segment of consumer goods manufacturers. The roadmap is based on research conducted mainly in Europe, and so is inevitably Eurocentric. This must be taken into account when applying it outside of Europe.

The master roadmap consists of the following elements:

- Content
    Industry trends
    Specific IT solutions required
    Roadmap specification
- Applications
    Roadmap tool
    Roadmap application model

In logical terms, the roadmap starts by defining and analyzing the main industry trends and environment, and then looks at what requirements these impose in terms of IT solutions. It then considers in detail what they actually mean in terms of technology and business management. The roadmap tool then puts these factors in the context of the individual company, customizing the approach efficiently and purposefully.

The complex nature of designing business processes in response to organization- and technology-driven innovation requires a clear guide through the multistage roadmap process. A simplified off-the-shelf approach is out of the question, if only because the changes we are looking at here will have a lasting impact on all aspects of a business. This is where the roadmap application model comes in, specifying a process model for using the e-transformation roadmap.

Using the roadmap is usually a multistage process that entails an increasing amount of detail at each new stage. In developing this tool, it was important to ensure that practical results could be achieved at relatively little cost in the initial stage. The roadmap tool is thus designed to work out key elements, in interaction with an FMCG company, based on an analysis period of just a few days, and to draw up the first draft of a holistic e-transformation roadmap with the help of the tool. The results obtained provide the foundations for the strategic renewal process, showing where innovation is particularly rewarding and promising. These results make it much easier to understand individual projects in the overall context and integrate them in medium- to long-term planning. They can then be further validated and worked out through a process of iterative improvement, in particular through continued use of the tool, both internally and together with external specialists.

The next steps in the roadmap application model involve progressively refining the results, with a view to internal communications as well as to implementing the projects identified.

5.6.3 Roadmap Content

As explained previously, three main trends have become evident:

1. Globalization
2. Increasing efficiency
3. Direct customer relationships

In this section, we look at what this means in terms of the IT solutions required.

Requirements

What are the strategic consequences of these trends? It may be useful here to go a level deeper and examine what each of these main trends implies in detail.

Globalization Requirements This is a complex subject, and there is not enough room here to do more than skim the surface. Mergers and acquisitions have a particular impact on brand strategies in terms of creating a strong and consistent international image. Merging different corporate structures also touches upon many general elements, such as cultural and organizational aspects, IT systems landscapes, and supplier relations. Even with aggressive organic growth though, the question remains whether the business model and technology employed are scalable. At present, many FMCG manufacturers are dealing with the question of how to organize themselves in response to key accounts with global operations, such as Wal-Mart, Ahold, and Carrefour, and to ensure prompt and meaningful global account controlling.

Efficiency Requirements There are two aspects that must be differentiated here:

1. *Increasing Efficiency in Internal Processes.* Although lasting improvements have been made in recent years, there is still a long way to go in speeding up and simplifying processes, focusing more clearly on the right processes, and creating an efficient communications environment. There is also a need to examine and classify processes in terms of their potential for being redesigned to accommodate an e-business approach.

2. *Increasing Efficiency in External Processes.* In the business of the future, the key will be to form intercompany partnerships on the sales and procurement side and in the value creation process. Possible tools here include such solutions as CPFR, collaborative transport management, vendor-managed inventory, and Extranets.

Direct Customer Relationship Requirements In the consumer goods industry, the value chain must become even more tailored to consumer needs than it has been in the past. For manufacturers, this means intensifying relations with retailers, as they are the ones that ultimately sell things and are in direct contact with consumers. On the other hand, Web technology provides another option for getting in touch with end consumers directly, thus allowing greater proximity to them. A third possibility is to build up a flexible value network to give customers more value, whether by making products more individual or offering complementary services.

The E-Transformation Roadmap—An Action Program for Structured Decision Making

The overall trends in the industry imply a certain portfolio of business management solutions from which companies must choose the building blocks that will make the greatest contribution to their individual goals. Supporting this selection process is where the actual roadmap model comes in. It is based on the considerations elaborated above and provides specific recommendations on the selection and sequence of the projects to be implemented.

The roadmap is divided into four areas that can be seen as the steps a company takes to become a network economy player. However, if these areas were "steps" in the strictest sense of the word, which could be taken only in sequence, the model would have missed its mark. Rather, this step approach is designed to serve as an intellectual framework, in which various self-contained individual projects can be grouped together in a meaningful way. By taking the financial, technological, and organizational considerations of a specific business into account, the four areas can then be arranged to form an individual innovation plan: a customized e-transformation roadmap.

The core areas of the roadmap mark out four steps in the development process, ranging from a more tactically oriented internal view, to collaborative processes in operations, to new value-creation approaches in a networked environment, and ultimately to redefining the business as part of the long-term vision of the network economy (see Exhibit 5.21).

Each of these areas has its own processes and scenarios with their potential for innovation. Today, these processes and scenarios are more or less crucial to a manufacturer's innovation process. Therefore, the master roadmap also offers a master set of options from which a business can design its own specific action program, in terms of both content and chronological priority.

In step 1, the focus is on optimizing internal processes and systems, doing the "homework," so to speak, to lay the groundwork for subsequent steps. This step is mainly about enterprise application integration (EAI) as a platform for technologies that enable automated communications and interoperability of various applications and business processes.

EXHIBIT 5.21. E-TRANSFORMATION ROADMAP FOR THE FMCG SECTOR.

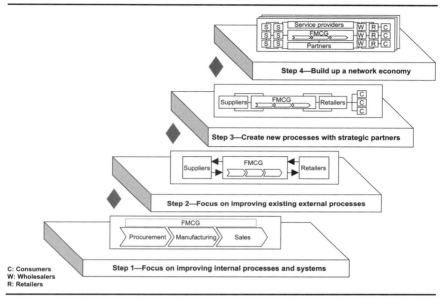

SOURCE: Roland Berger & Partner/SAP.

This rather technical aspect of step 1 should go hand in hand with a rigorous change-management program, which could be managed by temporary business integration teams, for instance.

In step 2, which can easily be run in parallel, existing external interfaces and processes are drawn into the optimization. Traditional issues such as EDI or, more recently, Web EDI are increasingly enhanced by implementing Extranets, which enable flexible communications with a whole host of business partners. Also, advanced planning and scheduling (APS) systems, which address problems of forecasting, planning, and execution, are becoming increasingly popular. Global open standards form a common language for exchanging information of all kinds and play a key role in these issues.

Step 3 is based on the idea of a collaborative platform (collaborative hub) with five key features:

1. Consumer/customer relationship management (CRM)
2. Vendor-managed inventory (VMI)

3. Collaborative Planning, Forecasting, and Replenishment (CPFR)

4. Supplier relationship management (SRM)

5. Collaborative transportation management (CTM)

This platform (see Exhibit 5.22) can be used to exchange information, products, and services via the Internet and provides the basis for using the collaborative features listed, integrating trading partners and service providers to the greatest extent possible.

Step 4 marks the realization of the network economy, in which companies focus strictly on their core competencies and competitive advantages, work closely with all kinds of business partners on the basis of global industry standards and open, intelligent technologies, and create real value for their customers in the process (see Exhibit 5.23).

If we consider the topics listed here in the light of the current debate, we find that the hottest topics, such as customer relationship management, supply chain management, and CPFR, are in step 3, that is, developing progressive collaborative processes. Here, the desire to implement innovative processes is driven by the potential they can in theory unleash. Whether this potential can be achieved in practice, however, is another matter. It is of little use, for instance, to sit down with customers to work out joint plans for CPFR if unavoidable changes of plan in response to unforeseen events mean that production

EXHIBIT 5.22. AN EAI PLATFORM IS AN EXCELLENT BASE FOR RUNNING COLLABORATIVE FEATURES.

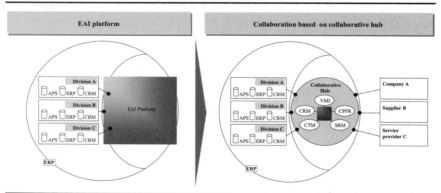

SOURCE: Roland Berger & Partner/SAP.

EXHIBIT 5.23. IN THE NETWORK ECONOMY, N-TIER TRADING PARTNERS WILL BE LIKED VIA COMPLEX NETWORKS.

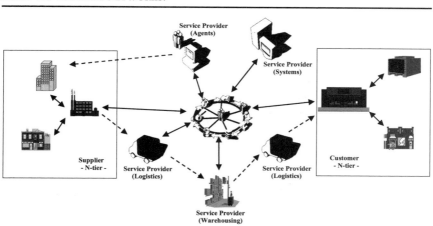

SOURCE: Roland Berger & Partner/SAP.

and distribution are unable to put such plans into action. Under these circumstances, it is best to identify where the greatest return can be achieved with the least effort, and to start there. The answer may be not introducing CPFR, but rather improving processes that may be peripheral yet indispensable for smooth operations.

The roadmap's real value added thus lies in considering the different development stages as a single whole. Put simply, it can be used to put the clean-up of the existing infrastructure—both organizational and technological—into the context of innovation that ensures enduring competitiveness. Securing and improving existing investments contributes directly to strengthening a company's competitive position without neglecting the medium- to long-term effects whose potential for improving processes is, in fact, the actual starting point and ultimately also the goal.

In the next section, we look at two process examples in greater detail to illustrate how the roadmap model can be used to develop a holistic innovation approach.

Process Example: Global Account Profitability

The process of globalization or, more accurately, internationalization in the retail industry is one of the greatest challenges consumer goods manufacturers face today. This trend is extremely evident in Europe in particular and is magnified even further by the transition to a single currency, the euro. Increasingly, retailers are becoming multinationals and are keen to present a consistent image that transcends national boundaries. On the procurement side in particular, many retailers see potential for lasting efficiency improvement in uniform prices, supply structures, and streamlined product ranges, and they want to tap this potential.

This trend presents both opportunities and risks for manufacturers. Those who can manage their customer relations actively and profitably in this context will be a step ahead of the competition. As always, here, too, the race will be determined primarily by the speed and flexibility with which manufacturers respond to the new conditions. The battle is not about size: It will be fast companies that win out over slow companies.

One of the fundamental requirements for success is that the profitability of customer relationships be transparent. This transparency makes it easier to decide with whom to work and on which areas to focus. If a manufacturer can determine and track how profitable its relationship with a given customer is, not only at the national level but also in the international arena, its negotiations with this trading partner will become much easier.

But how do we go about implementing global account profitability in a specific context? First, a detailed expert and technical analysis of the situation is needed. In many cases, the data are already available but are stored in multiple systems, or are difficult to consolidate because the structures are incompatible. In many cases, there are even systems available for use in calculating the indicators required. However, only the professionals and technology experts together can determine the details of the modifications, extensions, and new systems required.

This process was presented using the roadmap model for a consumer goods manufacturer. The results amazed everyone: The company already had virtually all the data it needed in its systems. All that was necessary to process it was to make proper use of powerful reporting and analysis tools. With this in mind, a data-warehousing tool was selected and applied to consolidate and store data and to put the financial and controlling solutions already available at the company to greater use.

Process Example: CPFR

Today, CPFR is probably the most promising model for collaboration between retailers and manufacturers in the supply chain process. In some cases, it has resulted in a 5–10 percent improvement in service, more precise planning (50–80 percent), less capital tie-up through inventory reduction (30–50 percent), and lower supply chain costs (15–25 percent)[2]. Accessing the resulting potential is one of the most pressing tasks for both retailers and suppliers.

It doesn't always work, though, as shown by the following example. A well-known manufacturer, whose CIO was quick to recognize how useful CPFR could be, launched a number of pilot projects that tested different aspects of such a collaboration. Success was not slow in coming, and the manufacturer decided to apply the processes right across the entire relevant product range. It soon found a solution provider and went to work. Some time later, however, after several attempts to link the existing systems to the new process element, it ultimately shelved the project altogether. So what went wrong?

Time and time again, the complex, incompatible data structures of the participating partners' systems, and the processes underlying them, resulted in the collapse of the collaborative process chain. Besides actually implementing the CPFR scenario, they had quite simply forgotten to address the necessary restructuring and harmonizing of the existing systems and processes. Even if this usually involves dry, abstract, detailed work in such "old-fashioned" but fundamental systems as sales, shipping, and billing, neglecting these matters could render the ultimate goal, namely the introduction of a complex process like CPFR, impossible.

The real point that emerges here is the increasingly prominent issue of e-readiness. Not every company is in a position to implement the latest cutting-edge processes. In fact, it is often the more humdrum "homework" that promises greater success in the short term, paves the way for lasting process innovation in the middle term, and enables the company to survive in a competitive environment in the long term. However well the actual process itself may be reflected, it is only when it is used in conjunction with linked processes or, as in this example, associated systems, that additional value added can be realized.

With CPFR, this is especially true of the associated processes within the participating companies from the retail and consumer goods industries, where many functional areas are not yet ready to live with an increasingly flexible process chain. The outlook is better for the relationship between manufacturers and their suppliers, which is why many of today's successful CPFR projects can be found in this area. In some cases, multinational manufacturers have even used CPFR scenarios as internal process control tools. Thanks to past supply chain projects, most of the subsidiaries involved have already coordinated their processes and thus find it very easy to use the results of improved planning to boost the performance of their business operations.

5.6.4 Roadmap Application Model

Let's return for a moment to the question of what keeps CEOs of consumer goods manufacturers awake at night when it comes to the future of their companies. The answer, we said, was the search for profitable growth. How, then, can the e-transformation roadmap be used in reality? Can it be used to develop the basis for choosing the right innovation route for a company in the context of today's financial and technological environment?

The first point to note is that the master roadmap presented is not, in itself, capable of satisfying a demand of such great scope. It first needs to be adapted to the company's specific circumstances; in other words, an individual roadmap needs to be drawn up. Above all, it must include company-specific data regarding size, customer structure, and any organizational obstacles that exist.

What needs to be developed is thus a logical sequence of business cases that clearly show the individual steps along the way, quantify the steps in terms of cost, time, and expected revenues, and allow individual decisions. The holistic approach of the analytical model and the fact that projects are considered interdependent from the outset ensure that investments in individual projects are safe.

The dynamics of today's world, however, also demand a change-management mechanism that will ensure that new developments and opportunities are included in the innovation plan as necessary. The name of the game is evolution, not revolution. Two key features of the roadmap make this possible: First, individual projects can be monitored separately, and are modular, so they can also be evaluated in terms of achieving the expected goals. This makes it possible to discern, in a timely manner, any revisions that need to be made to the strategy. Second, the projects are essentially independent of one another, so the strategy may be realigned at any time. For strategy revisions, an updated roadmap based on an extended master version is useful.

5.6.5 Prospects

The present approach provides a tool that enables consumer goods manufacturers to decide how best to transform themselves and evolve toward the network economy. A master roadmap supplies a portfolio of choices for this, drawn from best practices in the industry. Building on this, a company's strategic alignment and its organizational and technological constraints are taken as the basis for devising its individual innovation sequence. This provides top management with a tailor-made e-transformation roadmap laying out a sequence of business cases that can be implemented and decided upon on their own, plus a proposal regarding the timetable involved. Taken as a whole, these individual projects constitute a harmonious, compatible whole to ensure the company's short- and long-term competitiveness in the network economy.

At the end of the day, however, the success of the approach will have to be proven in practical applications. That is, after all, what it was designed for. The tool, with its combination of strategic and directly applicable implementation competence, has the potential to pave the way for strategic decisions in the holistic framework of the relevant technology context. This is undoubtedly what sets it apart from other, similar models, which either get too bogged down in strategy considerations or are too obsessed with technology to make a really convincing contribution to achieving profitable growth, a company's ultimate goal.

Unlike other approaches, this model's holistic aspect offers more potential than any partial approach such as supply chain management or customer relationship management models. The e-transformation roadmap blazes a trail through the jungle of options that companies have today when it comes to process innovation. It answers the question of whether a given project makes sense in light of alternative value-creating projects, that is, if it identifies the "low-hanging fruit" and shows the way toward more efficient, but also more sustainable, improvement.

In our opinion, this approach is a first step toward developing a collaborative innovation approach, combining strategic and operational process competence with extensive and technologically advanced IT expertise. In the future, a company's competitiveness will depend increasingly on its ability to establish a powerful innovation network. The task of this network will be to speed up the innovation in terms of decision making and implementation, and to improve the quality of the process. Our aim is to ensure that IT really is the enabler so many strategic process models consider it to be.

Notes

1. Roland Berger Strategy Consultants, ECR survey of 120 European manufacturers and retailers in the FMCG sector.
2. Roland Berger expert interviews and European studies.

Bibliography

Aaker, D. A.: *Strategic Marketing Management,* 6th edition, New York: John Wiley, 2001.

Ahlert, D.: "Vertikalisierung der Distribution—Die kundenorientierte Neugestaltung des Wertschöpfungsprozess-Managements," in *Distribution im Aufbruch* (edited by Beisheim, O.), Munich, 1999, pp. 333–350.

Ahlert, D.: *Distributionspolitik—Das Management des Absatzkanals,* 4th edition, Stuttgart/Jena/New York, 2001.

Ahlert, D. and **Borchert**, S.: "Prozessmanagement im vertikalen Marketing—Efficient Consumer Response," in *Konsumgüternetzen,* Berlin/Heidelberg: Springer, 2000.

Alvarado, U. and **Kotzab**, H.: "Supply Chain Management—The Integration of Logistics in Marketing," in *Industrial Marketing Management,* No. 2, 2001, pp. 183–198.

Alves, R.: "Integrierte Führung und Imitationsmanagement in Filialsystemen des Handels," Frankfurt, 1996.

A. T. Kearney Consulting and **PAP Consulting**: "Assessing the Profit Impact of ECR," *ECR Europe Study,* Brussels, 1998.

Bachl, T.: "Category Management—Erfolgsrezept für den Handel?" in *Coorganisation,* No. 3, 1995, pp. 22–25.

Barth, K.: "Architektur der Kundenzufriedenheit und Kundenbindung: Die drei Säulen," in *KSA News—Kundennähe realisieren* (edited by KSA), Düsseldorf, 1997, pp. 3–6.

Barth, K.: *Betriebswirtschaftslehre des Handels,* 4th edition, Wiesbaden: Gabler, 1999.

Bastian, R.: "Wachstum über Kundenbegeisterung," in *Marketing & Kommunikation,* No. 1, 2000, pp. 4–7.

Baumgart, G. and **Bieber**, D.: "Prozesskettenoptimierung vor dem Hintergrund sich verändernder Vertriebs- Informations-, und Logistikwege," in *VDI/VDE-IT: Schnittstellenoptimierung in der Distributionslogistik—Innovative Dienstleistungen in der Wertschöpfungskette,* 2000, unpublished.

Behrends, C.: "Category Management—Bestandsaufnahme und Perspektiven," in *Category Management—Neue Herausforderung im vertikalen Marketing? Edition: Arbeits-/Dokumentationspapiere der Wissenschaftlichen Gesellschaft für Marketing und Unternehmensführung e.V.* (edited by Meffert, H./Wagner, H./Backhaus, K.), Münster, 1995, pp. 5–29.

Belz, C., **Kramer**, M., and **Schlögel**, M.: "Supply Chain Management: Probleme, Strategien, und Lösungen," in *Thexis—Fachbericht für Marketing von dem Forschungsinstitut für Absatz und Handel,* No. 4/1994, St. Gallen, 1994.

Bertram, H.: "Data Warehouse—Trends bei Wal-Mart, Sears & Co," in Dynamik im Handel, No. 7, 1999, pp. 22–25.

Bickelmann, R.: "Henkel's Unique Combined Use of EPOS & Panel Data," in *European Logistics and Supply Chain Management,* 05.01.1999, pp. 8–9.

Biehl, B: "Tesco nimmt Hersteller ins Boot—Tesco nutzt Industrie und Berater-Know how für sein Category Management," in *LZ* 27.03.1998, pp. 46–48.

Biehl, B.: "ECR noch lange nicht am Ende—Die 4. ECR-Konferenz befasst sich in Paris mit dem Consumer Value," in *LZ* 16.04.1999 (a), p. 38.

Biehl, B.: "ECR und die Welt des Internets—Fünfte europäische Konferenz in Turin diskutiert EDI-Durchsatz und Global Commerce," in *LZ* 31.03.2000, p. 58.

Borchert, S.: *Führung von Distributionsnetzwerken—Eine Konzeption der Systemführung von Unternehmensnetzwerken zur erfolgreichen Realisation von Efficient Consumer Response-Kooperationen,* Wiesbaden: Deutscher Universitäts-Verlag, 2001.

Bösler, B.: "Regeln für den Brückenbau zwischen Edifact und XML—Ausschuss des Deutschen Instituts für Normung verabschiedet Standards für den Weg vom klassischen zum Internet-EDI," in *LZ* 3.11.2000, p. 62.

Brettschneider, G.: *Beschaffung im Handel unter besonderer Berücksichtigung von Efficient Consumer Response,* Frankfurt: Lang, 2000.

Brockman, B. and **Morgan**, R. M.: "The Evolution of Managerial Innovations in Distribution—What Prospects for ECR," in *International Journal of Retail & Distribution Management,* No. 10, pp. 397–408.

Brown, P. G. and **Visconti**, M.: "ECR Europe 1996 Tracking Survey—Progress to Date and the Way Forward," Kurt Salmon Associates, presentation at second ECR Europe conference in Amsterdam, 1997.

Bruce, R. and **Ireland**, R.: "CPFR: Only the Beginning of Collaboration," in *Supply Chain Management Review,* September/October 2000.

Buzell, R. D.: "Is Vertical Integration Profitable?" in *Harvard Business Review,* No. 1, 1983, pp. 92–102.

Cansier, A.: *Efficient Consumer Response aus kooperationstheoretischer Sicht,* Wiesbaden: Deutscher Universitäts-Verlag, 2001.

CCRRGE (Coca-Cola Retailing Research Group Europe): *Kooperation zwischen Industrie und Handel im Supply Chain Management,* Essen: Coca-Cola, 1994.

Centrale für Coorganisation: *Managementinformationspapier CPFR,* Cologne: Centrale für Coorganisation, 2001.

Centrale für Coorganisation: *Handbuch ECR Supply Chain Side,* Cologne: Centrale für Coorganisation, 2002.

Cooke, J. A.: "CPFR: The Countdown Begins," in *Logistics Management and Distribution Report,* Nov. 1999.

Corsten, D. and **Plötzl**, J.: *Efficient Consumer Response—Integration von Logistiketten,* Munich/Wien: Hanser, 2000.

Dantzer, U.: "Was ist und was bringt 'Efficient Consumer Response.'" in *LZ,* 08.11.1996, p. 82.

Dölle, C.: "E-Procurement—Neue Perspektiven in der Beschaffung—B2B-Marktplätze werden mit Einkaufskooperationen konkurrieren," in *LZ,* 3.11.2000, p. 63.

Doppler, K. and **Lauterburg**, C.: *Change Management,* Frankfurt: Campus, 1994.

ECR Europe: *Introducing Efficient Replenishment,* Brussels: ECR Europe, 1996 (a).

ECR Europe: *Efficient Replenishment Techniques,* Brussels: ECR Europe, 1996 (b).

ECR Europe: *Efficient Replenishment Trials,* Brussels: ECR Europe, 1996 (c).

ECR Europe: *Introducing EDI,* Brussels: ECR Europe, 1996 (d).

ECR Europe: "Newsletter for European Retailers, Suppliers, and Distributors," Amsterdam Conference Report, Brussels, 1997.

ECR Europe: *A Guide to CPFR Implementation,* Brussels: ECR Europe, 2001.

Eierhoff, K.: "Die Logistikkette als Wertschöpfungselement des Handels," in *Management der Logistikkette* (edited by Pfohl, H.-C.), Berlin, 1994, pp. 129–147.

Eierhoff, K.: "Efficient Consumer Response (ECR)—Ein neuer Weg in der Kooperation zwischen Industrie und Handel," in *Informationssysteme für das Handelsmanagement* (edited by Ahlert, D., et al.), Berlin, 1998, pp. 365–386.

Ester, B. and **Baumgart**, G.: "Cash Flow Aspekte bei der Supply-Chain-Gestaltung," in *Supply Chain Management* (edited by Pfohl, H.-C.), Berlin, 2000, pp. 141–160.

Fairfield, D.: "CPFR and the Collaborative Economy—Are You Ready?" in *Consumer Goods' Technology Magazine,* Vol. 10, No. 2, February 2001.

Feld, C.: "Category Management im Handel," Working paper No. 8 of the Faculty of Trade and Distribution, University of Cologne, Cologne, 1996.

Feller, M. and **Grossweischede**, M.: "Steht ECR am Scheideweg?" in *LZ,* 09.04.1999, p. 55.

Fernie, J. and **Sparks**, L.: *Logistics and Retail Management,* London: Kogan Page, 1998.

Figgen, B.: "Category Management und Efficient Consumer Response—Der Verbraucher steht im Mittelpunkt," in *Handbuch Efficient Consumer Response—Konzepte, Erfahrungen, Herausforderungen* (edited by von der Heydt, A.), Munich: Vahlen, 1999, pp. 181–193.

FMI (Food Marketing Institute): "Backgrounder: Efficient Consumer Response," in http://www.fmi.org/media/bg/ecr1.html (Internet), 18.10.1999.

Friedrich, S. A. and **Rodens**, B.: "Wertschöpfungspartnerschaft 'Handel/Industrie'—Gemeinsam Werte für den Kunden schaffen," in *Das Neue Strategische Management* (Hrsg. Hinterhuber, H. H. Ayad, A., and Handlbauer, G.), Wiesbaden: Gabler, 1996.

Galloway, J.: "EDI: Enabler of Business Process Re-engineering," in *Introducing EDI* (edited by ECR Europe), Brussels: ECR Europe, 1996, p. 11.

GCI: "VICS—Collaborative Planning, Forecasting, and Replenishment," GCI Recommendation, 2001.

Glendinning Consultans: "Der Verbraucher weiss, was er will— Glendinning Consultants untersuchen Warengruppen aus Kundensicht," in *LZ*, 16.04.1999, pp. 41–43.

Günther, A.: "Category Management und Efficient Consumer Response in der Kosmetikindustrie," in *KSA News—Kundennähe realisieren* (edited by KSA), Düsseldorf: Kurt Salmon Associates, 1997, pp. 10–12.

Hahne, H.: *Category Management aus Herstellersicht,* Cologne: EUL, 1998.

Hambuch, P.: "Category Management: der Verbraucher steht im Mittelpunkt," in *Perspektiven ökonomischen Denkens* (edited by Woratschek, H.), Frankfurt: Deutscher Fachverlag, 1998, pp. 41–51.

Hammer, M. and **Champy**, J.: *Business Reengineering,* 5th edition, Frankfurt/New York: HarperBusiness, 1995.

Heydt, A. von der: *Efficient Consumer Response,* 2d edition, Frankfurt: Lang, 1997.

Hill, R. W.: "Demand-Side Priorities & Vision," Andersen Consulting, presentation at second ECR Europe conference in Amsterdam, 1997.

Hillemeyer, J.: "Marktplätze als digitaler Brückenschlag—HIS-Tagung in Münster: Elektronische Kommunikation zwischen Handel, Industrie und Kunden," in *LZ*, 01.06.2001, p. 41.

Hinterhuber, H. H. and **Friedrich** S. A.: "Quo Vadis ECR?— Dated Effizienzstreben zur Kundenorientierung," in *Handbuch Efficient Consumer Response—Konzepte, Erfahrungen, Herausforderungen* (edited by von der Heydt, A.), Munich: Valen, 1999, pp. 332–346.

Hinterhuber, H. H. and **Friedrich** S. A.: "Wettbewerbsvorteile durch Wertschöpfungspartnerschaft—Paradigmenwechsel in der Hersteller/Handels-Beziehung," in *WiSt—Wirtschaftswissenschaftliches Studium,* 1999 (a), No. 1, pp. 2–8.

Hoffman, K. C.: "The Vision: Suppliers, Manufacturers, Retailers Collaborating as One," in *Global Logistics & Supply Chain Strategies,* June 1998.

Holland, H., **Hermann**, J., and **Machenheimer**, G.: *Efficient Consumer Response,* Frankfurt: Deutscher Fachverlag, 2001.

Holmström, J., **Hoover**, W. E., **Louhiluoto**, P., and **Vasara**, A.: "The Other End of the Supply Chain," in *The McKinsey Quarterly,* No. 1, 2000, pp. 62–71, in http://205.253.128.123/manuoper/oten00.asp (Internet) dated 24.04.2000.

Hughes, J., **Ralf**, M., and **Michels**, B.: *Supply Chain Management—So steigern Sie die Effizienz ihres Unternehmens durch perfekte Organisation der Wertschöpfungskette,* Landsberg/Lech: Verlag Moderne Industrie, 2000.

Industry Directions/Syncra Systems: "CPFR Survey—Findings & Analysis," April 2000, in http://www.cpfr.org/WhitePapers/SurveyResults.pdf (Internet) dated 07.02.2002.

Jarillo, J. C.: "On Strategic Networks," in *Strategic Management Journal,* No. 1, 1988, pp. 31–41.

Jirik, C. T.: "Supply Chain Management—Gestaltung und Koordination der Lieferkette," in *WiSt—Wirtschaftswissenschaftliches Studium,* 1999, No. 10, pp. 547–550.

Johnson, M.: "Collaboration Data Modeling—CPFR Implementation Guidelines," Syncra Systems publication, Reprint of 1999 annual conference proceedings of the Council of Logistics Management, in http://www.cpfr.org/WhitePapers/CollaborationDataModelingA.pdf (Internet) dated 07.07.2002.

Joint Industry Project on ECR: *Category Management Report,* Washington, D.C.: Food Marketing Institute, 1995.

Joint Industry Project on ECR: *Category Management II—Building Organizational Capability,* Washington, D.C.: Food Marketing Institute, 1999.

Jordan, P.: "Why Do You Need EDI" for ECR Europe, in *Introducing EDI* (edited by ECR Europe), Brussels, 1996, p. 2.

Kaas, P. N.: "Efficient Consumer Response—Kooperation und Wettbewerb auf dem Lebensmittelmarkt," in *Perspektiven ökonomischen Denkens* (edited by Woratschek, H.), Frankfurt: Deutscher Fachverlag, 1998, pp. 23–39.

Kalmbach, U.: "ECR Europe und ECR Deutschland—Ein Überblick," in *Handbuch Efficient Consumer Response—Konzepte, Erfahrungen, Herausforderungen* (edited by von der Heydt, A.), Munich: Vahlen, 1999, pp. 24–40.

Kaluza, B. and **Kemminer**, J.: *Dynamisches Supply Management und Dynamische Produktdifferenzierungsstrategie,* Duisburg: S&W Verlag, 1997.

Kansky, D. and **Weingarten**, U.: "Supply Chain: Fertigen, was der Kunde verlangt," in *Harvard Business Manager,* No. 4, 1999, pp. 87–95.

Kanter, R. M.: "Collaborative Advantage: The Art of Alliances," in *Harvard Business Review,* July/August, 1994, pp. 96–108.

Kapell, E.: "WWRE launcht globales CPFR-Projekt im Juni— Marktplatz für weitere Händler und Hersteller offen," in *LZ,* 6.04.2001, p. 33.

Kilimann, J. and **Schlenk**, H.: "Die ECR-Bewegung—Mehr Verständnis für den Kunden," in *Efficient Consumer Response—Strategische Waffe für Industrie und Handel* (edited by Tienes, E.-C., Kilimann, J., and Schlenk, H.), Stuttgart: Schaffer-Poeschel, 1998, pp. 1–10.

Klein, H. L. and **Lachhammer**, J.: "Efficient Consumer Response—Die Aufgaben des Beziehungs-Managements," in *Absatzwirtschaft,* No. 2, 1996, pp. 62–66.

Kohl, M. and **Zimmermann**, K.: "Wie Continental eine ECR-Initiative steuert—Projekt Scorecard," in *Absatzwirtschaft,* No. 6, 2001, pp. 36–40.

Kolodziej, M. J.: "Zur Kultur der Zusammenarbeit," in *Globales Handelsmanagement* (edited by Zentes, J. and Swoboda, B.), Frankfurt: Deutscher Fachverlag, 1998, pp. 429–448.

Koloszyc, G.: "Retailers, Suppliers Push Joint Sales Forecasting," in *Stores,* June 1998.

Korpiun, M. and **Kohl**, M.: "Supply Chain Management und Efficient Consumer Response als Herausforderung für ein effektives und effizientes Projektmanagement," in *Handelsforschung 2000/ 2001—Kooperations- und Wettbewerbsverhalten des Handels, Jahrbuch der Forschungsstelle für den Handel Berlin* (edited by Trommsdorff, V.), Cologne: Gabler, 2000, pp. 217–238.

Kotler, P. and **Bliemel**, F.: *Marketing-Management—Analyse, Planung, Umsetzung und Steuerung,* 10th edition, Stuttgart: Schäffer-Poeschel, 2001.

Kotzab, H.: "Distributionslogistische Kooperationsstrategien von Handelsunternehmen mit ihren Lieferanten in der Konsumgüterwirtschaft—Das Beispiel Efficient Consumer Response," in *ÖZV,* No. 1, 1997, pp. 58–67.

Kotzab, H.: *Neue Konzepte der Distributionslogistik von Handelsunternehmen,* Wiesbaden: Deutscher Universitäts Verlag, 1997.

Kotzab, H.: "Improving Supply Chain Performance by Efficient Consumer Response?—A Critical Comparision of Existing ECR Approaches," in *Journal of Business and Industrial Marketing,* No. 5/6, 1999, pp. 364–377.

Kotzab, H.: "Management by ECR—Internationale Bestandsaufnahme und empirischer Vergleich der Umsetzung von ECR," in *Thexis—Fachzeitschrift für Marketing,* No. 3, 2001, pp. 29–33.

Kotzab, H. and **Schnedlitz**, P.: "The Integration of Retailing to the General Concept of Supply Chain Management," in *Journal für Betriebswirtschaft,* No. 4, 1999, pp. 140–153.

KPMG: "Supply Chain Management-Studie," in *Logistik Heute*, No. 7/8, 1998, pp. 57–58.

Krieger, W.: *Informationsmanagement in der Logistik*, Wiesbaden: Gabler, 1995.

Kruger, R. M.: "Destination: Diapers—Category Management," in *Discount Merchandiser*, No. 3, 1998, pp. 57–58.

Kurt Salmon Associates: *Efficient Consumer Response—Enhancing Consumer Value in the Grocery Industry*, Washington, D.C.: KSA, 1993.

Kurt Salmon Associates: *Quick Response*, New York/Washington, D.C.: KSA, 1997.

Laurent, M.: *Vertikale Kooperationen zwischen Industrie und Handel— Neue Typen und Strategien zur Effizienzsteigerung im Absatzkanal*, Frankfurt: Deutscher Fachverlag, 1996.

Lee, H. L., **Padmanabhan**, V., and **Whang**, S.: "Der Peitscheneffekt in der Absatzkette," in *Harvard Business Manager*, No. 4, 1997, pp. 78–87.

Lord, S.: "CPFR Inter-Operability," White paper Procter & Gamble Maerz, 2001, in http://www.cpfr.org/WhitePapers/CPFRInter operability.doc (Internet) dated 07.02.2002.

LZ Spezial: "Die Viererbande auf einen Blick—CPGmarket, Global Net Xchange, World Wide Retail Exchange und Transora," in *LZ Spezial*, No. 1, 2001, pp. 16–17.

Manheim, M. L., **Vlahos**, N. J., and **Xie**, Y.: "Designing Team Support Applications to Meet Business Objectives," in *Groupware— Technology and Applications* (edited by Coleman, D. and Khanna, R.), Englewood Cliffs, N.J.: Prentice-Hall, 1995.

Margulis, R.: "CPFR Emerging from ECR's Shadows," in IdeaBeat, June 1998, in http://www.rampr.com/Articles.html (Internet) dated 17.02.2002.

Mattmüller, R. and **Tunder**, R.: "Ein neues Selbstverständnis der Hersteller gegenüber dem Handel—Theoretische Hintergründe und Umsetzungsalternativen," in *Handelsforschung 2000/2001—Kooperations- und Wettbewerbsverhalten des Handels, Jahrbuch der Forschungsstelle für den Handel Berlin* (edited by Trommsdorff, V.), Cologne: BBE, 2000, pp. 3–26.

McAfee, A. and **Ashira**, M.: "Syncra Systems," Harvard Business School Case Study, Boston, 2001.

Meffert, H.: "Einführung in die Problemstellung," in *Category Management—neue Herausforderung im vertikalen Marketing?* Edition: Arbeits-/Dokumentationspapiere der Wissenschaftlichen Gesellschaft für Marketing und Unternehmensführung e.V. (edited by Meffert, H., Wagner, H., and Backhaus, K.), Münster: University of Münster, 1995, pp. 1–4.

Meffert, H.: "Zwischen Kooperation und Konfrontation—Strategien und Verhaltensweisen im Absatzkanal," in *Distribution im Aufbruch* (edited by Beisheim, O.), Munich: Vahlen, 1999 (a) pp. 407–424.

Merkel, H.: *Logistik Managementsysteme,* Munich: Oldenbourg, 1995.

Merkel, H.: "Firmenübergreifendes Prozessdenken—Ein lohnender Ansatz," in *Efficient Consumer Response—Strategische Waffe für Industrie und Handel* (edited by Tienes, E.-C., Kilimann, J., and Schlenk, H.), Stuttgart: Vahlen, 1998, pp. 35–52.

Meyer, M.: "Efficient Consumer Response—Eine kritische Betrachtung," in *Handelsforschung 1999/2000, Jahrbuch der Forschungsstelle für den Handel Berlin* (edited by Trommsdorff, V.), Wiesbaden: Gabler, 1999, pp. 297–314.

Mierdorf, Z.: "Grundidee von CPFR ist ECR, Interview mit Zygmunt Mierdorf, Vorstandsmitglied der Metro AG," in *LZ,* 25.05.2001, p. 25.

Milde, H.: "Category Management—die stille Revolution," in *Markenartikel—Zeitschrift für Markenführung,* No. 7, 1994 (a), pp. 343–346.

Möhlenbruch, D.: "Kundenorientierung durch Category Management—Kritische Analyse eines Kooperationsmodells zwischen Industrie und Handel," in *Handelsforschung 1997/98—Kunden-orientierung im Handel, Jahrbuch der Forschungsstelle für den Handel Berlin* (edited by Trommsdorff, V.), Wiesbaden: Gabler, 1997, pp. 113–134.

Möhlenbruch, D. and **Nickel**, S.: "Kooperationsstrategien als Element der wettbewerbsstrategischen Konzeption von Einzelhandelsunternehmungen," in *Handelsforschung 1994/95—Kooperation im Handel und mit dem Handel, Jahrbuch der Forschungsstelle für den Handel Berlin* (edited by Trommsdorff, V.), Wiesbaden: Gabler, 1994, pp. 3–22.

Moll, C.: *Efficient Consumer Response,* Frankfurt: Deutscher Fachverlag, 2000.

Mouzas, S. and **Araujos**, L.: "Implementing Programmatic Initiatives in Manufacturer-Retailer Networks," in *Industrial Marketing Management,* No. 3, 2000, pp. 293–303.

Müller-Hagedorn, L.: *Der Handel,* Stuttgart: Kohlhammer, 1998.

Müller-Hagedorn, L., **Dach**, C., **Spork**, S., and **Toporowski**, W.: "Vertikales Marketing—Trends in der Praxis und Schwerpunkte der theoretischen Diskussion," in *Marketing ZFP,* No. 1, 1999, pp. 61–75.

Needel, S. P.: "Understanding Consumer Response to Category Management," in *Journal of Advertising Research,* No. 4, 1998, pp. 61–67.

Olbrich, R.: "Entwicklungsperspektiven des vertikalen Informationsmanagement zwischen Handel und Industrie," in *Handelsforschung 1995/96—Informationsmanagement im Handel, Jahrbuch der Forschungsstelle für den Handel Berlin* (edited by Trommsdorff, V.), Wiesbaden: Gabler, 1995, pp. 39–50.

Pfähler, W. and **Wiese**, H.: *Unternehmensstrategien im Wettbewerb,* Berlin: Springer, 1998.

Picot, A., **Reichwald,** R., and **Wigand**, R. T.: *Die grenzenlose Unternehmung—Information, Organisation und Management,* 4th edition, Wiesbaden: Gabler, 2001.

Porter, M. E.: *Wettbewerbsvorteile—Spitzenleistungen erreichen und behaupten,* 5th edition, Frankfurt/New York: Campus, 1999 (a).

Porter, M. E.: "Creating Tomorrow's Advantage," in *Strategische Unternehmensplanung—Strategische Unternehmensführung* (edited by Hahn, D. and Taylor, B.), 8th edition, Heidelberg: Physica, 1999 (b), pp. 944–952.

Pretzel, J.: "Gestaltung der Hersteller-Handel-Beziehung durch Category Management," in *Category Management—neue Herausforderung im vertikalen Marketing? Reihe: Arbeits-/Dokumentationspapiere der Wissenschaftlichen Gesellschaft für Marketing und Unternehmensführung e.V.* (edited by Meffert, H., Wagner, H., and Backhaus, K.), Münster: University of Münster, 1995, pp. 30–43.

Reda, M. and **Harding**, P.: "Demand Chain & Supply Chain Management," in *Supplement to Retail Info System News and Consumer Goods,* May 1998.

Reda, S.: "CPFR Takes Off," in *Stores,* February 2000, in http://www.stores.org/archives/feb00cover.html (Internet) dated 07.02.2002.

Ritter, S.: "ECR—Brücke zwischen Vision und Wirklichkeit?" in *Dynamik im Handel,* No. 4, 1999, pp. 39–40.

Rode, J.: "Tesco ermöglicht Lieferanten Zugriff auf EPOS-Daten—'Revolution' per Internet," in *LZ,* 27.03.1998, p. 48.

Rode, J.: "Trade Information Exchange: Workflow per Internet," in *LZ,* 01.10.1999, p. 46.

Rode, J.: "Supply Chain als Top-Aufgabe—VICS Vision Summit—Chefs globaler Unternehmen diskutieren Zukunft des Handels," in *LZ,* 23.04.1999 (a), pp. 44–45.

Rode, J.: "CPFR—Zauberformel für Turbo-ECR," in *LZ,* 22.01.1999 (b), pp. 14–15.

Rode, J.: "Drei Wege digitaler Daten—Metro wirbt Lieferanten für klassisches und WebEDI," in *LZ,* 12.05.2000, p. 44.

Rode, J.: "Die digitale Handels-Revolution," in *E-Commerce—Das Web revolutioniert die Handelswelt* (edited by *LZ Spezial*), No. 1, 2000 (a), pp. 8–22.

Rode, J.: "Schnelles Wachstum der B2B-Marktplätze—Handel grösste Anwenderbranche," in *LZ,* 1.09.2000 (c), p. 30.

Rode, J.: "CPFR begeistert ECR-Konferenz," in *LZ,* 18.05.2001, p. 26.

Rode, J.: "dm gibt POS-Daten frei—Extranet liefert Abverkaufs- und Perfomancezahlen," in *LZ,* 9.02.2001 (a), p. 28.

Rode, J.: "B2B—Ein langer Weg für die Branche—CPFR, die IT-Integration der Marktplätze und globale Standards fallen nicht vom Himmel," in *LZ,* 25.5.2001 (b), p. 51.

Rode, J. and **Weber**, B.: "Die Viererbande—Vier Giganten wollen die Konsumgüterwirtschaft aufmischen: GNX, WWRE, Transora und CPGmarket," in *LZ Spezial,* 2001, pp. 12–15.

Rode, J. and **Wolfskeil**, J.: "Planspiele im Web—Das Konditionsgerangel steht vor dem Aus," in *LZ Spezial,* No. 1, 2001, pp. 34–37.

Rodens-Friedrich, B.: "ECR bei dm-drogerie markt—Unser Weg in die Wertschöpfungspartnerschaft," in *Handbuch Efficient Consumer Response—Konzepte, Erfahrungen, Herausforderungen* (edited by von der Heydt, A.), Munich: Vahlen, 1999, pp. 205–221.

Roland Berger & Partner: "Category Management Enabling Components Workshop," presentation at the second ECR Europe conference in Amsterdam, 1997.

Roland Berger & Partner: "Die grosse Unbekannte—Out-of-stock-Situationen kosten einige Umsatzpotentiale," in *LZ,* 16.04. 1999, p. 46.

Roland Berger & Partner: "How to Implement Consumer Enthusiasm—Strategic Consumer Value Management," ECR Europe Study, Brussels, 1999 (a).

Roland Berger & Partner: "Efficient Replenishment Project—'Working Three-Gether'—Transport Consolidation with the Involvement of Logistics Service Providers," ECR Europe Study, Brussels, 1999 (b).

Roland Berger & Partner/The Partnering Group: "Category Management Best Practises Report," ECR Europe Study, Brussels, 1997.

Rotthowe, T.: "Category Management Deutschland: Kurz vor dem Durchbruch?" in *Dynamik im Handel,* No. 12, 1999, pp. 49–51.

Rudolph, T. and **Einhorn**, M.: "Herausforderungen im europäischen Einzelhandel," in *Thexis—Fachzeitschrift für Marketing,* No. 3, 2001, pp. 2–7.

Runau, R.: "Sicherheit im Datenmeer—Probleme und Risiken," in *LZ,* 3.11.2000, p. 66.

Schachtman, N.: "Trading Partners Collaborate to Increase Sales—CPFR Brings Companies Together to Share Data, Cut Product Cycle Times, and Reduce Inventory," in *Informationweek,* October 2000.

Schmitt, D. and **Taplick**, N.: "Elektronische Marktplätze—Mitmachen oder Abwarten?—WWRE und andere Branchen-Plattformen verändern die Geschäftsmodelle," in *LZ,* 3.11.2000, p. 58.

Schneckenberger, T. and **Plötzl**, J.: "Partner im Dilemma—Nutzen und Machtverlust beim Informationsaustausch—Ergebnisse einer Studie des Instituts für Technologiemanagement der Hochschule St. Gallen," in *LZ,* 14.05.1999, No. 19, pp. 44–46.

Schröder, H. and **Geister**, S.: "Internationales Category Management im europäischen Einzelhandel—Herausforderungen und Informationsgrundlagen," in *Thexis—Fachzeitschrift für Marketing,* No. 3, 2001, pp. 41–46.

Schröder, H., **Feller**, M., and **Grossweischede**, M.: "Kundenorientierung im Category Management," in *LZ,* 17.03.2000, pp. 60–61.

Schröder, V.: "Vertrauen und gemeinsamer Wille—Interview with Volker Schröder, Procter & Gamble Europe, About CPFR Pilot Projects," in *LZ,* 22.01.1999, p. 13.

Seifert, D.: "Efficient Consumer Response—Exploiting Cost Saving Potentials," unpublished study for a major Euopean manufacturer, Budapest, 1996.

Seifert, D.: "Chance ECR: Zuerst eine grundsätzlich strategische Neuausrichtung—Strategische Unternehmensführung von Industrie- und Handelsunternehmen in Zeiten dramatischer Veränderungen im Absatzkanal," in *Markenartikel—Zeitschrift für Markenführung,* No. 1, 2000, pp. 40–43.

Seifert, D.: "Efficient Consumer Response—Ein Instrument des Marketing Controlling zur Schaffung strategischer Wettbewerbsvorteile im Handel," in *Handbuch Marketing-Controlling* (edited by Zerres, M.), Berlin/Heidelberg/New York: Springer, 2000 (a), pp. 351–371.

Seifert, D.: "Einzelhandel—wie er strategisch optieren muss," in *Harvard Business Manager* (German edition of *Harvard Business Review*), No. 4, 2000 (b), pp. 22–27.

Seifert, D.: "Wal-Mart hat die Metro weiter im Visier—Studie: Der Weltmarktführer im Einzelhandel ist in Deutschland auf Übernahmen angewiesen," in *Die Welt,* 07.08.2000 (c), p. 16.

Seifert, D.: "On Your Mark—Global Retailing," in *Chain Store Age—The Newsmagazine for Retail Executives,* No. 10, 2000 (d), pp. 72–74.

Seifert, D.: "Die Besten der Besten—ECR-Studie Deutschland," in *Logistik Heute,* No. 5, 2001, pp. 58–59.

Seifert, D.: *Efficient Consumer Response—Supply Chain Management (SCM), Category Management (CM), und Collaborative Planning, Forecasting, and Replenishment (CPFR) als neue Strategieansätze,* 2d edition, Munich/Mering: Hampp Verlag, 2001.

Seifert, D.: "Efficient Consumer Response—Wie der Handel strategische Wettbewerbsvorteile erzielen kann," in *Handelsforschung 2001/2002—Jahrbuch der Forschungsstelle für den Handel Berlin* (edited by Trommsdorff, V.), Cologne: BBE, 2001 (a).

Seifert, D.: "Category Management Kompetenzführer im deutschen Handel und in der Industrie," in *Absatzwirtschaft*, No. 8, 2001 (b), p. 55.

Seifert, D.: "Die Kompetenzführer im Category Management—Ergebnisse der Efficient Consumer Response-Erfolgsfaktorenstudie Deutschland," in *Markenartikel—Zeitschrift für Markenführung*, No. 6, 2001 (c), pp. 24–28.

Seifert, D.: *Collaborative Planning, Forecasting, and Replenishment—How to Create a Supply Chain Advantage*, SAP-Preprint edition, Bonn: Galileo Press, 2002.

Seifert, D.: "Collaborative Planning, Forecasting and Replenishment—E-Marktplaetze als Katalysatoren fuer das Wertschoepfungsmanagement," in *Thexis*, No. 3, 2002 (a), pp. 15–21.

Seifert, D., **Gawlik**, T., and **Kellner**, J.: *Effiziente Kundenbindung mit CRM—Wie Procter & Gamble, Henkel und Kraft mit ihren Marken Kundenbeziehungen gestalten*, Bonn: Galileo Press, 2002.

Seifert, D., **Ketels**, C., and **Kracklauer**, A.: "Kooperatives Kundenbindungsmanagement—Potentiale einer neuen Zusammenarbeit von Handel und Industrie," in *Consulting 2002—Jahrbuch für Unternehmensberatung und Management* (edited by Breidenstein, F., et al.), Frankfurt: FAZ, 2002, pp. 125–131.

Seifert, D. and **Kracklauer**, A.: "Category Management—Stellen Sie die richtigen Fragen," in *Absatzwirtschaft*, No. 6, 2001 (a), pp. 52–55.

Seifert, D. and **Kracklauer**, A.: "Gemeinsam näher am Kunden—Wie Industrie und Handel kooperatives Kundenbindungsmanagement betreiben," in *Markenartikel—Zeitschrift für Markenführung*, No. 3, 2001, pp. 50–59.

Seifert, D., **Kracklauer**, A., and **Mills**, D. Q.: *Kooperatives Kundenmanagement*, Wiesbaden: Gabler, 2002.

Seifert, D., **Kracklauer**, A., **Mills**, D. Q., **Leyk**, M., and **Ruebke**, S.: "Was dem Handel aus der Krise hilft," in *Harvard Business Manager* (German edition of *Harvard Business Review*), No. 4, 2002, pp. 98–106.

Seifert, D., **Kracklauer**, A., and **Passenheim**, O.: "Mutual Customer Approach—How Industry and Trade Are Executing Collaborative Customer Relationship Management," in *International Journal of Retail and Distribution Management*, No. 12, 2001, pp. 515–519.

Seifert, D. and **Thiel**, E.: "Optimierung innerhalb der Supply Chain," in *Distribution—Logistik in Warenfluss und Verteilung*, edition No. 7/8, 2001, pp. 26–27.

Sherman, R.: "Collaborative Planning, Forecasting, and Replenishment—Realizing the Promise of Efficient Consumer Response Through Collaborative Technology," in *Journal of Marketing—Theory and Practice*, Special Issue, Vol. 6, No. 4, 1998.

Spaan, U.: "Tesco TIE—ECR in Perfektion," in *Dynamik im Handel*, No. 8, 1999, pp. 26–27.

Spalink, H.: "Erfolgsfaktoren bei der Einführung von ECR," in *KSA News—Efficient Consumer Response* (edited by KSA), Düsseldorf: KSA, 1996, pp. 14–15.

Spalink, H. and **Berten**, B.: "Kooperation schöpft Markt besser aus—Studie von Kurt Salmon Associates belegt die positiven Effekte von CPFR," in *LZ*, 28.01.2000, p. 50.

Speer, F.: "Verbraucherdaten als wesentliche Steuerungsgrösse—Category Management—Wasch-, Putz- und Reinigungsmittel," in *Dynamik im Handel*, No. 4, 1998 (a), pp. 78–81.

Strüber, H.: "Die neue Logistik—Hebel für mehr Effizienz," in *Efficient Consumer Response—Strategische Waffe für Industrie und Handel* (edited by Tienes, E.-C., Kilimann, J., and Schlenk, H.), Stuttgart: Schäffer-Poeschel, 1998, pp. 53–68.

Swoboda, B.: "Wertschöpfungspartnerschaften in der Konsumgüterwirtschaft—Ökonomische und ökologische Aspekte eines ECR-Managements," in *WiSt*, No. 9, 1997, pp. 449–454.

Swoboda, B.: "Globale Transaktion und Wertschöpfung durch Electronic Commerce—Eine Herausforderung für die Hersteller-Handels-Beziehung?" in *Globales Handelsmanagement* (edited by Zentes, J. and Swoboda, B.), Frankfurt, 1998, pp. 349–384.

Täger, U. C. and **Nassua**, T.: "Der Einzelhandel in Westeuropa— Struktur und Entwicklungstendenzen," in *Globales Handelsmanagement* (edited by Zentes, J. and Swoboda, B.), Frankfurt: Deutscher Fachverlag, 1998, pp. 25–52.

Teuscher, H. and **Engler**, G.: "CPFR—Der nächste Schritt von ECR," in *LZ*, 18.05.2001, pp. 35–36.

Thaler, K.: *Supply Chain Management—Prozessoptimierung in der logistischen Kette,* 3rd edition, Cologne: Fortis, 2001.

Theis, H.-J.: *Handelsmarketing—Analyse- und Planungskonzepte für den Einzelhandel,* Frankfurt: Deutscher Fachverlag, 1999.

Tienes, E.-C., **Kilimann**, J., and **Schlenk**, H.: *Efficient Consumer Response—Strategische Waffe für Industrie und Handel,* Stuttgart: Schäffer-Poeschel, 1998.

Tietz, B.: "Kooperation statt Konfrontation—Kontraktmarketing zwischen Industrie und Handel," in *Handelsforschung 1994/95— Kooperation im Handel und mit dem Handel, Jahrbuch der Forschungsstelle für den Handel Berlin* (edited by Trommsdorff, V.), Wiesbaden: Gabler, 1994, pp. 39–56.

Tietz, B.: "Efficient Consumer Response (ECR)," in *WiSt— Wirtschaftswissenschaftliches Studium,* 1995, No. 10, pp. 529–530.

Tochtermann, T. C. A. and **Lange**, E.: "Analyse kommt vor dem Profit—Wie Hersteller mit Category Management profitieren können—Das McKinsey Modell," in *LZ*, 22.05.1998, pp. 40–42.

Tomczak, T. and **Schögel**, M.: "Management globaler Hersteller-Handels-Beziehungen," in *Globales Handelsmanagement* (edited by Zentes, J. and Swoboda, B.), Frankfurt: Deutscher Fachverlag, 1998, pp. 327–348.

Töpfer, A.: "Efficient Consumer Response—Bessere Zusammenarbeit zwischen Handel und Herstellern," in *Handelsforschung 1995/96—Informationsmanagement im Handel, Jahrbuch der Forschungsstelle für den Handel Berlin* (edited by Trommsdorff, V.), Wiesbaden: Gabler, 1995, pp. 187–200.

Töpfer, A.: "Das ECR-Konzept als Anforderung an Theorie und Praxis," in *Handbuch Efficient Consumer Response—Konzepte, Erfahrungen, Herausforderungen* (edited by von der Heydt, A.), Munich: Vahlen, 1999, pp. 362–375.

Trommsdorff, V.: "Kooperation als strategische Option—Vorwort des Herausgebers," in *Handelsforschung 1994/95—Kooperation im Handel und mit dem Handel, Jahrbuch der Forschungsstelle für den Handel Berlin* (edited by Trommsdorff, V.), Wiesbaden: Gabler, 1994, pp. v–xv.

Tucher, F. W. von and **Wiezorek** H.: "Efficient Consumer Response," in *Management logistischer Netzwerke und Flüsse* (edited by Klaus, P. and Krieger, W.), Wiesbaden: Gabler, 1998, pp. 93–99.

VICS: *Collaborative Planning, Forecasting, and Replenishment Voluntary Guidelines,* VICS publication, 1998.

VICS: *Roadmap to CPFR: The Case Studies,* VICS publication, 1999.

VICS: "VICS CPFR XML Messaging Model," White paper VICS June 2001, in http://www.cpfr.org/VICS_CPFR_XMLMessaging Model0601a.doc (Internet) dated 07.02.2002.

VICS/Northwestern University: "Collaborative Transportation Management," A White Paper Based Upon the Wal-Mart, Procter & Gamble, J. B. Hunt Pilot, December, 2000.

Vitek, S.: "A Work in Progress—Category Management," in *Progressive Grocer,* No. 5, 1998, p. 17.

Völlmecke, U.: "ECR bei Karstadt," in *Dynamik im Handel,* February 1999, pp. 62–66.

Waldmann, J.: "Trends und Visionen in der Logistik—Das Spannungsfeld zwischen Industrie und Handel," in *LZ,* 01.09.1995, pp. 68–71.

Walton, B. and **Princi**, M.: "From Supply Chain to Collaborative Network—Case Studies in the Food Industry," in http://logistics. about.com/gi/dynamic/offsite.htm?site = http%3A%2F%2Fwww. ascet.com%2Fdocuments.asp%3FgrID%3D134%26d_ID%3D266 (Internet) dated 07.02.2002.

Weber, B.: "Die Marktplätze der Branche müssen umdenken— Wal-Mart's Extranet ist Vorbild," in *LZ,* 11.05.2001, p. 32.

Weber, B.: "Die Schaltstelle—Der Handel braucht eine einheitliche Internetsprache für den Datenaustausch," in *LZ Spezial,* No. 1, 2001 (a), pp. 24–26.

Wehrli, H. P. and **Krick**, M.: "Mit strategischen Netzwerken Kundennähe realisieren," in *Absatzwirtschaft,* No. 1, 1998, pp. 62–68.

White, A. G.: "Collaborative Data Modeling—CPFR Implementaion Guidelines from the Manufacturer's Perspective," White Paper Logility, in http://www.cpfr.org/WhitePapers/CPFRManufacturers Perspective.doc (Internet) dated 07.02.2002.

White, A. G.: "N-tier CPFR—A proposal, White Paper Logility, May 2001, in http://www.cpfr.org/WhitePapers/nTierProposal.doc (Internet) dated 07.02.2002.

White, A. G.: "The Rise and Fall of the Trading Exchange," White Paper Logility 2001, in http://www.cpfr.org/WhitePapers/Riseand FalloftheTradingExchangeR1.doc (Internet) dated 07.02.2002.

White, A. G.: "The Value Equation—Value Chain Management, Collaboration, and the Internet," White Paper Logility 1999, in http:// www.cpfr.org/WhitePapers/The_Value_Equation.doc (Internet) dated 07.02.2002.

Wiezorek, H.: "ECR—Eine Aufgabe des Beziehungsmanagements," in *Globales Handelsmanagement* (edited by Zentes, J. and Swoboda, B.), Frankfurt: Deutscher Fachverlag, 1998, pp. 385–402.

Wiezorek, H.: "Efficient Consumer Response—Kooperation statt Konfrontation," in *Informationssysteme für das Handelsmanagement* (edited by Ahlert, D., et al.), Berlin: Springer, 1998 (a), pp. 387–400.

Wildemann, H.: "Kooperationen über die Wertschöpfungskette," in *Handbuch Unternehmensführung* (edited by Corsten, H. and Reiss, M.), Wiesbaden: Gabler, 1997, pp. 743–765.

Wildemann, H.: "Kundennahe Produktion und Zulieferung—Empirische Bestandsaufnahme und aktuelle Tendenzen," in *Kundenzufriedenheit* (edited by Simon, H. and Homburg, C.), Wiesbaden: Gabler, 1998, pp. 97–126.

Zentes, J.: "Effizienzsteigerungspotentiale kooperativer Logistikketten in der Konsumgüterwirtschaft," in *Management der Logistikkette* (edited by Pfohl, H.-C.), Berlin: Springer, 1994 (a), pp. 105–126.

Zentes, J.: "Strategische Allianzen: Neuorientierung der kooperativen Wettbewerbsstrategien im Handel," in *Handelsforschung 1994/ 95—Kooperation im Handel und mit dem Handel, Jahrbuch der Forschungsstelle für den Handel Berlin* (edited by Trommsdorff, V.), Wiesbaden: Gabler, 1994, pp. 73–85.

Zentes, J.: "Erfolgsstrategie ECR: Potentiale und Voraussetzungen," in *KSA News—Efficient Consumer Response* (edited by KSA), Düsseldorf: KSA, 1996 (a), pp. 4–6.

Zentes, J.: "Von Pull- und Push-Strategien zum kooperativen Wertschöpfungsmanagement," in *Markenartikel—Zeitschrift für Markenführung,* No. 4, 1996 (b), pp. 162–165.

Zentes, J.: "Trends im Handel—Chancen und Risiken zwischenbetrieblicher Kooperationen," in *Informationssysteme für das Handelsmanagement* (edited by Ahlert, D., et al.), Berlin: Springer, 1998, pp. 345–351.

Contributing Authors

Dr. Ferri Abolhassan, cochair and CEO IDS Scheer AG
Dr. Ferri Abolhassan is responsible for the internationalization of IDS Scheer, an international consulting and software company that specializes in business process management and e-business. He joined IDS Scheer in January 2001. Abolhassan held several executive positions at SAP AG (Germany). During his tenure there, he served as senior vice president of IBU Retail, responsible for the retail industry worldwide. He has also held the position of chief executive officer at SAP Retail Solutions, and prior to that he managed the worldwide business development, sales, rollout, and implementation of all products for the retail and consumer products market as director of Global Business Development IBU Retail/Consumer Products. Abolhassan has earned a Ph.D. in computer science at the University of the Saarland in Germany.

Joseph C. Andraski, vice chair VICS CPFR and senior vice president OMI International
Joseph C. Andraski is a senior VP for OMI International and an adjunct professor at Michigan State and at Penn State University and serves as a

385

member of the Senior Advisory Board of the Schulich School of Business Supply Chain Executive Program, York University. He spent twenty-five years with Nabisco as an executive responsible for supply chain management and customer marketing and is globally recognized as an expert in his field. He is a board member of the American Marketing Association and the Voluntary Interindustry Commerce Standards (VICS) Association and vice chairman of the VICS CPFR Committee. He has been involved in the development and evolution of CPFR as a global, leading-edge business practice since its inception. He graduated cum laude from the University of Scranton.

Prof. Dr. Gerhard Arminger, professor at the University of Wuppertal and chief scientist SAF-AG

Prof. Dr. Gerhard Arminger is professor of statistics in the Department of Economics at the University of Wuppertal. He has taught at the University of California at Los Angeles, University of Arizona at Tucson, Indiana University at Bloomington, the Technical University of Vienna, Basel University, and the University of Salzburg. He has published ten books and over 100 articles in scientific journals. He is co-founder and chief scientist of SAF-AG, a Swiss-based company specializing in software for simulation, analysis, and forecasting of demand and order building for retail and manufacturing. For SAF, he mainly works in the areas of microforecasting with self-learning systems and in optimization methods for order generation on all levels of the supply chain ranging from SKU-store to CPFR forecasts. Customers of SAF software for computer-assisted ordering on the store level include dm-drogerie markt internationally and Metro Cash & Carry Germany.

Brian Bastock, director customer logistics, Manco

Brian Bastock is the director of customer logistics at Manco, Inc. He came to Manco in 1997 as transportation manager. He was promoted to director of information logistics in 1999 and director of customer logistics in 2001. His areas of responsibility, in addition to collaborative relationships, include transportation, customer service, distribution, and international logistics. Prior to joining Manco, he spent eight years at Roadway Services, Inc., where he held various roles in auditing and corporate marketing. Brian received a bachelor's in business administration from Ohio University in 1988.

Fred Baumann, senior director collaborative solutions, JDA Software

Fred Baumann directs collaborative solutions at JDA Software, a global leader in inventory management and replenishment solutions. Fred's previous career experience includes an application-training role at IBM and eight years' experience with The Pillsbury Company, where he served as a value chain manager. He was responsible for starting the collaborative inventory program with Wal-Mart for Pillsbury. He received his M.B.A. with a focus in logistics from the University of Arkansas, Sam M. Walton School of Business. Fred is affiliated with the CPFR VICS industry subcommittee and is a contributor to CPFR Guidelines, published in 1998. He is also an active member of, and speaker at, the Council of Logistics Management.

Gunter Baumgart, head of ECR–Supply Chain Management, Henkel

Gunter Baumgart is responsible for the international supply chain projects of Henkel with its trading partners in the fabric and home care department. He also heads research projects sponsored by the German government in the area of supply chain management.

Greg Belkin, senior editor, MoonWatch Media's *Supply Chain Alert*

Gregory Belkin is a senior editor of *Supply Chain Alert,* which provides in-depth case studies and other original, factual reporting on how leading retailers, suppliers, and transportation companies are designing collaborative relationships with their supply chain partners. He is a graduate of George Washington University with a bachelor of arts degree in English.

Christopher A. Brady, business process analyst, Safeway

Christopher A. Brady started with Safeway in 1983. He worked in retail operations for thirteen years. Since 1998 he has worked in supply chain management at Safeway. He earned his bachelor's degree at the University of California at Davis and his M.B.A. at California State University, Hayward.

Donald P. Brenchley, director of alliances and e-collaboration, JDA Software

Donald P. Brenchley started his career in retail management for Sainsbury, then studied business management. Afterward he became a customer service manager for Procter & Gamble. For the British supermarket chain Safeway, he ran an innovative supply chain partner program to reduce supply chain costs and to develop new operational methods. He served for three years as a logistics consultant for PE International, which gave him insight into various business problems faced by manufacturers, wholesalers, and retailers and the respective solutions providers. He is an active member of the British Institute of Logistics and Transport.

Robert Bruce, president, VCC Associates

Robert Bruce is a leading authority on the integration of corporate demand and supply chain strategies in the retail/CPG industry. He established VCC Associates to provide consumer value through strategic collaborative value chain advisory services. During his eighteen years at Wal-Mart, he served as vice president of corporate supply chain strategies, leading breakthrough initiatives in merchandising, replenishment, forecasting, supply chain, and logistics, optimizing decisions in a collaborative environment. He also led the development of VMI, CPFR, and other collaborative supply chain initiatives with suppliers. He was a partner at Surgency, Inc., formerly Benchmarking Partners, and a director of inventory management and replenishment for a division of Target Stores, Inc.

Michael E. Di Yeso, executive vice president and chief operating officer, Uniform Code Council

Michael E. Di Yeso joined the Uniform Code Council as executive vice president and chief operating officer in February 2001. Mr. Di Yeso is responsible for the UCC's global activities in standards development and maintenance and oversees the organization's EAN-UCC system strategy, standards development, standards management, and market development departments. He brings to the UCC nearly twenty years of proven experience in consumer and industrial business operations. Prior to joining the UCC, he served as vice president, global supply chain, for Black and Decker Corporation, a global manufacturer and marketer of power tools, hardware, and home improvement products. During his tenure at Black and Decker, he was responsible for all aspects of the company's global supply chain activities, including strategy development, demand planning, materials management, production scheduling, inventory planning and control, logistics, and customer service. He began his career in 1980 with the American Can Company, where he held several general management and financial management positions. Mr. Di Yeso obtained his master's in business administration from the University of New Haven, West Haven, Connecticut. He holds a bachelor of science in business administration from Pace University, Pleasantville, New York.

Ralph W. Drayer, chair, Supply Chain Insights and former chief logistics officer, Procter & Gamble

Ralph W. Drayer is chairman and founder of Supply Chain Insights, a supply chain strategy consultancy. Prior to that he was Procter & Gamble's chief logistics officer. During his thirty-two years with Procter & Gamble, he held a number of distribution, logistics, customer service, and customer business development responsibilities, both domestically and internationally. As P&G's first vice president of customer service/logistics, he was instrumental in the development of P&G's industry-leading supply chain capabilities. He has served as cochair of the Grocery Industry's ECR Best Practices Committee; as chairman of the GMA Distribution and Logistics Committee; and on the boards of the Uniform Code Council, VICS, and the Council of Logistics Management's Executive Committee. He was also a founding member of the Global Commerce Initiative. Mr. Drayer is the recipient of the Grocery Industry's first Path Forward Award for his industry-leading work on ECR and the Council of Logistics Management's Distinguished Service Award, the highest honor that can be bestowed on an individual for achievements in logistics.

Sergio Duque, process manager trade and sales services, Henkel Spain

Sergio Duque is a process manager of the trade and sales services department of Henkel Ibérica, a member of Henkel's CPFR Team, and a member of the ECR Europe working group on CPFR. Sergio is an industrial engineer specializing in industrial organization.

Georg Engler, manager, Accenture
Georg Engler is a manager with Accenture. He is based in the Frankfurt office and specializes in supply chain management and the development of CPFR solutions.

Dr. Birgit Ester, head of supply chain management, dm-drogerie markt
Dr. Birgit Ester joined the retail company in 1998. In 1999 she became head of supply chain management. She is responsible for the optimization of the value chain from the suppliers to the point of sale. Prior to joining dm-drogerie markt, she worked in the areas of logistics consulting and strategic controlling at well-known pharmaceutical companies.

Daren K. Fairfield, associate partner, Accenture
Daren K. Fairfield is an associate partner in Accenture's Consumer Goods & Service Market Unit. He is responsible for Accenture's CPFR market offering in North America and has assisted several clients with CPFR strategy and implementations. Mr. Fairfield is also an active member of the Voluntary Interindustry Commerce Standards (VICS) CPFR subcommittee. Daren is a published subject-matter expert on CPFR and is a member of the *Consumer Goods Technology Magazine* editorial board. Daren graduated summa cum laude from Hope College with a B.A. in business administration and a minor in communications.

Lawrence E. Fennell, vice president, Wal-Mart Stores
Lawrence E. Fennell has been with Wal-Mart more than twenty years. He served eighteen years in store operations, the last ten of those years as a regional vice president. In 1996 he was promoted to vice president of basic inventory. Since 2000 he has served as vice president for business development and is actively engaged in the implementation of Retail Link CPFR.

Julie Fraser, principal and director of market strategies, Industry Directions, Inc.
Julie Fraser has sixteen years' experience as a manufacturing systems industry expert. Before joining Industry Directions, she held a position

as vice president of marketing for Baan Supply Chain Solutions. Prior to that, she was the senior analyst on manufacturing execution systems and integration at Advanced Manufacturing Research (AMR). Fraser was the editor-in-chief of the *CIM Strategies* newsletter from the mid-1980s to the early 1990s, which built on her previous experience in production operations for an industrial goods manufacturer.

Thomas H. Friedman, president, MoonWatch Media Inc.

Thomas H. Friedman is founder and president of MoonWatch Media Inc., a global B2B events, publishing, and advisory company. He is publisher of *Retail Systems Alert Research Report, Supply Chain Alert Research Report,* and *Top of the Net Weekly Update.* He is author of some of the industry's most thought-provoking executive briefing papers, including "Global Retailing in the New Millennium" (1998), "SupplyWebExchange: The Changing Supply Chain Landscape" (2000), and "Sorting Through the Standards Maze" (2001, in conjunction with the Uniform Code Council). A magna cum laude graduate of Syracuse University, he continued his studies at London University, University of California, and Harvard University Extension. Mr. Friedman was recently selected by *RIS News* as one of the twenty-five most influential people in retailing.

Geoffrey S. Frodsham, divisional vice president, logistics, Canadian Tire Corporation

Geoffrey S. Frodsham joined Canadian Tire Corporation in June 1990. He is currently responsible for domestic and international logistics activities including forecasting and replenishment, operations planning, and supply chain process improvement initiatives. Prior to his current role, Mr. Frodsham was senior director of operations planning, senior director of information technology, and the reengineering director responsible for the process design and implementation of Canadian Tire's time-phased forecasting and replenishment processes. Mr. Frodsham has significant expertise in business process redesign, supply chain management, and electronic commerce. Mr. Frodsham holds an MBA and is a frequent speaker on logistics and electronic commerce in a number of industry forums. Also contributing from Canadian Tire were James McDonald, Nancy Rae, and Vicki Seto-Wright—all members of Canadian Tire's CPFR team.

Esteban Garriga, manager trade and sales services, Henkel Spain and cochair CPFR project (ECR Europe)

Esteban Garriga is the trade and sales services manager of Henkel Ibérica, with eleven years of experience in the company. Involved in different international projects, Esteban is the cochair of the ECR Europe working group on CPFR and a member of the GCI-CPFR advisory group. Esteban holds an MBA from ESADE in Barcelona.

Peter Hambuch, manager CPFR and demand process excellence Germany, Austria, Switzerland, Procter & Gamble

Peter Hambuch has been with Procter & Gamble since 1980 and has held several management positions in customer business development. In recent years his main focus has been on the implementation of such innovative concepts as category management and Efficient Consumer Response. His department is supporting multifunctional customer teams of Procter & Gamble Germany, Austria, and Switzerland. He studied mathematics at the University of Saarbruecken.

Dr. Gerhard Hausruckinger, partner, Roland Berger Strategy Consultants

Dr. Gerhard Hausruckinger graduated from the University of Regensburg, Germany in 1988, where he then spent three years as assistant professor of marketing. After working for the German retailer Karstadt in the corporate development department, he joined Roland Berger & Partners in 1994. From 1998 to 2001 he headed the consumer goods/retail competence center in the United Kingdom. He has been back in the Munich head office since August 2001. His focus areas are corporate strategy, e-commerce, and ECR/category management.

Ron Ireland, vice president, VCC Associates

Ron Ireland is an industry practitioner with a focus on best business processes and complementing-enabling technology. He has over twenty years of technical and functional experience. Ireland worked as a manager of MRPII application development at Martin Marietta Data Systems and as strategy manager of systems application and development responsible for replenishment and forecasting systems at Wal-Mart Stores and helped pioneer CPFR. Ron was also a director of systems development at J. D. Edwards and a partner at Surgency, Inc., formerly Benchmarking Partners.

Matthew F. Katz, principal and director of collaborative services, Kurt Salmon Associates

Matthew F. Katz has a broad range of experience helping clients realize improvements in supply chain performance through the adoption of B2B solutions and practices, business process reengineering, and organizational design. He leads engagements with leading global brands, vertical manufacturers, and department store retailers. His project teams assist in the architecture and innovation of collaborative supply chains, the development of global sourcing strategies, and the design of merchandising processes and organization. Matt manages KSA alliances with top-tier technology solutions. An active leader in the VICS-GCI CPFR Committee, Matt is regarded as a thought leader in CPFR and supply chain collaboration. He is a frequent speaker and author on supply chain initiatives. Prior to joining KSA, Matt worked in department store retailing for nine years. He managed information systems, led expansion/consolidation efforts, developed store-line strategies, and managed controller office operations while at Federated Department Stores.

Christian Koch, director, marketing consumer industries, SAP AG

After completing his studies in physics and economics, Christian Koch joined the former DACOS Software company (now SAP Retail Solutions) in Germany to work in consulting, business development, and sales for logistics and merchandise management solutions. In 1996, he moved to the SAP Industry Business Sector Consumer Industries, where he has been concentrating on the worldwide rollout of SAP's solution for these industries. Since 1998 he has been responsible for SAP's international marketing activities in the Consumer Industries.

Nick J. Miller, director, supply chain, GlobalNetXchange

As director of supply chain services at GlobalNetXchange, Nick J. Miller has been leading the development of CPFR and other collaborative services on the GNX retail exchange for over eighteen months.

Mr. Miller has over fifteen years' experience in supply chain management, with a focus on retail and manufacturing. Prior to joining Global-NetXchange, Mr. Miller was with PricewaterhouseCoopers, where he worked with numerous large, multinational organizations on strategic supply chain initiatives. Mr. Miller holds a B.S. in mechanical engineering and an M.S. in management science from London University.

Laura A. Mooney, director, solutions marketing, Manugistics
As part of Manugistics's supply chain management team, Laura A. Mooney is responsible for vision development, positioning, and solution strategy for Manugistics's collaborative forecasting, replenishment, and order management solutions. She has over twelve years of experience in the software industry with a focus on supply chain management, collaboration, and e-commerce technology. In addition to her tenure with Manugistics, Ms. Mooney has held senior leadership positions with Internet start-ups OutReach Technologies and SpaceWorks and spent several years with IBM. Ms. Mooney holds a B.A. in information systems from James Madison University and an MBA with a concentration in marketing from the University of Maryland, Smith School of Business.

Prof. Dr. Wilhelm Pfähler, chair of economic policy and industrial economics, University of Hamburg
Prof. Dr. Wilhelm Pfähler has held the chair of economic policy and industrial economics at the University of Hamburg since 1992. Previously he taught at Georgetown University in Washington, D.C., the Hochschule für Unternehmensführung (WHU) Koblenz/Vallendar, and the China-Europe Management Institute (CEMI). Since 1992 Professor Pfähler also has been a faculty member of Universitätsseminar der Wirtschaft (USW) Schloss Gracht and the China-Europe International Business School (CEIBS) in Shanghai. One of his areas of teaching and research is industrial economics (focus on business strategies). His current research focus is the international competitiveness of regions and companies.

Prof. Dr. Dawn M. Russell, assistant professor of business logistics, The Smeal College of Business Administration, The Pennsylvania State University
Prof. Dr. Dawn M. Russell's research focuses on the integration of information technology in a supply chain context to support collaborative

processes. Dawn is actively involved with the Voluntary Interindustry Commerce Standards (VICS) organization through participation on the CPFR Committee and the collaborative transportation management (CTM) subcommittee. She is also an active member of the Council of Logistics Management and has worked with the Supply Chain Council. Prior to joining Penn State in 2001, Dawn spent eleven years working both practically and academically in the areas of logistics and supply chain management with GE Aircraft Engines, Lockheed-Martin Aero & Naval Systems, Arthur Andersen, and Northwestern University. Dawn completed her Ph.D. in Transportation Engineering at Northwestern University and was a 1999 Eno Transportation Fellow. She earned her MBA at The Ohio State University and her B.A. in materials and logistics management at Michigan State University.

Christian Schick, supply chain manager, dm-drogerie markt

Christian Schick heads the continuous replenishment/vendor-managed inventory at dm-drogerie markt. He is a member of the CCG (Centrale für Coorganisation) boards of Joint Forecasting and CPFR. He is deeply involved in the research and development of supply chain management and CPFR at dm-drogerie markt.

Michael Seishoff, project manager, Centrale für Coorganisation (CCG)

Michael Seishoff has been a project manager at CCG since 1999. His focus is on ECR process management with national and international projects in efficient unit loads; optimization of information; and product flow in the consumer goods industry, forecasting, and CPFR. Before joining CCG, he worked for Bretzke Consulting and Klaus-Moers-Retail-Consulting. Mr. Seishoff studied Business Administration at the University of Duisburg.

Scott Smith, collaborative commerce project leader, Ace Hardware

Scott Smith manages the collaborative commerce program at Ace Hardware and is responsible for inventory management of import redistribution and quick response implementation. Scott has coordinated collaborative efforts along with JDA to develop their collaborative commerce program. Scott's previous career experience includes inventory and distribution roles with the Electro Motives division of General Motors and United Stationers. Scott has been responsible for developing business processes to improve and streamline the replenishment process. He received his undergraduate degree from Western Illinois University and an MBA from Benedictine University. Scott is an adjunct professor at St. Francis University, teaching quantitative analysis.

Jeffrey B. Stiely, principal, Kurt Salmon Associates

Jeffrey B. Stiely is a principal in Kurt Salmon Associates's supply chain services practice. During his twelve-year career with KSA, he has worked with leading suppliers and retailers in Europe, Asia, and the United States on product development, planning and forecasting, merchandising, and supply chain management initiatives. Mr. Stiely has worked with clients, consortiums, B2B software vendors, and industry associations in the development of collaborative business practices and has authored several articles and speeches on this topic. He led a KSA team in conducting a six-month study to assess the impact and role of collaborative relationships and technologies in the retail industry. He also chaired an industry committee composed of more than fifteen leading retailers, manufacturers, and textile suppliers in the area of collaborative product development. Prior to joining KSA, Jeff earned a bachelor's degree in management science from Virginia Polytechnic Institute & State University.

Hans Teuscher, manager supply chain management, Accenture Spain, coordinator ECR Europe CPFR project

Hans Teuscher is a manager in Accenture's supply chain management line of business, based in Barcelona. He is the coordinator of the ECR Europe project on CPFR and serves on the CPFR Advisory Committee of the GCI. He led various collaboration projects for clients in the retail and FMCG industry across Europe. Mr. Teuscher holds an MBA from IESE in Barcelona.

Saskia Treeck, senior project manager, Centrale für Coorganisation (CCG)

Saskia Treeck has been responsible for national and international supply chain management projects at CCG since 1997. Her main focus is on concepts like CPFR and ECR (efficient replenishment, efficient unit loads, and efficient replenishment upstream). She also coordinates ECR Europe and ECR D-A-CH (Germany, Austria, and Switzerland) committees. Prior to joining CCG she worked for UNIT Logistic Consulting and Thyssen Haniel Logistic. Ms. Treeck studied business administration at the University of Dortmund in collaboration with the Fraunhofer Institute for Product Flow and Logistics.

Nils Weisphal, consultant IDS Scheer AG and Ph.D. student
Nils Weisphal is currently working on his doctoral thesis at the University of Hamburg. His research focuses on CPFR. Simultaneously he works for IDS Scheer Consulting as consultant in the field of consumer goods industry and retailing. Parallel to his education and studies of business administration at the University of Hamburg with a focus on industrial economics, business information systems, and retailing, Weisphal started up his own business and built up a bakery chain in Hamburg. He also worked as a regional sales manager for a bakery chain with more than eighty outlets.

Index

399

About the Editor

Prof. Dr. Dirk Seifert is head of a CPFR research project and visiting scholar at Harvard Business School. In addition, he teaches management and marketing at the University of Massachusetts. Before joining the Harvard Business School he worked as a director with Bertelsmann, one of the world's largest media companies. Other senior positions he has held have been in the Category Management Department of Procter & Gamble and the International Marketing Department of Bayer (Pharmaceutical Division).

Prof. Seifert's research focuses on strategic retail management, category management, and supply chain management. He is the author of several books and numerous articles in major journals, such as the German edition of *Harvard Business Review* and the *Journal of Retail and Distribution Management*.